FIVE CENTURIES OF LAW AND POLITICS IN CENTRAL MEXICO

EDITED BY RONALD SPORES AND ROSS HASSIG

Vanderbilt University
Publications in Anthropology
No. 30
Nashville, Tennessee
1984

ISBN 0-935462-21-X

FIVE CENTURIES OF LAW AND POLITICS IN CENTRAL MEXICO

INTRODUCTION

The topics addressed in this volume relate to law and politics in Central Mexico from late pre-Conquest times to the present. When dealing with a temporal span of such dimensions and cultural-historical developments of such complexity, topics, articles, approaches, and perspectives reflected in this volume necessarily constitute a sampling of the scholarship in the field. However, the editors have attempted to present a balanced collection of articles reflecting current research relating to our specific thematic, areal, and temporal concerns, while seeking to fill some of the gaps in current knowledge of law and government in Mexico. We believe that these contributions represent significant additions to Mexican and Mesoamerican studies, as well as to the various academic disciplines represented—anthropology, history, and political science.

Scope. In an effort to delimit the scope of this book, we have restricted the geographical focus to central Mexico. Insofar as the present volume is concerned, central Mexico comprises the area from the Isthmus of Tehuantepec in the south to southern Zacatecas and San Luis Potosi in the north, and from the Gulf Coast to the Pacific Ocean. We have excluded the Maya area and the northern desert, or "Chichimec" area that did not fully share in the high culture of Mesoamerica or in the "full" hispanization of the colonial period. Major emphasis within the area has been placed on the central plateau, especially the valleys of Mexico and Puebla, with secondary emphasis on outlying areas, such as Oaxaca. At least three articles are concerned with larger domains: the Aztec Empire, the Mexican Republic. This delineation encourages sharper focusing of attention on specific political and legal functions, structures, patterns of change, and relations between political institutions and activities and social, economic, and ideological factors.

Overview. Within the thematic, spatial, and temporal boundaries of this volume, the articles vary, both in specific focus and in general approach. Except for the pre-Columbian era, where appropriate data are scarce, the articles have largely eschewed the macro-level approach traditionally employed, and examine political and legal functions and their impact at the local level alone or in relation to other levels. By so doing, they show how political society functioned in the lives of individuals and how they influenced, and were influenced by, the changing political situation.

Rather than seeing Indians, and later *mestizos*, as passive receptors of politically-inspired changes imposed from above, the articles present evidence of the way they operated within the politico-judicial system to maintain traditional rights and secure new ones as opportunity and shifting political principles allowed.

National-level studies have established the broad outlines of Mexican political and legal organization and principles, and development over time. But any leap from the actual or ideal operation of the system at the national level to the local level is conceptually unsound and empirically unwarranted. As the studies in this volume make clear, the form and function of Mexican politics at the local level are varied and their interaction with other levels active and mutually affective.

The articles have drawn on a wide range of sources. Traditional historical sources, such as the chronicles of the Conquest and colonial periods, have, of course, been used and offer much valuable information. But all too frequently, they paint with overly broad strokes, rendering the societies and conditions they present as seamless wholes, bereft of conflict or of variability. Values and attitudes often appear as though they were possessed by groups as entities rather than individually by their constituent members. Mexican archival material is rich in specific data on political, legal, social, and economic matters, and for the authors in this volume this has been the primary source of information.

Unlike traditional chronicles, archival data are seldom prosaic essays endeavoring to present comprehensive accounts. Rather, individually, they offer only partial glimpses of events and conflicts and require copious collection, culling, and analysis to flesh out the patterns of the events they suggest. Thus, the events and conditions depicted herein are not the result of some fortuitously uncovered archival treasure trove, but of careful examination of numerous, scattered documents revealing the many small interactions that general studies may overlook.

A dominating theme in this volume is the structure, function, and evolution of complex, multi-level systems of government in pre-Hispanic, Colonial, and Republican Mexico. Found wanting in terms of total comprehension are methods of analysis that focus only on the native community as a closed, autonomous, political entity or upon the imperial, colonial, or national levels of government while ignoring provincial/state, regional/district, or local-community levels of government and their articulation. The realities of political and legal needs, action, goals, power distribution, and decision-making are adequately perceived and understood only when seen from beginning to end, from center to periphery, from the top level of the political system to the bottom.

Another major theme is the interaction of formal political offices and mechanisms, on the one hand, and, on the other, informal, non-explicit, tacit, yet functionally effective actors and institutions that have evolved in the Mexican para-political arena since pre-Hispanic times. The significant role of native priests or the Catholic clergy, the *pochtecah*, Euro-American business interests, *encomenderos*, and other extra-official actors, while not always obvious, is clearly palpable and operative. The political and judicial functions, the "mixed" or "overlapping" jurisdictions, and the rivalry and balance between civic officials and the clergy, as perceived by Taylor in eighteenth-century Puebla politics, have their counterparts in kin group-military-religious-political functionaries in pre-Hispanic Tenochtitlan and Texcoco and in the relationship between business and government in nineteenth- and twentieth-century Mexico. As important determinants of political and legal behavior and institutions, such para-political elements deserve analytical attention.

All contributions deal with change, responses to evolving demands, shifts in dimensions of power, authority, and jurisdiction, and with the re-shaping of fields of political activity and alternating levels of centralization and regional or local autonomy. The complex interplay of groups, political action, and structure has been constant since ancient times. No comprehensive, longitudinal study of Mexican government and law can fail to ignore patterns of change and accommodation in the political system.

Articles. The articles have been arranged chronologically, in order to place them in the most immediately intelligible sequence, and so that changes may be followed through time. For the pre-Columbian period, Offner examines a legal system, and Hassig, a political one. In *The Distribution of Jurisdiction and Political Power in Aztec Texcoco: Subgroups in Conflict*, Offner examines the structure and function of Texcoco's pre-Conquest law, focusing on both the overarching legal system and that of constituent subgroups. He examines the structure of the judiciary, looking at jurisdictional bases and substantive laws, but puts them in an evolving political context, placing the growth or decline of various courts against the background of growing or declining significance of various subgroups in Texcocan society. Thus, law is seen not simply as a passive means of resolving disputes, but as a sensitive barometer of changing political fortunes within Texcocan society. In *The Aztec Empire: A Reappraisal*, Hassig examines the way the Aztec empire has been viewed. Under the traditional interpretation, it was seen as suffering from various shortcomings. By looking at the actual functioning of the empire, rather than stressing conceptually-based imperatives, he offers an alternative model in which political practices of the Aztecs and the subordinated groups are placed in a framework that makes their actions more readily understandable.

For the sixteenth century, Kellogg, in *Aztec Women in Early Colonial Courts: Structure and Strategy in a Legal Context*, and Cline in *A Legal Process at the Local Level: Estate Division in Late Sixteenth-Century Culhuacan*, both examine the operation of Spanish law and courts among the Indians of the Mexico City area. Kellogg concentrates on women's participation in the Spanish court system. She examines their legal rights before the Conquest and the way they used the Spanish system to expand both their rights and their participation in the judicial process, frequently playing pre-Columbian principles off the newly introduced Spanish legal concepts to enhance their status. Cline examines the process under which the political structure of Indian towns changed to accommodate Spanish organizational patterns, often resulting in the merging of Spanish and Aztec offices and practices. Among these was the Spanish use of testamentary disposition—bequests through wills. Although lacking pre-Columbian antecedents, this practice was readily adopted and implemented in ways favored by indigenous practices; it served as a mechanism for altering preexisting concepts of property and allowed municipal political units greater control over the alienation of local property.

The somewhat neglected seventeenth century is examined by Lewis, in *Indian Political Activities in Spanish Texcoco, 1570-1630*, and Zeitlin, in *Colonialism and the Political Transformation of Isthmus Zapotec Society*. Lewis focuses on the political structure of Texcoco and the natives' success in maintaining Indian dominance. Although Spanish introductions clearly altered the pattern of political authority, the occupants of the offices, and the real wielders of power, continued to be Indians, who actually increased in influence under the Spanish-recognized right of towns to own property. While the fate of Indians clearly declined throughout the colonial period, many towns were able to adopt Spanish political forms and exercise rights vigorously through them. In the Tehuantepec region, far removed from the Mexico City area, there is also evidence of the imposition of Spanish offices atop preexisting ones, but again, it was at the municipal level that Indians managed to maintain some degree of control. Regional integration was shattered and although towns remained vigorous entities, they did so in forms significantly different from their pre-Columbian antecedents.

For the eighteenth century, Taylor, in *Conflict and Balance in District Politics: Tecali and the Sierra Norte de Puebla in the Eighteenth Century*, and Haslip-Viera, in *Criminal Justice and the Poor in Late Colonial Mexico City*, look at different ends of the urban spectrum: the political situation of rural localities and the legal conditions of the urban masses. Rather than focusing on either national or local political offices, Taylor examines the intermediaries, emphasizing the roles of parish priests and royal magistrates and their struggles over control of the municipalities, and the strains introduced by political tensions between core and periphery. Haslip-Viera concentrates on urban populations in Mexico City, examining the penal-judicial system as a mechanism of social control reflecting less the operation of a dispassionate legal system than the political manipulation of that system for social purposes. He further considers the attitudes of the elite toward the poor and the non-Spanish majorities—Indians, *mestizos*, and *mulatos*.

For the nineteenth century, another relatively unexplored period, Kicza, in *The Legal Community of Late Colonial Mexico: Social Composition and Career Patterns*, and Spores, in *Multi-Level Government in Nineteenth-Century Oaxaca*, examine legal and political systems respectively. Kicza looks not at the functioning of the judicial system, but at the position of lawyers in Mexican society, seeing the law as influenced by its practitioners, and the role of attorney as one of the main avenues of social and political mobility by various elements of the society. Spores examines the changing political structure in the provinces, in relation to both higher national offices, and to lower local ones, and how these offices and powers changed through late colonial and, more especially, early Republican times.

The twentieth century has been well represented in the anthropological, historical, and political literature, but not thoroughly or completely. C. Lomnitz, in *Compliance and Coalitions in the Mexican Government: 1917-1940*, Corbett, in *Community Political Systems and the Expansion of the Mexican State 1940-1980*, and L. Lomnitz, in *Social Structure and Political Integration in Urban Mexico*, all examine facets of the Mexican political and legal scene, but from different perspectives. C. Lomnitz takes to task studies that neglect both spatial and temporal variations, proposing, and convincingly demonstrating, a model for Mexico between 1917 and 1940 that not only explains cyclical variations in the State's approach to political goals, but permits, and indeed demands, analytical consideration at all levels of the system. Corbett looks at the way Mexican political organization has been viewed from 1940 to the present, examining the role of local officeholders, traditional sources of authority, patronage, and political brokerage in relation to State penetration of the local communities. By focusing on the relationship between national and local polities, he reveals areas of local political erosion, as well as areas in which local offices are strong, phenomena inexplicable from a single-level approach. In her analysis, L. Lomnitz considers the class-based analysis of Mexico's urban political scene and, while not rejecting it outright, presents additional considerations. She examines both horizontal and vertical ties in a context of political brokerage and patronage to explain not only the functioning of the Mexican political system, but its flexibility and persistence as well.

This volume thus presents a survey of the changing politico-legal scene in central Mexico from the fifteenth century to the twentieth. In so doing, it draws on specific case studies to reach general conclusions, focuses on local and national levels of the politico-legal systems and their interactions, and presents the data and methodological concerns about the region of various disciplines. Thus, it offers new insights into structures and processes in central Mexico at various times—many of which throw light on events in other periods—and theoretical considerations with consequences for Mesoamerican studies in general.

THE DISTRIBUTION OF JURISDICTION AND POLITICAL POWER IN AZTEC TEXCOCO: SUBGROUPS IN CONFLICT

Jerome A. Offner

Introduction

The study of Aztec law has been notably neglected despite excellent data in the historical sources, particularly for the city of Texcoco. In ethnohistoric investigations, the structure and content of legal systems can serve as a reliable indicator of the dynamics of the social process and can also delineate the major power blocs in a society along with their interrelationships and struggles. This article describes the composition of the four highest councils of the Texcocan empire, delimits the areas of substantive law over which each had jurisdiction, and considers the range of social, cultural, and economic life with which each council was involved. Jurisdictional domains of these four councils are then investigated to illustrate the relative distribution of power. Finally, changes in the balance of power over eighty years are identified and analyzed. Although it has been popular to portray Aztec states as strongly centralized, often monolithic, organizations, careful consideration of the data leads to different conclusions.

The Four Major Councils of the Texcocan Empire

Ixtlilxochitl, Torquemada, and Veytia[1] provide the most detailed information on the structure and composition of the empire's four major councils: 1) Music, Arts, and Sciences; 2) Treasury; 3) War; and 4) Supreme Legal Council. Each council had its own quarters in the ruler's palace in Texcoco, as is shown on the *Mapa Quinatzin*.[2]

The Council of Music, Arts, and Sciences was composed of an unspecified number of specialists on poetry, rhetoric, history, astrology, and both good and evil magic and sorcery.[3] The composition of the War Council (*tequihuahcalli*) is better reported in the sources. Ixtlilxochitl[4] states that there were three noble captains and three citizen members from Texcoco as well as fifteen provincial representatives[5]. Torquemada[6] also mentions commoners in this council.

The Treasury Council[7] was made up of the ruler's *mayordomos* (*calpixqueh*, tribute collectors) and that most important merchants of Texcoco (presumably the long-distance traders or *pochtecah*). Ixtlilxochitl's description can be interpreted to mean that this council had a numerical and class composition very similar either to the War Council or to the Supreme Legal Council.[8] In either case, however, the council contained both nobles and non-nobles from Texcoco and representatives from the empire's fifteen provinces.

Textual information[9] on the structure of the Supreme Legal Council is highly divergent.[10] To summarize: (1) The Supreme Legal Council was composed of a minimum of twelve judges whose decisions could be appealed to at least two higher judges. The high judges, however, sentenced only with the approval of the ruler. (2) There were also a number of commoner judges.[11] But at least half of the judges were drawn from the nobility.

Ixtlilxochitl's "definitive" description[12] specifies eight "noble" (*nobles y caballeros*) and four non-noble judges. These officials functioned along with fifteen provincial judges in the "inner part" of a room[13]. In this room's "outer part" were four "supreme presidents" (*jueces supremos*) who were also the "supreme presidents" (*presidentes supremos*) of the four major councils.

Nezahualcoyotl, ruler of Texcoco (A.D. ca. 1473–ca. 1472) and architect of the Texcocan legal system, had close kinsmen in charge of each of the four councils. His son, Acapiotzin, commanded the War council, while two other sons, Hecahuehuetzin and Xochiquetzaltzin, headed the Treasury Council and the Council of Music, Arts, and Sciences, respectively.[14] Torquemada states that two brothers of Nezahualcoyotl, "Quauhtlehuanitcin" and "Ichantlatocatcin," headed a supreme legal council, while Ixtlilxochitl reports that "Ichuantlatohuatzin," a son of Nezahualcoyotl, was president of the Supreme Legal Council.

The composition of these councils argues against any outright imposition of this structure by a central authority or even by a single, unified ruling class. Instead, a process of accommodation to powerful subgroups and an attempt to balance the needs and demands of these subgroups are indicated. To begin with, the various commoner classes, and not just the noble class, were represented at the highest levels of government. In addition, the major political subgroups[15] of Texcoco were also represented at these high levels: the War Council was filled with military men; merchants formed part of the Treasury Council, and priests and craftsmen were among the members of the Council of Music, Arts, and Sciences. Furthermore, the ruler's own immediate family did not act in a unitary fashion. While the close kin ties among Nezahualcoyotl and the council heads might have been expected to ensure loyalty and coordinated action among the four councils, this did not prove to be the case. Playing upon their kinship and political positions, the council heads developed power bases among the subgroups in their respective councils and created considerable disorder within the empire, as will be seen below.

Substantive Law, Jurisdiction, and Political Subgroups in Texcoco

> The law of substance sets limits to permissible behavior and deals chiefly with the content of legal precepts, such as kinds of crimes and torts and their punishment . . . The law of procedure, on the contrary deals with the process of law, e.g. with problems of jurisdiction [and] allocation of authority . . .[16]

Jurisdiction is concerned, *inter alia*, with specifying which legal authority will decide which cases, and may rest on several bases: the territory in which a case arises, the qualities of persons involved in a case, the nature of the dispute in a case, and so forth. The following deals with the way jurisdiction over substantive cases was divided among the four major councils of Texcoco.

The legal systems of most societies possess a number of different legal levels and legal systems involved with their overall structures.[17] In the Texcocan empire, for example, numerous authorities existed on a number of lower legal levels and decided many minor legal matters. Only the more important cases reached the four major councils.[18] The most significant of these cases could be appealed to and decided by the supreme ruler of Texcoco, acting in consultation with the fourteen principal rulers of the empire and the heads of the four councils.[19]

As mentioned, Texcocan society contained a multiplicity of political subgroups. These political groups necessarily practiced a form of social control to preserve their integrity and ability to function effectively,[20] and the evidence indicates that each political group had its own legal system. These legal systems, each with its own idiosyncrasies, were all tied in to the four council structure in an attempt to resolve or preserve differences in their substantive and procedural law. An examination of the jurisdictional responsibilities of each of the four councils as they pertained to the substantive law of Texcoco, then, will reveal the Texcocan ruler's attempt to mediate conflict and distribute power among the various subgroups in his empire.

Ixtlilxochitl[21] says that the famous eighty legal rules of Nezahualcoyotl were divided into four parts for the four councils, and the document *Estas son las leyes que tenían los Indios de la Nueva España*[22] also exhibits distinct traces of a quadrapartite division appropriate to the four Texcocan councils.[23]

Ixtlilxochitl[24] relates that the jurisdiction of the Council of Music, Arts, and Sciences encompassed offenses involving "superstitions," witchcraft, and magic. One of these rules is apparently reported by Ixtlilxochitl himself,[25] who says that the death penalty and confiscation of goods was the punishment for the use of witchcraft and magic. The first chapter of the document *Estas son las leyes* ... , "which deals with witches [or wizards] and highwaymen"[26] contains five rules, three of which are of interest here. (1) Those who engaged in magic or witchcraft against a city had their hearts extracted in the sacrificial manner; (2) a witch or magician who enchanted the members of a household in order to rob and abuse them was strangled; (3) highway robbers were strangled and severely punished. The association of crime on the open road with other crimes involving magic and witchcraft is notable, since it indicates that the Texcocans viewed the open countryside and the roads as being filled with supernatural dangers. It is also noteworthy that theft and treason involving supernatural aid were punished by the council, rather than by the Supreme Legal Council which had jurisdiction over most other types of theft and treason.

The priesthood was closely associated with the Council of Music, Arts, and Sciences, which served as its highest legal level. Pomar indicates that priests were organized into hierarchies and were associated with temples. Some temples had up to forty priests, some only four or five, and others none at all. Each temple had a chief priest with the title *Quetzalcoatl*. The details of the hierarchy of priests in each temple and the overarching hierarchy of priestly hierarchies in Texcoco are not known,[27] but Pomar[28] records legal rules that illuminate some aspects of their organizational structure. The Texcocan ruler, who was the supreme religious authority, could appoint and remove any *Quetzalcoatl*. Priests could resign their positions at any time but remained celibate while in the priesthood. Violators were punished by expulsion from the temple and by headshaving, according to Pomar, or by death, according to Ixtlilxochitl.[29] Ixtlilxochitl also specifies the death penalty for drunken priests.

Such offenses were most likely punished by the priestly hierarchy itself, but the legal level at which this was done is unclear; perhaps the *Quetzalcoatl* of each temple passed judgment and the temple personnel executed the sentence, or perhaps the Council of Music, Arts, and Sciences reserved such judgments to itself. It is certain, however, that the priesthood administered justice to the youths of Texcoco in the youths' schools.

Veytia[30] provides additional information on the jurisdiction of this council, most of which seems plausible. He states that the council regulated the education of the youth. Licensed teachers saw that they were paid by their pupils' parents or relatives, and inspected the students' progress every year. The council also exercised censorship over works dealing with "astronomy, chronology, music, or painted history" and over all crafts. It could punish creators of defective works and products, and prevent their distribution. Thus, the Council of Music, Arts, and Sciences served as the highest legal level for the priesthood, for craftsmen, and for the various members of the nobility who pursued careers in the arts and sciences. Only the lower legal levels of the priesthood are traceable in any detail, but the other professions no doubt also had hierarchies and lower legal levels.[31]

Nezahualcoyotl yielded to this council jurisdiction over the pursuits and businesses of its members as well as over non-affiliated witches and magicians. The priesthood,in particular, was a force with which the ruler had to reckon, for they controlled the presentation of religion to the people, could most likely "discover" and punish witches and magicians, and oversaw the education of the more distinguished youths of the empire. Texcocan priests did not, however, have the power of the priesthood in Tenochtitlan. There is, for example, no one in Texcocan history who compares with the formidable priest Tlacaelel, the *cihuacoatl* of Tenochtitlan,[32] and priests are of only minor importance throughout Texcocan history.

The Supreme Legal Council had rather more far-reaching jurisdictional powers than the Council of Music, Arts, and Sciences. Ixtlilxochitl[33] states that crimes and disputes involving homosexuality, treason, sumptuary regulations, adultery, theft, drunkenness, slaves, property, lands, and the statuses of and differences between offices all came under the jurisdiction of this council. Not surprisingly, legal rules related to such crimes and disputes are grouped together and distinguished from crimes and disputes under the jurisdiction of the Councils of War and Music, Arts, and Sciences in the document *Estas son las leyes....* Veytia[34] points out that the jurisdiction of this council extended over the members of the other councils if they, or other priests, soldiers, craftsmen, artists, etc. committed crimes not within the jurisdiction of the other three councils. In addition, the close association of this council with the ruler of Texcoco (as described by Ixtlilxochitl and Torquemada) indicates that it was the most important of the four councils. It seems not to have been allied with any particular subgroup, other than with the hierarchy of legal specialists and their associated civil servants (bailiffs, scribes, etc.).

The War Council, of course, had jurisdiction over military affairs, but only a limited jursidiction. Two military rules in the document *Estas son las leyes...* are of particular interest in establishing the scope of its jurisdiction. One rule, which specifies the death penalty for anyone wearing certain insignia of the Triple Alliance rulers in a dance, party, or war, is comparable to a rule that was included under the jurisdiction of the Supreme Legal Council.[35] Nevertheless, this rule does not specifically mention the wartime wearing of such insignia. It seems that punishment of unauthorized wartime use of these insignia was within the jurisdiction of the War Council, but use of these devices in other situations was not. Indeed, Motolinía's[37] mention of this rule refers only to the theft of war insignia and/or the use of such insignia in wartime.

Similarly, another military rule of the *Estas son las leyes...* document specifies death by dismemberment along with the loss of goods and the enslavement of the relatives of a traitor who aided the enemy in wartime. Ixtlilxochitl[38] states that traitors were dismembered, their goods taken, their houses destroyed, their estates sown with salt, and their children and members of their households were enslaved "up to the fourth generation." These rules, then, are comparable but the military council seems to have had jurisdiction only over wartime treason, while the Supreme Legal Council tried all other treasonous offenses.

Thus, the *tequihuahcalli* had jurisdiction over all soldiers and related officials during a military campaign. Nezahualcoyotl did not concede any peacetime jurisdiction to the military, and he held them accountable for non-military crimes in the standard legal councils of the empire.

The last of the four councils to be considered is the Treasury Council. These personnel were charged with the collection and distribution of the imperial tributes, and its jurisdiction included all offenses relating to the collection, payment, and misuse of such tributes. Ixtlilxochitl specifies only one legal rule that this council enforced: tribute collectors who gathered excessive tributes were punished by death. However, there were doubtless many other rules included in this council's jurisdiction.

Pochtecah (merchants) were included on the Treasury Council because of their importance in the procurement of luxury goods and because the imperial tribute system as a whole depended to a large extent on ancient Mesoamerican marketing systems.[39] The merchants acted as spies for the various Aztec rulers and possessed considerable military power. Furthermore, their ability to pass through a variety of hostile political units, due in part to their international organization, made them an indispensable source of information and influence for the procurement of goods and commodities—by tribute or trade—from all areas.

In the words of Zorita,[40] the merchants "had some liberties, because it was said that they were necessary for the state." The privileges enjoyed by merchants varied from political unit to political unit in the Valley of Mexico. In Tlatelolco, merchants were for some time the predominant influence in their state's affairs.[41] The extent of the jurisdictional powers of the merchants in Texcoco is not known, but it might have been similar to those of the Tlatelolcan merchants who were able to try, sentence, and even execute fellow merchants and had considerable authority in that city's marketplace. The Texcocan merchants' position seems to have been better than that of the merchants of Tenochtitlan, where there was an acute rivalry between the merchants and the military. It is reported that in the time of Motecuhzoma Xocoyotl certain groups of merchants were falsely accused of crimes and were executed; their estates were then used to support the powerful and reckless military orders of *otomitl* and *cuachic* ("shorn one") warriors. It is not surprising, then, that the Tenochcan merchants sometimes took precautions to conceal there wealth from public view. Neither is it surprising that Nezahualcoyotl separated the jurisdictions of the military and the merchants from each other in Texcoco.

In summary, then, the four councils established by Nezahualcoyotl for the Texcocan empire had jurisdiction over an offense that depended neither on the status of the person committing it nor on the territory where it was committed, but on the type of offense and the circumstances under which it was committed. Through this arrangement, Nezahualcoyotl sought to balance power and authority among the major subgroups in the empire. These subgroups all possessed complex internal hierarchies, regulated their own affairs to some extent, and through their respective councils, they could regulate the behavior of all citizens under special circumstances (e.g., in the case of the War Council, on a military campaign). But the members of these groups all fell under the far-reaching jurisdiction of the Supreme Legal Council if they committed offenses other than those under the narrow jurisdictions of the other three councils. Consequently, there was no personality principle of law[42] that corresponded to these groups; soldiers, priests, craftsmen, and even merchants could not always depend on being judged by their fellows. Thus, the Supreme Legal Council was structurally the most powerful of the four councils, and was designed to serve, along with the highest legal level (the ruler and his advisors), as a check on the politcal power and ambitions of these other subgroups.

Changes in the Balance of Power

The stability of the balance of power among these four great councils of the empire depended in large part on the leadership of Nezahualcoyotl, for upon his death, various factions of the Texcocan ruling family (led in three cases by persons who were also heads of one of the four councils), attempted to take over the rulership of Texcoco. Their political position as heads of powerful political subgroups, as well as their genealogical position as potential successors to Nezahualcoyotl provided these individuals with the ability to contend for domination of the Texcocan political apparatus.

Nezahualcoyotl died in the year 6 *Tecpatl* or 1472,[43] shortly after expressing his preference that his favorite son, Nezahualpilli, succeed him. Since Nezahualpilli had been born only in 11 *Tecpatl* (1464) or 12 *Calli* (1465),[44] he was unable to rule alone, so Nezahualcoyotl appointed Acapiotzin, the president of the War Council, as regent until Nezahualpilli was able to rule alone.[45] As one of many sons of Nezahualcoyotl, Nezahualpilli had to avoid being done away with in his early years by the various factions of the royal family. Fortunately, he was able to count on the aid of Acapiotzin and of the Tenochcan ruler Axayacatl (ca. 1469–ca. 1481) so that, after considerable difficulties, he established himself as the ruler of the Texcocan empire.

Actually, the struggle for supremacy seems to have begun before Nezahualcoyotl's death and apparently led to the death of Nezahualpilli's full brother, Tetzauhpiltzintli, the successsor apparent to the Texcocan rulership. Ixtlilxochitl provides an elaborate account of how Tetzauhpiltzintli came to be accused of grave crimes through the machinations of Nezahualcoyotl's favorite concubine. According to this account, Tetzauhpiltzintli was ordered executed by the rulers of Tenochtitlan and Tlacopan whom Nezahualcoyotl had called in to determine guilt and sentence.[46] Ixtlilxochitl relates that Nezahualcoyotl was shocked at the severity of the action taken against his favorite son. (Here it must be noted that this favorite concubine had two sons: Xochiquetzaltzin, head of the Council of Music, Arts, and Sciences, and Ecahuehuetzin, head of the Treasury Council.)

Upon Nezahualcoyotl's death, Axayacatl, ruler of Tenochtitlan and, of course, a close relative of Nezahualpilli, acted firmly and quickly to ensure Nezahualpilli's security. He summoned Nezahualpilli and his three chief rivals, Ichautlatoatzin, Xochiquetzaltzin, and Ecahuehuetzin, to appear in Tenochititlan. It is reported that Acapiotzin also came (in order to protect Nezahualpilli). It should be noted again that the three chief rivals were not only Nezahualpilli's half-brothers, but were also heads of the Supreme Legal Council, the Council of Music, Arts, and Sciences, and the Treasury Council, respectively, and so possessed power second to Acapiotzin, who was the head of the War Council. In Tenochtitlan, it was made clear to the three chief rivals that Nezahualpilli was to be ruler of Texcoco, and even Ixtlilxochitl reports that Axayacatl frequently held court in Texcoco during the early years of Nezahualpilli's reign.[47]

From the beginning of his reign, Nezahualpilli followed the astute advice of Acapiotzin. The principal threat to his security continued to be the faction of the royal family centered around the favorite concubine of Nezahualcoyotl. Accordingly, her youngest son was made *grande* ("great lord") of Chiautla and was given extensive new properties in conquered lands. This faction seems to have been partially pacified by this extraordinary action.[48]

Acapiotzin also saw to it that Nezahualpilli built support among parties predisposed to favor both of them; thus, Nezahualpilli ordered that a special palace be constructed for his brother Axoquentzin, a close ally of Acapiotzin.

Nezahualpilli's brothers continued to plot against him for a number of years. Torquemada[49] says that Nezahualpilli's brothers conspired with the Chalcans to kill him, and also Nezahualpilli's narrow escape from death at the hands of the army of Huexotzinco. His brothers had shown his devices and armor to the enemy army so he could be easily recognized, sought out, and killed, but Nezahualpilli was informed of the plot and took successful precautions against it. Ixtlilxochitl tells substantially the same story.[50]

Nezahualpilli eventually eliminated all significant opposition by his brothers. He supported Acapiotzin against Xochiquetzaltzin in a public struggle to claim credit for a victorius military expediton. It is reported that when Xochiquetzaltzin and those of his faction saw Nezahualpilli side with Acapiotzin in public, they never again tried to claim credit for the expedition. Nezahualpilli, thereby, eventually silenced the most powerful and troublesome faction in the royal family.[51] Finally, Ixtlilxochitl[52] says that after Nezahualpilli severely punished one of his brothers for refusing to give him a daughter for a concubine and also, later, a drum (*teponaztli*), the royal brothers never again plotted against Nezahualpilli, in public or in private.

Over time, Nezahualpilli continued to change the laws of Texcoco in recognition of changes in the society as a whole.[53] For example, Nezahualpilli changed the adultery law in the case of a soldier convicted of the *tercera especie* ("third type") of adultery for which the penalty was death by strangulation for both parties. Nezahualpilli declared that although the adulteress was still to be strangled, the adulterer, in view of his profession, was to be sent out on perpetual military frontier duty; furthermore, he declared that this punishment was to apply to all similar cases in the future,[54] since the state would benefit from such military service.

There is an indication of a gradual shift in the balance of power among the subgroups in Texcoco towards the military. Only soldiers could escape death upon conviction for adultery. Acapiotzin's early support of Nezahualpilli seems to have been rewarded by a significant concession to the subgroup of which Acapiotzin was head.

Conclusion

The elucidation of Aztec political and legal administrative structures is a worthwhile goal in itself. Because of the nature of the historical sources, merely establishing hierarchical relationships among entities is a difficult task. The description of political and legal administration, however, is only a first step in adequately explaining Aztec law and politics, and reliance on such "one-step" descriptions can produce the impression of organizations with no significant internal dynamism. Unless the far less obvious references to political action involving competition for power among subgroups are carefully sought out, a false view of Aztec legal and political organization can result.

In the Texcocan case, irregularities and asymmetries in hierarchical relationships (e.g., the distribution of jurisdiction over substantive law) suggest that the political and legal administrative structures developed by the Texcocan ruler were artifacts of political action and struggles by and among powerful subgroups. Explicit references in the sources to the conflicting goals and needs of political subgroups, along with details of actual political struggles among the members of the ruling family who headed these subgroups, showed that the Texcocan polity was internally dynamic. Indeed, it is noteworthy that the second most important Aztec state was internally unstable to such an extent.

Centralization of power in Texcoco, then, was limited by political subgroups in competition for power. In addition, the framework in which they were competing was of recent construction. The balance of power had not been definitively established, and as the Texcocan empire expanded and experienced rapid social, cultural, and economic changes, new areas of contention among subgroups developed. The government of Texcoco was essentially exhibiting its youthful, untested character. As a product of political compromise rather than of regal *fiat*, Texcocan government resembled more a shifting series of political alliances than a type of "despotism."

NOTES

[1]Ixtlilxochitl 1952; Torquemada 1975; Veytia 1944.

[2]Aubin 1886.

[3]Ixtlilxochitl 1952 I:326, 496-97; II:178, 189; Torquemada 1975 I:146-47; Veytia 1944 II:182-83.

[4]Ixtlilxochitl 1952, II:178.

[5]See Offner (1980: n.d.a., chapter 2-4) for a discussion of the significance of the number fifteen in Texcocan imperial organization.

[6]Torquemada 1975, I:146-47.

[7]Ixtlilxochitl 1952, I:326, II:179, 193; Torquemada 1975, I:147.

[8]Veytia (1944, II:183) finds that the Treasury Council more closely resembles the Legal rather than the War Council.

[9]Motolinía 1903:280, 304-12; Pomar 1886-1892:31; Torquemada 1975, I:148, 168; II:354-56, 441; Ixtlilxochitl 1952, I:236 326; II:175-78.

[10]For a fuller treatment of this subject, see Offner n.d.a., chapter 2.

[11]E.g., Pomar 1886-1892:31.

[12]Ixtlilxochitl 1952, II:175-78.

[13]Veytia (see above) assumes that this description is also the composition of the Treasury Council. Also note this description's similarity to the make-up of the War Council.

[14]Ixtlilxochitl 1952 I:326; Torquemada 1975, I:146-47.

[15]The membership of the major political subgroups cut across class lines (see Offner n.d.a., chapter 4).

[16]Pospisil 1971:1.

[17]Pospisil 1971:97-126.

[18]This is particularly true for cases arising in the provinces.

[19]See Offner n.d.a, chapters 2-5.

[20]Pospisil 1971:106-7, 125.

[21]Ixtlilxochitl 1952, II:187.

[22]*Estas son las leyes...* (1886-1892). This document is closely related to the Texcocan legal tradition.

[23]In the second part of this document ("the accurate rules"), there is a strict separation of legal rules pertaining to war and legal rules pertaining to supernatural matters, both from each other and from the types of legal rules described by Ixtlilxochitl as coming under the jurisdiction of the Supreme Legal Council.

[24]Ixtlilxochitl 1952, II:187.

[25]Ixtlilxochitl 1952, I:238-39.

[26]*Estas son las leyes...* 1886-1892:310.

[27]Torquemada (1975, II, Books 8 and 9) presents data for New Spain in general while Acosta Saignes (1946) discusses the priestly hierarchies of Tenochtitlan. The applicability of these data to the priestly organizations of the Texcocan empire is problematic.

[28]Pomar 1886-1892:7, 22-23.

[29]Ixtlilxochitl 1952, I:238.

[30]Veytia 1944, II:182-83.

[31]Acosta Saignes 1945; 1946; Zantwijk 1970.

[32]Pomar (1886-1892:19) mentions a *cihuacoatl* in Texcoco and calls him a "principal priest," but the office seems not to have been nearly as important in Texcoco as it was in Tenochtitlan.

[33]Ixtlilxochitl 1952, II:187-89.

[34]Veytia 1944, II:181-82.

[35]*Estas son las leyes...* 1886-1892:312.

[36]Ixtlilxochitl 1952, II:188.

[37]Motolinía 1903:300.

[38]Ixtlilxochitl 1952, II:188.

[39]Calnek 1978; Berdan n.d.; Offner 1981a, 1981b.

[40]Zorita 1886-1892:156.

[41]Sahagún 1950-1969, IX:23-24.

[42]A personality principle of law specifies where and how a person will be tried according to certain qualities inherent in that person (e.g., class, ethnicity, sex). For example, the merchant hierarchy in Tlatelolco appears to have had exclusive authority to try merchants for all types of crimes.

[43] *Anales de Cuauhtitlan* 1945:296; Siméon 1889:132; Dibble 1942; Ixtlilxochitl 1952, I:322, cf. II:243.

[44] *Anales de Cuauhtitlan* 1945: 192; Siméon 1889:127; Ixtlilxochitl 1952, II:229.

[45] Ixtlilxochitl 1952, I:253-56, 497-98; II:241-42; Torquemada 1975, I: 173-74.

[46] Ixtlilxochtil 1952, II:220-22.

[47] Ixtlilxochitl 1952, II:248-50.

[48] Ixtlilxochitl 1952, II:253.

[49] Torquemada 1975, I:180, 183-84.

[50] Ixtlilxochitl 1952, II:275-77.

[51] Ixtlilxochitl 1952, II:293-94. The expedition is described in Ixtlilxochitl (1952, II:202-3); see Kelly (1952:269, n. 37) for the location of *Cuexteca que es Panuco.* In the time of Nezahualpilli, the two competing brothers, along with numerous musicians, friends, and allies, engaged in a series of public dance competitions in which each brother's party claimed credit for the Texcocan victory. Dances, then, had other purposes in Aztec societies besides religious celebration, education of the young, general promotion of "social solidarity," and so forth. This episode actually represents the use of dance for competitive, divisive, purposes. Fortunately, Nezahualpilli developed an unusual method of dispute settlement to resolve the situation—he and his retinue joined the dancers of the side he favored.

[52] Ixtlilxochitl 1952, II:298-99.

[53] Motolinía 1903:304.

[54] Ixtlilxochitl 1952, II:297-98.

THE AZTEC EMPIRE: A REAPPRAISAL

Ross Hassig

The Aztec empire has long been the object of scholarly attention, but in view of the swiftness of the Spanish intrusion and the ease with which the Aztec empire was divided and conquered, many interpretations have stressed the inadequacy of the Aztec political organization, emphasizing the empire's lack of internal cohesion, the frequency of revolts, and the apparent inadequacy of its military organization.

The theoretical underpinnings for this perspective derive from von Clausewitz,[1] whose basic premise is that war is inherently political—its purpose is not random violence, but the furthering of some goal of the polity. While von Clausewitz's works permit many arguments to be made, the basic principle extracted and applied to the Aztec case is that the enemy must be controlled after conquest—a task best accomplished by disarming the vanquished and occupying their territory.[2] The main concern of empires is territorial expansion, internal control, and the maintenance of secure borders. This entails the existence of a standing army, control of the enemy's will (most easily accomplished by control of the territory and leadership), and fortifications to guarantee territorial defense.[3] The Aztecs are generally regarded as not having effectively controlled vanquished territories. The cause, from a Clausewitzian perspective, is the absence of a standing army, on which garrisons and fortifications are, in turn, dependent.

It is the contention of this study that the nature of the Aztec empire and its military organization has been misconstrued due to overreliance, implicit or explicit, on the von Clausewitz view of empire. In order to assess the accuracy of traditional views of the Aztec empire, three related factors must be considered: the professionalism of the Aztec military, the existence of fortifications, and the presence of garrisons throughout the empire.

Traditional View

It is frequently maintained that Aztec warriors cannot be considered professional soldiers—despite the existence of military orders—because membership in the army was neither a means of support nor a full-time occupation.[4] Each time the need arose, the military was reconstituted from the populace. There was no permanent, standing force: without which, the political directives of the capital could not be effectively imposed on the conquered territories. Thus, political centralization was impossible.

Fortifications likewise require the presence of a sophisticated military organization.[5] Despite the numerous reports of fortified sites throughout Mesoamerica (implying military professionalization), Gorenstein[6] denies this status to the sites. The existence of walls does not imply the kind of military professionalism required for actual fortifications. Such strongholds as existed were simply matters of expediency and not permanent military installations. This is necessarily so if there was no standing army. However, Aztec garrisons were reported throughout the empire by the conquistadors to native accounts.[7]

Since garrisons imply a standing force, this concept has been the subject of reconsideration.[8] Gorenstein states, and Davies concurs,[9] that the original meaning of the term was not that now assigned to it. Referring to the Spanish term "*guarnición*," Gorenstein says, "A 17th century dictionary (Covarrubias 1943:665) defines it as 'soldiers guarding or protecting a place where they were,' not troops *stationed* at a fortification." She takes *guarnición* to refer to transient troops without reference to a location, which could easily exist without a standing army. In short, Gorenstein would dismantle the Aztec military qua military, by beginning with the recorded political fragility of the empire and then explaining it as the result of martial inadequacy.

A recent refinement of these general requisites adds further to our knowledge of the dynamics of empire by focusing on internal spatial variations of polities. Skinner[10] demonstrates a systematic relationship between space and defense. In the center of the polity, there is little governmental concern with defense, while at the frontier, the opposite is the case. This results from spatial variations of threats to security—low in the center where homogeneity is high and the likelihood of external support for revolt is slight; high at the periphery where heterogeneity is high, likelihood of external support for revolt is great, and a breakaway alliance with bordering polities is feasible. This spatial refinement of empire lends cogency to the stress on standing armies, border fortifications, territorial control, and the suppression of potentially subversive local governments.

However, these logical requisites are based, not on the way the Aztec empire functioned, but on a European conception (and type) of empire. The latter view entails the territorial expansion into previously sovereign areas (frequently ethnically and linguistically diverse) and the exercise of political domination—achieved and maintained militarily—not only to guarantee territorial integrity, but to replace or control conquered governments. In other words, empire seems to demand a standing army, territorial control, border and internal fortifications, and the removal or subordination of indigenous governments.

This basic concept of empire pervades the Mesoamerican literature.[11] But rather than viewing the Aztec empire as a deficient political entity, as this definition requires, an alternative organizational model displays the data in a better light.

Hegemonic Empire

In reanalyzing the Roman Empire, Edward Luttwak[12] has presented several alternative imperial models, the earliest of which—the Julio-Claudian system—is applicable to the Aztec case. Under this system, the empire was one of hegemonic expansionism. The Roman Empire did not fortify and man the frontier. Rather, beyond their nuclear zone of direct control (the territorial empire) lay an inner zone of diplomatic control, composed of client states, and an outer zone of diplomatic control, composed of client tribes. Unlike the passivity of true buffer states, the client states actively supplied auxiliary troops and provided peripheral security against "low intensity" threats. Roman troops were deployed as a field army, available to meet threats rather than being tied to territorial defense. The army was defensive, aimed at internal unrest. The empire was one of political rather than territorial control, buttressed by the threat, rather than the presence, of Roman military might, thus achieving great economy of force. As Luttwak states:

> By virtually eliminating the burden of maintaining continuous frontier

> defenses, the net "disposable" military power generated by the imperial forces was maximized. Hence, the total military power that others could perceive as being available to Rome for offensive use—and that could therefore be put to political advantage by diplomatic means—was also maximized. Thus the empire's political military power could be converted into actual political control at a high rate of exchange.[13]

While the similarities between the Romans and the Aztecs can be overstated, they did share certain characteristics: 1) expansion of political dominance without direct territorial control, and 2) a focus on the internal security of the empire by exercising influence on a limited range of activities within the client states, which was achieved by 3) retaining rather than replacing local officials in most cases. Because their imperial concerns were limited, maintenance of the empire was achieved with great economy of force, local resources being relied on for local security and order. The Aztec army did not have to maintain a presence. It was mobilized only for further conquests, rebellions, and other major disruptions. For lesser matters, the threat of its inexorable presence was sufficient to achieve compliance of the clients. In such a system, a standing army, garrisons, and fortifications take on a different significance than in a territorial empire. By adopting this alternative model, the heretofore "inadequate" pivotal characteristics of the Aztec empire can be profitably reanalyzed.

Aztec expansion was neither continuous nor smooth,[14] but punctuated by revolts and reconquest,[15] usually following succession of rulers. However, the Aztecs did engage in successful imperial expansion[16] and there was at least some internal cohesion.

Army

The Aztec army was drawn from both noble (*pipiltin*) and commoner (*macehualtin*) ranks, with the bulk coming from the *macehualtin*, and not the middle or artesan class.[17] In short, the *calpolli* (originally a kin group, but by the time of the Spanish Conquest, a residential and land-holding group) formed the basis of the commoner units (see Kellogg and Lewis, this volume). The nobles lacked an analogous organizational unit and fought as members of military orders.[18] Men were trained in schools, nobles in the *calmecac* and commoners in the *telpochcalli*, with brief retraining prior to a war.[19] Weapons were stored at the entrance to the temples, apparently in each barrio.[20]

The internal organization of the military is still imperfectly understood, but Piho[21] has established a provisional scheme distinguishing general grades of warriors, specific ranks, the administrative hierarchy, specific offices within either the military or administrative hierarchies, and military orders. There were seven general grades, varying by battle experience and the number of enemy captured, and fifteen specific ranks subdividing the general grades. Both military and administrative offices were occupied by warriors of various ranks, and the military orders—*otomih* and *cuachictin*—were composed of seasoned warriors. While nobility was a prerequisite for some of these ranks,[22] that alone was not sufficient—military valor was required.[23] In short, the Aztec military was complexly organized, distinguishing between higher noble and lower commoner ranks, each graded by valor and military success, and permitting limited penetration of the noble ranks by meritorious commoners.

Although technically a standing army may have been absent,[24] the existence of military ranks, grades, and offices clearly indicates a military infrastructure running through Aztec society, providing the organizational basis for mobilization. And while few military professionals per se existed—save military instructors in the *telpochcalli*[25]—such a distinction, although meaningful for the laboring commoners, lost significance among the nobility. The emphasis laid on martial valor, the prominence of military orders, and the existence of gathering houses for warriors, all indicate a professionalism that cannot be defined away simply because nobles received financial support for being noble rather than for being warriors. Such criticism would also deny the professionalism of European knightly orders.

A clearly differentiated military structure existed in Aztec society, patterned after Aztec social organization. Males were instructed in the art of war, public armories existed, and a quiescent chain of command lay ready. Atop this massive force stood highly trained, and largely noble, military orders that formed the vanguard and elite of the army. But only in time of war was it mobilized.

Fortifications

While fortifications may bear directly on the nature of the military, the issue in Mesoamerica is a thorny one, varying with one's basic assumptions. Central Mexico is dotted with sites that are arguably fortified. However, the designation of specific sites as fortified meets with less agreement.[26] Much of this is definitional, revolving around the role of fortifications in relation to the Aztecs' assumed military capacity. This condition is scarcely alleviated by the scant data of actual site use. The problem is complicated by the apparent lack of fortifications in many cities, including Tenochtitlan.

In Europe, the history of military constructions is reflective of the growth of political units, fortifications expanding from small strongholds dominating the surrounding countryside, to walled city-states, to fortified boundaries of centralized national states.[27] Applying this to archaeological data is problematic, however, particularly where the empire is heterodox and loosely tied. Archaeologically, political expansion may not be readily distinguishable from trade. Thus, sites in Mesoamerica permit an interpretive continuum from decentralized to centralized polities. Fortified cities may be interpreted as isolated polities maintaining their own defenses, but so too may large ostensibly unfortified cities, such as Tenochtitlan, which may not need fortification due to size or location.[28] On the other hand, unfortified sites may be regarded as the center of a state while fortified cities may be interpreted as occupying the political periphery, where contact with possible adversaries was likely.[29] Thus, while numerous arguably fortified sites exist, their significance is subject to different interpretations, especially insofar as their existence and dispersions reflect directly on imperial territorial extent.

For the period of Aztec dominance, historic and protohistoric sources clearly indicate some type of political empire in which the capital and constituent parts are detailed, so its expanse is known. However, the assumption that it fits the territorial empire has not been demonstrated. Furthermore, from the perspective of the hegemonic empire, a correlation between polity size and fortification distribution is less compelling. The extent to which these sites were permanent fortifications is pertinent only when territorial control is a goal. Where it is not, the role of fortifications is different and criticisms based on their inadequacy—judged as permanent fortifications—is hollow.

Garrisons

The issue of garrisons also bears directly on the nature of the military and is, to a large extent, definitional. In normal parlance, garrison (*guarnición*) may refer to either a place or to the troops manning it, but it is the conjunction of the two that makes the term's application to troops meaningful. And this is what Covarrubias intends, not only from the context of the full entry, but from the sentence in question, "*Guarnición de soldados, porque guardan y asseguran la fuerza o plaza donde estan.*"—Garrison of soldiers, because they guard and protect the fortress or place where they are. However, a debatable definition is a weak basis on which to rest an argument about the military structure of an empire. More light may be shed by examining *guarniciones* as revealed in sixteenth-century documents.

Despite an armed Aztec presence in many parts of central Mexico, and the existence of regular troop transit areas,[30] *guarniciones* were apparently limited to frontier areas: Tarascan, Gulf coast, and Chichimec.[31] In short, they were located adjacent to hostile polities and in areas of imperial expansion.[32] Rather than an accidental collection of transitory troop locations, the geopolitical distribution of *guarniciones* indicates an orderly pattern. *Guarniciones* were more than simply troops where they were, but that they were permanently manned fortifications may also be suspect.

Based on site surveys,[33] and sixteenth-century accounts,[34] *guarniciones* appear to have been strongly fortified sites, and to have had resident Aztec troops.[35] These troops were supported by royal tribute from subject towns in the region.[36] However, some, if not all, forts were unoccupied during peacetime,[37] and frequently, the manning of these forts fell to local towns in lieu of other tribute.[38] The obligation to supply troops varied according to the incidence of war [as did the obligation to send supplies],[39] and rotated among the subject towns, each manning the fort at intervals for a limited period.[40] *Guarniciones* entailed not simply troops, but locations that maintained armories.[41] In short, they were fortified strongholds where arms were kept, and which were manned as tribute by local communities on a rotating, periodic basis, and intermittently by Aztec troops. While *guarniciones* may have been less than armies from Tenochtitlan permanently stationed in farflung areas of the empire, they were considerably more than merely temporary camps for transient troops.

Logistics

The Aztec military organization was not simple, nor was its task. There was an effective army, but the nature of the hegemonic empire placed considerable burdens on it. Enforcing Aztec desires and defending tributary areas placed enormous stress on a military system lacking permanent occupying forces and suffered under the severe transportation constraint of having only human porters[42] to furnish supplies for large armies, not only in battle, but on marches of considerable duration. These problems were largely overcome by relying on resources of the local tributaries to maintain Aztec forces at minimal cost.

In the field, the Aztec army required, and received, considerable auxiliary support in the form of Aztec colonists relocated in potentially troublesome areas, supplies provided as tribute en route, allied troops from various places in the empire, and local troops manning the frontiers in lieu of tribute.

The difficulty of Aztec military logistics has led to the conclusion that their military efforts were greatly handicapped.[43] However, these constraints were largely overcome by royal granaries spread throughout the empire to store tribute grain,[44] and by local support in areas of transit. The local support, however, was not always reliable. In some instances, goods were freely supplied;[45] but in others, they were essentially extorted. If supplies were not voluntarily offered, they were seized and the towns' fields destroyed. The army often took what it needed, causing the people along the march route to hide their food.[46] However, this practice appears to have been more prominent in the early years, under conditions of little imperial consolidation.

With imperial expansion, lands (*milchimalli* or *cacalomilli*) were set aside for the support of the army, and, as part of their tribute, towns en route supplied both food and weapons to the army when it passed.[47] Food was also supplied to the *guarniciones*, as were arms, and lands (*itonalli*) were set aside for the provisioning of *guarniciones*.[48] Military supplies provided under the tribute system allowed the army to move through the empire relatively quickly and unencumbered.

The supply problem was further reduced by the use of local troops. Although most of the soldiers were drawn from the Triple Alliance (Tenochtitlan, Texcoco, and Tlacopan) and other cities of the Valley of Mexico,[49] they could be drawn from a larger area, and providing troops for the army when it passed through subject towns was common: Tepexpa, Totolapa, Alahuiztlan, Tetela, Atitalaquia, Tuchtepeque, Teticpac, Chichicapa, Petlaltzingo, Texaluca, Chilapa, and Sultepec.[50] Thus, supplies for the whole armed body for the entire march from Tenochtitlan to the site of the battle were not necessary, as many troops were added en route, which not only increased Aztec strength, but did so at a relatively low cost in supplies.

Added to the troops collected en route were frontier armies. Peoples occupying regions bordering such hostile groups as the Yopes, Tlaxcallans, and Tarascans, were exempt from the payment of tribute goods in return for military service: Acapetlaguaya, Teloloapa, and Tamazola.[51]

During the reign of Ahuitzotl, married men were recruited from various cities of the empire—most from Tenochtitlan, Texcoco, and Tlacopan, but also from subject towns—and sent to distant regions to settle.[52] This occurred in Oztuma, Alahuiztlan, and Teloloapan, in Tuchtepeque, and also in Oaxaca.[53] These colonies have been interpreted as the previously discussed *guarniciones*;[54] but the few colonies, in contrast to the oft-mentioned and scattered *guarniciones*, argues forcefully against their being the same in all instances, although an argument may be made in specific cases. At a minimum, the existence of Aztec colonists in distant settlements would have provided security for transient soldiers, local levees in time of war, and a loyal force to suppress possible revolts. Thus, the Aztec war complex consisted of a core army drawn from the cities of the Valley of Mexico, augmented by proportionally cheaper troops gained en route, and supplemented at the frontiers by loyal colonists and local armies providing border defense in lieu of tribute.

Internal Control

Despite the ingenuity exhibited by the Aztecs in overcoming some of the difficulties entailed in their imperial organization, such an organization necessarily permitted the existence of largely autonomous local governments. This limited imperial control thus led to the perception of the Aztec empire as an inferior political system—an inadequate, possibly embryonic empire.[55]

The inadequacy of the Aztec empire is indicated by endemic internal revolts. Unlike a territorial empire in which the threat to centralized control is greatest at the periphery of the system, in a hegemonic empire there is limited territorial integration and little comprehensive political structure to maintain greater cohesion at the core than at the periphery. Force and the threat of force supply the cohesion. The feasibility of revolt does not systematically vary by proximity to the center. In contrast to territorial empires, virtually all of the provinces that had revolted were near the center of the empire, not at the periphery.[56]

The Aztec empire cannot fairly be faulted for lack of proper local control or for the recurrent revolts.[57] Rather than flaws in a territorial empire, these were logical consequences of a hegemonic empire. Although hegemonic empires enjoy certain advantages over territorial empires, such as economy of force, greater expanse, smaller military, and greater economic return where that is a goal, their structure entails certain disadvantages as well. External threats of low intensity may be resolved locally without the intervention of imperial forces, but high-intensity threats can be dealt with by imperial forces only after the fact, in response.

Conclusions

Hegemonic empires are well suited to endemic threats, as forces can be deployed to specific areas for some duration; but sporadic threats, such as rebellion, are kept in check by the 'armed suasion' of absent imperial forces, or put down after the fact. Hegemonic empires do not rely on immediate force to deter revolt. Hence, its occurrence is not a failure of the imperial system, but an expected consequence of the hegemonic structure. Hegemonic empires are oriented toward maintaining tranquility, not maintaining fortified imperial boundaries, thus freeing forces for the former use. Backed by eventual imperial force, client states are largely responsible for their own security.

Despite intimations of fortified positions and border seiges,[58] the number of imperial soldiers, their placement, their permanency, the use of local auxiliaries in perimeter defense, and the intermittent nature of border fortifications argue strongly against a determined defense of the perimeter of the Aztec empire. Rather, these factors slowed intruders and acted as a trip wire for response. Territory could be penetrated by troops (slowed only by problems of logistics). Seizure and exclusive control of territory was not an Aztec goal. Cities and the control of populations were the objects of war, and defense was structured accordingly. The hegemonic empire focused on internal control, not on perimeter defense.

NOTES

[1]Clausewitz 1943.

[2]Clausewitz 1943:3-24.

[3]Finer 1975:85-86; Tilly 1975b:73.

[4]Gorenstein 1966:60-63.

[5]Bosch Gimpera 1966:14; Gibson 1971:392; Gorenstein 1966:46.

[6]Gorenstein 1966:53-55.

[7]Aztec garrisons are mentioned at Oztuma (PNE 6:105, 149), Alahuiztlan (PNE 6:123), Asuchitlan (Vargas Rea 1944-1946, 7/5:26), Chinantla (PNE 4:61-62), Oaxaca (PNE 4:120, 194), Cuestlauaca (PNE 4:165-166), Mixteca (PNE 4:185), Acatlan (PNE 5:113), Teozacualco (Gómez de Orozco 1927:175), Ayusuchiquilazala (Caso 1928a:147-148), Xilotepec (Frías y Frías 1906:21), Cotastla and Otopo (Ramírez Cabañas 1943:24), and Tepecuacuilco. Tarascan garrisons are mentioned at Taymeo (Vargas Rea 1944-1946, 7/1:104), Sirandaro and Guayameo (Vargas Rea 1944-1946, 7/8:20-21), and Meztitlan had a garrison on their frontier with the Aztecs (DII 4:532). Many of the "fortified" hilltops served as refuges to which village populations retreated when threatened (Spores 1965).

[8]For Gorenstein, the fates of a standing army, garrisons, and specialized fortifications are interwoven. If any exist, the others may exist, but if none are supposed to exist, as her perspective demands (Gorenstein 1963:125, 138, 148, 161-62, 167, 168, 178), the admission of any is detrimental. Davies (1972:219) likewise contests the existence of garrisons, but the consequences of error are not so telling on his general view.

[9]Davies 1972:219.

[10]Skinner 1977b:308-45.

[11]Bernal 1966; Borgonio Gaspar 1954-55; Bosch Gimpera 1966; Caso 1966; Corona Núñez 1966; Davies 1972, 1977a; Gorenstein 1963, 1966; Jiménez Moreno 1966; Paddock 1966a, 1966b, 1966c; Palerm 1956; Phillips 1979.

[12]Luttwak 1976.

[13]Luttwak 1976:19.

[14]Despite attempts to analytically differentiate eras (Berdan 1975:238-39; Katz 1972:151), Aztec imperial growth does not readily lend itself to periodization beyond kingly reigns (Gibson 1971:378-80; Holt 1979). Furthermore, claims of conquest are often ambiguous as to success of the campaign, permanence of the conquest, and which city merits primary credit. Prior to the rule of Itzcoatl (ca. 1427 to ca. 1440), the Aztecs were under the domination of the Tepanec empire, so early victories are best interpreted as Tepanec conquests in which the Aztecs played a subordinate role.

The earliest claimed conquests occurred within the Valley of Mexico during the reign of Acamapichtli (ca. 1376 to ca. 1396), aimed at Xochimilco, Cuitlahuac, and Mixquic to the south, and at Xaltocan to the north. Further campaigns were waged against Cuauhtinchan in Puebla and Cuernavaca in Morelos. Huitzilihuitl (ca. 1396 to ca. 1417) participated in attacks on Tula to the north and on Texcoco, Acolman, Otumba, and Tulanzingo to the east, but the following reign (Chimalpopoca, ca. 1417 to ca. 1427) was largely uneventful.

The Aztecs formed the Triple Alliance (of Tenochtitlan, Texcoco, and Tlacopan) during the reign of Itzcoatl and overthrew the Tepanec empire. Conquests were carried out in an area bounded on the north by

Tula, on the west by Huitzitzilapan, on the south by Xiuhtepec, and on the east by the Texcoco area, as well as in northern Guerrero. Under Mocteuczomah I (Mocteuczomah Ilhuicamina, ca. 1440 to ca. 1469), enormous thrusts were carried out. The immediate vicinity was consolidated, including Chalco, the northern Tepanec towns of Xilotepec, Tula, Atotonilco, Hueypuchtla, and Itzcuincuitlapilco, and Aztec armies expanded further into Guerrero, Morelos, central Puebla, northern Oaxaca, upland central Veracruz, and conquered the Gulf coast cities of Tuxpan, Tlatlauhquitepec, Cempoala, and Quiahuixtlan. Tlatelolco was conquered during the reign of Axayacatl (ca. 1469 to ca. 1481), as were the towns of Atlapulco, Capuhuac, Xatlatlauhco, and Ocoyacac to the west during what was primarily a period of consolidation in central Puebla, central Veracruz, and the Tuxpan region. During Tizoc's reign (ca. 1481 to ca. 1486), Toluca and Yanhuitlan were conquered, but his rule was largely without appreciable gains, a fact Davies (1977a:157) suggests may have led to Tizoc's early (and possibly involuntary) demise. His successor, Ahuitzotl (ca. 1486 to ca. 1502) was responsible for another period of major expansion, conquering such farflung areas as southern Guerrero, Oaxaca, southern Chiapas, and the Tehuantepec area, as well as the cities of Huejotla and Coatzacoalcos. The interior, however, remained incompletely controlled until the reign of Mocteuczomah II (Mocteuczomah Xocoyotzin, ca. 1502 to 1520), who also conquered additional areas of central and southern Oaxaca, northern Puebla, Veracruz, and Soconusco. Despite these conquests, the Aztec empire bordered, and frequently encircled, independent regions: Michoacan, Meztitlan, Tlaxcala, Yopitzinco, Cholula, Huejotzingo, Acapulco, and Acatepec.

[15]Holt (1976:61) lists the revolting provinces as follows:

[province number (based on Barlow 1949), name, number of revolts]

2	Tepequacuilco	2
3	Tlachco	1
7	Quahuacan	1
10	Quauhtitlan	2
11	Xilotepec	1
18	Tlapacoyan	1
19	Atotonilco el Grande	2
21	Chalco	4
22	Quauhnahuac	3
23	Huaxtepec	1
26	Tlatlauhquitepec	1
27	Quauhtochco	1
28	Cuetlaxtlan	2
32	Yoaltepec	1
35	Coayxtlahuacan	1
37	Citlaltepec and Tlatelolco	2
38	Petlacalco	2

[16]Gibson 1971:378-80; Holt 1979.

[17]Davies 1972:213.

[18]Davies 1972:214; Gorenstein 1966:58.

[19]Borgonio Gaspar 1954-55:383; Davies 1972:214.

[20]Davies 1972:214; Gorenstein 1966:57.

[21]Piho 1972, 1974.

[22]Borgonio Gaspar 1954-55:383.

[23]Stenzel 1976:180.

[24]Contra Kurtz 1978:177-78.

[25]Piho 1974:174.

[26]For instance, see Hardoy (1973:91) on Xochicalco, and Armillas (1942-1944:165) and Gorenstein (1966:55) for opposing interpretations of Oztuma.

[27]De la Croix 1972.

[28]Armillas 1951:80.

[29]Palerm 1956:194-95.

[30]Caso 1928b:170.

[31]PNE 6:105, 147; Ramírez Cabañas 1943:24; Frías y Frías 1906:21.

[32]PNE 4:61-62.

[33]Armillas 1942-1944.

[34]PNE 6:105, 110, 147, 257.

[35]PNE 6:123; 4:61-62.

[36]Caso 1928a:147-48.

[37]PNE 4:85.

[38]PNE 6:116, 257.

[39]PNE 4:61-62, 165-66.

[40]PNE 6:147.

[41]PNE 5:113.

[42]Transport was by *tlameme* porters, each carrying two arrobas (22.5 kilograms, or 50 pounds), five leagues per day (Díaz del Castillo 1974:99). Also see Hassig n.d.

[43]Davies 1977b:299; Gorenstein 1966:58.

[44]Hernández Xolocotzi 1949:160-63.

[45]Durán 1967, II:165.

[46]Durán 1967, II:167, 180.

[47]Barlow 1947:264; Caso 1928b:170, 1963:869; PNE 4:90, 165-66, 5:70, 74, 76, 6:149.

[48]Caso 1963:869.

[49]Mexicalzingo (PNE 6:196), Chimalhuacan (PNE 6:70), Acolman (PNE 6:213), Tenochtitlan, Texcoco, Tlacopan, Xochimilco, Chalco, Culhuacan, Ixtapalapa, and Huitzilopochco (Durán 1967, II:319).

[50]PNE 6:235, 6:8, 6:102, 6:133, 286, 6:206, 4:61-62, 4:111, 4:117, 5:70, 5:86, 5:178, 7:11.

[51]PNE 6:116, 6:147, 4:84.

[52]Durán 1967, II:351-55.

[53]PNE 6:105, 4:61-62.

[54]Davies 1972:215-17.

[55]Davies 1972:217, 220; Gorenstein 1966:60-63.

[56]Contrary to Davies' (1977b:342) assertion, revolts were closer to the center of the empire, which may relect the length of time the provinces have been incorporated into the Aztec empire: the greater the time, the more the revolts. However, this does not appear to be the case. Duration may present more occasions for revolt, but this is only one factor and does not directly correlate with incidence of revolts.

[57]Gorenstein 1966:61-62.

[58]Davies 1972:217; Stanislawski 1947.

AZTEC WOMEN IN EARLY COLONIAL COURTS: STRUCTURE AND STRATEGY IN A LEGAL CONTEXT

Susan Kellogg

When Angelina Verónica, an Aztec Indian woman, appeared before the *Real Audiencia* in Mexico City in 1585, she went as the guardian of her two grandchildren. In that capacity, she sued to protect certain property rights belonging to her grandchildren. She was not unique in going before the *Real Audiencia* (functioning in this instance as a court). In fact, numerous Indian women produced legal documents and participated in legal suits. The question that immediately arises is why—why did so many Aztec women come before the *Real Audiencia*?

To understand the extent of Indian women's participation in the early colonial court system, it is useful to discuss some general background about pre-Hispanic Tenochtitlan (now Mexico City). From 1325 until the Conquest, this city was the Aztec capital and seat of an expanding empire. Much of what is understood about Tenochtitlan and the Aztecs themselves, is based on the classic ethnohistoric sources. This documentation reveals a great deal about the more spectacular aspects of Indian society such as human sacrifice, religion, war, government, and the huge marketplaces. But information on actual lives, beliefs, and behavior of native peoples is more difficult to find. It is particularly difficult to assess women's lives and social roles from these sources.

There are other, infrequently consulted ethnohistoric sources, however, that allow us to undertake profitable investigation of Indian social organization and social history in the late pre-Columbian and early colonial periods. In an effort to elucidate the fate of native women in the Spanish legal system, this article utilizes one kind of administrative record: property suits tried before the *Real Audiencia.*

The *audiencia*

> ...functioned, above all, as [a] court of appeal; the viceroy or governor dealt with government, war, the supervision of the Royal Treasury, and ordinary justice (exercised by the lieutenant-governor, who was a *letrado*). The viceroy was also president of the *Audiencia* but he was not permitted to intervene directly in specifically judicial matters; these were left to the *oidores*. The *Audiencia* sometimes operated as an ordinary law court of first instance, especially in litigation between natives and Spaniards, which were considered privileged "court cases."[1]

Most of the cases discussed come from the *ramo de Tierras* of the Archivo General de la Nación in Mexico City, the section containing the majority of native property litigation of the colonial period. This body of documentation contains abundant information on Indian social organizational in the sixteenth century. The data found in *Tierras* are particuarly useful in analyzing Indian legal behavior and strategies in the early colonial period. These documents permit better understanding of the relationship between formal procedures of law and legal behavior.

Fifty-five cases gathered for this study came from the *ramo de Tierras*. Four additional cases came from other sources. Case selection was based on three criteria. The first was that the owners of the property were natives of Tenochtitlan-Tlatelolco. The second was that the suits originate in the sixteenth century. The dates of the litigation used here range from 1557 (the earliest suit found) to 1601. The final criterion was that at least one of the parties to the suit be Indians. Eleven suits were over rural lands owned by inhabitants of the city. Two were over urban garden plots (*chinampas*), and forty-six concerned house sites or the boundaries between house sites.

In working with these documents and especially in analyzing inheritance patterns, I became aware of the striking number of women participating in litigation, a fact previously noted by Calnek and Carrasco (personal communications). This observation was borne out by an analysis of the wills, in which eighteen of twenty-nine extant wills were made by women and the remaining eleven by men. Actually, the eighteen women's wills were made by fifteen women; two women made five different wills. But this does not change the observation that a majority of the extant wills were by women.

Why were Aztec women active in the Spanish legal arena in early colonial central Mexico? In answering this question there are a number of diverse pieces of evidence that must be examined: (1) the legal rights of women under Spanish law; (2) Aztec women's activities in the early colonial legal arena: (3) the status and role of women in Aztec society prior to the Conquest; and (4) the status and role of Aztec women in early colonial Aztec society. Both pre-Hispanic property rights and legal rights introduced by the Spaniards influenced women's abilities to manipulate the system and use power in the early colonial period. The implication is that, at least in the legal arena, Aztec women won somewhat greater power in the early colonial period than they held during the pre-Hispanic era. Yet, paradoxically, this improvement in the legal situation of women was not matched by improvement in other sectors of their lives.

Women's Legal Rights Under Spanish Law

To understand Aztec women's participation in these legal proceedings, it is important to examine their standing in the courts and their legal status under Spanish law. The legal situation of Indian women was still further complicated by the fact that they *were* Indian and that they resided in a colony far from Spain where Spanish law had to make certain compromises with Indian law, customs, and practices. Two aspects of the relationship between Indian women and Spanish law will be examined here: (1) Spanish law and women in general; and (2) the institutional framework of Spanish justice as it affected Indians in the New World.

Spanish law, as well as Spanish intellectual thought, regarded women and men as different types of beings with different legal and social rights and duties.[2] A basic assumption of Spanish law was that women were dependent members of domestic groups, living under the authority of their fathers or husbands; widowhood, of course, could alter this status. Ots Capdequí, in his study of Spanish law in the Indies, comments that widows enjoyed "full civil capacity."[3] Women needed the permission of their husbands to participate in a contract or other legal matters, such as appearing in court, but a judge could force a husband to give this permission.[4] Overall, it can fairly be said of women's position in early

Spanish law codes that

> ...only in truly exceptional situations was the full civil capacity of women recognized; the rule of family law so absorbed the personality of the women that only under very special circumstances could the woman emphasize her individuality with full responsibility for her actions.[5]

This picture is supported by the work of Bernal de Bugeda.[6]

The legal status of women in Spanish possessions in the New World was not so simple.[7] Recent scholarship,[8] based on detailed examination of dowries and wills (1640-1790) of women of Puebla and Guadalajara, demonstrates several ways in which women had more power, either in codified law or in actual practice, than contended: Ots Capdequí

> 1. While women were under the control of fathers, then husbands, they could, if widowed, be appointed as guardian for their children.
>
> 2. A woman' s dowry property remained legally hers "...and could not be alienated without her permission."
>
> 3. Of great interest here is that upon the death of the husband "...the wife was entitled to half of the wealth accumulated during the marriage, her dowry, and whatever property she may have owned separately. These rights gave the woman, in practical terms, an economic edge over the potential rights of the children."[9]

Thus, Spanish women had more of a basis for strategic maneuvering than might be expected given our stereotyped view of the Spanish legal framework. The essential point is that while this framework was certainly limiting to women, it was not absolutely limiting.

We are dealing with *Indian* women here, and the question arises as to what extent the institutional framework of Spanish justice affected Indians in the New World. There are several studies that treat this issue,[10] but none deals in detail with the specific place of Indian women and their legal problems, needs, or issues in the Spanish institutional framework. On the one hand, evidence in the *Tierras* documents indicates that Indian women were subject to certain Spanish rules and restrictions. Thus, married women often (though not always) had letters of permission from their husbands to go before the *Real Audiencia*. On the other hand, because the Aztec kinship system and inheritance rules differed from those of the Spanish, the *Real Audiencia* had to make some accomodation to this fact in its rulings. Ots Capdequí[11] has pointed out how Spanish justice might be influenced by Indian law or custom, due to the decree by Spanish monarchs that Indian law stand in areas where it did not interfere with Spanish law and important interests. *Tierras* evidence points to the fact that there was a period of adjustment and compromise in which Spanish law and Indian law and practice accommodated each other. Yet, at the same time, there can be no doubt that long range trends obliterated the native ruling elites and eventually drastically changed the culture and way of life.[12]

The *Tierras* evidence is important because it represents a body of data in which generalizations or hypotheses about the interactions of Spanish law and Indian cultural beliefs and practices might be tested. That is one purpose of this paper. Nevertheless, it remains true, as Borah has pointed out, that indigenous practices were probably responsible for settling most disputes:

> Even though few records have been found thus far and most proceedings may never have been committed to written record, it seems likely that local custom would continue to be important at the lowest levels of native litigation and justice. The Indian *alcaldes* would be better versed in it than in Spanish law and would rely upon what they knew. Moreover, the Community itself would insist upon its own custom.[13]

Borah[14] classifies the types of litigation that arose as ecclesiastical and royal cases, subdividing the royal cases into three groups: civil, criminal, and administrative. The *Tierras* suits fall into the civil category since they were not criminal proceedings, nor were they decided by administrative decree.

We can now ask: what can be learned about Indian women's legal position and behavior from these documents? Additionally, the question of cultural change and accommodation between two very different bodies of law, will also be examined.

Aztec Women in the Early Colonial Legal Arena

Gómez de Cervantes, a judicial official who travelled in central Mexico during the sixteenth century, wrote of Indian women:

> When some Indian has a dispute, though the Indian may be very important, able and skilled, he will not appear before the court without bringing his wife with him, and they inform and speak that which by reason of the lawsuit it is necessary to say, and the husbands are very timid and quiet; and if the court asks something that it wishes to know, the husband responds: "here is my wife who knows it"; and in such manner it has happened to me upon asking one Indian or indeed many, "what is your name?", and before the husband responds, his wife says it; and thus in all other things; thus they are, men who have submitted to the will of the woman.[15]

Analysis of the case material gathered for Tenochtitlan-Tlatelolco bears out Gómez de Cervantes' observations about the participation of Indian women in the legal matters handled by the *Real Audiencia.* Fifty-three of the fifty-nine cases studied involved actual litigation. In thirty-eight of the fifty-three suits the main participants were both males and females. In eleven cases the main participants were exclusively male, and in four they were exclusively female. Males and females might be on opposing sides, or they might sue jointly. Sometimes these were husbands and wives, but there are also examples of brothers and sisters or mothers and children (sons and/or daughters), suing jointly. Women were plaintiffs as well as defendants.

In fact, forty+ women were plaintiffs (the + means that several women in one case sued jointly, but the exact number was not stated). Of these forty+ women, eight were widows, sixteen were married, and sixteen were either minors (two) or were of unidentified marital status. It is likely that many of the latter were actually widowed since no husbands were mentioned. Twenty-six of the women won their suits, nine lost, and for five there was no decision. Fourteen women sued kinspersons, and eleven of these fourteen were females suing by themselves or with other females (i.e., not with husbands). Eleven women who were kin and thirteen who were not were sued (twenty-four in total). Of the fourteen kinspersons sued, thirteen were affinally related, and all the property at stake was inherited property of some kind. Forty-one women were defendants, fourteen were widows, nine were married, and eigthteen were either minors or had no identifiable marital status. Seven female defendants won suits in which they were involved, twenty-three lost, and there was no decision for eleven.[16]

Forty+ men were plaintiffs (here the plus refers to more men than women because there were four suits in which large groups of men sued but the number was not cited). Except for those cases in which married couples sued toegether, it is more difficult to elaborate on the marital status of these men because it was often unstated. Not surprisingly, marital status was not a relevant characteristic of men's legal status. Of these men, fifteen won their cases, eight lost, and for seventeen there was no decision. Seven males sued kinspersons, and four of these were males who did not sue with wives. These seven sued six related females and three related males (nine). Eight were affinally related, and all the property contested in these suits was inherited. Forty-two+ males were defendants, Seven won, twenty lost, and there was no decision for fifteen. One note of importance is that while much of the property involved in lawsuits was inherited, some of the litigation concerned property that had been sold (twenty out of fifty-three cases). Thirteen of the twenty cases involving sale occurred after 1575 (i.e., in the final quarter of the sixteenth century).

Several important points emerge from the numerical data:

1. The number of male and female plaintiffs and male and female defendants is roughly equal.
2. Women were somewhat more likely than men to be involved in suits with kinspersons.
3. Women plaintiffs had a much better chance of winning than women defendants, and this pattern is very similar to the pattern for men.
4. The pattern of significant participation in legal affairs by women, at least in relationship to property, is also seen in the wills.

Despite the involvement of native women in legal affairs, women were second class citizens in the court in certain respects. For example, women infrequently participated as witnesses. While women did occasionally serve as witnesses, they did so significantly less often than men. Female witnesses tended to be widows, although there are rare examples of married women providing testimony. Women were not more likely to call upon female rather than male witnesses; in fact, the reverse is true. Moreover, women were seldom called as witnesses in cases involving only men as the principal litigants or in cases involving large, rural estates.

The case of Angelina Verónica[17] mentioned at the start of this article, is useful in illustrating various aspects of Aztec women's participation in the legal arena of early colonial society and the legal strategies they employed. Angelina Verónica, a widow, was the maternal grandmother of Bonifacio Maximiliano and Bernardina Francisca. In 1585 she went before the *Real Audiencia* on their behalf to protect part of their inheritance. Some land the children had inherited from their paternal great-grandmother was being usurped by a second unrelated party. The children had inherited several properties from this great-grandmother, Angelina Martina. When she died, she left a will that provides fascinating details on the large amount of property she amassed during her lifetime. It was introducted into evidence by Angelina Verónica to support the children's claim to the specific piece of land in contention.

Angelina Martina left the largest amount of property of any woman making a will and about as much as the wealthiest males for whom wills still survive. While other women tended to leave their personal house compound, various small properties such as cloth, thread, domestic implements, or money, and more rarely, small amounts of rural land to which they held rights, Angelina Martina left significant land holdings and large quantities of each of the other categories of property. She apparently was not a member of the noble stratum, but rather had close ties to the merchants. Her will extends for some eight pages, and in it she leaves numerous amounts of "personality," such as cloth and thread as well as realty, consisting of lands and houses. She left at least four house sites, most of which were urban. She also left sixteen pieces of land, some containing houses. Some of the land and houses were properties that she had inherited, while others she had purchased.

The details of the litigation are that another woman, doña María Coatonal, a noble who was also the plaintiff in a separate complex and lengthy suit, apparently mistook one of the plots of land that Angelina Martina left to her great-grandchildren as her own and collected the proceeds from it. Angelina Verónica then went to the *Real Audiencia* to assert the claim of her grandchildren. The court called several witnesses including a man, then in jail, who had worked the land as a *terrazguero* (farm laborer). His wife's father had previously worked the property. The *terrazguero* testified that the land had belonged to Angelina Martina. Besides presenting such witnesses, Angelina Verónica presented the will as evidence, as well as a bill of sale dating from 1551 in which it was stated that Angelina Martina bought the land from its previous owner, who had himself inherited it. Doña María Coatonal claimed that she had inherited the property from her grandfather through her father. Her father's brother took control of the property for her and her sisters (who were children at the time) and kept it. Doña María Coatonal mistook the children's property for her own and attempted to collect the fruits of the land. Angelina Verónica then sued her in the name of Bonifacio and Bernardina.

This case illustrates several aspects of women's participation in property litigation heard by the *Real Audiencia*. We see that a widow was able to act as guardian for her young grandchildren and sue in their behalf. Both Angelina Verónica and doña María based their claims to the land in question upon inheritance. Angelina Verónica spoke on behalf of her grandchildren who had inherited the land from their paternal great-grandmother. Doña María claimed that she inherited the land from her father. Claims based on inheritance were by far the most common type lodged by both men and women. Both sexes generally went into court trying to prove that they were entitled to property based on inheritance and often gave much genealogical data to support such claims. It was very common for Indians to sue on the sale of seemingly vacant land or houses, claiming rights to property, and often they were able to succeed in having sales or grants of property overturned.

An example of such a situation can be seen in *Tierras* 55-5 (1564). Around 1539, Pablo Maquex and his wife were given a grant of land and *chinampas* upon which they built houses. This grant was given at the time of their marriage in gratitude for services Pablo had performed for the *principales* of the *barrio*. Ana Xoco, and her husband, Pedro Xochitl, brought suit in 1564, claiming the property as hers. The *gobernador* and *alcaldes* of the *barrio* (San Pablo Tlachcuititlan) investigated the case. They were told by five *tepixques* of the *barrio* that the land originally belonged to the brother of Ana's grandfather and that Pablo had taken the property on which he built his house. They awarded Ana five *chinampas* and a small piece of the property, and gave the rest to Pablo because he had held it for a "long time." The suit continued because Pablo and some of his relatives continued working the land. The *Real Audiencia* eventually gave the entire property to Ana on the basis that, in fact, she truly held the rights to the property through inheritance.

Yet another example is a case involving land rather than houses. In 1579 the widow María Juana and some of her *terrazgueros* sued the *Colegio de San Pablo* and doña Barbola Marta over lands in Huehuetla (250 by 40 *brazas*). María Juana had been married to don Diego de Tapia. Doña Barbola was the daughter of don Pedro (former governor of Izcuicuitlapilco) and doña María de Tapia, sister of don Diego de Tapia and don Hernando de Tapia, from whom doña María had inherited this land. María Juana had workers laboring on the land, but doña Barbola had donated the land (by *capellanía*) to the *Colegio*. There is no final decision in the case, but the fact that there was a set of appeal documents by María Juana indicates that either the *alcaldes* or the *Real Audiencia* ruled against her. Thus, it appears that doña Barbola's claim of inheritance from her mother was upheld against María Juana's claim of inheritance from her husband. But this is not merely a case in which a consanguineal tie was upheld as the basis for inheritance over an affinal tie. In *Tierras* 37-2 the siblings of don Hernando de Tapia, were given shares in land, among them this property. *Tierras* 46-4 indicates that the shares were divided with each sibling having a share in a specific part of the land so that doña Barbola would be the proper heir in this instance. How did Bonifacio, Bernardina, Ana Xoco, and doña Barbola come to have the property rights they successfully asserted before the *Real Audiencia*?

Women in Pre-Hispanic Aztec Society

Aztec women had significant inheritance and property rights in pre-Hispanic society. Aztec residence groups were formed by units that were often larger than nuclear family groupings, based on a parent-child or, more often, a sibling tie. Inheritance patterns supported these residential groupings because more than one person, usually siblings, received rights in residential sites, as well as other parental property.[18] Male and female siblings inherited *equivalent* rights in these parental estates, indicating that their kinship system was cognatic. Other lines of evidence, including kinship ideology and the structure of certain kin units, indicate this as well.

It is not difficult to demonstrate that the ideology of the Aztec kinship system was cognatic. Evidence from the *Florentine Codex* shows that a child was believed to share the substance of both mother and father.[19] This biological connection was stressed metaphorically in other realms of social organization. For example, leadership was often characterized as being like motherhood and fatherhood. A noble, addressing the inhabitants of

Tenochtitlan upon the installation of a new ruler, said "... it is assuredly true that he is thy real mother, thy real father. Thy mother is not thy mother, thy father is not thy father."[20] When parents addressed the leaders of the *telpochcalli*,[21] the parents referred to the children as *amoconetzin* ("your child") and *amopiltzin* ("your child"). *Conetl* is the word for child used by a woman, *pilli* by men or women, and the prefix *amo-* means "your." Thus, the parents implied that the leaders of the *telpochcalli* were to be both fathers and mothers to the children. The structural equivalence of men and women is further exemplified by the belief that women who died in childbirth were like men who died in war. They went to the same afterworld, and young warriors were said to want a finger from the body of such a woman, or some hair, so that they might place such relics on their shields and be brave in battle. Continuing the metaphor, after a woman had a child,

> ...the midwife shouted; she gave war cries, which meant that the little woman had fought a good battle, had become a brave warrior, had taken a captive, had captured a baby.[22]

In making an equivalence between war and birth, an equivalence between men and women may have been implied.[23]

This structural equivalence is also seen in the organization of the relatively shallow, lower level corporate descent units that existed in pre-Hispanic and early colonial Aztec society. Both men and women were members of such groupings and could transmit membership in these descent units. One unit was referred to by the term *tlacamecayotl* (meaning literally "rope of people"). The indigenous concept is similar to what Periano calls a "descent line"[24] and expresses the relationship between an ancestor and his or her descendant(s), traced through one or more connecting links. Such descent lines appear to have been the basis for shallow descent groups. These descent lines were traced from either male or female ancestors and included men and women.[25]

The term *tlacamecayotl* appears in Book Ten of the *Florentine Codex* where it is used to describe a group of kin including an ego's grand-children, male and female children, mother, father, and maternal or paternal grandmother, grandmother, grandfather, great-grandmother, great-grandfather, and great-great-grandparents.[26] Either male or female links could be used to trace an ego's connection to a specific ancestor. The use of such tracing is clear in the *Tierras* documents when individuals provide genealogical information to support their claim (on the basis of inheritance) to property.[27]

The term *teixuiuan*, on the other hand, was a descendant rather than ancestor focused concept, and literally meant "someone's grandchildren." The literal meaning is an important clue to the kin unit and descent implications of the term. It referred to a "group of cousins"[28] and, thus, had a group referent. This descent-unit meaning is further supported by Spanish translations of this or related terms (*noxhuihuan*, or *iixhuihuan*, literally "my" or "his/her grandchildren") in several early colonial documents as *un deudo descendiente*, *parientes*, or *todo sus descendientes*. *Tierras* documents indicate that in either its literal or extended meaning it could include males and females.

The point that emerges from this discussion is that Aztec women's property rights were patterned after the structure of the Aztec kinship system. It was very different from the Spanish kinship system, even though both may be termed "cognatic." The Aztec system emphasized descent and inheritance units composed of groups of siblings; each sibling then passed on rights to his or her own children. The Spanish system emphasized the lineal transmission of rights to one descendant, preferably male, in the inheritance of houses and land, with collaterals receiving money rather than shared rights. But what was the native, pre-Hispanic legal system like, and how did women participate in it?

Offner[29] has provided a detailed description and analysis of the Texcocan legal system, and also comments on the legal system of Tenochtitlan-Tlatelolco. That there was a hierarchy of judges and courts is clear,[30] but there is little extant information on its actual structure. More is known about some types of crimes heard by judges, including adultery, drunkenness, theft, and business offenses and related punishments.[31] Divorce, likewise, took place in a judicial context, with judges often attempting to persuade a couple to reconcile (at least in Texcoco). Women were liable for their actions in such crimes as adultery,[32] but their participation in the hierarchy of the court system is unclear. There are indications that women might have been able to hold certain judicial positions. Women were known to be marketplace "directors," overseeing prices and fairness in the markets.[33]

While it is frustrating that more cannot be learned about the legal activities of Aztec women in the pre-Hispanic era, there are suggestions that women did play important public roles, even though their public status appears to have been declining during the late pre-Hispanic era.[34] Ethnohistorical evidence does not indicate much female participation in the highest political levels of society, but women were very important in the religious realm as deities, priestesses, and practitioners of life-cycle ritual. The latter two roles are of most interest here.

While women who participated in the Aztec religious hierarchy have traditionally been described as nuns, rather than priestesses,[35] their titles and activities indicate that they would best be viewed as priestesses. Clavijero said, in describing the women of the temples:

> Neither was the priesthood limited to the masculine sex; there were also women dedicated to the prompt service of the temples; they offered incense to the idols; they watched the sacred fire; they swept the courtyard, and prepared the offering of food that was made daily; they even presented it themselves to the idols; but they were excluded from the ministry of sacrifice and from preeminent dignities of the priesthood.

There were at least two distinct types of women's participation in religious institutions and in the religious, priestly hierarchy. One type consists of those women, attached to the *calmecac* (school for priests and noble children), who "guarded" and taught young girls. These women may be thought of as teachers. The girls were dedicated by their parents to a deity, and would live and serve in that deity's temple for a certain period of time. The women, called *cuacuacuiltin* or *tlamacauhqueh*,[37] were older, unmarried, and permanently attached to one of these temples. Durán refers to these women as *abadesas* (abbesses) under whom young girls in the temples served, being taught to worship, sweep, fast, light the incense, weave, and spin.[38] Weaving and spinning were the only exclusively female activites in which they were engaged and may have had both ritual and economic functions. Female children could also be entrusted to the *telpochcalli* (school for commoners and warriors). Here they were trained by female teachers or leaders called *ichpoctiachcauh* ("leaders of girls").

The other type of religious specialization was the female functionaries. There were at least two kinds: the *cihuatlamacazqueh*, women who participated in the monthly calendrical ritual, and the *cihuacuacuilli*, women who had specific responsibilities to certain deities such as Toci. A woman entitled *Iztac Cihuatl Cihuacuacuilli* kept watch over those who swept and kept the fire at Toci's temple, Atenchicalcan. She also attended others who served at this temple.[39] According to Sahagún, "...any who made supplications [to the goddess] spoke to the Iztac Ciuatl Ciuaquacuilli."[40]

Women also played important roles in life-cycle ritual. For example, they were very active in all ceremonies after the birth of a child. The midwife proclaimed that a child was born and led the ceremony where the child's umbilical cord was buried, and then ritually greeted the child. In these rites, symbols of the child's sex were displayed. For a male, symbols of his father's profession, such as a soldier's weapon or artisan's tools, were displayed. A spindle, workbasket and broom were displayed for a female child. The child's name was then given by the midwife.[41] As Hellbom has pointed out, it is important to notice the essentially equivalent and parallel nature of male and female birth ceremonies.[42] This parrallelism is seen here as a reflection of the fundamentally cognatic nature of the kinship system, as are women's property rights.

Women also played important economic roles.[43] They were extremely important in the domestic economy of individual households and were often the merchants in local markets. Angelina Martina's wealth, as mentioned earlier in this article, attests to the ability of some merchant women to control large amounts of property, even in the early colonial era; and her will indicates that it was she (not she and a husband) who held control and amassed her wealth.

Women in the Early Colonial Era

Thus far I have argued that one basis for women's assertion of property rights in the *Real Audiencia* lay in the kinship of structure of pre-Hispanic Aztec society. I then suggested that this structure can be used as a basis for understanding women's rules in, and indeed the organization of, other realms of pre-Hispanic society such as the religious sphere. But kinship structure alone is inadequate to explain women's participation of legal proceedings. Women's legal activities during the early colonial period were also the product of the Spanish legal system in the New World that opened up an arena of legal action and manipulation for women. Two questions may be raised here: First, why did women need to go to court if they held these property rights? Second, how did the status of Aztec women change during the early colonial period?

The first question is very difficult to answer. There are great similarities in the strategies used by men and women to assert or protect claims; rights of ownership (especially rights of alienation) rested upon establishing a genealogically valid claim to such ownership and such a claim was particularly strong if it could be traced back into the pre-Hispanic era. Because both women and men used this method of arguing for and supporting their rights, and because of the tremendous importance, of this strategy (used in over 90 percent of all suits), they are presumably arguing for rights based in the indigenous kinship and inheritance system. But it is clear that there was tremendous social dislocation during the early colonial period. People were killed and many house sites (particularly in Tenochtitlan) were destroyed during the Conquest, and epidemics occurred several times in the sixteenth century. The *Tierras* documents describe situations of virtual squatting. They also mention vacant sites being sold by persons who may or may not have had legitimate rights to do so. Sellers in these cases were often persons related distantly by kinship or marriage to the site's earlier owners. Subsequently, litigation might occur as individuals claiming to be either owners or other descendants and heirs attempted to win back their ownership rights. If the validity of such a claim could be proven to the satisfaction of the *Real Audiencia*, that claim overrode any subsequent transactions regarding the property. Thus, sales could be overturned even when there were no means by which the buyer could recover his money. Women often asserted rights to property they were not actually occupying, but frequently they were taken to court, especially if they were single or widowed, by another claimant. Nevertheless, reliance on indigenous (pre-Hispanic) or, at least, inherited, property rights as the basis of a legal claim to property is true of both women and men.

The traditional view of Indian women's rules and status in the early colonial period is that while their status was not very high in the pre-Hispanic period, it fell further during the early colonial period.[44] The complexity of the issues involved are indicated by Nash:

> Thus, the half truth that the conquest of the Americas was the conquest of women can be restated in terms of an analytical separation of forms of reproduction. A more accurate statement would be that the conquest was not one of women, but of Indian male control over the productive power of women, with the result that Spaniards claimed the right to recruit the children born of their relations with Indian women as heirs or laborers. The advantages men enjoyed while their sex was in short supply were eroded as the caste society emerged.

Burkett[45] discussed the status and roles of Indian women in early colonial Peru and found that, generally, indigenous females were in positions of closer contact with Spaniards than were indigenous males, and that women were able to "... strengthen their economic and social position"[46] through their economic activities and social alliances (particularly with Spanish males). Silverblatt[47] has also written of Indian women in early colonial Peru who were able to draw upon their pre-Hispanic religious activities (which were based, to a large extent, in the structure of the kinship system) and the Spanish restructuring of society to emerge powerfully in native resistence to Spanish colonial administration. Nash recognizes the complexity of the situation of Indian women as cultural brokers in the early colonial period. Their status is not totally advantageous, however, for they become trapped by their sex, race, and emerging class position. Greater emphasis must be placed on the various ways women in native Latin American societies were able to maneuver and engage in strategic planning. Even those who owned relatively little property or were not closely allied with individual Spanish men should be considered.

Aztec women's status did not decline in any simple way during the early colonial period. They used new legal forms to defend property rights based in the indigenous kinship system. Their participation in the Spanish legal system had little to do with individual connections to particular Spaniards. Instead, it was a manifestation of the disruption of property rights, perhaps older legal mechanisms, and the creation of new legal institutions in which women sought to participate and to appeal to indigenous kinship norms and practices.

Women's status appears to have been fluctuating, but declining in the late pre-Hispanic era due to the increasing complexity of the Aztec state.[48] But the diverse strands of evidence—economic, religious, kinship—examined here indicate women controlled aspects of life with which they were concerned. Evidence suggests that this control extended to certain aspects of the legal system such as the marketplace judiciary.

During the early colonial period, Indian women were able to use some of their rights as a basis for participating in the Spanish legal system which probably coexisted with a truncated native system for much of the sixteenth century. Examination of the role of Aztec women in property suits from early colonial Mexico leads to three conclusions:

1. Women had legal standing before the *Real Audiencia.*
2. Marriage modified women's legal rights, but, in practice, women retained most of their rights and were not reduced simply to a childlike (or minor) status.
3. Women invoked certain traditional rights in order to legitimate their claims.

The early colonial period in Mexico witnessed a series of profound dislocations in Indian life. One of the many results of these dislocations was that "new" and "old" claims to property were thrown into opposition. The indigenous system of property rights influenced the colonial system to the extent that indigenous rights were recognized by that colonial legal system. Indian women inherited property differently than did Spanish women, and the *Real Audiencia* implicitly recognized this fact, as can be seen in the records of its cases and judgments.

NOTES

[1]Góngora 1975:89.

[2]Fitzmaurice-Kelly 1927; Bernal de Bugeda 1975; Lavrin 1978a.

[3]Ots Capdequíl975:95.

[4]Martínez Alcubilla 1885:II; *Novísima Recopilación* X-I-11-13.

[5]Ots Capdequíl975:95; my translation.

[6]Bernal de Bugeda 1975.

[7]I cannot comment on Spain itself, since I have not examined Spanish evidence on this question. However, I would predict that if one did investigate such evidence, the peninsular situation would also be complex.

[8]Lavrin and Couturier 1979.

[9]Ots Capdequí1975:282, 287.

[10]Gibson 1964, 1966; Haring 1947; Ots Capdequí1975; MacLachlan 1974; Góngora 1975; Borah 1982.

[11]Ots Capdequí1975:11.

[12]Borah 1982.

[13]Borah 1982:273.

[14]Borah 1982:274.

[15]Gómez de Cervantes 1944:135; my translation.

[16]Nader (1967) analyzed sixty court cases from the Zapotec town of Ralu'a. While the types of cases vary much more (from "familial" cases to various types of clearly criminal "complaints"), there are some interesting contrasts to the data presented here. Of forty-seven men, seventeen were plaintiffs and thirty were defendants; of thirty-four women, twenty-two were plaintiffs, and twelve were defendants. There was, thus, significant female participation, but many more women were plaintiffs than defendants. Nader attributes women's high participation to lack of a male relative to participate for them. Women's suits were more often with kin (particularly affines) and men's with non-kin.

[17]AGN-T 49-5, 1585.

[18]AGN-T 46-4.

[19]Sahagún 1950-1969, VI:175, 216.

[20]Sahagún 1950-1969, VI:79.

[21]The *telpochcalli* ("young men's house") was a school for young men, commoners, training them to be warriors. Girls did attend these but the nature of their participation is not really clear (see, for example, Soustelle's discussion, 1961:73).

[22]Sahagún 1950-1969, VI:167.

[23]This statement does not mean men and women are "equal" in terms of status. It simply means that for the establishment of rights and claims or one's place in a line of descendants, men and women are considered equivalent.

[24]Sahagún 1950-1969, X:97.

[25]There was a patrifiliative bias here since males were claimed as the ultimate ancestor to whom a house claim was traced three times as often as females (thirty-four/eleven); in land claims, males were claimed as such four times as often (fifteen/four).

[26]Sahagún 1950-1969, X:1-6. Offner (1979:409-10) disagrees with this emphasis on lineality by arguing that the terms were polysemous, thereby automatically designating collaterals as well. This might be true but archival evidence indicates that collaterals were often marked in special ways, particularly by the use of the term *huehcapan, lejano/a* in Spanish, "distant, far" in English. Carrasco (1966) has analyzed the meaning and use of the term *huehcapan* in some detail.

[27]In claims to house sites, equal numbers of male or female links were used (twenty-two); with land, males were used as links twice as often (thirteen/six).

[28]Carrasco 1966:155.

[29]Offner 1979 and in this volume.

[30]Veytia 1944, II:186; see also *Antigüedades de México* 1965, I, *láminas* 68, 69, pages 143, 145.

[31]Offner 1979:522-566.

[32]Motolinía 1971:356.

[33]Sahagún 1950-1969, VIII:67-69. Gómez de Cervantes' observations about litigious women in the early colonial period are supported by the *Códice Mendocino's* rendering of scenes of pre-Hispanic litigation (*Antigüedades de México* 1965, I, 1964, *láminas* 68, 69, pages 143, 145). In two scenes a judge or judges are depicted as male, but in each picture the disputants are shown as males and females (*lámina* 68: three men, three women; *lámina* 69: two men, two women).

[34]Nash 1978.

[35]Las Casas 1958:24; Durán 1967, II:544.

[36]Clavijero 1976:168; my translation.

[37]Hellbom 1967:129-30.

[38]Durán 1967, II:544.

[39]Hellbom 1967:129-30.

[40]Sahagún 1950-1969, II:197.

[41]Clark 1938, I:89.

[42]Clark 1938, I:153.

[43]Bialostosky 1975; Nash 1978.

[44]E.g., Nash 1978, 1980.

[45]Burkett 1978.

[46]Burkett 1978:123.

[47]Silverblatt 1980.

[48]Nash 1978; Leacock and Nash 1977.

A LEGAL PROCESS AT THE LOCAL LEVEL: ESTATE DIVISION IN LATE SIXTEENTH-CENTURY CULHUACAN

S. L. Cline

A consistent feature of early colonial life in New Spain was that Indian government regulated many aspects of local life. One area of governmental involvement was the division of estates of deceased residents of native towns. Nahuatl testaments and related documents indicate that native town government was concerned that citizens make proper wills, take measures to preserve testaments in a central place, and participate in actual estate division. Since testators were usually citizens of the towns in which they resided (and died), and since much that the land testators owned was within the bounds of the *altepetl* (the county-sized Indian political division), local Indian government assumed jurisdiction in the matter of estate division. Frequent references to wills, and the inclusion of the actual documents in property disputes indicates the importance of testaments.

The basis for this study of estate division is the *Libro de Testamentos de Culhuacan*, the largest extant corpus of sixteenth-century Nahuatl testaments and documents from Culhuacan.[1] The wills in the *Libro de Testamentos de Culhuacan*, some 65 of them, were drawn up primarily in 1580 and 1581, with a few dating to 1582-1599.[2] It is not clear what the criteria were for the preservation of the sixty-five Culhuacan wills. Doubtless, many more people died there between 1579 and 1599 than is indicted by the number of testaments. The major concentration of wills is for two years, 1580 and 1581, known years of epidemic conditions.[3] Thirty-four of the forty-nine dated wills (69 percent) were made in 1580 and 1581. Another seven undated testaments were likely made in this period.[4] There is a clustering of testators from a few wards (*tlahxilacalli*).[5] Other wards had a few of their members' wills preserved.

Spanish administrative structures and legal procedures were introduced to Indian communities in the early sixteenth century. Indian towns established *cabildos*, or town councils, patterned after Spanish municipal government, but shaped by pre-existing indigenous practices.[6] The native ruler, or *tlahtoani*, usually became the *gobernador* (governor), the highest town official, and from the town's male elite were chosen the other officials, the *alcaldes*, *regidores*, and *alguaciles*. Spanish titles were used to designate municipal offices, but all officeholders were Indians. An important functionary was the Indian notary or *escribano*. Although not officially a member of the *cabildo*, the notary was nonetheless a vital participant in the local administrative process. His role in the testamentary process and estate division is particularly significant.

In the Spanish world, notaries were essential to civilized life, Spanish society being highly legalistic and litigious. A whole range of acts and transactions were recorded by notaries. No expedition of conquest or even a forlorn whaling operation was complete without its notary.[7] In colonial Indian towns, native notaries also became indispensable, with good reason. Pre-Hispanic Nahua culture had a highly elaborated legal system[8] and there were pre-Hispanic precedents for scribes and written records. Specialists called *tlahcuilohqueh* were trained in writing and interpreting (or reading) native pictographs.

Records such as tribute lists, cadasters, genealogies, censuses, and so on, were kept. In the colonial era, Nahua scribes quickly adopted the Latin alphabet for much of their recordkeeping,[9] keeping the same general types of records they had in the pre-Hispanic era. A number of legal records and instruments were introduced by Spaniards. Among these are minutes of *cabildo* meetings, bills of sale, receipts for payment, and testaments. Pre-Hispanic Nahua society was accustomed to setting down important matters in pictographic form. In the colonial era, the introduction of new legal instruments and Spanish writing may have expanded the role, as well as the number of notaries.

In Indian towns, there were numerous notarial offices, and in some places, multiple notaries served at the same time.[10] Often the same individuals held several offices at once, and used different titles. Most frequently found in the Culhuacan wills is the simple title *escribano*, abbreviated *esc°*, but other titles existed, such as *escribano nombrado* (appointed notary), *escribano público* (notary public), and *escribano de la iglesia* (notary of the church). The same notary could sign a will with any of his various titles. In different wills, for example, the Culhuacan notary Miguel Jacobo de Maldonado identified himself as *escribano del la iglesia* and *escribano nombrado.* It is not known at present how Culhuacan notaries were selected. In Tlaxcala, *escribanos del cabildo* were chosen by the active members of the *cabildo.*[11] In general, notaries acted as ex officio *cabildo* members and were of the same social stratum as *cabildo* officials.[12] At times, Culhuacan notaries actually served on the *cabildo*, as in the case of Miguel Jacobo de Maldonado, who served as *alcalde* for a one-year term.[13] Others held church offices, such as Marcos Jorge, who recorded one testament when he was *topil del coro* (official in charge of the choir), but who later held the offices of *escribano público* and *escribano nombrado.*[14]

Since literacy was not widespread in Nahua society, notaries played an important role in legal procedures requiring documentation, such as estate division. If an Indian wanted to make a testament, it is likely he or she would be incapable of making a holograph will. Some Nahua noblemen had very competent signatures, indicating they may have been fully literate; others could barely scrawl their names. Some were explicitly illiterate and made a cross instead of a written signature. Women's signatures, even noblewomen's, seldom if ever appear.[15] Notaries were the main group of literate Nahuas, and were, without exception, males. Notaries and other literate people who could have written holograph testaments did not do so. Along with everyone else, notaries made their bequests through a notary. Although this was primarily to properly legalize the testament, there was pre-Hispanic precedent in publicizing important acts.

Notaries acted in a narrow sense as scribes, setting down testators' bequests; however, their role goes beyond simple inscription. The formulation of testators' desires in a proper legal format and wording, and the validation of the will by a notary, transforms the final statements into legal documents. The validity of testaments depended in part on the verification by the notary of the accuracy of his transcription. Typically there appears the phrase "the invalid ordered his testament well and true, and I verify it with my name and signature." In some cases in the later colonial period, when the notary of record subsequently died, this may not have sufficed. In eighteenth-century Nahuatl records from Amecameca, the validity of a will entered in a legal proceeding was contingent on someone verifying the hand of the deceased notary.[16]

Indian notaries not only wrote testaments and other documentation, but were in charge of keeping the records in good order.[17] In Culhuacan, it is clear that the collection of testaments was preserved together, just as books of certifications of baptism and burial were. Notaries made annotations concerning the disposition of the estates of testators whose wills are preserved. Usually these notes consisted of the amount of money delivered from testators' estates to religious officials. The notations were often written below the will itself, or on a new page immediately following. There are examples of transactions relating to the testaments that occurred up to fifteen years after the death of the testator.[18] In addition, in the *Libro de Testamentos de Culhuacan*, there is cross-referencing of some testaments of people related to one another.[19] The orderly preservation of the *Libro de Testamentos de Culhuacan* is doubtless due to the notaries' efforts.

Notaries were involved in estate division, often delivering the monies from an estate to the church. The estate of one notary, Miguel García, shows other aspects of the notary's role.[20] Listed in his will are a number of transactions for which he was responsible. These included keeping valuable property belonging to Culhuacan ward officials, acting as the agent for the payment of someone's debts, and accepting money from testators for the purchase of goods for the Church. The latter two are direct involvement in estate division. In the cases where García was in charge of money matters, he seems to have kept the money for awhile for his own use, ordering the payments made only on his death. Significantly, however, he did enumerate his obligations in his will, and was attempting to act in good faith, if not promptly.

Having testaments kept by native notaries presented an opportunity for fraud and mishandling of funds. Similar problems are found among Spanish notaries in charge of testaments.[21] In Culhuacan, one Indian notary, Miguel Jacobo de Maldonado, hid some of the testaments he had written. For that reason, in 1585 town officials took the book of testaments away from him and gave them to another notary.[22] However, Miguel Jacobo's lapse of ethics did not prevent him from serving as notary in 1602, *alcalde* in 1603, and notary again in 1604 and 1605.[23] How his suppression of testaments came to light is not known, but once discovered, town officials did take steps to better preserve the book of testaments. This served to underline local government's role in preservation of testaments for future use.

The Nahua practice of notarial involvement in estate division was influenced by Spanish practice. In the early sixteenth century, the Spanish Crown set up the *escribanía de bienes de difuntos* (notariate of the goods of the deceased) to act as custodians for the estates of Spaniards who died in the New World. This *escribanía* was the only newly created notariate for the Indies. Abuses by the tribunal and complaints by heirs marked the history of this body, and it ceased to exist as a separate office after 1584.[24] During the period that the bulk of the Culhuacan wills were drawn up, however, there existed a Spanish notariate exclusively concerned with estate administration, and this may have influenced procedures in Indian towns.

Notaries were not the only town officials customarily involved in estate administration. Many wills are witnessed by men called *albaceas* (executors). In the Spanish world, *albaceas* were usually trusted individuals named by the testator to administer the estate. In Indian Culhuacan, however, *albaceas* were town officials. They usually identified themselves as *diputados* (deputies). At times, these officials called themselves by the general Nahuatl word for officials in charge of something, *topilehqueh*, but also by the dual title, *albaceas/topilehqueh.* The use of the dual title may indicate some pre-existing native equivalent to the role of *albacea.* Notaries also at times described themselves as *albaceas.*[25] Officials functioned as executors, but it seems to have been a role rather than an actual office or title.

Wills were probably not a pre-Hispanic type of record,[26] but by the mid-sixteenth century, Nahuatl wills began to appear with some frequency in colonial documentation (usually lawsuits). The natives' early, enthusiastic adoption of this legal instrument may indicate some kind of pre-Hispanic testamentary tradition.[27] Wills were called by the Spanish word *testamento,* however. At the very least, there were pre-Hispanic customs governing property division.[28]

Nahuatl wills follow a standard format, modeled after Spanish wills, consisting of a religious invocation, identification of the testator by name and place of residence (*tlahxilacalli*), and formula passages concerning the person's body and soul. Testators' bequests of land, houses, and movable goods came after the opening formulas. Following the bequests is a list of witnesses. The final section of the will is a formula statement by the notary who wrote the will, affirming the validity of his record, followed by his signature.

Wills served as the legal instrument to set testators' affairs in order. Most important were the bequests of property to chosen heirs, provision for masses for the souls of the testators (and sometimes the testators' relatives), and directives for collection and payment of debts. Testators could also make statements concerning special arrangements concerning the estate or individuals named in the will.

Although serving the civil function of distributing property, according to the Philippe Ariès,[29] "a will was primarily a religious document, required by the Church even of the poorest persons." Excommunication and denial of burial on consecrated ground were possible sanctions applied to those dying intestate. In spite of this, by the sixteenth century, even in Europe, notaries had replaced curates as those in charge of testaments In Culhuacan, only occasionally does a notary identify himself as *escribano de la iglesia;* more often, he was called by the civil title of *escribano nombrado.*

The making of wills in Culhuacan was not restricted to those owning large amounts of property. Testaments were also made by people of humble circumstances. If someone did die intestate, the town government at times took it as its duty to make posthumous testamentary declarations concerning the deceased, even when the estate consisted of a few movable goods and little else. Perhaps this was in line with religious necessity of making a will. Often the sale of the deceased's goods, even in insignificant amounts, resulted in funds forwarded to the church for masses.

Colonial Indian testaments were generally made immediately before death or when someone perceived death was near. The formulaic statement that the testament was made "on the verge of my death"[30] could be quite literally true. At times the time of death was miscalculated. For example, the Culhuacan testator Juan Tezca[31] thought he would die immediately and made his will. It was a false alarm; he lived on. The will was entered in the *Libro de Testamentos de Culhuacan,* but the notarary indicated in the margin of the testament "[the testator] from Santa María has not yet died." Given the epidemic conditions of the late 1570s and early 1580s, someone could easily perceive a serious illness as potentially fatal and make a testament. In Mexico City, one Nahua woman made multiple testaments, some well in advance of death.[32] Perhaps she had three serious illnesses and made a new will on each occasion, changing and updating the original instrument.

When people miscalculated the time of death and died intestate, town officials could become involved in settling the estate, as noted previously. Culhuacan officials made declarations concerning the estates of deceased citizens' land, houses and movable property. In one case, Culhuacan officials demanded an explanation of why one man died intestate. The deceased's brother-in-law, Josef de San Marcos, said that he had sent for a notary at the time of his relative's death, but no will was made. Instead, the deceased gave an oral declaration before he expired.[33]

It is clear that notaries made house calls. Indeed, several testators stated that they were bequeathing the houses in which they lay sick. In 1579, in nearby Huitzilopochco, the Christian sacrament of Extreme Unction was administered to Indians at home because of the risk of their dying en route to church.[34] No wills indicate the presence of the local curate, but likely the notaries were at testators' residences as they lay dying. One Culhuacan Indian dictated a lengthy and detailed will as he lay mortally wounded in the town's hospital, but his is the only such case.[35]

Nahuatl testaments were modeled after Spanish wills. Nahuatl invocations were direct translations of Spanish legal formulas. For example the Spanish testamentary invocation, "*Sepan cuantos esta carta vieran y lean*" becomes "*Ma ixquichtin in quittazqueh in quipohuazqueh inin amatl*" ["Know all who see and read this document"]. Once formulas were translated into Nahuatl, they were learned by succeeding generations of notaries without reference to the Spanish original. There were variations in formulas from one town to another, and variations over time.[36] In Culhuacan, formula invocations were mainly from a given notary's repertoire, but some wills indicate that testators could shape wording of invocations. Most often, opening formulas include a religious invocation. Usually the Holy Trinity or Jesus and Mary were invoked,[37] but there were other variations in texts, some of which indicate truncations of lengthier formulas.[38] Although in theory the religious invocations and dispositions of property had equal weight,[39] one Culhuacan notary merely put the Spanish loanword abbreviation, "*etc.*", to take the place of some religious formula phrasing.[40]

Although the overall structure of Nahuatl wills closely parallels their Spanish models, there are some differences between the two in tone, phrasing, and legal intent. Some formula-phrasing appearing in Nahuatl testaments prohibits breaking of the will's provisions. Phrases such as "let no one take it from her," "let no one covet it of him," "let no one break my will,"[41] may indicate that testators expected difficulties in the smooth transfer of property. Indeed, disputes over estates were common, and testaments were included in legal cases to assert and prove ownership of property. Although the phrasing of the prohibitions is formula, it may have real legal import. Such prohibitions may have been inserted only when the testator expected property in dispute. In this regard, it should be noted that Spanish wills lack such prohibitions.[42]

Another characteristic of Nahuatl wills is their anecdotal digressions and lapses into colloquial language. Most testaments are written in the first person, but much of the text is dry formulary enumerations of individual bequests. A typical bequest is "I say I have a field in [placename] that is [x] long and [y] wide; I give it to my [relative]; no one is to covet it of him/her." However, highly personal and very human observations by Nahua testators are often found in Nahuatl wills, observations of a type not found in Spanish wills. While they are often anecdotal, they are more than just intimate glimpses into the lives of individual Indians. Often they relate directly to property disposition and disinheritance of potential heirs. One Ana Juana,[43] for example, vented her spleen about the behavior of her good-for-nothing third husband. She called him a "great scoundrel" and accused him of carrying on business without consulting her, being stingy and unsympathetic to her. The intent of her tirade was to disinherit her spouse and make sure her son got her entire estate. Recorded in another will is a direct verbal exchange between the testator and her heir. Ana Tiacapan (b)[44] bequeathed a canoe to her daughter. "But then the daughter said," the text of the will continues, "it cannot be that I take the canoe; I give it with all my heart to my father, because with it he gathers the zacate tribute and he will go on using it."[45] There is no response by the testator to this change in recipient; seemingly she accepted her daughter's reassignment of ownership. In another case, a testator complained about some relatives and praised others. One María Tiacapan (b)[46] claimed her uncles had abandoned her and her sister to the care of strangers when they were orphaned. "Those uncles of mine, my relatives, never said 'Our nieces are poor, they just live in the corners of other peoples' [houses], by their walls, just humble, they are poor and perhaps they have nothing to eat.' And neither did my uncles say 'Our niece is sick, let's go see her'." María's grandmother took over the job of raising her, and María began a speech lauding her efforts. The notary did not see fit to record the speech but left it as, "My grandmother was praiseworthy during the whole time we were left orphans *etc* [sic]." In all three cases mentioned above, the anecdotes relate to property disposition, giving specific reasons why some potential heirs are excluded while others are considered worthy of bequests. Elsewhere, I have suggested that this happens with greater frequency in the testaments of women, because their wills were more open to dispute.[47]

One criterion for making a will was status as an adult. Unfortunately, civil status was not usually explicitly stated in wills,[48] although it loomed large for tribute purposes. No one actually said how old he (or she) was, but there are indications of testators' ages. Most were married or had been married at some point in their lives. Of the 65 testators, only four men and four women seem never to have married by the time of their deaths. This is suggested by their mentioning no spouses and no lineal descendants, the products of marriage. Likely, those who had not married were young. This hypothesis is bolstered by the fact that most single people left their goods to older relatives such as uncles—and in one case, a vigorous grandmother.[49] Many bequests to children place the surviving parent as guardian and custodial recipient of the property. When the children came of age, they would take full legal control of the property. Presumably, those who made testaments did have the full legal right to ownership of property and were legal adults.

A factor that was not a criterion for making a will (or having it preserved) was gender. Approximately equal numbers of Nahua men and women made wills, bequeathing the property they held as individuals. Although in the Culhuacan collection more testaments of men (37) than women (27) have been preserved,[50] there are more extant native women's wills from sixteenth-century Mexico City than men's.[51] The numbers are about the same in Calimaya-Tepemaxalco.[52] Women as well as men held property in their own names, meaning that, regardless of gender, making a will was important for civil reasons.

There is some evidence that women's testaments were more open to challenge than men's, so that making a will was particularly important for women.[53] In Culhuacan, single and widowed women comprise more than half the women testators, while not quite a third of the men were single or widowed at death.[54] Women without a husband may have been especially concerned with preserving their heirs' interests by making a will. In addition, marital discord may have prompted women to make testaments. Ana Juana, mentioned previously, clearly made her will to exclude her husband from sharing in the estate.[55]

Although the wills preserved in the *Libro de Testamentos de Culhuacan* have a bias toward the wealthy and titled,[56] many testators had very modest estates. It is difficult to judge with absolute certainty the wealth of testators, mainly measured in the amount of land owned, but general etimates can be made.[57] Both women and men held large and small estates. The size of estates did not vary by gender.

The notary and the testator are obvious participants in the testamentary process, but almost invariably, wills include a list of witnesses. As indicated previously, important transactions were done before witnesses in the pre-Hispanic period, so it is not surprising that colonial Nahuatl testaments were witnessed. By the late sixteenth century, witnesses were identified by the Spanish word *testigos*, and individual witnesses were named.[58] The *albaceas* were almost mandatory witnesses to wills, and they were acting in an official capacity. Other witnesses to wills were relatives of the testator, recipients of bequests, the testators' creditors or debtors, those owning fields neighboring the testators', and an array of others whose connections to the testator is not determined. Most likely these were the testators friends and neighbors, but even relatives were often not identified as such. Usually, testators had both men and women witnessing wills, including a number of married couples. Men were usually listed first, then women. Women's names were recorded, often followed by their husbands' names. In Culhuacan, no identifiable minor children witnessed wills, although seemingly there are instances elsewhere of Nahua youngsters acting as witnesses.[59] Men were witnesses more frequently than women for both men's and women's wills. However, two male testators' only witnesses were female relatives, one listing two, another three.[60] It should be noted that to be valid, Spanish documents needed three adult male witnesses and a notary, and that women seldom if ever appear as witnesses, though they could issue documents and give testimony.[61] Although Indian men do appear more often as witnesses to wills, which may indicate their word had more legal force, nonetheless, the standard inclusion of women as witnesses is significant.

Witnesses were often relatives of the testator. Male testators often had as witnesses their spouses and (adult) offspring, while women testators seldom did. Children of women testators are not often listed as witnesses, even when they received bequests. Perhaps the children were not adults and could not be counted for legal purposes. Only one woman with a surviving spouse had him witness her will, and he received bequests.[62]

Having close family members witness testaments may have been a device to insure the estate was not challenged. In the case of Joaquín Matlallacan,[63] his entire estate went to his son, but his wife and his mother acted as witnesses to the will. The two women were in effect disinherited, but by acting as witnesses to the will, they may have been acknowledging and acquiescing to the act. In another Culhuacan will, the witness seems also to have been expected to acknowledge and comply with the terms of a will. Simón Moxixicoa[64] left property to his wife with the undertanding that she stay and raise the children there. María witnessed the will, perhaps implicitly agreeing with his wishes.

However, she subsequently left the marital residence, taking her personal belongings.

Some witnesses may have been included for legal reasons, to insure that transactions were completed. One woman owed money to the testator Luis Tlauhpotonqui.[65] He mentioned the unpaid debt in his will and she acted as witness to the document. In this way, she may have affirmed her responsibility to pay the debt. Sometimes those owning fields neighboring those of testators were witnesses to wills. These people may have been included to insure orderly transfers of land to testators' heirs, and to avoid boundary disputes. Another legal reason for having someone as a witness may have been to insure completion of work. One woman had contracted for construction work which was not completed at the time of her death, and the mason was a witness to her will.[66]

Other witnesses to wills knew about previous transactions of testators. For example, a witness to Melchor de Santiago's will[67] knew about a grant of land given Melchor by the *tecpan* (place or community house) of the Culhuacan ward of Coatlan. The witness, Pedro de San Nicolás, had mesured the land originally and was to take care of the sale of the land after Melchor's death.

A final important category of witness is the *tlahxilacalehqueh*. At times, the term seems to refer to ward heads or ward elders, or, in other instances, simply to the people of the ward.[68] In two wills, the same group of men and one woman was listed as the *tlahxilacalehqueh*,[69] but in most others, they appear to be a random collection of people. Having the *tlahxilacalehqueh* witness wills is not surprising. Wards regulated aspects of their residents' lives, such as property transfers, permission to reside, and collection of tribute.[70] They also assisted residents with cash loans,[71] apparently a practice common enough that some testators denied they had contracted such debts.[72] In one case, *tlahxilacalehqueh* seemingly affirmed the denial of indebtedness by acting as witnesses to the statement.[73]

There are differences in the functions of European and Indian witnesses. Spanish wills had three adult male witnesses who affirmed that the testator performed the act of ordering his or her will. They were not necessarily called upon to attest to the validity of what was said. Nahua witnesses appear to include a number of people who could attest to the validity of the testators' right to bequeath property, as well as affirm that the testators made the wills. If a testator bequeathed property before witnessess who did not object, this might be presented as proof that the testator had the legal right to do so. Property rights were asserted through means of bequest. This helps account for the large numbers of native testaments contained in lawsuits.

Instructions to third parties to dispose of property or take care of special arrangements are typical in Nahuatl testaments but not in Spanish wills.[74] Usually the third parties were the testators' kin who were to care for minor children and to sell property for masses. These were informal instructions and exhortations, not backed by any administrative hierarchy. Often the testators went so far as to set prices to be paid for land, houses or movable goods. This may simply be the testators' estimation of value, having no relation to the actual prices paid. And since the orders of the testators are often all the information available, sale prices cannot be determined. The *albaceas* often acted as the sole executors of the estates, but the *tlahxilacalehqueh* also acted as third parties in some instances, selling land for masses, accepting donations of land from testators in order to reassign it to poor people without land,[75] and accepting land assigned to the ward's saint.[76] Third parties were also called upon to insure that the will's provisions were carried out. For example, the notary Miguel García[77] wanted the *tlahxilacalehqueh* to make sure his goods were sold immediately and his debts paid, and Vincente Xochiamitl wanted the *tlahxilacalehqueh* to speak in his son's behalf so that no one would trick him out of his inheritance.[78] Individuals were also called upon to speak on the behalf of heirs. The most colorful case is that of thrice married Ana Juana, who wanted her *alcalde compadre* to make sure her son got her property, not her spendthrift scoundrel of a husband.[79]

A paradigm of the most uncomplicated case, then, is that a moribund Indian had a notary summoned to the deathbed scene. After the notary wrote out a series of religious and legal formulas, he proceeded to take direct testimony from the invalid, at times shaping the wording, at other times recording verbatim what the testator said. The testator bequeathed his or her property to a variety of heirs, usually including their spouses and children, as well as others, including siblings and nephews and nieces.[80] Witnesses verified the fact that the testator made the will and the property rights were valid. Town officials acted as witnesses to the will. The notary wrote closing formulas, and verified the transcription of the will. The notarized will was kept by the municipal authorities. Heirs took possession of their property, and property to be sold was disposed of by the *albaceas* or third parties. The money received was forwarded to the church, and the curate would certify that he received the monies and that the proper number of masses were celebrated.

There are more complicated situations in the Culhuacan documentation. One which did not involve disputing parties shows how deeply involved town government could be in estate division. Separate from the *Libro de Testamentos de Culhuacan* is documentation dealing with the division of the estate of the Culhuacan noblewoman, doña Luisa Juana, a member of the Moteucçoma (Montezuma) family, who died in 1580.[81] The estate was large and was complicated by the fact that much of doña Luisa Juana's property came from a previously undivided estate. Doña Luisa Juana's grandmother had died earlier, leaving her property to her two daughters. These two did not divide the estate, but seemingly shared it. Subsequently, doña Luisa Juana's mother died, leaving her shares in the estate to doña Luisa Juana. The estate, now shared with her aunt, continued undivided. When doña Luisa Juana made her will, she left her property to her father, an alcalde. After the lady's death, the estate was actually divided, after two generations of women had shared it.[82]

The division of doña Luisa Juana's estate was accomplished amicably and with the supervision of the town government. The documentation of the transaction is seemingly complete, and may be typical of the division of a large complicated (but undisputed) estate. The will of doña Luisa Juana was brought before the *juez-gobernador*, the highest town official, who declared it valid, and in typical native fashion, ordered that no one break its provisions. Only this will was entered in the proceedings and not the wills of the mother and grandmother.[83] In November of 1580, six months after doña Luisa Juana's death, her father and aunt appeared before the *cabildo* with an agreement to divide the estate. The *juez-gobernador* saw the declaration of the two and gave an order to the *alcalde* to give legal possession to them on the basis of the agreement. The *alguacil mayor* was to put stakes in the fields to show which parts belonged to each. Actual legal possession was shown by the *alcalde* taking Juan de San Miguel, doña Luisa Juana's father, by the hand to each of the fields to give him possession. Juan de San Miguel showed possession by digging in the four corners of each field with a digging stick. Only the legal possession of Juan de San

Miguel is documented, and it is not clear whether the other party to the agreement, doña Luisa Juana's aunt, simply retained what was left without any further legal action by the town council. The act of taking legal possession is a practice introduced by the Spaniards, indicated by the term for it, *posesión*. Spanish rituals of taking possession were readily assumed by Nahuas,[84] and there may be pre-Hispanic precedents for it.

In addition to the division of the estate between Juan de San Miguel and his sister-in-law, there is documentation on the disposition of the rest of the estate. In her will, doña Luisa Juana gave land to her father and stepmother, but ordered her house and some lands sold in order to pay for masses for her, her mother, and her grandmother. The house was something quite grand by Culhuacan standards, valued at 40 pesos, about ten times the price of the average Culhuacan house.[85] In accordance with the will, the house was offered for sale but no Indian could afford it. Juan de San Miguel found a buyer, the brother-in-law and sister of the Culhuacan curate. Since sales to Spaniards were in theory restricted, a license (called in the Nahuatl documentation by the Spanish word *licencia*) had to be obtained from the town council. The *cabildo* readily approved the sale, and there is documentation of Juan de San Miguel's transmission of the money to the curate for masses. Most of these transactions occurred within a year or so after doña Luisa Juana's death. However, some of her land was sold in 1594, fourteen years later, and the *teniente* made the transcription of her testament and bill of sale.

Disputes concerning estate division were handled at two levels. If local officials could not resolve a dispute, the case would be argued before the court in Mexico City. The *Libro de Testamentos de Culhuacan* provides information on the settlement of local disputes. One such case is that of Simón Moxixicoa.[86] The dispute and its resolution were written directy after the testament, indicating that the book of wills was not simply an archive of testaments, but was actively used by town government. In this case, mentioned previously, Simón left property to his wife María, with the understanding that she raise his children. She was a witness to the will, and seemingly did not raise objections at the time to the arrangement. Subsequently, however, she changed her mind and left. Simón made his testament in January of 1581; in May, María and her relatives appeared before town officials to contest the will. The officials included two *alcaldes*, an *alguacil*, and the *fiscal*, as well as the notary who recorded the proceedings. María and her relatives said to the officials, "let us hear the testament that the deceased ordered," at which point the will was found and read. The disputants contested the inclusion of some corn María claimed with the goods Simón gave his children. The *alcaldes* found for María, and ordered her to leave the house, take firewood, her "woman's things" (*cihuatlatquitl*), and the maize. She was to take the goods under the supervision of the *alguacil mayor*, who set fines for anyone contesting the decision. The setting of fines and penalties for going against the decision of authorities was typical of Nahuatl testaments, and was not a Spanish practice.

Redress for disputes could be found in Mexico City courts. Kellogg's study of Nahua women in Mexico City (elsewhere in this volume) analyzes some 56 cases of Indians before the Spanish courts. For Culhuacan, only one such case is known.[87] Perhaps in a less central place, such as Culhuacan, this avenue of redress may have been sought only in extreme cases. The Culhuacan case is typical of cases involving estate division. The suit was carried on in Spanish, through interpreters, but a Nahuatl testament,[88] a native genealogy, and a native house plan were included in the documentation. The case concerned property rights of two sets of relatives. The Nahuatl will is by Cristina Tiacapan, a widow of Miguel Huitznahuatecatl, who left her property to a variety of people. The relationship of these heirs to Cristina is not specified, but some of them acted as witnesses to the will. One person Cristina failed to mention entirely was her husband's daughter by a previous marriage. Suit was brought in the 1590s, some fifteen years after Cristina's death, by the stepdaughter against Cristina's heirs. The stepdaughter claimed ownership of the house and lands through her relationship to her father. Not surprisingly, Cristina's stepdaughter did not act as witness to her stepmother's will. The outcome of this dispute is not known.

Summary and Conclusions

Although testamentary statements do not appear to have been a pre-Hispanic type of record, they became a standard Nahuatl document from the mid-sixteenth century on. Spanish wills were used as models, but the Nahua testamentary process has a number of distinctly native features and possible indications of native precedents. Most salient here is the extensive role of native government in estate administration. This is seen in the functioning of the notary, the *albaceas*, and ward and town officials, and in the broad role of the witnesses. Transmission of property was ordered through the legal instrument of the will, with the document itself being kept by municipal authorities. Orders of the testators were carried out by both formal and informal means. At times, heirs took formal possession of property, under the supervision of town authorities, when there were disputes. Property was often sold by town officials to pay for masses for the testators' souls. In this way, the *altepetl* could keep control over the land within its jurisdiction.

The legal system available to Nahuas allowed for redress at the local level, but also provided satisfaction to outside authorities. If the paucity of extant Culhuacan suits in the archives is an indication of the frequency with which suits were brought before Spanish authorities for decision, this avenue of redress was sought only in extreme cases. The *Libro de Testamentos de Culhuacan* indicates that municipal authorities could and did successfully mediate disputes. For this study of native patterns, sources such as the Culhuacan wills is invaluable, since it shows typical local level processes rather than the conflict-ridden cases that could not be resolved locally.[89]

NOTES

[1]These include a testament and division of an estate (AGN-T 58-4, and the *Proceso de Culhuacan*, BNP 110). My thanks to Susan Kellogg and H. B. Nicholson for these materials.

[2]S. L. Cline 1981:33.

[3]Gallego 1927.

[4]The *Libro de Testamentos de Culhuacan* (LTC) is generally ordered chronologically. The seven wills are

found between wills of the two major years.

[5]Two of the wards may, in fact, have been one, with some form of dual organization. The two wards are Santa María Magdalena Cihuatecpan and Santa María Tezcacoac. In one will, the ward is called Cihuatecpan Tezcacoac (LTC f. 74v).

[6]Gibson 1952; 1964.

[7]A good deal is known about Spanish notaries. Generally, they attained their office by purchase from the Crown, and in the sixteenth century, sale of public office was a major source of revenue for the Crown. Those who purchased offices had to acquire the title *escribano real* (royal notary) and to produce evidence of honesty, professional competence, and *limpieza de sangre* (i.e., "old Christian" heritage). Those able to purchase office were wealthy and viewed their offices as an investment, to be sold or bequeathed (Parry 1953 ff.). Spanish notaries in Indian towns followed the general Spanish pattern of acquisition of office by purchase. And, according to Charles Gibson (1952:78), "Probably no other single officeholder in colonial Tlaxcala possessed so little sympathy for Indian welfare, or exploited to such an extent the Indians' credulity and inexperience in Spanish law, than the [Spanish] escribanos públicos."

[8]Offner 1979.

[9]Indians' control of Latin orthography was developed early. Sixteenth-century documents written by Indians have a distinct, chiseled style. Usually letters are carefully formed, and the effect at times is quite elegant. In the *Libro de Testamentos de Culhuacan,* the Nahuatl wills are carefully penned, while the notations in Spanish by the Augustinian friars are barely legible scrawls. Examination of the Culhuacan notaries' orthography indicates a great similarity in style. Perhaps one taught the other.

[10]Gibson 1952:114.

[11]Gibson 1952:114, n. 68.

[12]One Culhuacan notary is identified in a will with the noble title *don,* but he never used the title when signing a will. Notaries and other *cabildo* officials in Culhuacan all had thoroughly Spanish names, which in the sixteenth century was an index of nobility (S. L. Cline 1981:224).

[13]LTC f. 108v.

[14]LTC f. 104v, 105r, T-58-4-7r.

[15]An agreement between two Culhuacan residents (T-58-4-9r) includes the name, and possibly the signature, of doña Luisa Isabel. Similarly, documentation from Texcoco includes the name of one noblewoman, but whether she signed it herself cannot be established (López y Magaña 1980:76, 80).

[16]Karttunen and Lockhart 1978:166-67.

[17]Gibson 1952:114.

[18]E.g., LTC f. 98r, T-58-4.

[19]LTC f. 84v, 64v.

[20]LTC f. 56r.

[21]Artiles 1969:501-3; Parry 1953; Gibson 1952:78.

[22]LTC f. 90r.

[23]LTC f. 108v.

[24]Artiles 1969:501-3.

[25]E.g., LTC f. 41v.

[26]Motolinía 1971:134-35.

[27]León-Portilla 1976:17.

[28]Motolinía 1971:134-35; Gómara 1943:222-23.

[29]Ariès 1981:189.

[30]LTC f. 43v.

[31]LTC f. 12r.

[32]Kellogg 1979.

[33]LTC f. 52r. Final words of dying persons, even when not transcribed, could be construed as legally binding testaments. The earliest testamentary statement presently known is an oral native testament from Mexico City ca. 1534 that was entered in evidence for a later lawsuit (Edward Calnek, personal communication). However, final words had more legal effect when written and notarized. Written testaments were entered in evidence in lawsuits from the 1560s on, and oral testaments, if common in an earlier period, gave way to written documents. In modern ethnography of the Zapotecs, Diskin (1979:212-13) has noted the phenomenon of the chat (*plática*) versus a conversation with deeper legal implications. He notes that after a few minutes of conversation, Zapotec villagers would say

> "This is only a chat" (*Esta es solamente una plática*). After two years of experience there, [Diskin] understand[s] this expression to mean "This conversation is an idle one from a legal standpoint. If it were more significant and involved any binding agreements, it would be the occasion to create a legal, witnessed document."

[34]Gárcia Pimentel 1897:226.

[35]LTC f. 88r.

[36]Cf. Anderson *et. al.* 1976:44-75.

[37]Some French scholars have inferred changes in religious beliefs over time from testamentary formulas (Vovelle 1978), but such an analysis is not possible for the Culhuacan wills, which were written in a concentrated period (1580-81) by a few notaries. There is, of course, the problem that formulas were written the elite and do not necessarily reflect the beliefs of the testators.

[38]S. L. Cline 1981:65-67.

[39]Ariès 1981:189.

[40]LTC f. 70v. The use of the phrase *et cetera* is most often seen with truncations of formulas, indicating that they occasionally got tired of writing out the same phrases over and over. However, in one case (LTC f. 65v) discussed in the text of this paper, the notary got tired of the longwindedness of one of the testators who launched into a speech about her wonderful grandmother. The Spanish loanword *et cetera* appears in very early documentation from the Cuernavaca area (MNA-AH 549, 550, 551) as an entire category of tribute goods *amo ets* ("no *et cetera*"), probably meaning nothing else.

[41]LTC f. 42v, 57r, 38v.

[42]Lockhart 1981:12.

[43]LTC f. 49r.

[44]LTC f. 54r.

[45]The translations from Nahuatl to English are mine.

[46]LTC f. 65v.

[47]S. L. Cline 1983.

[48]María Tiacapan (LTC f. 4r) and María Icnocihuatl ("widow") (LTC f. 50r) were explicitly identified as widows. Women were often identified in relation to their male relatives.

[49]LTC f. 65v.

[50]The sum is 64, not 65; one of the testator's gender cannot be determined from the testament fragment.

[51]Kellogg 1979.

[52]Loera y Ch. 1977.

[53]This may account for the number of Indian women's testaments that have survived, in the records of civil litigation. See Kellogg's paper on Mexico City native women elsewhere in this volume.

[54]S. L. Cline 1981:75.

[55]LTC f. 49r.

[56]For an extended discussion of the biases in the *Libro de Testamentos de Culhuacan*, see S. L. Cline 1981:73-93.

[57]S. L. Cline 1981:80-81; 1983.

[58]In the early colonial period, groups of Nahuas whose individual members were not named acted as witnesses to wills (Lockhart 1981:12).

[59]Lockhart 1981:12.

[60]LTC f. 42v, 68r.

[61]Lockhart 1981:12.

[62]LTC f. 77v.

[63]LTC f. 91v.

[64]LTC f. 71r.

[65]LTC f. 66v.

[66]LTC f. 54r.

[67]LTC f. 61r.

[68]S. L. Cline 1981:132-34.

[69]LTC f. 64v, 65v.

[70]LTC f. 46v, 83v, 88v, 98r, 104v, 107v.

[71]LTC f. 49v.

[72]LTC f. 82r, 83v.

[73]LTC f. 83v.

[74]Lockhart 1981:12.

[75]LTC f. 46v, 88v; cf. Zorita 1963.

[76]LTC f. 107v.

[77]LTC f. 57r.

[78]LTC f. 60r.

[79]LTC f. 49r.

[80]S. L. Cline 1981:322-39; 1983; Kellogg 1979; Loera y Ch. 1977.

[81]AGN-T 58-4.

[82]For how long they shared it is not clear.

[83]These wills are not extant, and may never have existed.

[84]Lockhart 1981:14.

[85]S. L. Cline 1981:312-13.

[86]LTC f. 71v.

[87] *El Proceso de Culhuacan*, BNP 110.

[88] This will is the only one with a colonial Spanish translation made for the suit.

[89] E.g., the *Proceso de Culhuacan* (BNP 110).

INDIAN POLITICAL ACTIVITIES IN SPANISH TEXCOCO, 1570-1630[1]

Leslie Lewis

Post-Conquest Texcoco shared many characteristics with other regions situated in or near the Valley of Mexico: a large Hispanic population, well-developed Spanish political institutions, a mature estate structure, and an economy stimulated by Mexico City. Nonetheless, despite the presence of Hispanic society in Texcoco, many pre-Conquest political entities, social practices, and trade patterns survived into the colonial period. This article considers some of the continuities of native society in colonial Texcoco, Indian political activities through the local town councils, and landholding patterns.

The region of Texcoco was an ancient pre-Conquest state of imperial stature. The province had several urban centers, of which the largest were Texcoco, Huexotla, Coatlichan, Tizayuca, and Chiautla. The population was composed primarily of Nahua-speaking peoples, with a large Otomi minority. At the time of the Spanish Conquest, the city of Texcoco was the capital.

Texcoco's pre-Conquest prominence and Texcocan aid to the conquering Spaniards (provided especially by factions dissatisfied with Tenochtitlan's dynastic choices) gave the town a favored position during the colonial period. Texcoco was one of the four Indian towns in the Valley of Mexico of sufficient stature to be designated "city," and was one of the first to have its own town council and governor. Coatlichan, Huexotla and Tizayuca were designated sub-*cabeceras*, positions they strongly protested. It was, in part, the granting of "city" status to Texcoco that allowed many overt native practices to continue and to be grafted onto Spanish political structures.

It was on the social, political and economic practices of the *altepetl* and its surrounding *calpollis* that the Spanish built their society. Pre-Conquest place names remained unchanged and no new political towns were founded. Although soon after the Conquest a sizeable Hispanic population resided in the province, the native communities maintained much of their political integrity. The exact organization and the relationships between the *calpollis* and the *altepetls* remain to be fully defined. What is known is that the *calpollis* were communities in their own right, usually outlying villages. There is strong evidence that the *calpollis* had their own communal lands, governmental organization, and internal laws governing the operation and distribution of lands among its members. The native community remained a complex social entity, including among its members nobles, agriculturalists, laborers, and traders. The bulk of the population was agriculturalists who cultivated maize on communal, private and rented lands for their own subsistence and to fulfill their households' tribute obligations. Despite the intrusion of European practices into the indigenous society, the native community, in the corporate sense, operated much as it had in the pre-Columbian period.

The political differences between *calpollis*, *parcialidades*, and *barrios* in the Texcocan region are just beginning to be studied. There is a lack of uniformity in the terminology used in the various documentary bases studied. Hicks, deriving most of his data from the chronicles and legal cases, writes that *parcialidades* were ethnically based, and there were six of them within Texcoco: Chimalpan, Tlailotlacan, Mexicapan, Colhuacan, Tepanecapan, and Huitznahuac. Hicks indicates that these names were derived frm six ethnic groups which arrived in the Acolhuacan region at various times, and were given lands on which to settle.[2] In the notarial records from Texcoco, *barrios* were districts located within or immediately outside an urban center. They were primarily social groupings. There were Indians and Spanish *barrios* early in the colonial period, but kinship and occupational specialization were not necessarily prerequisites for living in a particular barrio. By the early 1600s most of the *barrios* were inhabited by *mestizos*, with a few purely Indian *barrios* functioning on the very fringes of Texcoco proper. There was a proclivity for the less Hispanized Indians—those newly arrived from the countryside—to live in the outlying *barrios* with relatives who had arrived earlier. In the local documents the words *estancia* and *barrio* are never confused—*estancia* always referred to a humble Spanish landholding located outside of the city. Through the colonial period, *calpollis* remained Indian communities, political entities unto themselves, whose major economic activity was agriculture. These organizations were politically and socially united by a complex set of political, family, clan, and landholding relationships that are not clearly defined in the documents. But the notarial records and Indian wills from the region never confuse the words *barrio* and *calpolli*, indicating that local Texcocan *escribanos* and notaries saw these entities as distinct and different.

Overview of Texcocan Indian Society

Prior to the Conquest, Indian society was a complex structure. It is significant that in the colonial period, Indian society continued to be both multileveled and interregional, but new sub-levels developed as Spanish social, economic, and political processes became entrenched in Central Mexico.

The top stratum of the region's post-Conquest native society was composed of the direct descendants of the Texcocan ruling house. They were the *tlahtohqueh* or heads of the *altepetl* of Texcoco, and hence much more powerful and higher ranking than the *pipiltin*, *principales*, or nobles, who with the *tlahtoani* families of the smaller towns of the Texcocan region made up the bulk of the native elite. The highest *tlahtohqueh* were the descendants of Nezahualcoyotl and Nezahualpilli. Only a handful of families were direct descendants of the Texcocan kings, and could therefore claim membership in the province's *teccalli* (table 1 is a partial listing of those known members of the *teccalli*). The Spaniards called these individuals *señores y caciques de Texcoco.*

Native nobility during the pre-Conquest period functioned in an interregional context, and many interprovincial social and economic activities continued after the Conquest. Most of central Mexico's noble houses were related because of the extensive intermarriage that had taken place between the *tlahtoani* regimes. The practice of intermarriage did not cease with the Conquest, but continued to be used to buttress political, social, and economic prestige within both the Hispanic and Indian worlds.[3] This was certainly true of the second-level nobility: *caciques.*

Caciques' ties to Texcocan society, and forms of articulation remain to be fully studied (table 2 lists second level native elites mentioned in the local notarial records). *Caciques* held a distinguished position within Hispanic society. As early as the 1530s, *caciques* were apparently highly Hispanicized. Nonetheless, they never fully denied their Indian backgrounds. The two major sources of their political and social power were their noble patrimonies and their dominance of the Texcocan town council. Indian nobles, whether biologically Indian or *mestizo*, were highly conscious of their group identity when it came to controlling these traditional sources of economic and political power.[4]

Operating on the margins of the *cacique* class were several families who held respected but less prestigious positions within Indian and Spanish society. Many of these families were *mestizo*, the illegitimate and legitimate offspring of Spaniards and noble Indian women. Although most members of this marginal group culturally identified with Hispanic society, their position within Valley society was determined by their family's socio-political-economic status during the pre-Hispanic period. Many families' ties to Texcoco's *teccalli* were not as strong as those of the *caciques* because members' mothers or grandmothers were concubines of Texcocan native nobility. This marginal group grew in size through the colonial period as Indian nobles from the *cacique* class married Spaniards, and *tlahtoani* regimes became fragmented.

The bottom level of Texcoco's Indian elite was composed of individuals who were called *principales.* These were Indian nobles who were related to the numerous fragmented *tlahtoani* lines but who were not *tlatoque. Principales* ranked far below the top two levels of the native society. They were more active in the provincial society than the first and second level nobility. Their lives centered in the province, where they collected the imperial tribute, trade maize and livestock, and bought and sold houses. This group never severed its ties with the Indian community. The key to their local economic success was their influence in the native sector, combined with their ability to mediate between the Indian and Spanish communities. The majority of these people spoke only Nahuatl and married Indian women from similar class backgrounds. By the seventeenth century, the title of "*principal*" had become cheapened. Those *principales* who attempted to protect their noble lineage began to call themselves *principal legítimo.*[5]

The majority of the Indian population was composed of *macehualtin*, or commoners. Information on this group is very scarce. Most of them were agriculturalists who cultivated maize on communal, private, and rented lands for their own subsistence and to fulfill their household's tribute obligations.[6]

Indian Town Councils

Texcocan Indians, and especially village elders, maintained tight control over their communities and outlying hamlets through their own councils. Soon after the Conquest, Spanish-style municipal councils were established in central Mexico. The councils were headed by governors and included *alcaldes* (or judges), councilmen, constables, and a notary. The officials were entrusted with keeping the peace, maintaining the community treasury, watching over village lands, and collecting the royal tribute. Since most council business was conducted in Nahuatl, an interpreter, usually a *mestizo*, was kept on staff, as an *escribano* (notary), to record council business in Nahuatl. In pre-Conquest Mexico there was no political institution quite like the Spanish town council, and the Indian's dominance of the colonial town councils in Texcoco provides insight into how pre-Conquest political institutions and practices intertwined with those introduced by the Spanish.

The native aristocracy's political functions grew out of traditional prerogatives. In Mesoamerica, the most powerful nobles were entrusted with overseeing dynastic succession and the collection of the imperial tribute. The native aristocracy viewed the duties of the Spanish town council as a continuation of many pre-Hispanic practices. Members of the *teccalli* dominated the local political machinery. The full town council rarely met, and only the most powerful figures made political decisions. Some council members even went so far as to call themselves *herederos y sucesores de Neçahualcoyotl y Neçahualpiltzintli* after listing their names and offices. The inter-regional nobility, or their offspring, who were often *mestizo*, dominated Texcoco's town council through most of the colonial period. The powerful families rotated the office of governor among themselves. By the late sixteenth century, the influential Pimentel family dominated the governorship of Texcoco (see table 3).

In the outlying *cabeceras* of Tepetlaoztoc and Huexotla, continuation of pre-Columbian political practices is even more evident. In Tepetlaoztoc, town council members were elected from the four major *calpollis* (see table 4). Councilmen referred to themselves as *pilli*, indicating that they were of lesser status than Texcoco's city council members. In Tepetlaoztoc and Huexotla, meetings were never convened unless one representative of each *calpolli* was present. The position of governor rotated among the four *calpollis*. Any attempts by *calpollis* or nobles to disrupt the established political practices caused long and drawn-out disputes. Well into the colonial period the *cabeceras*' municipal councils were dominated by Indians who conducted all their business in Nahuatl. Indian councilmen viewed any Spanish intrusion on their councils as erosive to their community's solidarity. In early seventeenth-century Tepetlaoztoc, a Spaniard held the office of governor, but was either absent from all council meetings by choice, or the council chose to meet without him. The councilmen ignored all complaints by the governor that meetings were conducted in Nahuatl.[7]

An overview of the province's town councils shows how the Spanish political framework provided a structure within which pre-Conquest political practices were sustained. Members of the imperial nobility dominated the municipal council machinery in the outlying *cabeceras*. Such patterns of political office holding went on uninterrupted well into the seventeenth and eighteenth centuries. The town councils were instrumental in exercising the Spanish political and legal structures to support their positions within their provinces and their noble pretensions within Texcoco and Mexico City society. Frequently, these actions concentrated on land ownership, both private and communal.

Indian Landholding in Texcoco

The Indians learned very quickly how to manipulate and use Spanish law to protect their private and communal landholdings. The basic landholding unit for the Indians was the *calpolli*, which held both private and communal land. And within the *calpollis* there were also patrimonies (mixtures of private and communal lands, and tribute-paying Indians held by an individual family or jointly by several families).[8] The *calpollis* controlled the majority of the valuable land in Texcoco—that located along the lake front and the major roads leading to Mexico City. *Calpolli* elders strictly forbade the selling of communal or privately owned land to anyone outside or inside the community. Political and social practices within the *calpollis* worked to retain the control of lands in Texcoco. But, as will be discussed, the Indians constantly violated this practice, leading to long, drawn out litigation with both Spaniards and Indians. For instance, in 1725 the council of Huexotla attempted to initiate legal action against some local Spanish agriculturalists. To do so they needed and requested copies of viceregal orders giving them clear possession of the lands in question. According to the councilmen, the orders were in the Texcocan archives. To judge by some of the partial copies shown by the council, the orders really had existed. So the council searched for any relevant documentary support in Huexotla and succeeded in recovering several critical items. The council took these documents to Mexico City to have them translated from Nahuatl into Spanish by the interpreter of the Royal *Audiencia*. Interestingly, the interpreter's translations are not as close to the original vocabulary and content as translations made by local inhabitants. The interpreter probably knew that the documents were not germane to the case and that all that was needed was some original document or other to initiate the litigation. Accordingly, the councilmen of Huexotla returned to Texcoco and induced the *alcalde mayor* to act. The land dispute was settled in favor of the Indians.[9]

Village lands in Texcoco were dispersed throughout the province, just as they had been in pre-Conquest times. The lands were worked in common to meet the community's assigned tribute and by individual households for their own subsistence. Indian households also held private lands that were owned prior to the Conquest. In addition, they occupied vacated *calpolli* lands and purchased lands from other Indians and Spaniards. Indians, particularly commoners, used the Spanish legal system to protect those lands. Documents written in the Indian towns and villages of Texcoco province repeatedly show that the Indians understood Spanish laws, and actively used those laws to initiate lawsuits against each other and Spaniards over private and communal lands. In the late 1570s, there arose a dispute over whether a certain piece of land in Huexotla had been handed down in the same family before the Conquest, or whether the land should go to Francisco de Santa María, the husband of the direct heir, or to the latter's nephews, Elias de San Pedro and Melchor de Rojas. Despite the small amount of land (17 *brazas* by 7, which cannot have been more than some 140 by 60 feet), the dispute continued for more than twenty years, until finally, in 1597, both parties went to the *alcalde mayor* of Texcoco. His appeal to stop arguing over a "thing of such small value" went unheard. Francisco de Santa María then petitioned the council of Huexotla, and received a favorable judgement. The nephews, however, persevered to the extent of getting a letter signed by the viceroy of New Spain and appealing the entire matter to the Royal *Audiencia* in Mexico City, not once but twice. Yet Francisco de Santa María, who had better connections with the members of the council of Huexotla, won every time.[10]

The practice of alienating village lands reveals that frequently the distinction between village and privately-owned lands was blurred and that Indian economic enterprises were deeply entwined with those of the village. The statement from land litigation brought by the village against an Indian commoner in 1710 illustrates the tenacity with which Indians held onto their village lands through the colonial period and how the process of selling communal lands operated within the structure of the native landholding community and the Spanish legal system.

> ...truly you must know that I left the land, and now the townspeople say that I sold it, but I did not sell the land, for I only lent it to the late Diego López. But the widow says that he (or she) bought it, but from whom did he buy that land that cannot be sold, as I declare before God, so that God will not punish me in the future. And you must know that when I lent him (the land) the judge-governor don Juan de la Cruz chased me away on account of these lands, when a person named Cristobal was trying to take them from me. I showed them the testament, and they did not favor him; the former father minister fray Baltasar de Castillo knows of it, for it was read in his presence five times. And the lord governor went to see the land; then he told me: "only one person is to take the land; well, since you are not to take it, you are to leave the land." And it is true that because of this I went to lend it to Diego López. When I went to see him he said to me: "Don't worry about what I will plant on the land, for I will give you a yoke of oxen; but he did not give them to me..."[11]

Although the Indian commoner, Diego Tomás, insisted that the land was lent to Diego López and his wife, his statement leaves no doubt that others felt that he was selling village lands, and that López's widow saw the property as now belonging to her. The community elders met with some success in making sure that village lands were not alienated. Sometimes they would banish an Indian who was caught trying to sell village lands. And they successfully fought Spaniards in court to regain control over alienated lands. Yet, they tolerated many sales. Village elders, who frequently sat on the town councils as representatives of their community, sold and rented communal lands to Spaniards. They drove hard bargains, and many times made handsome profits for the community.

Conclusions

Frequently, Spanish institutions contributed to the native community maintaining its political and social solidarity. This is certainly true with the municipal town councils. The town council meetings were conducted in Nahuatl, and councilmen were drawn from the community's leading families. The fact that the Spaniards recognized the right of Indian community's and individual Indians to own land further supported the Indian communal structure in Central Mexico. Native communities similar to those found in Texcoco also existed in the regions of Tlaxcala, Toluca and Coyoacan. In Tlaxcala, the town council was composed of noble Indians drawn from the four *cabeceras*. Spaniards held no political posts other than those of *alcalde mayor*, constable, and sometimes, interpreter. And the members of the council carefully monitored local Spanish and Indian activities.

It is still too early to draw broad conclusions concerning the social, economic, and political status of Indian groups living in post-Conquest central Mexico. One general theme that keeps repeating itself is that native communities maintained much of their cultural and political integrity through the colonial period. The recognition by the Spanish of pre-Conquest political entities and the nobility enabled Indian political practices to continue in the post-Conquest period. But such continuation of native practices does not imply that the institutions in which these activities occurred were Indian. The political towns and *calpollis* were Indian, but the town councils and their structure were Spanish. And it was native practices that conformed to these structures.

NOTES

[1]This article is based on research done for my doctoral dissertation (L. Lewis 1978).

[2]Hicks 1978.

[3]The prominent Pimentel family had the greatest success with establishing a prestigious position for themselves in the Valley of Mexico based on their Indian noble pretensions and socioeconomic ties to Spanish society. As descendents of Nezahualpilli and supporters of Cortés, the Pimentel family found itself in a favored position in colonial society. It was awarded several patrimonies in the province and dominated the office of governor in Texcoco through most of the period studied. The Pimentels buttressed their position in colonial society through marital alliances with prosperous and prestigious members of Indian and Spanish society. As early as 1530, members of the family appeared to be highly Hispanized, for all had adopted Spanish patronyms, and some were fluent in Spanish (AGN-T 3594, exp. 2; 676-678; 2522, exp. 7; 2726, exp. 123; 1577; AN, Juan Pérez de Rivera, March 2, 1602; Feb. 10, 1604; Feb. 12, 1604; *Carta de don Hernando Pimentel cacique principal de Texcoco, al rey don Felipe II...* in ENE 6:70-75.

[4]MNA, Jan. 5, 1576; Feb. 28, 1576; Nov. 19, 1576; Feb. 7, 1577; Jan. 15, 1578; Aug. 11, 1578; Nov. 28, 1578; March 3, 1610; May 15, 1613; AGN-T 5, exp. 81; 3, exp. 991, 3780, exp. 3.

[5]AGN-I 5, exp. 81; 3, exp. 991; 3, exp. 780; AGN-T 5, exp. 81; 3, exp. 991; MNA, Jan. 5, 1576; Jan. 27, 1576; Feb. 28, 1576; Feb. 7, 1577; Jan. 15, 1578; Aug. 11, 1578; Nov. 28, 1578; Jan. 31, 1579; March 3, 1610; May 15, 1613.

[6]MNA, April 12, 1578; March 1, 1590; AGN-I 2, exp. 818; 5, exp. 394; 6, exp. 325.

[7]AGN-T 1520, exp. 10; MNA, Dec. 31, 1578; Jan. 10, 1579; Feb. 16, 1616; Feb. 17, 1616; AGN-I 2, exp. 596; 2, exp. 818; 5, exp. 394; 6, exp. 325).

[8]Patrimonies formed one important cornerstone of a native family's wealth. It is not clear from the documents what constituted a patrimony. Some, it appears, were mixtures of private and communal lands, and included Indian retainers who paid labor and tribute to the *cacique*. Grants were made to Indian families according to their noble house's pre-Conquest communal and private landholdings and the number of tribute-paying Indians they had. Patrimonies were held by individual families or by several families whose members were descendents of the same *teccalli*. For instance, the Alvarado, Pimentel, Luna, Guzmán, and Pomar families shared a patrimony in Texcoco. Many holdings were run like Spanish estates. The Indians added to their holdings by purchasing additional lands from both Spaniards and Indians, and they also usurped vacated *calpolli* lands. The owners raised maize and fruits for both Spanish and Indian markets, and extracted tribute from Indian retainers (AGN-T 676-678; H. F. Cline 1966; 1968; 1972).

[9]Significantly, a close examination of the documents reveals that it is quite possible that they were redone

long after the events described in them, and that wholesale falsification is a distinct possibility (AGN-T 1520, exp. 6).

[10]AGN-T 1520, exp. 6.

[11]AGN-T 1520, exp. 6.

TABLE 1
KNOWN MEMBERS OF TEXCOCO'S *TECCALLI*, 1575-1630

Name[1]	Date of Appearance in the Documents	Residence
don Pedro de Alvarado	1578-92	Texcoco
don Juan de Alvarado; husband	1592	Texcoco
of doña Antonia Pimentel	1581-92	Texcoco
don Gabriel de Ayala	1952-95	Texcoco-Mexico City
don Pedro Mexica de Bocanegra	1592	Texcoco-Mexico City
don Lorenzo de Luna	1585-1630	Texcoco-Mexico City
don Francisco Pimentel	1578-1606	Texcoco-Tlaxcala-Mexico City
doña Isabel Pimentel	1578-1595	Texcoco-Mexico City

[1]The relationship between each member of the *teccalli* is not clearly defined in the documents. It is known that there were two Pimentel families in Texcoco, and that the founders of the families were brothers. There was extensive intermarriage between *teccalli* members, which complicates tracing the relationships between the members.

Sources: MNA, rollos 1 and 2.

TABLE 2
KNOWN MEMBERS OF TEXCOCO'S SECOND-LEVEL NATIVE ELITE, 1545-1630

Name	Known Dates When Living	Residence
(don)[1] Fernando de Alva Ixtlilxochtil	1550-1612	Texcoco-Mexico City
Fernando Cortés Ixtlilxochtil	?-1579	Texcoco
Juan Bautista Pomar	1550-1606	Texcoco
(don) Simón de Santo Tomás	1578-?	Texcoco
María Teyeuhtzin	1520-1545	Coatlichan
Alonso Teyeuhtzin[2]	1545-?	Coatlichan

[1]The title of *don* was not used consistently.

[2]Alonso Teyeuhtzin was the son of María. He referred to himself as *señor de Coatlichan*.

Sources: MNA, rollos 1, 2, 3. Ixtlilxochitl 1952, II:248-50.

TABLE 3
KNOWN MEMBERS OF TEXCOCO'S TOWN COUNCIL IN 1578[1]

don Francisco Pimentel	Governor
don León Arido de Santiago	Alcalde
don Baltasar de Santa Francisca	Alcalde
don Jusepe de San Miguel	Alcalde[2]
don Pedro de Alvarado	Alguacil
don Gabriel de Ayala	Alguacil
don Simón de Santo Tomás	Regidor
don Lorenzo de San Miguel	?
Pedro Contro	Notary
García Gómez	Interpreter

[1]There is no indication from the documents as to the size of Texcoco's town council. If the entire council ever met, there is no record of it. Also many positions and who filled them are not recorded here.

[2]It is not clear in the documents if the *alcaldes* on Texcoco's town council were *alcaldes mayores*, who were appointed by the viceroy. Two Spaniards, appointed by the viceroy, were known *alcaldes mayores* in Texcoco. They were don Lorenzo de Castilla and don Alonso Villanueva Cervantes.

Sources: MNA, Dec. 31, 1578.

TABLE 4
KNOWN MEMBERS OF TEPETLAOZTOC'S TOWN COUNCIL, 1614-1616[1]

NAME	BARRIO	POSITION
don Alonso Jímenez de Castilla Pérez (Spaniard)		Governor
Diego de Morales	San Miguel	Alcalde
Juan de San Gerónimo	San Gerónimo	Alcalde
Pedro de San Gabriel	San Gabriel	Alcalde
don Juan	?	Alcalde
Juan de Santa María	Santa María	Alcalde[2]
Domingo Salazar	?	Regidor Mayor
Bartolomé Tellez	?	Regidor Mayor
Juan de Mendoza	?	Alguacil Mayor
Lucas Martín	?	Alguacil
Sánchez de Quiñonez	?	Notary
fray Juan Núñez[3]		

[1]There is no indication from the documents as to the size of Tepetlaoztoc's town council. If the entire council ever met, there is no record of it.

[2]The known *alcalde mayor* was Juan de Ayala.

[3]The priest sat on the town council as a non-voting member. He occasionally signed for councilmen.

Sources: MNA, July 4, 1614; July 26, 1614; July 27, 1614; Feb. 15, 1616; Feb. 17, 1616.

TABLE 5

KNOWN MEMBERS OF HUEXOTLA'S TOWN COUNCIL, 1640-1641[1]

NAME	BARRIO	POSITION
don Diego Cerón		Governor
don Gabriel López[2]		Governor
don Juan Pérez		Alcalde
Juan de San Miguel		Alcalde
Alonso Martín		Alcalde
Luis de San Francisco		Alcalde
Juan Mateo	Caolhuacan	Alcalde
Juan Pablo	Tlayllotlacan	Alcalde
Juan Lucas	Tlatocan	Alcalde
don Pedro		Alcalde[3]
Diego de San Miguel	Mexicapa	Alguacil Mayor
Pedro Gaspar		Alguacil Mayor
Diego Lucas		Alguacil Mayor
Juan Martín		Regidor
don Lorenzo de Zamora		Alguacil Mayor de la Iglesia
Juan Bautista		Mayordomo
Pedro López		Notary
don Juan Pérez		Fiscal

[1]There is not indication from the documents as to the size of Huexotla's town council. If the entire council ever met, there is no record of it.

[2]Don Gabriel López disputed the election of don Diego Cerón. In 1641, it was ruled that don Gabriel should be the governor of Huexotla.

[3]There was one known *alcalde mayor* in Huexotla, a Spaniard named Capitán don Juan Leonel Gómez de Cervantes.

Source: AGN-Cr 260-10.

COLONIALISM AND THE POLITICAL TRANSFORMATION OF ISTHMUS ZAPOTEC SOCIETY

Judith Francis Zeitlin

In human history perhaps no single event has had the combined cultural, demographic, political, and ecological impact as that occasioned by the discovery of the New World by bands of adventurers from the Old. In Mesoamerica as in the Andes, where indigenous societies rivalled their sixteenth century European counterparts, the consequences of military defeat and Spanish colonial rule were complex and far-reaching. Recent studies by historians and anthropologists have focused on the reaction of ethnically distinct native groups to the particular economic and political presssures placed upon them by regional interests.[1] While not altering our general perception of widespread population decline, economic hardship, and cultural dislocation in the first centuries of Spanish rule, these fine-scale studies highlight the importance of considering the local context in which colonial institutions operated before assessing their toll on native society.

A case in point is Taylor's[2] exhaustive study of native and Spanish land use systems in colonial Oaxaca. Taylor found that, unlike the situation of northern Mexico where the growth of entailed estates reduced the Indian population to debt peonage on vast Spanish *haciendas*,[3] native groups in the Oaxaca Valley remained sufficiently strong to resist the encroachment of colonial landholders and prevent the breakdown of community life. Subsequently he proposed that the Oaxaca pattern may be typical of southern Mesoamerica, where the absence of strong regional states in late pre-Hispanic times and a relative isolation from the most intense pressures of early colonial economic interests permitted the survival of many languages and cultural institutions at the community level.[4]

Two hundred fifty kilometers southeast of the Oaxaca Valley stretches the Pacific plain of the Isthmus of Tehuantepec, where more than 80,000 speakers of native languages continue to pursue lives much influenced by a pre-Columbian heritage.[5] Like the Oaxaca Valley, the southern Isthmus is populated by Indian communities that survived the ravages of disease and economic exploitation that followed the Spanish Conquest. Place names mentioned in Aztec tribute lists or military accounts often reappear in sixteenth- and seventeenth-century documents or on modern maps and historical censuses without interruption. The fact of such strong community stability is in itself noteworthy, for Spanish land usurpation and its attendant ecological transformation were felt even more severely in the Tehuantepec region than in neighboring Oaxaca.[6]

Rather than attempt to delineate the complex array of economic variables that permitted native communities to retain the agricultural land base necessary for their survival, as Taylor did for the Oaxaca Valley, I would like to examine another issue of colonial Indian history; the extent to which native groups such as the Isthmus Zapotec were transformed into colonial societies that differed structurally from their pre-Columbian counterparts, despite the physical continuity of Indian land-holding units. My thesis is that the social and political effects of post-Conquest population loss, colonial rule, and cultural suppression drastically altered the nature of southern Mesoamerica's indigenous states and in so doing restructured social interaction in the surviving native community.

Isthmus Zapotec Society Before the Conquest

To better understand these colonial developments, let us first outline the pre-Conquest history and sociopolitical organization of the region's dominant Indian group. The Zapotecs were not the original inhabitants of the hot, fertile plains of Tehuantepec, as evidenced by their own narrative accounts, archaeological data, and historical linguistics. The entire Isthmus of Tehuantepec may have been the aboriginal homeland of Mixe-Zoque language speakers, whose modern-day distribution reflects the prehistoric encroachment of Nahuatl groups in the northern Isthmus and Zapotec and Huave peoples in the south.[7] Arriving on the Pacific coast sometime in the mid-fourteenth century,[8] Zapotec groups from the Oaxaca Valley established a base at the former Huave settlement of Tehuantepec and gradually penetrated what may have been Zoque territory along the Tehuantepec and Perros drainage systems.

Zapotec accounts of their Isthmian conquest offer no explanation for this migration. Great population movements appear to have been wide-spread in the turbulent political climate of the Postclassic era, in which interethnic hostilities and territorial aggrandizement were dominant themes throughout much of Mesoamerica. Whether the Zapotecs moved to take advantage of the southern Isthmus' strategic position along the coveted Soconusco trade route or whether they were compelled to emigrate because of political and economic presssures at home is uncertain. Lending support to a less opportunistic motive may be the migration's timing close to the late thirteenth-century date given for the first wave of Mixtec groups that moved into the already densely populated Oaxaca Valley. By the late 1400s, Zapotec losses in a new round of intercommunity competition forced the lord of Zaachila, paramount ruler among the petty Zapotec polities, to join in the established settlement in Tehuantepec, leaving many of his former tributaries subject to the Mixtecs at nearby Cuilapan.[9]

His retreat signaled neither a permanent decline in the Zapotec lord's fortunes nor some fatal weakness in the Zapotec state. Through familar cycles of warfare, conquest, and reconquest, the exiled Cosijoeza prospered from his Isthmian throne, acquiring large numbers of subjects from coastal communities allied to Tehuantepec and amassing rich private estates on the choicest lands in the province. The Tehuantepec ruler's authority extended over a region that the mighty Aztecs, thwarted in their efforts secure its control, considered to be "one of the richest and most powerful" regions in Mesoamerica.[10]

Cosijoeza derived his power and wealth from a sociopolitical system that placed the hereditary ruler at the apex of a highly stratified society in which an individual's position was largely determined at birth. Unfortunately, surviving documentary sources—while often rich in colorful details about isolated customs—leave many gaps in our knowledge of this system's functioning. Available evidence suggests that Zapotec society was structured according to principles familar to other Mesoamerican states, whether community-based, as among the Mixtec[11] or composed of vast territorial aggregates, as among the Aztec.[12] In drawing the following brief sketch of the pre-Columbian state centered at Tehuantepec, I have relied upon a diverse array of historical, linguistic, and archaeological sources to piece together elements of the native sociopolitical system. My purpose here is to amplify certain features developed in other syntheses of Zapotec society.[13] and to draw particular attention to its Isthmian manifestation.

Producers for the Zapotec State

Zapotec society was split into two major divisions, the nobility (or *principales*) and the commoners (or *macehualtin*), to use the Hispanicized Nahuatl term quickly adopted by colonial authorities. A *macehualli* (Zapotec *pèniquéche*, literally "person of the village"[14]) was the productive backbone of society, the laborer or tributary (*huèni chijna, copàci*) who produced goods and services for the support of the family, the non-producing nobility, and the supernatural world.

Among the Aztecs, whose social organization was recorded in considerable ethnographic detail by Zorita, Sahagún, and others, that labor was organized through the *calpollis*, which were kinship-linked residential units with landholding, administrative, and other corporate functions.[15] Attributes of a similar system are suggested for the Zapotec as well through isolated linguistic and descriptive data. In his sixteenth-century *Vocabulario* Córdova[16] provided Zapotec glosses for "lineage head, *padre grande principio de linaje*" (*pixózehuechijbatija, hueçòbatija, cozàanatáo huellàpitija*), a leadership position that may imply some corporate features for Zapotec lineages as well—a feature corroborated by other sixteenth-century sources. The presence of residential wards, or *barrios*, which have remained an important feature of community organization among the Isthmus Zapotec in modern times, is documented by Baltasar de San Miguel, who recorded 49 *barrios* for Tehuantepec during his 1550 *visita* to the province.[17] With an average of 16 extended family households per *barrio* from the 817 houses counted in this early census, Isthmian *barrios* can be correlated loosely with the *tijapèniquéche* or lineages. Our sources do not mention any landholding functions that the Zapotec *barrio* may have held comparable to those of the *calpolli*, but there are indirect suggestions. Since tribute payments to the nobility were assigned on a ward-by-ward basis rather than through the community at large, it seems reasonable to conclude that the *barrio* may also have played a role in distributing the means of production.

Not all commoners were full-time farmers. Whitecotton[18] attributes the following occupations listed by Córdova to the *pèniquéche*: "day laborers, free servants, weavers, dancers, musicians, sculptors, metal workers, painters, interpreters, diviners, curers, merchants, and peddlers, among others." While some individuals with specialized skills may have served the Zapotec nobility exclusively, others sold their products or services to the community at large through the periodic market or *quíya* (equivalent to the Aztec *tianquiztli*), for which major marketplaces were found at Tehuantepec, Miahuatlan, Coatlan, and other Zapotec centers.[19] Long-distance merchants from Tehuantepec traded widely in such local products as salt, cotton, cloth, and dried fish and shrimp, hiring porters from as far away as Ixtepeji in the northern Zapotec highlands to transport their merchandise to market.[20]

It appears that not all who wished to farm had access to community lands or to lands in sufficient quantity to support themselves. Córdova lists a number of Zapotec terms for the landless poor: *pénizaanijani* (peon), *pénicopéezéhe* (person without lands other than a *solar* or houselot), *pèniconeto, penihuezábiñaani* (one who hires himself out because of poverty). Among the Aztecs, the rule of primogeniture in inheritance and rapid population growth combined to produce a sizeable group of commoners without access to *calpolli* lands. They supported themselves by renting land from the nobility or from individuals of another ward where arable land may have exceeded its own members' needs.[21]

The social status of these landless individuals is enigmatic. Among the far better documented Aztecs, tenant farmers or *terrazgueros*, who worked the private lands of nobles, constituted a social class, the *mayehqueh*, separate from the *macehualtin*, for whom usufruct rights to *calpolli* land was a major criterion of membership. *Mayehqueh* were permanently attached to the private lands they cultivated, remaining on the property upon the death of the landowner and transferral of tenancy rights and obligations to his heirs. In return for providing agricultural produce and some personal services to the landlord, tenants were absolved of any obligation to pay tribute to the *cacique.*[22]

Because private property itself is generally thought to have originated among the Mexicans in the course of warfare and territorial expansion, it is not clear how pervasive the formation of a *mayehqui* class might have been outside of the expansionistic Aztec state. Spores[23] is convinced of the existence of indentured servitude among the Oaxaca Mixtec, finding as many as 2000 *terrazgueros* bound to the *cacique* of Yanhuitlán alone. Reviewing the evidence for a Zapotec *mayehqui* class, Whitecotton[24] notes the difficulty of distinguishing real serfs in colonial documents from *macehualtin* who simply worked lands belonging to *caciques* and *principales* as a tribute obligation, without being bound individually to any particular private tract. For the Isthmus Zapotec, there are many early colonial examples of Indians working the nobility's lands, such as the 1563 complaint by the Tehuantepec *cacique's* heirs that their patrimonial *macehualtin* were not fulfilling their obligations.[25] My own view is that such complaints may allude to the customary duties of *terrazgueros* rather than those of ordinary tributaries. Supporting linguistic evidence for the existence of a serf class among the Zapotec similar to that known for the Aztec state is found in Córdova's *Vocabulario*, which offers two words for renter or tenant, *pènitàholàa* and *pènicozàaca*, the latter meaning "foreigner" and suggested by the compiler to be appropriate because "frequently they are foreigners."[26] We might conclude from his comment that Zapotec *terrazgueros* also originated principally through the assimilation of foreigners or foreign lands, although the disenfranchisement of local *pèniquéche* probably added to their number.[27]

Serfs, particularly those belonging to non-Zapotec ethnic enclaves, must have existed somewhat outside the normal structure of social interaction, since that interaction was shaped largely by the web of kinship ties. Even more estranged, of course, were slaves, whose very existence within society could be transitory. Those taken captive in warfare (*péniquij* or vanquished man, also *péniyèxóyáa*) were marked for early sacrifice. If ritual cannibalism was performed, such a slave was called *xoyàaquij*. Córdova[28] provided some grisly culinary detail on this subject when describing *xoyàaquij* as those sacrificial victims who were "stewed or boiled or roasted for eating." That such a custom was indeed practiced by the Tehuantepec population is affirmed by Burgoa's account of Cosijoeza's battle with the Aztec ruler Ahuitzotl, in which, throughout a seven-month siege by the Mexican army, Zapotec forces subsisted on the flesh of captives taken back to their mountaintop fortress of Guiengola.[29] Slaves used as domestic servants (*chóco, pinijni, xillàni*) could be procured in slave markets, such as Miahuatlán's in the southern Zapotec highlands, where there was a brisk trade in war captives taken from all parts of Mesoamerica.[30]

The Cacique and his Subjects

At the opposite end of the social spectrum stood the hereditary Zapotec nobility, which the Spaniards divided into the ruling aristocracy or *caciques* and the lesser nobility or *principales* throughout New Spain. While this division glossed over some of the subtle distinctions Indian themselves drew between different sectors of the nobility, it reflected accurately the primacy of the royal family in Mesoamerican state organization. Among the Zapotec each independent town or *cabecera* had its own *cacique* (*coquì* in Zapotec), with the ruler of a more important town known as *coquìtào* (great lord) or *coquìtào huezàquiquèche* (lord conqueror). Marriages contracted between the royal families of powerful towns both preserved the integrity of royal blood lines and promoted political alliances among rivalrous petty states.[31] Among the polygynous nobility, first-born sons of *caciques* normally inherited the throne, but primogeniture was not an invariable rule. An elder son might be passed over if he lacked the personal qualifications deemed important for a ruler or if political considerations favored the son of a junior wife, as was the case in the inheritance of the Tehuantepec *cacicazgo*.

The choice of Cosijoeza's successor is chronicled in a rare early sixteenth-century codex, the *Lienza de Guevea*, described and analyzed by Edward Seler[32] from two hand-painted later copies. This document served to validate land titles from Santiago Guevea by establishing the Isthmian mountain community's long-standing fealty to the hereditary ruler of Tehuantepec. In one section of the codex a column of named chieftains (presumably from Guevea) faces a column of figures representing the pre-Columbian princes of Zaachila and Tehuantepec. According to Seler's interpretation of the hieroglyphs and transcribed Zapotec names associated with the second column, two of the figures represent not Cosijoeza's ancestors but his eldest sons, whose unsuitability for royal office is remarked upon in the text, for example "the eldest son attracted suspicion," thus validating Cosijopi's ascension to power in place of his elder brothers.[33]

More than personal ability and character may have favored the younger brother. Born of the marriage contracted in 1502 between Cosijoeza and Moctezuma's daughter Ichcatlaxoch, Cosijopi must have been an adolescent at the time of his installation as ruler of Tehuantepec in 1518. While he was too young to have yet proved himself in battle, the prince had powerful maternal family connections to support his candidacy for office, if not to require his selection. Although Zapotec narrative history described the circumstances of the alliance between Cosijoeza and Ichcatlaxoch differently,[34] Aztec accounts suggest that the marriage contract may have been part of the Tehuantepec ruler's belated acknowledgment of Moctezuma's suzerainity.[35] As Gibson[36] points out, one way the Aztecs imposed indirect rule on a conquered province was through an arranged marriage between the local *cacique* and a legitimate daughter of one of the Triple Alliance rulers. Provincial succession then passed to a son of this marriage, regardless of any prior claims to the throne by the *cacique's* older children. The continuation of hostilities between the Aztecs and Isthmus Zapotecs during the remainder of Moctezuma's reign, however, reminds us that this was not a very effective means of political control.

Marriage and inheritance patterns that preserved the purity of royal blood lines were but one measure of the separate status accorded the Zapotec *cacique*. In life he was lavished with every luxury provided by native artisanry. He wore delicately woven cotton cloth and colorful feather cloaks and headdresses, with jewelry of gold and precious stones adorning his body. He ate special food denied to the common populace and lived in many-roomed palaces attended by a large staff of servants and noble retainers.[37] He sat on a jaguar skin throne and was carried about his domain on a litter borne on the shoulders of a dozen men.[38] At death, a great lord and his wife were buried in richly appointed, stone-lined tombs, archaeological remains of which are among the greatest Mesoamerican treasures. Sacrificial victims (*pénitòoga*) were dispatched to accompany them to the supernatural world, a pair of men for a *cacique* and a pair of women for his wife.[39] Even after death they continued to be venerated, for among the Zapotec, who believed in the spiritual power of ancestors to intercede on behalf of the living community, deceased royalty were often regarded as divine beings themselves.[40]

The authority that demanded these acts of sacrifice and subservience stemmed from the *cacique's* position as supreme political, military, judicial, and religious leader. It was he who waged war, made peace, and entered into alliances with rival states; he who directed the affairs of the community, set taxes, and resolved disputes. While many of these functions, in fact, were routinely carried out by the *cacique's* appointed agents or, as in the case of priests, by individuals with special training in esoteric knowledge and ritual, he was the ultimate arbiter in all matters. Burgoa[41] relates separate incidents when the Tehuantepec ruler personally consulted oracles and performed special rites of sacrifice and propitiation at times of community crisis. Depicted on a throne attired in priestly garb,[42] the Zapotec *cacique* embodied the moral and political conscience of society, and his name was synonymous with his domain.

In turn, the community was obliged to provide labor and material support necessary to affect the ruler's decisions and to supply his private needs. The latter were met by regular tribute, or *chijna*. Among modern Isthmus Zapotecs the word still connotes work, labor, or office,[43] a meaning implicit in sixteenth-century renderings for worker *hueni chijna* and office *quela chijna* or *xichijñaya*. In the 1580 *Relación Geográfica*, informants declared that prior to Cortés' arrival they had given tribute to Cosijopi in the form of gold dust and jewelry, precious green stones, feathers, tiger skins, cotton cloth, turkeys, corn, chile, beans, honey, deer, fish, local fruit, an all kinds of hunted game.[44] From practices that survived and were sometimes disputed in the colonial period, it appears that the *pèniquéche* also were obliged to perform domestic services, repair houses, and provide labor on the *cacique's* lands.[45] Apart from these customary tribute payments, the *pèniquéche* could be mobilized for additional services. They provided warriors for battle and laborers and material for public works. When the Tehuantepec ruler built his mountaintop fortress at Guiengola, thousands of laborers were drafted to create its walled complex of temples, palaces, ballcourt, and plazas. Although we do not have documentary evidence for the conduct of such labor drafts, the Zapotecs very likely followed a common Mesoamerican practice of supplying workers on a rational basis through the residential ward organization.

Tribute obligations to the *cacique* were incurred not only by the populace of the *cabecera* and its subject hamlets, for which he was hereditary ruler, but also by the inhabitants of independent towns subjugated through force. Before his exile to Tehuantepec, the Zaachila lord held several Zapotec communities in the Oaxaca Valley tributary, with some possessions later falling into Mexican or Mixtec hands and others continuing to provide payments and services to Cosijoeza and his son in Tehuantepec.[46] For the southern Isthmus itself, the extent of the Tehuantepec *cacique's* domain is less clear, since we have no documentary evidence from Zoque, Huave, or even other Zapotec towns to counterbalance the sixteenth-century picture of Tehuantepec's complete domination. The 1580 *Relación Geográfica* for the province states that all 31 villages were "small and subject only to the cabecera, the *villa* of Tehuantepec."[47]

Archaeological evidence from one intensively surveyed section of the Isthmian coastal plain sheds some additional light on native regional politics. Prior to the fourteenth century, the Río de los Perros area had enjoyed several centuries of population growth and cultural florescence, with scattered hamlets and villages under the domination of a single regional center. This pattern of growth abruptly ended with the Zapotec invasion. The primate center was abandoned, population declined, and settlements along the river floodplain dispersed into smaller communities, whose material remains reflected strong influences from the Oaxaca Valley.[48] As was the practice in wars of conquest, the Tehuantepec *cacique* expropriated for himself some of the most productive properties in the conquered territory, from profitable salt mines near the coast to choice irrigated lands in the Río de los Perros piedmont. After the Spanish Conquest, Cosijopi's daughter deeded some of these properties inherited from her father's estate to the Dominican convent at Tehuantepec, including bathing pools near Laollaga and extensive orchards covering over half a league.[49]

As clear-cut as the subjugation of some parts of the province was, it would not be unexpected if similar evidence of cultural and political dominance does not emerge everywhere in the archaeological record. Some villages may have escaped conquest while others made regular tribute payments to the Zapotec *cacique* and still others were subject to the Aztec tax collector. Even Cosijoeza was put in the uncomfortable position of giving tribute to Ahuitzotl following a decisive military loss, but his subjugation was not permanent.[50] In postclassic Mesoamerica, the local landscape was typically a shifting mosaic of independent and conquered towns owing allegiance to two or three victorious rulers.

Principales and the Administration of the State

Only the *cacique* and his direct descendants were accorded highest rank in Zapotec society. The remainder of the nobility—the *joàna* or *principales*—enjoyed many of the same social privileges as did the royal family, but apparently held no vested authority other than that conferred on them individually by the *cacique*. They too were permitted to wear fine clothes, eat the richest foods, and dwell in spacious houses. Commoners were obliged to address them using special deferential language, and they preserved their noble status through rank endogamy.[51]

In central Mexico, *principales* were organized into noble houses or *teccalli*, which were ostensibly like the commoner *calpolli*, but in fact embodied more clearly the corporate and kinship features of a lineage.[52] Small enough for their members to all claim descent from a common founding ancestor, the *teccalli* owned land that was farmed by *terrazgueros* or by *macehualtin* in fulfillment of tribute obligations. It appears that some noble lineages were by right of custom associated with particular offices in the Aztec state organization; upon the death of an officeholder, family members elected his successor among themselves, but their nominee had to be confirmed by the ruler.

Unfortunately, our own sources do not permit a comparable description of the *tijajoàna* or Zapotec noble lineages, but they hint at some likely shared attributes. Patrimonial estates and tributary allotments of *pèniquéche barrios* survived among the Tehuantepec *principales* into the sixteenth century.[53] Hierarchical ranking of the noble lineages as is known for the Aztec[54] might be inferred for the Zapotec as well. Córdova[55] distinguishes not just the *tijacoquij* or lineage of great lords and the *tijajoàna* or lineage of lesser lords ("*como caballeros*"), but also the *tijajoànahuíni* (literally "lineage of the little nobility") or *tijacollàba* as the lineage of lowest nobility ("*como de hidalgos*"). Since this division was not maintained systematically in the *Vocabulario*, for the present we can only speculate on the nature of any internal stratification within the Zapotec nobility. We do not know if this society permitted the degree of upward mobility documented for the Aztecs, among whom commoners who distinguished themselves in warfare could enter the nobility, passing on any achieved rights and privileges to their heirs.

A nobleman was also a *péniquela*, a person of authority. It was from the noble lineages that individuals were drawn to fill administrative, religious, and military offices vital to the community's maintenance. Our evidence for religious offices is the most complete,[56] for the Dominican priests whose writings provide the best description of Zapotec culture were keenly interested in the workings of their outlawed pagan rivals. Much less attention was paid to the organization of secular offices in antiquity. Responses to the *Relación Geográfica* questionnaire on the subject of pre-Columbian native government were brief and typified by this Tehuantepec example:

> ...the lord of this province of Tehuantepec, the aforementioned don Juan Cortés [Cosijopi], governed as its natural lord and appointed one of the foremost men for his lieutenant, and this individual had account with the natives of the province, collecting and gathering the revenue which they gave to don Juan Cortés...[57]

This chief lieutenant or *mayordomo* was known as the *collàbachijna quìhui*, an office with no precise Spanish counterpart, but one equated with the Mexican *tequitlahtoh* or provincial governor. Each *barrio* or hamlet of the town had its own *collàbachijna*, who collected taxes and settled disputes.[58]

Whether or not other formal offices (apart from war leaders) existed within the Zapotec state is more controversial. Whitecotton[59] concludes that the prince and his *tequitlahtohqueh* constituted the entire governmental bureaucracy, for he notes that the Zapotec were unable to provide non-overlapping equivalent terms for the offices of *gobernador, regidor* and *alcalde* instituted under colonial rule. While the Zapotec may indeed not have conceived of government in terms of the discrete separation of official powers intended by the Spanish, there are suggestions of some system of decision making and administration more complex than that described in the *Relaciones Geográficas*. That this system did not survive 60 years after the Conquest probably reflects its capitulation to imposed colonial forms.

In central Mexico, the native ruler was assisted in decision-making matters by a council of important leaders whose members were drawn from the highest nobility.[60] Córdova[61] hints of a similar unit among the Zapotec in a set of linguistic cognates for a council, *quelahuexijatícha*; a group of men forming a *cabildo, penihuexijaticha*; and the members of an *audiencia, láhuihuexija* or *lahuihuiñaticha*. Unlike their efforts to translate *gobernador* and other Spanish offices, in which they often seem to have been grasping for comparable meanings, in this case his informants appear to have had a very clear idea of what constituted the authority and domain of such a council. The Zapotec root *tica* (cf. *tíchapéa*, meaning law or power) suggests that it was a judicial body, but probably not in a narrow, legalistic sense. Many of the words Córdova glosses for both administrative and judicial offices or roles, such as *alcalde, gobernador, corregidor*, judge, lawyer, and even learned person are related forms (*huetògoticha, huecuècheticha, huezàalàoticha, coquìlleticha, quichijñoticha*) and might refer to the members of this council or their assistants.

We have too few threads of evidence even to suggest what the duties of other offices listed in the *Vocabulario* may have been. Although existing documentation for the Zapotec provides few avenues for reconstructing how native government operated, diverse linguistic and historical data permit us to conclude that the nobility functioned actively in administrative and judicial matters. The political organization of the native Zapotec state seems then to have paralleled society's division into stratified classes, but its purposes were not wholly the exploitation of the many by a powerful few. In large towns, such as Tehuantepec, hierarchical government served not only the self-interests of the nobility but also the harmonious integration of the general population, whose numbers were too great for kinship institutions alone to forestall and resolve conflict or to direct public effort toward common ends.

At the time of Cortés' capture of Tenochtitlan in 1521, Cosijopi had been installed by his father as lord of Tehuantepec. The young ruler was quick to ally himself with this powerful new force in Mesoamerican politics and sent emissaries laden with rich gifts to greet Cortés' first exploratory party to reach the Pacific Coast. Cortés, a useful friend in Cosijopi's struggles with traditional enemies, dispatched Pedro de Alvarado to subdue the Mixtecs of Tututepec after they attacked Tehuantepec. The following year Cosijopi reciprocated the favor by treating Alvarado with great courtesy and hospitality when he passed through the southern Isthmus in pursuit of a victory over Soconusco and Chiapas.[62]

This felicitous relationship between native *cacique* and Spanish conqueror persisted for many years. Cortés coveted the coastal province both for the sheltered harbors it afforded his exploratory voyages in search of new lands and profitable shipping routes and for the potential of its natural resources. He secured the province for his private domain, the Marquesado del Valle, which Charles V conferred on him in 1529 as a reward for his services to the Crown. This quasi-feudal state within New Spain included many of the colony's choicest highland properties, but Tehuantepec was the Marqués' sole coastal province.

Like any *encomendero*, the Marqués del Valle had tribute rights over the native population alloted to him and permission to exercise a free hand in promoting private economic ventures on lands not farmed by Indian communities. On the southern Isthmus, Cortés instituted a diverse set of enterprises that included building ships on the lagoon shore, mining for gold in the nearby mountains, and raising cattle and mules on the coastal plain. These activities were supported with labor and supplies exacted as tribute from the Tehuantepec natives.[63] Unlike other *encomenderos*, the Marqués himself enjoyed the privilege of granting allotments of tributary Indians within his domain to Spaniards in his favor and the right to appoint an *alcalde mayor* and lesser administrative officials to oversee Indian affairs and tribute collection.

The immense wealth and autonomy that the Marquesado permitted Cortés aroused the suspicion and jealousy of New Spain's colonial government from the beginning, and rivalries intensified under the regal posturing of the second Marqués, Martín Cortés. After repeated efforts to limit Cortés' tributary income, the *audiencia*, under Viceroy Luís de Velasco, finally succeeded in having the Tehuantepec province removed from the Marquesado in 1563. The ostensible grounds for its removal were the Crown's belated acknowledgment that the province contained a port and was therefore too important to remain in private hands.[64] Despite the loss of seignorial powers in the southern Isthmus, the Cortés family continued to maintain an active economic interest there through its private cattle and mule ranches.

For the Tehuantepec *cacique*, life under the Marqués' authority was not without its advantages, at least initially. Under the *pax hispánica*, Cosijopi was relieved of the Aztecs' persistent demands for tribute and was at last able to consolidate his own authority as native ruler of the entire province. Cortés *alcalde mayor* concerned himself primarily with tribute collection and with the management of the Marqués' business enterprises, leaving internal affairs of the native population alone, albeit under the watchful eye of the Dominican mission in Tehuantepec. By an arrangement that the Crown permitted only in select cases where the native ruler had been especially helpful to the Spanish conquerors, Cosijopi continued to receive much of his income from tribute paid him directly by subject towns in the province. Some communities paid tribute to the *cacique* and some paid to the Marqués.[65] In the Marqués' 1542 tax assessment, this income was sufficiently large for Cortés to levy a quarterly surcharge of 92 1/2 pesos from the *cacique*, an annual sum amounting to over 20 percent of the total tributary income he received from the Tehuantepec natives.[66]

Cosijopi's outward identification with Spanish rule had several manifestations. He accepted Christianity as part of his new allegiance to the Spanish monarch, adopting the baptismal name of Juan Cortés and providing the dominican mission in Tehuantepec with a sumptuous convent and everything needed to support their activities.[67] Permission to acquire the trappings of the Spanish nobility sweetened the taste of European domination. Don Juan, as he was known historically, eagerly adopted such Western fashions as wearing tailored clothing and riding on horseback. The *Lienzo de Guevea*, in its historical record of the Tehuantepec kings, depicts his transformation into a Spanish-style *hidalgo*, with Cosijopi and Cosijoeza pictured in priestly garb and seated on jaguar-skin cushions. At the top of this column of figures is don Juan, sitting with his legs crossed in a Spanish chair and wearing a hat, shoes, pants and cloak.[68] The rest of the native nobility quickly followed suit in the *cacique's* emulation of Spanish ways. Mid sixteenth-century archival records for the province are replete with official decrees granting individual *principales* the right to keep and ride horses.

Trivial privileges such as these were overshadowed by the larger economic and cultural price the Tehuantepec natives paid under their Spanish masters. While the nobility was exempt from tribute obligations throughout New Spain, the Marqués exacted heavy levies from the *macehualtin* in food and supplies for his household and business ventures, this in addition to the customary tax in gold. Slaves working at Cortés' Isthmian mines were supplied with staples, poultry, and clothing from Tehuantepec, shrimp from Ixtaltepec del Mar, fish from Huazontlan, and lime from Tepehuazontlan. The Tehuantepec *barrio* of Cía provided laborers for charcoal manufacturing. Coastal shipbuilding depended on an integrated system of Indian labor from several communities, in which those of the mountains fed and serviced Spaniards and black slaves operating the Marqués' animals, while riverine towns transported the finished masts, beams, and planking to the lagoon-shore shipyard, where yet another community supplied food and labor services to the Spanish carpenters.[69]

Cortés' tribute demands were gradually curtailed, at first as the *audiencia* removed labor drafts from *encomenderos* and regularized tribute schedules under the New Laws of 1542-43, and finally as the Isthmian population gained successive tribute adjustments in response to declining population figures.[70] More far-reaching consequences for Zapotec society than the immediate loss of goods and labor in tribute, however, arose from demographic and institutional changes brought about under colonialism. The first of these resulted from the colonists' unwitting transmittal of Old World diseases to an immunologically defenseless population. The second was the conscious outcome of colonial policies that sought to transform Indian society into a Christianized peasantry.

Colonial Population Decline in the Southern Isthmus

Epidemics of smallpox, measles, plague, and typhus swept through the New World after the Conquest, attended by malnutrition and weakened resistence to respiratory disease. One of the severest attacks came from the pandemic of 1545-47, variously identified as typhus or pneumonic plague. The presence of this scourge on the southern Isthmus is affirmed in records from Cortés' Tehuantepec mines, where declining revenues were attributed to the high death toll among the mines' slaves from *cocoliztli*,[71] a Nahuatl word referring to a great pestilence rather than a particular form of disease. Porters bearing food and supplies to the mines from coastal communities would readily have transmitted the disease back to their home villages, if indeed they were not already infected from other sources.

The first census for the region, made during Baltasar de San Miguel's 1550 *visita*, postdates the major impact of this epidemic. His careful enumeration of 16,726 men, women, and children must represent a substantial colonial population decline for the southern Isthmus. Smallpox alone has been observed to produce a 30 percent mortality rate in previously unexposed populations.[72] If we consider the combined effects of smallpox, plague, typhus, and measles outbreaks documented for neighboring parts of Chiapas and Guatemala three times prior to the 1545-47 *cocoliztli* siege,[73] the death rate during the first decades of Spanish rule must have been extremely high. A pre-Conquest population of about 50,000 for the Tehuantepec province would be compatible with archaeological data and with an estimated two-thirds population decline calculated by contemporary observers of the 1550s in the Valley of Mexico.[74]

Demographic data comparable to San Miguel's are unfortunately rare. For the remainder of the sixteenth century we must rely on tribute records for the province, in which tributaries not individuals were counted. Borah and Cook[75] arrived at a standard ratio of total population to tributaries of 2.8 to 1, based on census data from a large sample of central Mexican towns. If we calculate an independent ratio for Tehuantepec from the 1550 census, which counted married couples, unmarried adults, and children separately, we derive a conversion factor of 2.7, a number not very different from that of Borah and Cook.

Using this local population-to-tributary ratio, we can interpret Crown tribute records and obtain our next population estimate for 1560, when documents listing the tribute paid by native communities under private *encomienda* indicated a value of 2200 pesos for the Marqués' Tehuantepec jurisdiction.[76] Recent tribute reforms had regularized the amount of tribute assessed Indian communities by eliminating tribute payments to *caciques* and by scheduling the tribute rate at one peso of common gold and one-half *fanega* of maize for each full tributary or married couple and half that amount for widows, widowers, and unmarried adults.[77] On that basis, the amount of gold paid in tribute ought to equal the number of tributaries for the province, and the total 1560 population should number 5940, if we employ the 2.7 population conversion factor. Even boosting this figure by 10 percent or 20 percent to include the tribute-exempt nobility, we are left with a 1560 population estimate that is less than half that enumerated ten years earlier.

Such a profound demographic decline in a short period would seem suspect were it not for the existence of an independent source for a compatible population estimate. In a report on the Oaxaca diocese's native communities written in the mid-1560s, probably shortly after Tehuantepec was removed from the marquesado, Bishop Albuquerque of Antequera gave a figure of 2500 tributaries for the province, a figure that converts to a total population estimate close to our own calculation. Moreover, the prelate noted that a tremendously high mortality rate in the three to four years preceding this writing had sharply reduced the native population; "and so I believe that almost half the people are missing that ought to have been there before this time."[78] Since Albuquerque himself had earlier served in the Tehuantepec mission, he can be considered a particularly reliable informant. While no cause of this demographic catastrophe was noted, it appears that Tehuantepec had been hit by a localized epidemic of some disease.

The social, psychological, and economic repercussions were severe from what may have been a 90 percent population decline in the southern Isthmus during the first half-century following Cortés' conquest of Tenochtitlan. In 1580, when the demographic nadir had been passed, Tehuantepec informants for the *Relación Geográfica* claimed that 20,000 heads of households had lived in the province 30 years before.[79] Although this oral account may have compressed several of the early epidemics into the most recent crisis, the overall scale of disaster seems correct. Local people attributed the *pestilencias* to a number of changes in their way of life since the coming of the Spaniards: an unhealthier diet, increased use of alcoholic beverages, poorer work habits, and the congregation of Indians into nucleated settlements.[80] The significance of this last cause is underscored by population figures for the *cabecera*, where much of the imposed population concentration probably occurred. As might be expected, a large, densely populated center such as Tehuantepec was more severely affected by disease outbreaks that swept quickly through its crowded streets and extended family households than smaller communities.[81] In 1550, Tehuantepec and its *barrios* held over 70 percent of the region's population.[82] By 1580, the demographic balance had shifted to the rural communities, where 62.5 percent of the province lived.[83] While Tehuantepec remained the largest center in the region, with 1200 *vecinos*, it had lost two-thirds of its earlier population. By contrast, rural communities may even have experienced some population gains. The Spanish *alcalde mayor* reported 2000 *vecinos* in the countryside, an increase from the 1554 tributary equivalents recorded by San Miguel. Although the latter figure was probably an estimate, real differences in the demographic fortunes of town and country ought to be anticipated. Less crowded living conditions might have inhibited the spread of disease in rural communities, and may also have met an influx of migrants from Tehuantepec seeking to escape the ravaging pestilence.

Relación Geográfica informants complained of drunkenness, idleness, and vagabondage among the Tehuantepec natives following their conquest.[84] Such complaints were common in colonial New Spain, where the dissolution of ancient moral codes under Catholicism and the collapse of established social networks under uncontrollable population losses were widespread. Although, as Taylor[85] rightly warns, Spanish disapproval of these forms of Indian behavior does not by itself measure fragmentation of the colonial native community, other documented examples of individual rebellion and misconduct point directly to a profound dislocation of Zapotec society. Our evidence comes from two separate historical incidents, which I hope to demonstrate, and reflect not just uniquely dramatic events but the generalized impact of Spanish colonial institutions on the sociopolitical structure of a depressed Tehuantepec population.

Spanish Rule and the Demise of Native Government

In Tehuantepec, as in other native regions of Mesoamerica, the staggering population losses of the early decades of European contact brought into sharp relief the ambivalent relationship between colonial authority and native political institutions, despite their early accommodation to one another. In justifying the imposition of Spanish rule, the Crown adopted much the same sense of moral purpose that it held in the reconquest of Spanish territory from the Moors. It sought to establish Christian society and secure government in place of heathen rule, a formidable task for which the cooperation of a Christianized local leadership was considered essential.[86] Economic and political considerations, however, underlay and often undermined these ideals. As the conquered Indian population diminished in repeated waves of epidemic disease, the Crown kept jealous watch on its revenues and power, while *encomenderos* and newly arrived colonists competed for Indian labor and land. An image of a New World Christian utopia grew more distant as the sixteenth century progressed.

Caciques found themselves in an ambiguous position as brokers between their communities and Spanish authority. Like the Zapotec *coqui*, native rulers throughout Mesoamerica traditionally embodied the moral and political leadership of society. Under colonialism, the *cacique's* right to rule by inheritance was acknowledged by the Crown, which safeguarded legitimate succession for his heirs and granted him special privileges in accordance with his status as native ruler. At the same time, however, the Crown demanded that he exercise his right according to Spanish standards of moral behavior and political institutions. In order to rule, *caciques* were required to be perfect exemplars of Christianity and mete severe punishment for idolatrous practices.[87] The domain over which a native ruler held authority was reduced from the vast network of tributary dependents constructed by pre-Conquest imperial states to the local sphere of an individual head town and its subject hamlets. Even within the *cabecera* the colonial *cacique's* early authority as *gobernador* in the newly imposed political hierarchy gradually eroded as the Crown restricted his power to collect tribute and eventually succeeded in transferring the patrimonial office to that of an elected position on the Spanish-model *cabildo*.[88]

A dramatic illustration of this process is the case of don Juan Cortés, hereditary ruler of Tehuantepec who, despite his initial accommodation to colonial rule, found his patrimonial rights and personal privileges increasingly constrained. In the 1550s, Crown interference in local affairs peaked as the renewed initiative by Viceroy Luís de Velasco to remove Tehuantepec from the Marquesado spurred a series of official *visitas* to the province and a rash of viceregal edicts, which in part served to circumscribe the *cacique's* powers. While don Juan was confirmed in his traditional role as *cacique* and *gobernador* of all villages in the Marquesado, new limits were set on the amount of tribute he could collect.[89] Unpaid labor services in his household and on his estates were forbidden.[90] The population base of tributary subjects from which a native ruler's power and prestige traditionally derived shrank even further in the ensuing decade, a loss which exacerbated the erosion of *cacique* privileges mandated by the colonial government.

Don Juan's reduced circumstances might be seen as a measure of early colonial native society's fragility. By the early 1560s, individual efforts to accommodate traditional cultural values and social institutions to the imposed colonial forms were stretched to the point of collapse. Tehuantepec Indians accelerated the performance of surreptitious ritual sacrifices dedicted to familiar religious forces, and don Juan, assuming his pre-Conquest role of priestly leader, became a central figure in these outlawed activities. Eventually the nightly arrival of Indians from surrounding communities laden with rich offerings and animals for blood sacrifice at the royal palace aroused the suspicions of a local Spaniard, whose report to the Dominican friars led to don Juan's capture *in flagrante delicto*, as he performed pagan services with the assistance of six high priests from Mitla, the ancient Zapotec religious capital. Burgoa recounted with some sympathy don Juan's defense of his actions:

> ...and he was persuaded that, giving the tribute and the silver and gold that he was asked of them in compliance with their subjugation, they would be left to live according to their own law. And the truth of the matter was that some Spaniards gave occasion to believe that to be the case, because the pattern was to speak much [to the Indians] of gold and nothing of God...so that in many places the Indians think that the God of the Spaniards is gold...[91]

In 1563 the Bishop of Antequera, Bernardo de Albuquerque, summoned two of the Dominican order's most respected prelates, Juan de Mata and Juan de Córdova, compiler of the Zapotec dictionaries, to serve in the inquisitional court that would judge don Juan's heresy. The *cacique*, however, refused to be tried by a religious tribunal and demanded that his case be heard before the king's own representatives, the Viceroy and *Audiencia*. The protracted proceedings in Mexico City finally ended with don Juan confessing his guilt and forfeiting his political office and customary rents and tribute as punishment for idolatry. He died on the journey back to Tehuantepec.[92]

Don Juan's heretical conduct served as a convenient pretext for the *audiencia* to sever any remaining links between colonial Indian government in the Tehuantepec province and the pre-Conquest political state. The office of *gobernador* on the Spanish-style *cabildo* was separated from the hereditary *cacicazgo* in 1563, with the election of Pedro Pimentel to replace the dishonored *cacique*.[93] Don Juan' heirs retained the honorific title of *cacique* and income derived from rents on their patrimonial estates, but no longer reserved claim to an active political role. The democratically elected *cabildo* offices were a poor substitute for effective political leadership under the native *cacique*, for they heralded the dissipation of any remaining province-wide political authority and failed to provide a base within communities from which individuals might consolidate their leadership. Isthmian towns that held only *sujeto* status during don Juan's reign elected their own *gobernador, alcaldes* and *regidores* in the decades following his death and increasingly pursued independent paths for the remainder of the colonial period.[94] But even within populous towns such as Tehuantepec, these offices seem to have been a poorly developed vehicle for political leadership, as the infrequent reappearance of names of native officeholders among the scattered documents pertaining to Indian affairs suggests. Short one to two year terms inhibited the use of office for cementing personal power, although an individual with prestige and influence acquired in other endeavors might be elected or reelected on that basis. Already stressed in the mid-sixteenth century by the loss of commoner tribute obligations recently transferred to the Crown, the native nobility would have found small recompense in these salaried *cabildo* positions. Increasingly, the advantages of officeholding rested not in the authority assigned such positions within the native community, but in what pragmatic alliances they might provide with a growing Spanish population in the southern isthmus.

Despite persistent efforts by the *audiencia* to curb the most blatant examples of Spanish cooption, such as the election of non-Indians to office, opportunities for the coercion of native officeholders were many and probably frequently exercised by powerful local Spaniards. Pressures on the Indian community intensified as the Isthmus became a new focus of colonial economic exploitation during the late sixteenth-century ranching boom. By the mid-1600s, when the Crown issued no further *estancia* grants to private individuals, documented Spanish landholding totalled an area greater than 1300 square miles.[95] Tehuantepec had been transformed from an Indian *cabecera* to a Spanish *villa*, briefly renamed Guadalcazar. From 25 resident *vecinos* recorded in 1580,[96] the Spanish population had swollen to 500 households by 1629, when fray Bernabé Cobo passed through the province en route to Mexico from Peru.[97]

Economic and social pressures felt by the native population are documented in repeated complaints against negligent ranchers who allowed their untended cattle to trample Indian *milpas* or in opposition to greedy Spanish officials who too frequently visited native communities as a pretext for exacting fines and extra taxes.[98] One dramatic incident of this period underscores the extent of Indian exploitation and the weakness of native political forces. Begun as a spontaneous protest against the cruelty and avarice of one colonial administrator, the Tehuantepec rebellion of 1660 brought to the surface tensions that permeated native society during the seventeenth century.

Juan de Avellán, *alcalde mayor* of the province at this time, utilized his official position to amass great wealth through profitable *repartimientos* of Indian labor and commerce. According to native testimony, Avellan first squeezed 20,000 pesos from the Indians for the sale of unwanted merchandise, then instituted an impossible monthly production quota of 1500 lengths of cloth. Failure to comply or to produce goods of acceptable quality resulted in the flogging and imprisonment of *principales* and commoners alike. After an *alcalde* from La Mixtequilla was whipped and the *cacique* of Tequisistlán died following a severe flogging, public anger could no longer be contained by such passive forms of protest as the refusal to plant crops that had previously met Avellán's exploitation. On March 22, 1660, crowds of men and women—perhaps 6000 in all—gathered in the streets of Tehuantepec in a shouting and rock-throwing melee that ended with the death of Avellán and two others, while the terrified Spanish population and standing Indian *cabildo* took refuge in the Catholic church. Although the outgoing viceroy, the Duke of Albuquerque, and his appointed investigator, fray Alonso de Cuevas Dávalos, were sympathetic to the Indians' suffering and apparent contrition, Albuquerque's successor, the Marqués Conde de Baños, sided with the Spanish *vecinos* of Tehuantepec who demanded retribution. Lest "*haremos Tehuantepec*" continue to be heard as a rallying cry for Indian mutiny throughout Oaxaca, the new viceroy swiftly dispatched Juan Francisco de Montemayor in a surprise round-up of the rebellion's participants. Fifty-three men and women received sentences of death on the gallows, loss of a hand or ear, perpetual exile, or forced labor in the mines. The remainder of the population received a general pardon from Conde de Baños on July 4, 1661.[99]

My interpretation of the events of 1660 is that the uprising was a spontaneous general reaction to intolerable political and economic oppresson, rather than a well-coordinated Indian revolution. Efforts by a handful of native leaders to form a replacement government following the death of Avellán appear to be no more than an *ad hoc* attempt to reinstate order in the aftermath of chaos, provide a conduit for negotiation with the *audiencia*, and forestall Spanish fears of Indian anarchy. The extent to which indigenous political forms had been abandoned is reflected in the election of a complete Spanish-style *cabildo* to replace the loyalist government that allied itself with Avellán. A respected elder of the community, Marcos de Figueroa, was elected *gobernador*; this is the only individual about whose life and social position we have any information. A 1598 *estancia* petition mentions Figueroa as a *principal* of Tehuantepec who owned a mule ranch near Tepehuazontlan.[100] Quite old by the time of the 1660 rebellion, his figurehead role in the rebel *cabildo* was acknowledged even by Montemayor's judges, who sentenced Figueroa to exile rather than death, the judgement passed on other rebel officials. With the briefly united Indian opposition destroyed, hopes for the resurgence of effective native leadership dissipated as well, and the pro-Avellán *cabildo* was reinstated in office.

Tehuantepec and Models of Colonial Indian Society

In many respects the physical survival of the majority of Isthmian communities into the seventeenth century in itself seems a remarkable instance of the Mesoamerican Indian's tenacious grasp on his ancestral homeland in the face of an unrelenting attack by colonial officials and entrepreneurs. A combination of historical factors operative during what Gibson[101] has referred to as the "positive phase" of Spanish colonialism doubtlessly aided the native population transition to an imposed socioeconomic system and enabled it for the most part to retain its agricultural subsistence base. Aside from the generally supportive role played by the Crown as an early advocate of Indian rights throughout New Spain, the Tehuantepec region benefitted from two major protective factors in the first decades of Spanish rule: 1) the Zapotec ruler's quick embrace of Spanish authority, a fact that spared the region much bloodshed and placed it among a privileged group of native provinces, and 2) the Marqués del Valle's monopolistic hold on the southern Isthmus, which insulated its inhabitants from an early onslaught of competing Spaniards looking for wealth in Indian land and labor.

As Taylor[102] has pointed out, regional examples such as Tehuantepec are common in southern Mesoamerica, where Indian communities have remained agriculturally self-sufficient repositories of native languages and customs. According to Taylor, Indian communities in the south survived while their northern counterparts were drawn irrevocably into *mestizo* society, in part because of historical circumstances and in part because of the different structural basis of southern states. Among the latter, pre-Hispanic political hostilities isolated towns into autonomous units rather than drawing them into strong regional networks based upon Aztec models of military conquest. The colonial survival of these units as closed corporate communities is considered to be primarily a function of the pre-existing defensive posture toward the outside world.

In my view, Taylor's characterization of southern Indian society underestimates the complexity of pre-Columbian polities and the degree to which native communities were internally reorganized in places like Tehuantepec. As evidenced by ethnohistorical data summarized in this paper, the Zapotec state centered at Tehuantepec was a conquest, tribute-based entity, whose social and political organization reflected a hierarchy of inherited privileges and responsibilities. It differed from the Aztec state more in size of population than in kind of social interaction, more in extent of military success than in intent to subjugate other communities. Despite an early period of mutual accommodation, the continued existence of this, like other indigenous states in Mesoamerica, was ultimately at odds with the aims of Spanish conquest and colonization. Indian population losses, cultural dislocation, and political subordination combined to effect the structural transformation of native society in the southern Isthmus. Individual communities certainly did survive, but they did so based upon different organizational principles.

An examination of the transition period from an Isthmian perspective underscores some general features of the adaptation of Indian communities made to colonialism. Most dramatic among these was the loss of native political institutions extending beyond the independent town and its subject villages, a loss that exercised its greatest toll among the imperial states of central Mexico, but one that was also felt in the periphery of New Spain. Interested in administrative efficiency, the Crown had no use for the convoluted networks of tributary relationshps created by pre-Hispanic warfare nor for the native bureaucracy that oversaw long-distance tribute collection. Consequently, it preserved only the most localized aspects of intercommunity dependencies. Even in Tehuantepec, where Cortés' reliance on the Zapotec ruler for the delivery of Indian labor and goods promoted regional integration during the early decades of colonialism, political decentralization was an established trend by the early seventeenth century.

Secondly, although Indian communities retained some degree of authority over their internal affairs, they were obliged to do so through unfamiliar governmental and judicial institutions such as the *cabildo* and colonial *audiencia*. While more democratic in form than the indigenous system of inherited position, the *cabildo* was not bound to native cultural values and standards of leadership like its pre-Columbian counterpart. Its dependency on colonial government for legitimacy and on individual Spaniards for various perquisites of office created a situation in which real community interests might easily be shortchanged by these new cultural brokers. To protect itself against the actions of Spaniards or other Indian groups, the community was dependent upon formal litigation through the cumbersome colonial appeal system. Although Indians throughout New Spain seem to have mastered the intricacies of Spanish legalism at a surprisingly early date, the successful outcome of any particular suit rested not only on the legal merits of the case but also on the *audiencia's* limited ability to enforce its own decisions.

Within the native community the fabric of social interaction was greatly altered by demographic loss and socioeconomic change, the effects of which are manifest at many social levels. In Mesoamerica, where daily life was structured by a web of kinship based rights and responsibilities, the loss of family members to fatal disease in epidemic after epidemic have been particularly traumatic. As Gibson[103] notes, the staggering population losses of the sixteenth century undoubtedly triggered the widespread adoption of the Spanish *compadrazgo* system of fictive kinship as a means of protecting potential orphans. The economic survival of the Indian nobility was threatened by an ever dwindling pool of commoners who could support them with tribute or rents. Like the Spanish *encomenderos* of the late sixteenth century, those *principales* and *caciques* who desired to maintain the wealth and prestige formerly linked to their inherited titles had to do so by finding new sources of income less dependent upon Indian labor; in the Tehuantepec region the most enterprising did so by entering the colonial ranching economy. The retention of such class distinctions as *caciques, principales*, and *macehualtin* reflects the continuation of a social hierarchy within Indian communities, but in a greatly abridged form. While the loss of serf and slave classes may not be one to bemoan, the richness and complexity of native culture suffered from the disappearance of many specialized occupations. Colonial New Spain had decreasing use for picture-book painters, goldsmiths, lapidaries, feather-workers, long-distance traders in native luxuries, or for the great majority of non-utilitarian artisans and their skills. Lost forever were esoteric forms of knowledge articulated by outlawed native priests and promoted in special schools attended by the pre-Columbian nobility. The substance of Zapotec high culture, like that of other Mesoamerican states, was destroyed either by design or by subversion of its structural base.

What persisted were community-based folk cultures. Eric Wolf[104] originally characterized this social form as the "closed corporate community" and argued that its predominance in rural areas of Mesoamerica today reflects not the widespread survival of aboriginal community types, but a common adaptation by depressed Indian populations to the political and economic conditions of Spanish colonialism. In his view, hostility toward outsiders—Indian and Spaniard alike—and fierce defense of community lands are behavioral forms representing native response to continued Spanish incursions on a hard-pressed subsistence base; they are not surviving attributes of pre-Hispanic city-state rivalries. Some aspects of Wolf's thesis need qualification. Not all colonial Indian societies were as "closed" to the movement of individuals among communities as his definition assumes,[105] and we might question the universal importance of *congregación* in creating local land pressure. Nonetheless, it is a persuasive general model for the formation of peasant communities in New Spain under the complex demographic, economic, and political circumstances of colonialism.

For such societies, the retention of native languages and customs probably reflects both the inherent resiliency of these forms to change and their manipulation by the population as symbols of ethnic identity and community membership. They are aspects of behavioral norms in closed peasant societies that promote group survival and individual well-being through limited reciprocity and wealth-leveling mechanisms, behavior that serves to provide the community's members with a kind of minimal subsistence insurance.[106] A number of social historians have drawn attention to the basic incompatibility of these goals and associated norms with the values and economic pressures they regard as sparking the fires of peasant revolt.[107]

Whatever the merits of this theory as a world-wide model of peasant revolt may be,[108] it highlights inherent tensions in the relationship between colonial Indian communities and the economic institutions of New Spain. Nascent capitalism's direct impact was limited in places far from the center of creole entrepreneurial activity such as Tehuantepec.[109] Yet even where Indians were not drawn into *hacienda* or *obraje* labor, the exaction of cash values in tribute and *repartimiento* threatened the peasant community's standard of living. In prehistoric times, tribute or rent was assessed locally by designating particular lands to be cultivated on behalf of the *caciques* and *principales*, a system in which both commoners and the nobility shared the risks of a poor harvest. But the payment of fixed amounts of tribute and the forced purchase of unwanted merchandise compelled Indian households to convert agricultural produce to cash, even when there was little that might be considered surplus production. When those demands were execssively onerous, as they were during Juan de Avellán's tenure in the southern Isthmus, conditions were ripe for peasant revolt.

NOTES

[1]E.g., Farriss 1978; Gibson 1952, 1964; Osborn 1973; Spores 1967

[2]Taylor 1972.

[3]Chevalier 1952.

[4]Taylor 1974.

[5]Pickett 1960; Diebold 1969; Wonderly 1947.

[6]Zeitlin 1982.

[7]Thomas 1974.

[8]The date recited in Zapotec historical accounts (Burgoa 1934) is matched by lexicostatistical data indicating a separation of Isthmus and Valley Zapotec dialects approximately 600 years ago (Fernández, Swadesh, and Weitlaner 1960).

[9]Barlow 1945:23, 25.

[10]Ixtlilxochitl 1952, I:289.

[11]Spores 1967, 1976.

[12]Carrasco 1971; Katz 1966.

[13]Spores 1965; Whitecotton 1977.

[14]Colonial Zapotec terminology cited in this paper is drawn from J. Córdova (1942).

[15]Carrasco 1971; Monzón 1949.

[16]J. Córdova 1942.

[17]PNE 1:312.

[18]Whitecotton 1977:149.

[19]Caso 1928b; PNE 4.

[20]PNE 4:17.

[21]Katz 1966:43.

[22]Carrasco 1971:355f.

[23]Spores 1976:210-13.

[24]Whitecotton 1977:151.

[25]AGN-M 6-418.

[26]J. Córdova 1942:352r.

[27]Cf. Spores 1976:212.

[28]J. Córdova 1942:292r.

[29]Burgoa 1934:342.

[30]PNE 4:127f.

[31]Whitecotton 1977:145.

[32]Seler 1908.

[33]Seler 1908:189.

[34]Burgoa 1934:343.

[35]Durán 1951:438.

[36]Gibson 1971:390.

[37]Whitecotton 1977; PNE 4.

[38]Seler 1908:figs. 28a and b; Oviedo 1905b.

[39]J. Córdova 1942:292.

[40]Flannery and Marcus 1976; Marcus 1978.

[41]Burgoa 1934:351, 355.

[42]Seler 1908:fig. 28.

[43]Cf. *dxiiña*, Pickett 1965:79.

[44]Caso 1928b:169.

[45]AGN-M 4-142; 4-143; AGN-I 3-408; 6-2-223.

[46]PNE 4.

[47]Caso 1928b:168.

[48]Zeitlin 1978:253f.

[49]Burgoa 1934:378.

[50]Durán 1957:373.

[51]Whitecotton 1977:143.

[52]Carrasco 1976.

[53]AGN-M 8-8v; PNE 1:312.

[54]Carrasco 1971:353.

[55]J. Córdova 1942:246r.

[56]See Marcus 1978.

[57]Caso 1928b:169f.

[58]PNE 4:199.

[59]Whitecotton 1977:308f.

[60]Katz 1966:128.

[61]J. Córdova 1942.

[62]Gómara 1966; Ixtlilxochitl 1952; Burgoa 1934.

[63]Moorehead 1949; Berthe 1958; ENE 11; *El Libro de las tasaciones* 1952:373f.

[64]ENE 9:48.

[65]PNE 1.

[66]*El Libro de las tasaciones* 1952:374.

[67]Burgoa 1934:378.

[68]Seler 1908.

[69]*El Libro de las tasaciones* 1952:373f.

[70]*El Libro de las tasaciones* 1952:374f.

[71]Berthe 1958:126.

[72]Crosby 1967:325.

[73]MacLeod 1973:fig. 8.

[74]Gibson 1964:136ff.

[75]Borah and Cook 1960:102.

[76]ENE 9:6.

[77]Borah and Cook 1960:64.

[78]García Pimentel 1904:72.

[79]Caso 1928b:166.

[80]Caso 1928b:171f.

[81]According to San Miguel's census figures, Tehuantepec residences housed an average of 14.5 people, including 6 children under the age of 15, compared with a smaller average household size of 6, including 2 children among its subject towns (PNE 1:312f).

[82]PNE 1:312f.

[83]Caso 1928b:165.

[84]Caso 1928b:172.

[85]Taylor 1979:45.

[86]Gibson 1960:175.

[87]Gibson 1960:173f.

[88]Gibson 1964:167.

[89]AGN-M 4-138; 4-142.

[90]AGN-M 4-143.

[91]Burgoa 1934:356.

[92]Burgoa 1934:358.

[93]AGN-M 7-108v.

[94]AGN-I 1-153, 56; 27-317; AGN-M 8-100v.

[95]Zeitlin 1982.

[96]Caso 1928b.

[97]Cobo 1944:197.

[98]AGN-M 6-419v; 4-27; 40-86v; AGN-I 13-116.

[99]García 1907.

[100]AGN-M 21-176v.

[101]Gibson 1960.

[102]Taylor 1974.

[103]Gibson 1964:152.

[104]Wolf 1957.

[105]Farriss 1978:203.

[106]Scott 1976:13ff.

[107]Hobsbawm 1959; Moore 1966; Wolf 1969b.

[108]See Popkin (1979) for a different view of peasant society under stress.

[105]As part of a test of the "incursion" hypothesis' validity in explaining a nineteenth-century Isthmian rebellion, Tutino (1977) briefly considered the 1660 Tehuantepec revolt as well. My analysis of the economic and political context of this event differs from his.

CONFLICT AND BALANCE IN DISTRICT POLITICS; TECALI AND THE SIERRA NORTE DE PUEBLA IN THE EIGHTEENTH CENTURY

William Taylor

In the last thirty years historical studies have gradually moved away from the black and white legends of Spanish motives as a major issue that defined Latin America between Conquest and Independence and a view of the State and the Church as monolithic and preeminent. Those earlier approaches to colonial Latin America implicitly took Spanish monopolists of land, merchant capital, and high office to be the only real actors in the colonial process. *Encomenderos*, landlords, and royal agents loomed too large in such studies to convey much about the range of activities and relationships in colonial life. We had from them only the vaguest ideas about what most Indian subjects thought and did except in their formal dealings with Europeans; and even then we knew mainly the story of what Europeans did to Indians. Recent scholarship has, in particular, revised the older notion of great estates dominating rural life from beginning to end and the dualism of inward and outward-oriented segments of colonial society and economy–with colonial towns, cities, mining areas and commercial farms as outward oriented, and the rest of the rural areas where most people lived as inward-oriented, filled with helpless victims of the market system and colonial government.

There has been a delay in communicating this new work to a wide audience for it is still common in social science literature that draws on colonial history to find claims that great landlords were the only figures connecting inward-oriented, dependent peasant villages to the outside world as if the life of peasants were a simple dichotomy of a village and the "outside world" with all important contacts between the two controlled by a local *hacendado*.[1] The delay is partly because the implications of these recent studies of colonial land tenure have not yet led to the next step in research: close regional studies of the specific and changing connections between rural villages and the State and other powerful outsiders to whom the villagers were subordinate. This essay is a small entry into this subject of regional political history in the late colonial period. Political history here is less concerned with dynastic struggle and top-level events and policies than with the extension of a complex, sometimes contradictory, colonial bureaucracy into the Indian countryside and its interaction with local society and politics. My point of entry is the intermediaries who connected Indian villages and individual peasants to the larger society and economy in several parts of Puebla during the eighteenth century. I am particularly concerned with parish priests and royal magistrates at the district level (the *corregidores*, *subdelegados*, and their lieutenants), the officials who were in face-to-face contact with Indian villagers. Evidence for the place of priests and magistrates in the affairs of villages and districts consists of three long investigations into village defiance of *corregidores* and *subdelegados* and other political disputes in which parish priests had a central part. The three investigations document district politics in four places and times: Santiago Tecali in 1734-37, Zacatlán de las Manzanas in 1787, Tetela de Xonotla in 1793-98, and San Juan Quimixtlán in 1799.[2] As often happens, it is moments of crisis that leave a written residue of local behavior, relationships, and values. In tapping the record of these events, I am not mainly interested in the moments of crisis themselves. Rather, I have used them to reveal something of the nature of district-level politics and the activities of colonial officials in the local affairs of Indian communities.

The first section presents the cases separately while the second section describes three broad patterns in the records and offers some observations about district-level politics that distinguish what was specific to the time and place of the investigations from what may have been common to districts with Indian peasant majorities in Mesoamerica.

Tecali and the Sierra de Puebla

The four places represented in these investigations share a similar landscape and colonial social formation. Zacatlán, Tetela de Xonotla, and Quimixtlán are located in the Sierra de Puebla, a rugged, partly forested area some fifty miles north of the city of Puebla and about 125 miles from Mexico City. There are great variations in climate within each district.[3] Altitudes range from over 3,000 meters in the mountain valleys down to about 200 meters, producing hot, steamy weather in the low canyons and cold, dank conditions in the high country. But in nearly all places rainfall is abundant. Above temperate Zacatlán at 2,000 meters, mist and rain are almost constant, and the temperate lands are good for raising maize and beans and fruit trees. The dense pre-Hispanic population there followed the usual pattern of decline from epidemic diseases in the sixteenth and early seventeenth centuries, but Indians still outnumbered non-Indians by about five to one in the 1740s. The Indians were village farmers, traders, and artisans scattered in dozens of communities in the temperate and high valleys. Most still spoke native languages and needed interpreters when they testified before colonial magistrates. The Spanish, *mestizo*, and *mulato* families clustered in the district seats, in the few modest *haciendas* and *ranchos* nearby, and in the silver mines of the Xonotla district after the 1660s. Zacatlán and Tetela each were seats of *corregimientos* from the sixteenth century, and Quimixtlán was within the *corregimiento* of San Juan de los Llanos. All three were first evangelized by Franciscans, but parish duties were assumed by secular priests before the mid-seventeenth century.

Tecali is closer to the city of Puebla (to the southeast less than twenty miles) but similar to the Sierra districts in its social makeup. Situated mostly in fairly flat terrain at about 2,200 meters, Tecali's climate is temperate but cold in the winter and drier than the Sierra de Puebla. Seasonal rains are more erratic, and there is little surface water except for the Atoyac River at the bottom of a deep canyon. Aside from marble quarries, local production was mainly in maize farming, some ranching, and aviculture, and local people were drawn more to the market of Tepeaca than to Puebla. Tecali was mainly an Indian district in the mid-eighteenth century, with sixteen pueblos and about 1,500 tributaries. Only forty non-Indian families were reported in this district in 1743, mainly in the town of Tecali and on the five *haciendas* and twenty *ranchos* of the district. Franciscans had been the local priests there for a century—from 1540-1641. At the end of the seventeenth century, Vetancurt spoke of the Indians of Tecali as exceptionally "devoted to the Divine cult and to the service of the priests."[4] Early in the eighteenth century three subject villages had become the seats of separate parishes with their own resident secular priests. The *corregimiento* was founded later in Tecali than in the Sierra de Puebla, in 1664. A private *encomienda* continued after 1696 and part of the tribute was still collected privately in 1803.

In the mid-1730s resistance by three *sujetos* of Santiago Tecali to payment of tribute, *repartimiento de mercancía* debts, and land rents to the *cacique* of Tecali, and their opposition to the slaughter of their young cows by the *corregidor* led to a flurry of lawsuits against him and violent confrontations with the Indian officials of Tecali.[5] These episodes of confrontations and costly litigation culminated in a long royal investigation to determine the cause, punish those responsible, and restore order. The testimony of witnesses and other evidence assembled in this investigation uncovered a small host of rivalries and countervailing outside pressures on the Indian villages that complicated colonial government in this district.

At the center of this trouble was the subject village of Santa María Toxtepec. For years Toxtepec, an independent parish, had petitioned for political separation from Tecali. Finally, in 1734, a verdict came down from the *audiencia* in Mexico City: Toxtepec would not be made the seat for another *corregimiento*. At about the same time, the priest of Toxtepec, Matías González de la Cruz, posted on the church door a royal *cédula* of 1723 prohibiting *repartimientos de mercancías*, a lucrative monopoly of the *corregidor* on the sale of bulls, mules, horses, seed grains, brandy, wool, and chile in his district. Late in 1734, and again in 1773, the Indians of Toxtepec sought the priest's protection against the detailed list of abuses they claimed to suffer from the *corregidor*, Joseph Cárdenas, and Tecali's *cacique* and Indian *gobernador*, Cayetano de Tovar. Specifically, the Indians accused Cárdenas of overcharging tribute, forcing them to pay high prices for unwanted *repartimiento* goods (including starved and sick bulls), extracting one or two pesos a week from each family as payment for the *repartimientos*, and slaughtering Indian cows in large numbers without license as additional payment for *repartimiento* debts. The Indians also complained of forced contributions to the headtown of Tecali and to the *cacique*, from whom they rented their farmlands. Father González de la Cruz informed his bishop (because of the tithe on newborn calves, the bishop had a direct interest in the slaughter of the Indians' cows), helped the village leaders draw up a formal complaint against the *corregidor*, and enlisted the services of an attorney in Mexico City (according to the *corregidor*, Toxtepec and its allied villages spent 20,000 pesos on these various lawsuits against Tecali!). Early in 1735, the people of Toxtepec refused to make any payments to the *corregidor* or the *cacique*, and ceased the customary services in Tecali. Sometimes two or three, sometimes as many as six of the other sixteen villages subject to Tecali joined Toxtepec in resisting payments and opposing the *corregidor* and *cacique*.

Since his main responsibilities and source of income were challenged by these acts, the *corregidor's* response was predictable and swift. With two to four hundred armed Indians from Tecali, he went out to force the disobedient villages into submission. The people of San Miguel resisted with rocks, sticks, and machetes, but were driven back by the *corregidor*'s gun-bearing guard. The troops from Tecali invaded the church and attacked those who had hidden there, killing four and wounding many others.[6] The community chest was broken open and the money seized; and cattle were taken and buildings were set on fire. On the night of April 4, similar sacrileges were committed by the Santa Isabel, San Lorenzo, and Santa María Toxtepec. Accompanied by the Lt. General of Tecali, the lieutenant entered the churches swearing to drink the priest's blood and kill the Indians of the parish, and proclaimed "Now you'll see, Father, whether there are men here." Most of the Indians fled, but one was killed, others were wounded and, as in San Miguel, local men were arrested for failing to meet their tribute payments. Indians of Toxtepec ran to Puebla to tell the bishop, who ordered the excommunication of the *corregidor* and his lieutenants, and conducted a secret investigation of the events in August 1735.

Officials on all sides had gone too far for a local deal to be struck; ten of the district pueblos were in violation of the *corregidor's* orders; and the Spaniards in the district feared a general Indian revolt. At this point, the *audiencia* stepped in with the support of the Viceroy-Archbishop of Mexico, arresting the *corregidor* and *cacique*, removing the priest of Toxtepec from his parish, and appointing an independent judge to investigate the whole affair. The Archibishop urged exemplary punishments for the leaders, whom he judged to be village *alcaldes*, *fiscales*, and scribes, and declared that, as instigators of rebellion, they had no right to the immunity of the church. Notaries and magistrates once again occupied center stage and even though there were further reprisals by Tecali Indians, resistance by some villages in late 1735 and 1736, and renewal of the old issues of taxes and the *repartimiento* by Cárdenas's successor and a new priest of Toxtepec, the way to a traditional solution that would diffuse anti-colonial feelings was clear. The priest was transferred and reprimanded for inciting the Indians to costly litigation and rebellion; the *corregidor* was found guilty of abuses in the *repartimiento* and involuntary labor but was exonerated from responsibility for the violence. Toxtepec and the other pueblos received no relief beyond the *repartimiento* payments, since their political ambitions were judged to have caused the confrontation.

Incidentally, and despite the apparent suborning of some witnesses, the detailed inquiry into the troubles in Tecali sheds light on the sources of tension between rural villages and district officials there and the important but largely undefined role of the parish priest in district politics in the eighteenth century. There may have been an ethnic side to the conflict (the Chocho-speaking villages of the district were all in the parish of Toxtepec), but politically-dependent communities such as Toxtepec, now with nearly the population of the *cabecera* and already semi-independent in ecclesiastical matters, were restive over the costs, inconvenience, and humiliation of subservience to another town. The Spaniards' equation of the municipal "*república*" with civilization, their willingness to receive petitions for founding new *municipios*, and their preference for a divide-and-rule colonial system gave hope to ambitious communities.[7]

The people of Toxtepec expressed their ambitions and frustrations when they decried various forced contributions to the officials of Tecali, including labor service at fiesta time and a 20 1/2 *reales* annual payment per tributary. This contribution was unusually high, but Indian witnesses from the *cabecera* and other *sujetos* agreed that it was a very old tax that had been paid without objection until recently. Even during this period of protest, most villages in the Tecali district raised no objection to the contribution. The refusal of Toxtepec and its parish villages to hold their community elections in Tecali, as was the custom, was another sign of hard feelings about political subordination. The old rites of service would no longer be completed without question. After 1734, Toxtepec balked at sending two live deer to Tecali for the fiesta de Santiago at which Tecali Indians dressed as Chichimecs and chased the deer, and refused to supply the usual food, towels and money for Easter week celebrations in the *cabecera*. The priest of Toxtepec had his own reasons for supporting the Indians in their petition for *cabecera* status. Like many rural priests, he was irritated by the self-serving demands of a remote *corregidor* and his officious lieutenants. But as a priest with his own parish set within a larger *corregimiento* to which his parishioners owed much of their time and money, he had another reason to favor political separation, especially since his annual stipend (which was only one-third that of the priest of Tecali) was paid to him by the *cacique* of Tecali out of the 20 1/1 *reales* contribution of his Indian tributaries.

Cacique Tovar's authority was quite unusual. He owned the farmlands worked by Toxtepec and other *sujetos*; he collected the customary contributions from all tributaries in the district that paid for the priests' stipends, Tecali's lawsuits, the publication of Papal Bulls, the fiestas of Tecali, and the annual office-taking ceremony in Tecali for village officials throughout the district. He collected the tribute and other village fees (such as payment for his permission to cultivate *magueyes* or hold dances); and villages in the *corregimiento* were expected to bring him chickens and flowers at Easter (just as they did for the priest) and to provide him with household servants. These responsibilities and privileges, derived from his inherited position, were enhanced by personal skills, longevity, and close association with the *corregidor*. Literate in Spanish and Nahuatl, he was assigned responsibility for keeping the records of public collections and expenditures. At the time of the unrest in 1734, he had been reelected *gobernador* of Tecali nine consecutive times with the *corregidor's* support, in violation of royal orders against consecutive reelection. To the Indian *sujetos* he was closely associated with the *corregidor* since he provided hundreds of armed Indians from the *cabecera* for the magistrate's sallies into the countryside and collaborated in the slaughter of the villagers' cows.

The priest of Toxtepec and the *corregidor* of Tecali held conflicting views of the priest's political duties and the *repartimiento de mercancías*. Father González de la Cruz saw himself in the heroic role of the protector and father of the Indians in temporal as well as spiritual matters, a role dating from the "Spiritual Conquest" of the sixteenth century. The villagers in his district looked to him for this kind of guidance and, as witnesses, spoke of him as their father and the only outsider who could be trusted to help them. Before the violence of 1734, villages within the parish of Toxtepec had written to him pleading for his protection against the burdens of the *repartimiento*; and to this priest, the *corregidor's repartimiento* was "the unhealthy cancer." He could see that the *corregidor's* demands for payment of one peso a week from every Indian family against the *repartimiento* advances forced them to beggar themselves at the magistrate's bidding. To keep up with the payments, the Indians often sold cheap the cattle they were forced to buy from the *corregidor* at inflated prices. By 1734, González de la Cruz was ready to act on appeals like this one from the Indians of Santa Clara:

> We work all year yet we can hardly clothe ourselves; often if we eat dinner, there is no supper and we are even robbed of sleep worrying about how we can find so much money.... Together, all of your children in this pueblo plead with you, kneeling at your feet, to look upon us with eyes of mercy; we fervently hope that our curate and pastor will defend us from such cruelty and hardship.

Father González de la Cruz was correct in posting the royal law of 1723 against the *repartimientos*—the law specified that the parish priests were to tell their Indians of its provisions every six months—but, in the view of the *corregidor* and later of the *fiscal* of the *audiencia*, the priest had exceeded his authority by taking up the Indians' cause against the *corregidor* and aiding them in their lawsuits. Since Toxtepec had no interpreter other than Father González, the priest as defender of the Indians felt that he could not stop with the bureaucratic act of posting the law.

Corregidor Cárdenas naturally saw the issue in a different light. The *repartimiento* was his main source of income. The priests' temporal role should be limited to helping the Indians understand their place in colonial society and teaching them to obey; or, as he put it, "good education, submission, and instruction of the Indians." Cárdenas complained of the priest making the Indians of Toxtepec completely dependent on him, and of the Indians showing favoritism to Father González. González seems to have been the effective judge in his parish, operating a jail and inflicting whippings and time in the stocks at his own discretion. All of these activities were detrimental to royal justice and the King's jurisdiction, said Cárdenas, who saw them as the source of Indian disrespect to him during the previous two years. Higher colonial authorities later agreed, condemning González's "influence and passion" in the temporal affairs of the Tecali district.

Although there are only hints of the connections in these records, this conflict between priest and *corregidor* was more than strictly local. Non-Indians in the regional center of Tepeaca were involved on both sides. Several merchants of Tepeaca who financed the *repartimiento* as *aviadores* were involved on the *corregidor's* side while rival merchants, two captains, and the priests of Tepeaca and Cholula who were personal friends of González encouraged the petitions and complaints against Cárdenas.

The *repartimiento de mercancías* of the *corregidor* also was related to another *tumulto* and long investigation for Zacatlán de las Manzanas in the Sierra de Puebla in 1787. In this case, the *repartimiento* was one of a series of district-level problems brought on by the serious food shortages and epidemic of 1785-86, problems that might be smoothed over in times of plenty.[8]

Trouble began in August 1785 when frosts destroyed much of the maize crop in the district. Grain was especially expensive and in short supply in the *cabecera* of Zacatlán with its 14,000 residents, and in Chinauapan. To insure against shortage the following year, the *corregidor*, Captain Manuel Esteban Sánchez Tagle, ordered that an extra crop be planted in early 1786 on untilled lands of *ranchos* and Indian villages, and that the lands be worked with communal labor. The Bishop of Puebla donated 90 percent of the money needed to provide five hundred *fanegas* of seed maize,[9] and Sánchez Tagle depended upon the resident priests in the eleven parishes of the district to oversee the planting, prevent black marketeering, and deliver the crop to Zacatlán. Meanwhile, villages were ordered to sell some of the maize they had saved from 1785; but according to the *corregidor*, the priests and villages held back nearly all of the maize that was stored in the *cofradía* granaries. Late in June the special crop of nearly 50,000 *fanegas* was harvested in the mountain villages and some 1,500 Indians were transporting their maize to the *alhóndigas* (public granaries) of Zacatlán and Chinauapan for sale at a fixed price of 4 1/2 pesos per *fanega*. Compliance was compelled under threat of arrest or physical punishment from the lieutenants who patrolled the districts with squads of twenty-five armed militiamen. Sánchez Tagle claimed that he had ordered this military supervision because the Indians would not sell enough of their grain to the needy towns unless coerced. Maize was to be distributed to all at a fixed price from the Zacatlán *alhóndiga* under Sánchez Tagle's control. The Indians wrote to their priests objecting to this forced sale of their entire crop to Zacatlán. The priests informed Sánchez Tagle, but these rumblings of what was to come went unheeded.

On July 5 at 9:00 a.m., a crowd of Indians, mainly women from other villages, went on the rampage in Zacatlán—releasing prisoners from jail, breaking the grain measures at the *alhóndiga*, harvesting the community maize plot of the *cabecera*, breaking open the granary and selling the maize there as they pleased. Sánchez Tagle hid for four hours in a wardrobe in the priest's residence and, on July 9, fled the district. Indian control over the maize market and granary lasted until the evening of July 6 when the women obeyed the soothing words of the local vicar. From Puebla, Sánchez Tagle wrote to the viceroy that, for fear of another *tumulto*, he would not return to Zacatlán without an escort of twenty-five militiamen. He claimed that the mountain Indians had risen up because they had planted too much maize in the special harvest and now were angry because Zacatlán no longer would buy it at a high price. The investigation, however, revealed that the Indians who had come to Zacatlán that morning were angry about being forced to sell their entire crop to Sánchez Tagle without being able to buy back enough for their own needs. Sánchez Tagle admitted under oath that just before the violent protest, little grain was available for sale to the Indians and the price had risen to 10-12 pesos; this in spite of the fact that the granary was full and the price paid to the Indians for their maize had been 3 1/2—5 pesos. Sánchez Tagle denied the rumor that he was removing maize from the granary and selling it at night at 12 pesos a *fanega*. His reply then went on to claim that the high prices were the result of priests in remote parishes hoarding the grain to continue the shortages and then selling at high prices outside the *alhóndiga*. He claimed that he was only trying to protect the *cabecera*, to insure an adequate supply of maize throughout the district, and to provide a surplus for shipment to needy districts elsewhere in central Mexico. The viceroy concluded that the Indian women revolted because the *alhóndiga* would only sell them one-third of the maize they needed and at an inflated price. In spite of the serious allegations by the priests and the *corregidor*, Sánchez Tagle remained in office after 1736, as did the priests in the eleven *doctrinas*. An uneasy peace had been restored without resorting to Sánchez Tagle's recommendation that the troops be sent in, two or three leaders of the violence be sentenced to service in the fortifications of San Juan de Ulúa, and another ten or twelve be whipped for good measure.

The investigation into the *tumulto* and the charges against Sánchez Tagle exposed a structure of tension between parish priests in outlying areas and the *corregidor*. As early as March 1785, Sánchez Tagle had been warned by the *fiscal* of the *audiencia* to preserve harmony in his relationship with the curates. Both the priests and the *corregidor* had attempted to influence the elections of officials in the remote Indian villages.[10]

As in the Tecali case, Indian villagers looked to their parish priests for help in resisting what they thought were illegal innovations and abuses by the *corregidor* and his lieutenants, and in launching formal written complaints against them. The *corregidor* seemed to be unconcerned about the Indians' suffering from the famine and epidemic and showed little interest in their plea for temporary relief from the tribute tax. The pressing issue was Sánchez Tagle's interference with the usual way of selling maize: for the special crop of 1786 the Indians had to sell the entire harvest to the *alhóndiga*; they could not keep what they wanted and sell where and when they chose, as they were accustomed to do. This crisis and the investigation that followed a formal complaint brought other abuses to light. The forced sale of expensive mules by the *corregidor* to the villagers appeared prominently in the testimony of Indians witnesses, although without the detailed complaints of the Tecali Indians about inferior cattle or the various other monopoly goods distributed by the *corregidor* of Tecali. The rural priests seem to have primed the Indians for this issue, publicizing the royal law against *repartimientos* issued in 1784 and urging villagers not to accept the mules delivered by the *corregidor*. In one case, the lieutenant of Tecoyuca reported hearing the priest instruct his Indians to pay their legal debts on time, to pay what they owed to the *cofradías*, to pay their clerical fees, and to support their families, but under no circumstances to accept the *repartimiento* mules because the *corregidor* was an outrageous usurer. Sánchez Tagle retaliated by telling the Indians they did not have to obey the priests in any but spiritual matters. In Tlapacoya, the *corregidor* threatened fifty lashes and imprisonment in Mexico City to Indians who joined the local priest in his lawsuit against the *repartimiento de mulas y toros*. As a result, said the priest, only about one-third of his parishioners would attend mass any longer or confess durng Holy Week. Sánchez Tagle claimed that he received no salary and none of the usual fees for his judicial services from village subjects. The *repartimiento*, he said, was his only source of income and he was loath to give it up. And, he added, the profits from the *repartimiento* were not nearly as great as his opponents claimed (it was rumored that the *repartimiento* yielded a 50 percent profit). By his account, sales of *repartimiento* livestock produced 30,000 pesos a year but his expenses were 25,940 pesos plus 900 pesos *alcabala* tax on the sale, leaving a net profit of 3,160 pesos, or just over 10 percent. Besides, argued Sánchez Tagle, he was providing an important service in making these animals from distant places available to his district.

The *repartimiento de mercancías* was unusually important in this district because it was connected to the lucrative market in chicken eggs. Mules and horses were advanced to Indians who, in turn, were obliged to pay off their debts in eggs which the *corregidor* shipped to Mexico City. If Indian producers did not accept the *repartimiento* animals, they were sometimes forced to sell their eggs to the *corregidor* on credit. Sánchez Tagle was careful not to divulge his profits from the egg sales. He justified this sweet purchase arrangement on the grounds that he was, again, performing a vital service to the capital; that the practice was as old as the *corregimiento* of Zacatlán; and that priests and other non-Indians were busy wholesaling eggs, too, through old women they commissioned to buy for them. The *corregidor's* lieutenants were also accused of forcing Indians to sell them their eggs and exacting the sale of other local products, including nuts, at low prices. These forced sales were especially irritating to the Indians of this district because they had long been traders of eggs, nuts, *chile totonaco*, maize, fruits, and lard to distant markets.

The *corregidor*, in turn, supplied witnesses to support his charges that at least three of the eleven parish priests in his district were hoarding grain for profit, telling their Indian parishioners not to pay the *repartimientos* or obey the lieutenants, making insulting remarks in public about the *corregidor*, and being the evil geniuses behind the Indians' formal complaints, lawsuits, and disobedience to him. The administrators of the *alcabala* and tobacco monopoly had joined the priests against him, he said, because of his vigorous campaign against Indian drunkenness. Sánchez Tagle's major complaint against the priests, dating back to 1784 and 1785, centered on their interference in village politics, and it is in the investigation of these charges that the record provides information about the influence of priests and district officials in local elections.

The records of three village elections that went wrong in 1786 were included by Sánchez Tagle in his defense of 1787. In the case of San Baltasar in the *doctrina* of Tepezintla, a group of Indian men wrote to the *corregidor* in February and March asking that the *gobernador*, Francisco Antonio, be removed because he had been re-elected in consecutive years, was not a native of their town, and was cruel, drunk, and despotic. The Indian petitioners wanted new elections to be held in Zacatlán, rather than in Tepezintla where the curate resided, because of what they claimed was the priest's interference in previous elections. It was customary in this pueblo for the priest to propose three candidates for election to *gobernador*. But now the previous *gobernador* had simply been "elected" by the curate without a vote, and the Indian petitioners wanted a younger man in office. To investigate this dispute, Sánchez Tagle sent the Indian *gobernador* of Zacatlán who heard witnesses on both sides disagree about the charges against Francisco Antonio. The *corregidor's* representative ordered new elections that the parish priest, Joseph Mariano de Ortega, refused to attend. Three candidates were named, and the elections produced a new *gobernador*, Antonio Bernabé. Technically, the results were invalid since Father Ortega declined to certify them. Sánchez Tagle's intervention in San Baltasar may have been prompted by Father Ortega's suit against the *corregidor* in 1785 for his egg monopoly and his management of the maize shortage. The disputed elections for Huitlapan and Ahuacatlán in December 1786 echo the San Baltasar case. Ordinarily the curate proposed three candidates for election. The elections were held in the parish seat, although, for the most distant villages, elections could be held on the day of the annual fiesta of the patron saint when a priest went there to celebrate mass. However, in Huitlapan in 1784, 1785, ad 1786, the priest nominated only the illiterate old *gobernador*, declared him elected, and insisted that elections be held in his *casas curales* rather than the *casas reales*. New elections were ordered for 1787 by Sánchez Tagle and supervised by his lieutenant. Predictably, the curate refused to certify them. The elections in Ahuacatlán and its *sujetos* also had the curate insisting on the *casas curales* for the vote and failing to attend or certify the elections convened by the *corregidor's* lieutenants in the *casas reales*.

The irregular election of the *gobernador* in the *cabecera* of Zacatlán in November 1786 did not involve the priest. There it was the *corregidor* who had the privilege of nominating the three candidates for election. Sánchez Tagle proposed three elders who had served for many years in various offices including *gobernador*, but the Indian voters wanted a fourth man, Anastasio de la Cruz, whom Sánchez Tagle considered a *mulato* and a leader of the July *tumulto*. Fearing another violent incident, he allowed the election to go forward, witnessed by the lieutenant and the priest. Sánchez Tagle then raised his objection with the *audiencia* but an investigation showed that de la Cruz was registered as an Indian, not a *mulato*, and there was no firm evidence that he had taken part in the *tumulto*. The election was allowed to stand.

The 1790s produced a series of violent episodes and disputes between village priests and district officials in the Puebla area. Two of these for the Sierra region are described in a lengthy royal investigation and defense of the priests by the Bishop of Puebla in 1799.[11]

The priest of San Juan Quimixtlán, Manuel de Arenas, and the *subdelegado's* lieutenant for this town, Rafael Ramos, were at odds in 1798 over the adultery of Ramos's daughter with his married assistant. In pursuing this matter and the lieutenant's habit of gambling in the *casas reales*, allowing his wife to appear drunk in public, selling *aguardiente* on Easter Sunday, and allowing the Indians to drink a forbidden *tepache*, Father Arenas stated that he was merely fulfilling his priestly duty to oversee the public morals. On January 5, 1799, the dispute became a public scandal as the two officials argued in the town plaza. According to the Bishop's account, Lieutenant Ramos insulted Father Arenas—Ramos reportedly told him "*que se fuera a la mierda*"—and shouted to the Indians not to obey the priest, but to tie him up as mentally deranged, and to carry on sexually as they wished with the certainty that their lieutenant would protect himself. He ordered that the church bells be rung—calling the Indians to assembly—and went into a rage, biting the earth, fulminating against the townspeople for disobedience, declaring the lieutenant excommunicated, and threatening to whip him until two local Spanish men and the lieutenant's wife pleaded on their knees for the priest to relent. Arenas then ordered the Indians to arrest Ramos, threatening them with excommunication if they refused, and to take him to the town jail where he was held for three days.

Under oath, the Indian *gobernador* of Quimixtlán later told his version of the encounter between Ramos and Arenas. Although he did not speak much Spanish, the *gobernador* could see that it was a heated argument. The lieutenant ordered him to arrest Arenas but the Indians refused because he was their priest. The *gobernador* got down on his knees and pleaded with the curate to stop shouting, but Arenas only became more enraged, threatening to bring down the heavens, dry up the rivers, make the earth tremble, and refuse his Indians the last rites unless they arrested the lieutenant. The *gobernador* denied personally arresting the lieutenant but all of the other witnesses testified that several unnamed local Indians obeyed the priest's command.

In his defense, Father Arenas said that he ordered the arrest only because of the public insults, the end product of the lieutenant's flouting of the priest's position of respect and arbiter of the public morals. After this incident, Arenas continued to make intemperate accusations that Ramos was a depraved enemy of religion and was fully supported in his imperious, immoral conduct by his superior, the *subdelegado* of San Juan de los Llanos.

The Bishop of Puebla rose to the curate's defense, warning of the results for other Indian communities of this lieutenant's example of low morals and highhandedness. But the *fiscal* of the *audiencia* was more impressed by the priest's excessive rage—"like that of a rabid dog"—and his temerity to arrest an agent of the king. The *fiscal* censured the priest and warned darkly of the death penalty as the prescribed punishment for treason.

Reading between the lines, the root of the problem between Arenas and Ramos was not the insults or the specific case of adultery but, rather, a serious jurisdictional dispute and the priest's fear that his position in the community had been undermined. The lieutenant had not permitted the priest to whip the adulterers in question and he had released from jail other men and women the priest had placed there for adultery. The lieutenant's action was less a stand on public morality than a declaration that he alone had the authority to make such arrests and mete out the punishment. As the lieutenant had said to Arenas, "You are not my judge." In an earlier provocation, the lieutenant had boasted that the curate had jurisdiction only in his church, to which Arenas tried to reply with his fists.

In the second case, from Tetela de Xonotla in 1793-95, another curate was temporarily suspended from his duties on suspicion of inspiring a village uprising. The real scoundrel turned out to be the overbearing *subdelegado*, Antonio O'Farrill. Chased out of Xonotla by the local Indians in June 1793, O'Farrill lodged a formal complaint against the parish priest, José Antonio Martínez de Segura, as the force (or "motor" as the petition reads) behind this movement against the King's judge. O'Farrill returned and Father Martínez de Segura remained, but the investigation into the charges dragged on for six years. The results of the investigation were clear and a little surprising. All of the witnesses, including O'Farrill's successor as *subdelegado* of Teziutlán, as well as Indians from Xonotla, cleared Martínez de Segura of any responsibility for the *tumulto* of 1793. They had only the highest praise for the priest's unselfish service and personal sacrifices in the parish over more than twenty years. He had distributed maize in times of famine, had bought land for the landless, protected Indians from excessive tribute, performed burials without charge, pardoned all clerical fees during the recent epidemic, and treated the non-Indians just as well. In short, he was judged "an example of love and humility," venerated and respected by the citizens of the district. Rather than inciting the violent protest against O'Farrill, he had stepped in to restore calm. O'Farrill had provoked the protest himself by ordering fifty lashes for eight local Indian nobles when he was not met on the outskirts of Xonotla by a grand welcoming party. Halfway through the public whippings, the assembled crowd of Indians in the plaza took up rocks and drove O'Farrill out of town.

The inquiry into the *subdelegado's* conduct in office revealed that he demanded far more than the usual Indian service and contributions. He had forced Indians in the district to provide him with fish, bread, *aguardiente*, and other scarce supplies. For two years he had resided in Puebla rather than Xonotla and had demanded household servants from his district. These Indian laborers were neither paid nor fed by O'Farrill and were reported to have sold their clothes while in the city just to buy tortillas. During his residence in Xonotla he sent Indians back to Puebla on errands every few days, again without pay. He demanded cash contributions from the Indians to finance his lawsuits against Father Martínez de Segura. Finally, at the end of 1798 the *subdelegado* went too far. In the December elections for the 1799 Indian *cabildo* of Xonotla,

O'Farrill refused to certify the results and ordered a new election with his favorites, the Básquezes, as the candidates. Only the Básquez relatives voted; the rest of the Indians formed a menacing crowd at the *casas reales* and O'Farrill once again fled for his life. At the time, Father Martínez de Segura had been away from Xonotla for five months, so it was clear that the priest was not responsible. When Martínez de Segura returned—as reported by O'Farrill's grateful successor, José Rubén de Celis—he preached brotherly love, forgiveness, and respect for royal authority.[12]

Three Patterns and Some Observations

1. A striking, but not surprising, political pattern in these eighteenth-century investigations is that the parish priests in remote places enjoyed greater loyalty and affection of the rural villagers than did the *subdelegados* and lieutenants. Indians in these cases turned to the priest for protection against arbitrary acts of the district officials, and against the depredations of the the *repartimiento* system. Forced to choose between obeying the priest, the lieutenant, or the *corregidor*, Indian peasants usually followed the priest, even if they questioned his motives and feared the consequences, as in the arrest of the lieutenant of Quimixtlán. Respect for the position of the priest did not mean that curates were not in conflict with their pueblos—the example of local factions complaining of the priest's interference in their village elections is documented here—but it does suggest that the rural priest cannot be understood only as a solitary figure in the countryside, an inconsequential religious specialist and civil servant whose position "as a representative of the government gained him little respect from the exploited Indians."[13]

Naturally, the power of the rural priest in his remote parish varied from village to village and from one district to the next. The opportunity for special influence, however, was built into the circumstances of the rural parish priest. Indian villages of Puebla were reputed to be exceptionally devout and inclined to follow their curate if he established himself among them. The rural priest usually was the only state agent who lived and travelled regularly among peripheral Indian pueblos. The *corregidor* and lieutenants, by contrast, usually lived in the *cabecera* and spent as little time as possible in the remote parts of their district in the eighteenth century. Because the bulk of their actions would have been hidden from secular superiors, the rural parish priests enjoyed a partial independence as territorial agents. Often the priest was the only literate resident who understood colonial law. His position as intermediary between Indian laymen and God, and between laymen and the saints, and his primary role in the rituals of commemoration, morality, rites of passage, redemption and fertility, and the threat of excommunication helped to plant his spiritual authority deep into the daily lives of the faithful, even if they had their own syncretic beliefs, too.

Whether a particular parish priest exerted much influence on villagers in his area depended quite a lot on his personal qualities. The saintly Martínez de Segura who spent over twenty years as the curate of Xonotla had an extraordinarily loyal following. The hot-headed Arenas of Quimixtlán, with less than five years in the parish, got his way with the Indians in that moment of truth but it was clear that he was more feared than loved or trusted and probably had used up whatever good will his office carried with the local Indians. Matías de la Cruz of Toxtepec actively defended his parish's interests against the *corregidor*, but his fatherly motives were mixed with obvious political interests in wanting to separate himself and his parishioners from dependence on the *cacique* and *cabecera* of Tecali. It is not clear whether he commanded much personal support from the Indians of his district.

Generalizations about parish priests' attitude toward their work and its reflection in their behavior clearly will not hold for all curates or necessarily for any one of them. Still, it seems generally true that the idealistic sense of mission of the friars in the "Spiritual Conquest" of the sixteenth century was less often found in the eighteenth-century clergy. Late colonial curates were more likely to lodge complaints against their Indian parishioners than before, and to be occupied with family affairs and their private property. Failure to instill the subtleties and richness of Spanish Catholicism in Indians after the first great conversions later bred disillusionment among clergymen about the capacity and intentions of Indians and an estrangement inspired by the cultural distance between inward-looking Indian villagers and city-trained priests. "Limited capacity or intellectual stupidity" was the usual way for Spaniards of the late colonial period to characterize Mexican Indians;[14] their willful idolatry made the priest's duty to educate them an "invisible war." Many more young men took the cassock in the eighteenth century, to the extent that there was an oversupply of ordained clergymen and much competition and influence-peddling for chaplaincies and the better parish assignments.[15] Nearly all Mexican priests were trained in the nearest cathedral city, such as Puebla, or in Mexico City. They were educated as part of an urban, intellectual elite and most never left off wishing to return to the civilized city and its comforts and the conversation and company of their equals. There was great diversity in a curate's length of service in one parish, but the tendency—especially among younger priests in the late colonial period—was to move from place to place every few years, to spend as much time as possible in the cathedral city competing in the periodic *oposiciones* for tenured posts and mantaining contacts, hoping against hope to secure one of the prized salaried positions in the Cathedral Chapter.

One parish priest of the mundane sort in late eighteenth-century Puebla, José Miguel Guridi y Alcocer, has left a wonderfully candid and detailed autobiography in which he examined his early career and his feelings about parish service.[16] Born a creole Spaniard of humble origins near Texmelucan in 1763, Guridi showed little interest in learning or religion before he was sent to the seminary in Puebla at the age of eleven. He earned the baccalaureate degree in theology at nineteen but was not yet committed to the religious life. He says that he spent much of his time during those early years writing poetry, reading fairly widely in history, philosophy, and literature, falling in love with a cousin in Mexico City, and striving to curb his temper, vanity, and penchant for argument. The poor results of his subsequent legal studies in Mexico City and the marriage of his cousin to another suitor kindled his plans for the priesthood. He became the star pupil in his seminary class, moving quickly through his studies, receiving a chaplaincy and scholarship in theology, serving as an instructor in philosophy and the scriptures and becoming a Professor (*catedrático*) of Sacred Scriptures in Mexico City. Following his ordination in Puebla in 1791, he held a professorship in the seminary there and was assigned a small parish in the city. Late in 1791, instead of being named rector of the seminary as he hoped, Guridi was awarded the tenured post of parish priest (*propietario*) of Acaxete, an Indian parish less than a day's walk from Puebla. As Guridi realized, it was unusual for such a young, inexperienced priest to receive a permanent post like this with a guaranteed, if modest, income. But he was restless and dissatisfied. Few of his parishioners spoke Spanish, and as a "sociable man," Guridi saw the post as a kind of purgatory, "a wasteland, a solitude, ..., a sandy desert, ... a *páramo*."[17] Father Guridi left the parish whenever he could, politicking in Puebla for a prebend's post, earning a doctorate in canon law in Mexico, practicing in Mexico City, and holding the part-time legal position *promotor fiscal* in Puebla. He continued to keep his parish post but was rarely there during his eleven years' tenure. Finally, the bishop ordered him to return or renounce his rights to the parish, and ordered him not to leave Acaxete without his express license. Having "left my heart in Mexico City," Guridi reconciled himself to life in Acaxete, but just briefly. The autobiography ends in 1802 with the thirty-nine year old Guridi headed back to Mexico City as the curate of the villa de Tacubaya, "handing myself over to Providence."[18] Probably few parish priests of Puebla were as ambitious or as successful as Guridi, but many of them must have shared his hopes, his private feelings, and his restlessness. If so, this concern for career and the amenities of city life, and the long absences from the parish would have separated them in an important way from the needs and trust of their Indian parishioners (although their stronger contacts with public figures in the cities might also have made them even more effective as brokers).

Whatever his personal qualities, the curate had traditional responsibilities that brought him into the public affairs of his parish. He was the *padre manso*, the strong but gentle father, the teacher. Summoning his view of the ideal parish priest, Archbishop Lorenzana, in a pastoral letter of October 5, 1766, spoke of "the good and zealous curate contributing in large part or *in toto* to the spiritual and political government of a pueblo...; the prudence of the *párroco* as Father moderates and orders the actions of his children."[19] He was charged with informing superior colonial officials of local behavior that violated royal law. The right to judge and punish crimes against canon law was within his authority from early colonial times. His role as judge and protector of the Indians extended into what today would be considered civil and political matters: supervising and certifying local elections, protecting Indians against extortion by merchants, and against abuses by the *corregidor*; and he had special responsibility to prevent excessive drunkenness and protect the integrity of the family.[20] Eighteenth-century bishops and archbishops were not reluctant to speak out on the civic responsibilities of the King's Indian subjects. Lorenzana, for example, published a special letter to the Indians on June 30, 1768 in which he spoke of their specific obligations to insure the good order of their pueblos, including a job for every man over twenty-five years old, and the duty to marry and build a home.[21]

2. The customary public and political responsibilities of the priests inevitably overlapped with those of the *corregidores*, *subdelegados*, and lieutenants. This was true in the general sense of looking out for the good conduct and protection of Indian subjects and in some very specific matters, such as drunkenness and overseeing elections, where the priests and district magistrates were to share these responsibilities. But in the last decades of the colonial period, royal orders cut away much of this overlapping authority, doing so at the expense of the rural curate. Public drunkenness became a problem to be dealt with by the *subdelegados* and lieutenants. Priests were forbidden to use the whip—as they had done for more than two centuries—as punishment for Indian drunkenness and moral transgressions. Priests as teachers of literacy in Indian districts were being replaced by *maestros de escuela* (primary-level school teachers) who were salaried from the village treasury and generally allied with the *subdelegado*. The campaign to promote spoken and written Spanish throughout the viceroyalty was accompanied by orders for priests to preach and communicate with their Indian subjects in Spanish, and elimination of the requirement that curates speak the Indian language of their district. Where enforced, these changes would have reduced the curate's strategic role as interpreter and cultural broker.

Finally, in the *Ordenanza General...de Intendentes* of 1803, only Spanish judges could convoke, preside over, and certify local elections.[22] Curates were still to communicate royal decrees to their parishioners and to report to the colonial government on local affairs,[23] but they were losing many of their formal responsibilities under the law. Mexico's Archibishop in 1803, Francisco Xavier de

Lizana y Beaumont published a letter to his priests on September 1, 1803 tacitly supporting these changes. In ordering that the priests obey their royal superiors he remarked that "the ministers of God cannot be ministers of the world and its occupations."[24] But the line between affairs of state and the responsibilities of the parish priest had never been clear in practice. For moral as well as conservative political reasons, parish priests in rural Puebla could not step back as passive spectators of the worldly affairs of the *doctrina*. Their moral responsibilities had always been partly temporal and the farther they were from a provincial capital the more difficult it was to enforce the new provisions or for the state to get along without the curate's active participation in public affairs. One result was more disputes between priests and district magistrates of the kind documented in these investigations.

The growing conflicts over dominion between curates and district magistrates at the end of the eighteenth century also had to do with the magistrates themselves, encouraged by the royal decrees that worked to enlarge the secular state and promised to extend the authority of the royal agents, and which seemed to many priests to be a frontal attack on the traditional partnership of the Church and the State. *Subdelegados* like O'Farrill and lieutenants like Rafael Ramos in the 1790s treated the priests in their districts as inferiors rather than partners in the work of colonial administration, imperiously and inflexibly encroaching on the priest's customary authority and *subdelegados* and lieutenants proclaimed their superiority, told Indians not to obey the curate, and insulted priests in public. These were not new events but they happened with a new frequency and animus in the last decades of the colonial period. District magistrates now were quick to blame the parish priest for any disorder directed against them, and they were just as quick to respond with force instead of negotiation. If Sánchez Tagle and Ramos are representative, perhaps this was because more of the district officials in the late eighteenth century were military officers and fewer were lawyers. Viceroy Revillagidedo's instruction to his successor in 1794 spoke of his *subdelegados* as ignorant persons, knowing little of the law.[25] He blamed this situation largely on their reduced income since the elimination of the *repartimientos de mercancías* (they were now paid a salary of 5 percent of the tribute collected, plus judicial fees for services rendered).

The delicate balance of overlapping responsibilities, rivalries, and cooperation between rural priests and district magistrates that had operated in a clumsy, perhaps unplanned but often effective way for generations seemed to be breaking down at the end of the eighteenth century, with unsettling results for the rulers and the ruled. *Audiencia* judges and viceroys deplored the tyranny of the parish priests and the vehemence with which they answered the changing government policies and the growing authority of the *subdelegados* but they also worried about abuses of office by the magistrates that could have equally disruptive effects on Indian villagers. Above all, they feared that the violent confrontations and numerous disputes between curates and *subdelegados* or *corregidores* served as a bad example for the Indians, opening the way to rebellion and "perpetual disobedience."[26]

The Bishop of Puebla in 1799 saw the disputes and unsettled circumstances of district government leading to Indian unrest and insolence, but he placed the blame on patron withdrawal, on the end of the traditional services of the parish priest, and on the bold and irresponsible conduct of the magistrates:

> This humble and religious education which the temper of our time calls paltry and timid has been most useful to the government. For about three centuries these domains of Your Majesty have been held without

> need of armed force, in the firmest peace, showing love for the sovereign and the constant loyalty of the best vassals in the world. But since the authority of the *párrocos* has been limited, forbidding them to mete out moderate punishment which as fathers and teachers they used for the correction of their parishioners, and since those in charge of justice in the pueblos—true parasites of the state, men usually without roots or good habits (like the one in Quimixtlán)—have made a point of persuading the Indians that the priest can only confess and preach, the Indians have begun to become insolent. There is not an hacienda owner who has not complained of their false pride and poor service. When they are notified of government orders that do not suit their taste, their disturbances are continuous. And if they lose respect for the Church (which will inevitably happen if imprisonment of priests continues and the ecclesiastics lose their voice in public life) there will be no choice but to resort to force to contain a people who on the outside are extremely humble and submissive but underneath are filled with boundless malice and unalterable hatred for their conquerors.[27]

3. Another notable pattern to emerge from this evidence, perhaps less confined to the late eighteenth century or to the Indian districts of Puebla, is the political tension between center and periphery within districts. This tension was expressed especially in the problematic relationship between the *cabecera* and the *sujetos*. In the Puebla cases and elsewhere in central and southern Mexico, the *cabecera* was the center of the non-Indian world in the district, the place that was most regularly connected to provincial and vice-regal interests and influences. It was the center of colonial authority and the home of the *corregidor* or *subdelegado* (if he lived in the district). His relatives usually gathered there, along with the Spanish merchants, shopkeepers, tax collectors, lieutenants, and *casta* artisans. The Indians of the *cabecera* were more often able to communicate in Spanish, and Indian "*caciques*"—noblemen, men of authority—were concentrated there.

The authority of the *cabecera* extended out to the *sujetos*, to the obvious advantage of the *cabecera*. Indians from outlying areas in the district were required to do service in the *cabecera*; taxes were paid to officials from the *cabecera*; the *corregidor's repartimiento* was an especially onerous demand from the district center that interfered with the local economy. Even the saints were partisans in this hierarchy of center and and periphery. Santiago was the patron of the *cabecera* of Tecali "and its district" which meant that *sujetos* with their own patron saints to support must supply food and money for the *fiesta titular* in Tecali whether they wanted to or not.

Despite being the meeting point for many of the district's ties to the larger colonial world, the *cabecera* was spiritually isolated from its outlying communities. Like Father Guridi, the *cabecera*'s non-Indian residents viewed their town more as an enclave that looked out to the provincial and viceregal capitals rather than toward the hinterland that made them important. The *corregidores* and *subdelegados* were temporary appointees who rarely ventured outside the *cabecera*. They were known to Indians in outlying villages mainly as the distant figures who demanded tribute payments through their collectors, who required them to buy their cattle, and who passed judgment in serious violations of colonial law.

The *sujetos*, by contrast, were more Indian and ordinarily out of touch with district politics.

Few non-Indians lived there and few of the villagers spoke Spanish. Lieutenants of the *corregidores* sometimes resided among them but it was the parish priest who, if he remained for more than a few years, most embodied the formal colonial system in the Indian pueblo as interpreter of the imperial language and law, as figure of paternal authority, as priest of the new religion, and as potential adviser. And it was the parish priest who protected his own authority by confronting the *corregidor's* and the *cabecera's* infringements on local interest and failing to implement some district orders. The *corregimientos* and *subdelegaciones* were divided into smaller parish units that acquired their own poltical identities with the encouragement of their priests and sometimes sought independence from *cabecera*. There was some tension in being a parish seat but not a district capital. The case of Toxtepec documented here was not unique. Many *doctrinas*, especially ones that became larger than their *cabeceras* in the late eighteenth century, chafed at serving the interests of an unheeding district center and began to pressure the colonial government to grant them their own district status. These villagers would have understood Miguel de Unamuno's observation about Madrid that it was "a stomach, not a brain."

Perhaps more than any other cleavage, center and periphery shaped district politics in colonial Mexico. Ethnic and bureaucratic cleavages were important in these Puebla cases, too—Indian *sujetos* and partly non-Indian *cabeceras*; priests as authorities in the outlying areas, *corregidores* and *subdelegdos* in the *cabecera*—but the perceived interests of the center working against the periphery usually overrode these other divisions: in none of the Puebla cases did the parish priests in the *cabeceras* join their brothers in the countryside to oppose the *corregidor*. The Indian *caciques* and *principales* of the *cabeceras* (and Indians still outnumbered non-Indians in these *cabeceras*) also supported the *corregidor* in district affairs. They were the temporary soldiers who joined him in occasional expeditions into the district of collect unpaid taxes and demand obedience to his orders. It was the Indian *gobernador* of Zacatlán whom the *corregidor* sent as his special representative to investigate purported violations of election procedures in San Baltasar.

Conclusion

The overlapping responsibilities and rivalries between curate and *corregidor* that were inherent in the colonial administration of New Spain before the late eighteenth century held potentially explosive tensions, but they also provided an important check against personal power and arbitrary acts of either official. This helps explain how the Spanish state ruled in remote districts without a standing army or a large police force. Ideally a balance of polite but cautious cooperation should exist between the curates and district judges that would prevent either outright conflict or collusion between the two. Such countervailing power served the interests of the Crown as a way to check arbitrary rule by royal agents and ensure that serious disputes at the district level would be appealed to higher courts more directly connected to the king, thereby preserving at least a semblance of justice that could reduce the chance of an anti-colonial war by Indian subjects. Some competition among district officials also could benefit from the Indian pueblos. It gave them an opportunity to manuever for their own benefit in the administrative hierarchy. Unless the priest and magistrates were in league, there would be a natural ally for the Indians in one or the other when local disputes arose. And both the priests and the higher levels of the Spanish state shared an interest in maintaining corporate Indian villages as social and political units to counter the independent position of large private estates.

This hypothesis of rivalry and balance in district politics needs verification for other places and periods. It may be that as peninsular or creole Spaniards with urban ties, the priests and magistrates had more of an affinity for each other in the midst of Indian strangers than the Puebla investigations indicate.[28] One of the complaints in the *comunero* rebellions of Nueva Granada in the 1780s was that *corregidores* and parish priests worked together to exploit the Indians.[29] This complaint in itself suggests that checks and balances between these officials were expected and desired. For Nueva Granada, a structural reason existed for complicity: the salary of priests in Indian parishes there was paid from the Indian tribute tax collected by the *corregidores*. To my knowledge, Mesoamerican parish priests were not financially dependent on the *corregidores* in this direct way.

The Bourbon political reforms may have strengthened the Crown's hand in America and conceived the state in more modern, categorical terms, but by reducing the influence of curates in public affairs they led to sharper disputes between parish priests and district magistrates, and the weakening of a traditional hierarchy of patronage and authority that threatened the old ideal balance between competing and overlapping political agents.[30] The *subdelegado's* formal authority grew at the expense of rural priests. The *subdelegados*—tied to the *cabecera*, tax collection, and military organization—embodied the center in the periphery. They were enforcers of the King's law, often inflexible and unimaginative in the way they went about it. Few were trained in law or interested in mediating between impersonal, abstract colonial decrees and the specific needs and exceptional circumstances of their subjects. The curates who, as the Bishop of Puebla recognized, were the true political intermediaries between colonial centers and the Indian village periphery, were losing their formal position in the political system under the later Bourbons. After 1790 their wordy written objections to the encroachments and abuses of *subdelegados* no longer carried much weight and state agents now looked upon their more dramatic political gestures on behalf of tradition and village autonomy as treason. They were on the way to becoming a professional class instead of active partners in the enterprise of the state. Here, in a small way, is the trend that Charles Hale has illuminated so well for the nineteenth century in Mexico: the rise of the secular state at the expense of the Church and the local community and its culmination in the Liberals' War of Reform and the Porfirian system.

For Indian villages, the declining leverage of parish priests in the colonial bureaucracy and the growing importance of the *subdelegados* meant a loss in local political resources, new difficulty in limiting the extractions of the market, and greater estrangement from the colonial state. The logical extension of this process has been described by Sidney Tarrow in his study of politics in peripheral communities of Italy and France: "Where local political resources are weak and the mechanisms of local-national relations dominated by the center, to the burdens of peripheral decline will be added the indifference of the state."[31] The War of Independence interrupted this process of domination and weakened the state, but the beneficiaries in political power over the next century appear to have been the *hacendados* and political bosses more than villages and priests.

NOTES

[1]Migdal 1974:35-36.

[2]Each investigation fills at least one AGI legajo: AM 839-841, Tecali; AM 1939, Zacatlán; IG 3027, Tetela de Xonotla and Quimixtlán.

[3]Information in this and the following paragraph comes from Gerhard (1972:255-56, 388-89), *Puebla en cifras* (1944), *Memoria sobre la administración*...(1850), and *Regiones económico-agrícolas* (1936:732-47).

[4]Vetancurt 1960-1961, III:187-88.

[5]All information for this section on Tecali comes from AGI-AM 839-841.

[6]This is not the first time that district officials had burst into the church without the priest's permission. Witnesses said that lieutenants were in the habit of entering during Mass in search of Indians who owed tribute.

[7]I have discussed the divide-and-rule approach and the central place of the pueblo in colonial government in Taylor (1979, chapters 5 and 5), and in "Colonial Land and Water Rights of New Mexico Indian Pueblos," a report to the U. S. District Court of New Mexico (Exhibit JP-16) in State of New Mexico v. Aamodt (U.S. Civil No. 6639).

[8]All information for this section on Zacatlán comes from AGI-AM 1939.

[9]The special planting was distributed among the following Indian communities:

	Town	Fanegas	Almudes
1.	Zacatlán	50	
	Barrio Xicolapa	4	
	San Cristobal	10	
2.	Santiago Chinauapan	8	
	Aguistla	4	3
3.	Auacatlan	10	6
	San Marcos	4	6
	San Francisco	5	
	San Andrés	5	
	San Antonio	12	
4.	Tepezintla	17	
	San Baltasar	4	
	Tonalisco	10	
5.	Auistlan	12	
	Tecpatlan	8	
	Tugupango	7	
	Coyayango	6	
6.	Comacautla	3	
	San Bernardino		9
	Tapayula	7	
	Coatepec	6	
7.	Zapotitlan	6	
	Zongosotla	6	
	Huisila	14	
	Nanacatlan	5	
	Tustla	3	
8.	Atlequisayan	4	6
	Concepción	2	6
	Osenolacasgule	6	

	Cashucan	6	6
9.	Huitlalpan	9	6
	Chipahuatlan	6	
	Zitlala	6	
	San Martinito	3	
	Yxtepeque	12	
10.	Olintla	14	
	Huehuetla	14	
11.	Xopala	13	
	Chicontla	8	
	Patla	14	
	Tlaclantongo	8	

[10]The priest of Zacatlán in this case and the priest of Tecali in the preceding case took no part in the protests against the district magistrates.

[11]All information for this section on Quimixtlán and Tetela de Xonotla comes from AGI-IG 3027.

[12]These problems between priests and district officials over jurisdiction, political power, and personal ambition in the late eighteenth century were not confined to the Sierra region of Puebla. AGI-IG 3027 contains another lengthy case from 1797 for Chietla in the sugar-producing low country of southwest Puebla in which the *subdelegado*, Domingo Saavedra, violated the immunity of the local church, cursing and shouting as he arrested a vagrant there during Mass. Witnesses called in this case consistently testified that Saaveda was threatening and provocative toward local priests, declaring himself to be "the Pope, King, and Bishop," and demanding that the priests do strictly as he ordered. Four lieutenant priests had left the parish during his short tenure. One other jurisdictional dispute between a parish priest and a *subdelegado* is recorded in this *legajo*: against Vicente Zapata, the curate of Huatusco, for a whipping and other infringements on the royal jurisdiction.

[13]Brooks 1976:15, 41.

[14]Moxó 1837:16-17.

[15]Brading 1981:5-26.

[16]Guridi y Alcocer 1906.

[17]Guridi y Alcocer 1906:71.

[18]Guridi y Alcocer 1906:155. This was just the beginning of Father Guridi's public career. He served as a deputy of the Cortes of Cadiz in 1811, became a canon of the Cathedral in Mexico City in 1821, and signed the first federal constitution of Mexico in 1824. He died on October 4, 1828.

[19]University of Texas, Nettie Lee Benson Latin American Collection, Mexican Manuscripts (UT), G-15, "Documentos relativos al clero en la Nueva España, 1756 a 1817."

[20]The manual of responsibilities of parish priests in late colonial Spanish America that was studied by many Mexican curates is the fat *Itinerario para parochos de indios...* by Alonso de la Peña Montenegro, 2nd ed., Amberes: 1698 (a third edition was printed in 1754). It is an excellent, detailed guide to the traditional expectations and duties of the parish clergy.

[21]UT G-15, June 30, 1768, "Reglas para que los naturales de estos reynos sean felices en lo espiritual y temporal."

[22]"Ordenanza general...de intendentes" 1803:47.

[23]"Ordenanza general...de intendentes," 1803:46-47.

[24]UT G-15, Sept. 1, 1803.

[25]IVNE 1873, II:45.

[26]AGI-AM 839-59.

[27]AGI-IG 3027.

[28]Stein and Stein (1970:81) posit that *corregidores*, priests, and town officials combined to form a solid core of political power at the local level.

[29]Loy 1981:250.

[30]Valenzuela (1977:156) has a good discussion of patron-client and categorical forms of association in local politics.

[31]Tarrow 1977:3.

CRIMINAL JUSTICE AND THE POOR IN LATE COLONIAL MEXICO CITY

Gabriel Haslip-Viera

> The multitude is composed of many racial types, and these are naturally vicious. Their greatest inclination is towards drunkenness, gambling, lust and the love of luxury. There are many thieves among them, who are vulgarly known as *macutenos.* These individuals are inclined to use knives, called *belduques,* which are used, along with stones, to assault and cause injury.[1]
>
> The Viceroy, Marqués de Croix
> to Antonio María Bucareli,
> September 1, 1771

Crime was a major concern of Mexico City's urban elite throughout the late colonial period. Government officials, clergymen, intellectuals, property owners, and other influential persons complained constantly about the prevalence of theft, burglary, assault, murder, and other crimes. They also commented unfavorably on the large number of beggars, vagrants, public drunks, gamblers, and other suspicious persons who were constantly seen wandering about the streets or loitering in front of churches and public buildings. For the colonial elite, crime and social disorder were to be found everywhere and appeared to be out of control. Urban society and even civilization itself, seemed to be threatened and on the verge of chaos. At the same time, law enforcement officials were constantly reminded of their responsibilities and admonished to implement policies to reverse the pernicious trend towards rampant social disorder.[2]

In response to the challenge of crime and social disorder, colonial officials periodically initiated programs to improve the administration of justice and reduce the level of criminality. These efforts included the formulation of new criminal statutes, the expansion of the judiciary and law enforcement agencies, and the adoption of more effective correctional procedures. Some of these measures may have been successful, at least for a brief period of time, during the final decades of the colonial regime. From the early 1780s to the decade of the Wars for Independence, the level of official complaint appears to have subsided somewhat. It is true that crime continued to be a serious problem, but it seems that its threat to society was no longer perceived to be as great. Colonial officials were apparently pleased, if not completely satisfied, with the improved performance of the criminal justice system and its ability to control the level of criminality.[3] The present article will examine the problem of crime in late colonial Mexico City from two general perspectives. At the beginning, there will be a discussion of the origins and the characteristics of urban criminality and its effect upon society. This will then be followed by a survey of the various programs that were implemented to reduce the level of crime and an assessment of their overall effectiveness.[4]

During the late colonial period, Mexico City possessed all the economic and social conditions that were necessary for the rise of crime and the creation of a criminal class. With a population that ranged from 135,000 to 140,000 inhabitants in the late 1790s, Mexico City was geographically the largest and most populous city in the Americas. Its size and importance was largely the result of its role as an administative and commercial center for the Spanish Empire. The city functioned as a distribution point for the commerce that crossed the Atlantic between the Viceroyalty of New Spain and the mother country by way of mercantilist economic institutions. It was also the administrative and political center for all the kingdoms, provinces, and jurisdictions that constituted Spain's empire in Central and North America.

From the outset, the maintenance of social control in Mexico City was made difficult by its highly complex and stratified economic and social structure. A largely Spanish and creole elite, along with a small urban middle class, was situated at the top of the social hierarchy. These two groups monopolized commerce, manufacturing, the professions, most of the trade guilds, and all of the appointments to administrative positions and the clergy. The urban masses, living in abject poverty, with little security and hope for advancement, were at the bottom of the social structure and consisted of Indians, *mestizos*, *mulatos*, as well as a considerable number of poor Spaniards and creoles, the lower class was divided into its own peculiar hierarchical structure which was based on occupational status and ethnic classification. Small tradesmen, stallkeepers, and the higher status journeymen artisans were at the top of this hierarchy, while the lower status artisans, the city's itinerant street venders, and the unskilled day laborers occupied the bottom.[5]

The people in the upper levels of the lower class were in a precarious, but relatively privileged position, because their income was generally higher, and they had a greater degree of economic flexibility. The small tradesman or the artisan in one of the higher status professions could earn wages of between 6 and 8 *reales* a day or between 200 and 300 pesos a year in a society where the average annual cost of living for a family of four ranged from 130 to 265 pesos.[6] Consequently, individuals or families at the top of the lower class had relatively greater financial opportunities and could look forward to the possibility of higher economic or social status and improved living conditions. Such was not the case with the urban poor, and as we shall see, it was this group that provided most of the individuals that were arrested by the criminal justice system.

The urban poor, when employed, normally earned subsistence wages of between 2 and 6 *reales* a day, or between 60 and 200 pesos a year. These wages compelled many individals in the lower class to look for additional sources of income to support themselves and their families. Observers in the late colonial period noted that many artisans and day laborers were required to find supplementary employment. They also noted that the wives and children of artisans and day laborers were frequently obliged to work in order to purchase food and other necessities, but this supplementary employment, in itself, was often insufficient.[7] As a result, the urban poor were frequently pre-occupied with the day-to-day problems of mere subsistence.

Throughout the late colonial period, visitors and residents alike never tired of commenting on the precarious condition of the urban poor. Poor diet, ill health and horrendous living and working conditions were everyday facts of life. Rising food costs, a continuous migration to the city from rural areas, and major difficulties in certain sectors of the manufacturing economy led to a decline in wage scales and an increase in unemployment.[8] Such conditions increased the potential for social disorder to a significant degree. As a result, crime became an important aspect of daily life in Mexico City during the late colonial period.

Unfortunately, there is no way that we can precisely measure the actual amount of crime in Mexico City at any given time. There is a sense that urban criminality was a serious problem because government officials and other influential persons constantly complained of thefts, burglaries, assaults, murders, and other crimes. Surviving quantitative records, however, tend to be fragmentary and unreliable.[9] These records, although voluminous, account for only a small fraction of the total law enforcement activity in Mexico City in any given year. They are also inclined to reflect administrative realities, such as adjustments in personnel, the formulation of new criminal statutes, modification in law enforcement procedures, and changes in attitudes towards various kinds of crime by law enforcement agents, government officials and the judiciary. Nevertheless, despite their inherent shortcomings, the statistics compiled by Mexico City's law enforcement agencies can still provide valuable information on the nature and the extent of criminality in the late colonial period if their inadequacies are duly recognized.[10]

The figures in table 1 clearly indicate that, at various times during the eighteenth century, certain crimes were prosecuted with greater vigor than other crimes. For example, in 1710, indebtedness and the failure to pay tribute accounted for 36 percent of all the arrests made by the municipal authorities. The same transgressions, however, accounted for only 10 percent of the arrests made in 1741 and 7 percent in 1796. In fact, records indicate that no one was taken into custody for failure to make tribute payments in 1741 and 1796. The dissimilarities in the figures can be explained by administrative concerns, rather than by prevailing economic and social conditions. The years 1710 and 1741 were similar in that they were characterized by severe economic difficulties. Bad weather and poor harvests drove the price of maize and other foodstuffs to astronomical levels. At the same time, epidemics of smallpox and "fevers" afflicted the urban population, and were undoubtedly followed by the closure of manufacturing enterprises, a rise in unemployment, shortages of basic necessities, and other difficulties.[11] Yet, the similarities that characterized conditions in 1710 and 1741 are not reflected in the arrest records of the same years. Indeed, the proportional decrease in the number of arrests for indebtedness, the selling of prohibited liquors and the failure to pay tribute in 1710 and 1741, and the proportional increase in the number of persons arrested for vagrancy, public drunkenness, gambling, and sex crimes between 1741 and 1796, demonstrates that the activities of law enforcement agents were inclined to reflect peculiar concerns or administrative decisions to a significant degree.

Tables 2 shows that young adults were arrested in disproportionately greater numbers than persons in other age groups. Nevertheless, these statistics are not unusual, and may, in fact, be characteristic of criminality and law enforcement procedures at any time. Modern criminologists, for example, have observed that young adults are easily alienated by a social system that is characterized by rigid economic and social inequality. They also note that, among all age groups, young adults are more inclined to express their discontent through actions that are considered a threat to the social order.[12] Throughout history, ruling classes or elite groups have been fearful of young adults and their potential for deviant or rebellious behavior. Traditionally, they have been perceived as the most potentially dangerous group in society. As a result, law enforcement agencies have always placed special emphasis on the control of deviant behavior by young persons; fact supported by the statistical data for Mexico City in the late colonial period. Young adults between the ages of 16 and 25 accounted for 47 percent of all the arrests made by the municipal authorities in 1796. At the same time, persons between the ages of 16 and 39 acccounted for 83 percent of all arrests, even though this same age group comprised only 46 percent of the total population of Mexico City in 1790.

Reflecting the prevailing social attitudes of late colonial Mexico, more men were arrested by the municipal authorities than women. Although females were implicated in every type of crime, from public drunkenness to homicide, they were considered more delicate, less dangerous, and less inclined to participate in crimes and social disorders than men. Prevailing public opinion and elite attitudes towards female criminality were even reflected in the architectural configuration of the jails. A 1788 report indicated that the viceregal prison could accommodate up to 1,000 men and 500 women, which meant that law enforcement agents expected no more than 33 percent of the prison population to be composed of women. Prison records for the late colonial period demonstrate that women were arrested and incarcerated at near the expected level of 33 percent. Thus, it is also not surprising to find that men accounted for 73 percent of the persons arrested by the municipal authorities in 1796, while women accounted for only 27 percent of those arrested.[13]

In addition to the view that women would be less inclined to participate in crimes than men, it was also expected that few women would be arrested crimes that involved physical exertion, such as, assault, burglary, armed robbery, and murder. On the contrary, women were expected to be implicated in offenses of a moral nature, such as fornication, concubinage, prostitution, adultery and disputes with their spouses or lovers. In 1771, the Viceroy, Marqués de Croix, observrved that there were many disputes between spouses and that these conflicts were often motivated by the desire of the husband or the wife to live as "libertines." Viceroys Bucreli and first Conde de Revilla-Gigedo (1746-1755) supplemented this view with the observation that "prostitution" and adultery were the most common offenses committed by women.[14] The statistical data for 1796 demonstrates that the pattern of arrests was in conformity with the general assumption that women were more likely to be implicated in offenses of a moral nature than men (see table 3). In 1796, 54 percent of the women were arrested for family disputes, adultery, fornication, and other sex crimes, while only 28 percent of the men were arrested for the same infractions.

As in the case of women, the relationship between crime and ethnic classification was influenced by elite preconceptions and law enforcement procedures. In general, Indians, *mestizos*, and *mulatos* were expected to commit crimes more frequently than Spaniards and creoles. Considering their relatively low economic and social status, these groups were looked upon as being "naturally vicious," and inclined towards theft, violence, drunkenness, gambling, and other activities considered a threat to the social order. At the same time, certain ethnic groups became identified with specific crimes and behavior patterns. Indians, for example, were expected to participate in thefts, drunken brawls, or in crimes of a petty or juvenile nature, because of their presumed ignorance, irrationality, and distance from Spanish culture. At the same time, *mestizos* and *mulatos* were expected to participate in thefts and violent crimes to a disproportionate *degree* because of their alleged opportunistic, manipulative and immoral character. In contrast to the Indians, it was assumed that these latter groups understood the norms and values of Spanish culture and their accountability under the law.[15] It is, therefore, perhaps surprising to discover that the arrest records for late colonial Mexico City do not necessarily reflect the prevailing attitudes towards crime and its relationship to ethnicity. As expected, the 1796 arrest records (see table 4) indicate that Indians were overrepresented, and that Spaniards and creoles were underrepresented.[16] Yet, contrary to prevailing public opinion, the figures for *mestizos* and *mulatos* prove to be inconclusive. As expected, *mulatos* are overrepresented in the category of property crimes, however, *mestizos* are not significantly overrepresented in this area, while both groups are unexpectedly underrepresented in the category of violent crimes.[17]

Although the statistics on ethnicity prove to be inconclusive, alternative occupational data effectively demonstrates the relationship between crime and socio-economic status. The figures in table 5 show that 96 percent of the persons arrested in 1796 were listed as holding occupations that placed them in the lower class. At the same time, the figures also indicate that 30 percent of those arrested were unskilled laborers, itinerant street vendors and the unemployed. As the most destitute segment of the urban population, it is not surprising that this group, by itself, constituted almost one third of the total number of persons arrested by the municipal authorities in 1796. Nevertheless, the large number of low status artisans, constituting almost one half the total arrested, is perhaps more significant, because it better demonstrates the greater psychological impact that increased economic and social inequality might have had on this group during the late eighteenth century. The difficulties that afflicted certain sectors of the manufacturing economy in the late colonial period, and the apparent decline in artisan living standards probably conspired to produce an increase in unemployment, underemployment, and criminality among lower status artisans. The overrepresentation of lower status artisans in the arrest records is demonstrated by the fact that they were arrested for 39 percent of the property crimes and 58 percent of the violent crimes, and 50 percent of all charges related to indebtedness. In fact, the arrest records for 1796, clearly indicate that most of the lower status artisans were employed in occupations that had experienced a loss of prestige or were afflicted by chronic unemployment and underemployment. Specifically, 34 percent of all the persons arrested in 1796 were either masons, carpenters, bakers, weavers, tailors, shoemakers, or spinners of cloth. At the same time, these same individuals accounted for 21 percent of the property crimes, 45 percent of the violent crimes, and 40 percent of all the arrests related to indebtedness.[18]

In their effort to suppress or control thefts, burglaries, assaults, murders, and other crimes, the urban elite formulated criminal legislation, established correctional procedures, and expanded law enforcement agencies. In the area of criminal legislation, all magistrates were expected to consult various law codes for guidance in all criminal procedures. The Laws of the Indies, codified in 1680, and again in 1791, as the *Recopilación de leyes de los reynos de las Indias*, contained a number of criminal statutes; however it was understood that these statutes could not be relied upon in the prosecution of criminal cases. All magistrates, as a result, were expected to use the Spanish legal codes in addition to the Laws of the Indies. The *Recopilación* of 1791 established procedures for consulting the Spanish law codes when the Laws of the Indies could not be used in a particular case. At the outset, all magistrates were expected to consult the *Nueva Recopilación de Castilla (1569)*. If this procedure failed to produce a suitable statute, the magistrates were expected to consult the Laws of Toro (1505), which contained a further ranking of legal codes, including the *Ordenamiento de Alcalá (1348)*, the municipal *fueros*, the *Fuero Real (1255)*, and finally, the *Siete Partidas* (1265). Thus, the criminal statutes found in the Spanish law codes and the Laws of the Indies, along with the decrees of local officials, viceroys, and the crown, constituted the entire corpus of criminal legislation available to the colonial magistrates.

To a significant degree this body of criminal law and its medieval tradition reflected or determined many of the attitudes that judges, prosecutors, law enforcement agents, and government officials had towards crime throughout the colonial period. The law was generally seen as an instrument of authority: the divine authority of "his Catholic Majesty." As a result, attitudes towards criminal behavior almost always focused on the actions of individual lawbreakers. Theft, burglary, assault, murder, and other crimes were seen simply as anti-social behavior. Therefore, all lawbreakerss were treated as anti-social beings who violated the norms and values agreed to by the controlling elements of society. There was little or no emphasis placed on the social and economic background of individual lawbreakers. Likewise, there was little or no concern over whether or not convicted criminals should be rehabilitated or helped to re-enter society as productive citizens. Simply stated, all lawbreakerss were responsible for their actions and were, thus, expected to receive instant retribution for any crime or damage that they might inflict upon society.[19]

Variations in attitudes towards lawbreakers and their anti-social behavior were also reflected in the criminal laws. As a result, wealthy persons or persons of noble birth were accorded special consideration because of their status in society; individuals who enjoyed special corporate privileges or *fueros* were exempt from prosecution in the regular courts; and juveniles, women and the infirm were given special consideration and treatment in deference to their age, sex, and physical condition. At the same time, Indians were also accorded special consideration. Indians were considered physically weak, dullwitted, and inherently irrational ("*gente sin razón*"). As a result, they were relegated to a perpetual guardianship status in colonial society, entitled to special treatment and protection by the crown. Accordingly, crimes committed by Indians were considered less serious than crimes committed by Spaniards, *mestizos, mulatos*, and other ethnic groups. As irrational beings, Indians were not considered totally responsible for their actions and, as a result, they were to be treated as legal minors in the colonial courts. The law prescribed that Indians be punished less severely than Spaniards, creoles, *mestizos, mulatos*, and blacks for the same offenses.[20] In reality, however, this was not always the case. Despite the special consideration accorded to certain kinds of individuals or ethnic groups, responsibility for the criminal act still focused on the individual who committed the crime. As individuals, Indians, juveniles, women, and the infirm were still considered responsible for their actions. The attitudes that were associated with the criminal behavior of each status and ethnic group amounted to distinctions based on the degree of responsibility for the criminal act, not on any fundamental conceptual consideration.

For most of the colonial period, there was little change in the prevailing attitudes towards crime. In fact, the belief in individual culpability, a well as the belief that certain groups should be accorded special treatment, was reinforced by several popular theories. In the sixteenth century, a belief in the existence of criminal types was promoted by the science of physiognomics, or the study of the relationship of the mind and behavior to the body.[21] This was followed in the seventeenth and eighteenth centuries by theories of evolution which reinforced the belief that certain races and ethnic groups were physically and culturally inferior. In New Spain, these theories were combined to produce a belief that Indians, creoles, *mestizos, mulatos* and blacks were inherently inferior in varying degrees. As a consequence, all of these status groups were considered degenerate, weak willed, lazy, and manipulative when compared to European born Spaniards. At the same time, they were thought to be naturally inclined toward theft, vagrancy, assault, murder, and other crimes.[22]

At times, the relationship between poverty and crime was recognized by the colonial elite. Nevertheless, from the early sixteenth to the early eighteenth century, poverty was considered a problem beyond the power of society to resolve. Traditional Catholic dogma, while recognizing the suffering and misery experienced by the poor, nevertheless bestowed special virtues upon poverty. Religious manuals instructed the more fortunate to view the impoverished as "...poor men of Christ...who represent the Lord, and who are made poor in this world for our benefit." In this sense, poverty was seen as a condition to be alleviated by the more affluent through almsgiving. Thus, the relationship between poverty and crime was not considered important enough to merit special attention or analysis during the early colonial period. Any attempt made by the poor to alleviate their miserable living conditions through thefts, burglaries, and other property crimes was seen as a revolt against divinely imposed will. The poor were expected to "support their condition with patience," and to embrace their poverty "...with delight, as men of God."[23]

A more profound analysis of the relationship betwen poverty and crime was initiated by the

Bourbon reformers of the early eighteenth century. Influenced by the ideas of the Enlightenment, the Bourbon reformers believed that crime and a host of other problems were generated by poverty and the monopolistic structure of the economy. They called for basic reforms in the mercantilist economy and advocated the establishment of state sponsored manufacturing enterprises in the urban centers as part of an overall effort to provide employment for the idle poor. They also called for the arrest, confinement, and rehabilitation of recalcitrant beggars and vagrants. Accordingly, all beggars and vagrants were to be drafted into the army or confined to poor houses (*hospicios*), where they would be taught self-discipline and proper work habits. The confinement and rehabilitation of beggars and vagrants was considered an important aspect of the proposed reforms because it was also looked upon as being a valuable tool that could be used in the effort to control criminality. Juan Meléndez Valdés, the eighteenth-century Spanish poet and scholar, reflected the sentiments of many influential persons when he wrote: "There is but one short step from vagrancy to petty theft and grand larceny, and another from grand larceny to the death sentence."[24]

In Mexico, colonial officials and other influential persons were quick to adopt the new Enlightenment ideas on the relationship between poverty and crime. In the early decades of the eighteenth century, several viceroys observed that the emphasis on rigid mercantilist economic policies and the exploitation of precious metals limited the number of enterprises capable of employing a growing population. As a result, the elite class of merchants and large landowners were considered partially responsible for the growth of chronic unemployment, underemployment, and vagrancy. In turn, these problems were seen as a principal cause of criminality.[25]

Throughout the colonial period, new laws were issued against any activity that appeared to be even remotely connected to crime. There were decrees against the sale of stolen property, the carrying of arms, and the granting of asylum to lawbreakers in churches. By the middle of the eighteenth century, however, criminal legislation began to reflect the new Enlightenment attitudes toward poverty and its relationship to crime. Many of the laws that were issued during the second half of the eighteenth century were directed against begging, vagrancy, and public drunkenness, also known "...as the mother of many vices." In 1748, colonial officials initiated a comprehensive campaign against public intoxication which continued, with varying intensity, for the remainder of the colonial period. Several years later, a 1766 decree ordered all able bodied persons to demonstrate that they were gainfully employed within a thirty-day period. All persons who failed to demonstrate gainful employment at the end of the designated time period were to be arrested by law enforcement agents, and either confined to an *hospicio*, drafted into the army, or sentenced to serve as convict laborers on government sponsored public works projects.[26]

Along with the campaigns against beggars, vagrants, and public drunks, colonial officials also inaugurated economic measures designed to employ the idle poor. In Mexico City, there was a significant increase in the number of public works projects: new roads were built, bridges and aqueducts were repaired, and many of the city streets were paved. The crown also established a Royal Tobacco Factory (1769), in part, to provide increased employment possibilities for the idle poor. During the final decades of the colonial regime, the Tobacco Factory employed thousands of men, women and children, alleviating, somewhat the problem of chronic unemployment and underemployment in the city. The success and profitability of the Tobacco Factory encouraged colonial officials and the crown to sponsor the development of other state enterprises, but, most of these later efforts met with little success.[27]

In addition to the formulation of special criminal legislation and the establishment of public works projects and state enterprises, colonial officials modified the punishments that were given to convicted criminals. Jail sentences, whipping, mutilation, amputation, hanging, and other corporal punishments were increasingly replaced by convict labor and other correctional procedures considered more "rational," or more "effective." To a significant degree, the increased use of convict labor reflected the influence of the new Enlightenment ideas; notably those of the Italian criminologist, Cesare Beccaria. Criticizing the existing penal codes as ineffective and the "mere tool of the passions of some," Beccaria insisted that the establishment of humane laws and punishments, based on "the compact of men," would result in a decline of criminality. To this end, he recommended a thorough reform of the legal codes, the elimination of inhumane punishments, and the establishment of more "rational" correctional procedures designed to "rehabilitate" criminals. Beccaria's proposal to reform the legal codes in a more egalitarian manner was largely ignored but his proposal to establish more humane or rehabilitative forms of correction had considerable influence among the Bourbon reformers. Torture, mutilation, amputation, and other brutal punishments declined during the eighteenth century, while the use of convict labor, houses of correction, and other, more "rehabilitative" forms of punishment increased. Although the Bourbon reformers were quick to cite the rehabilitative aspects of these correctional procedures, the emphasis on rehabilitation was ignored in actual practice. With few exceptions, moral guidance, vocational training and other measures designed to rehabilitate lawbreakers were never incorporated into the correctional programs.[28]

Already important during the seventeenth and early eighteenth centuries, the use of convict labor increased significantly during the second half of the eighteenth century. In Mexico City, persons convicted for vagrancy, indebtedness or for serious crimes, such as murder and grand larceny, were sold to private employers for terms of up to eight years to help defray the cost of operating the criminal justice system and to provide the city's artisan workshops with a relatively inexpensive alternative to wage labor.[29] Convicts were also used on government sponsored public works projects, usually in work that was unsavory, dangerous, and otherwise unattractive to wage laborers. In the 1790s, for example, persons convicted for minor offenses, such as public intoxication and disorderly conduct, were sentenced to serve in one of the city's sanitation brigades for periods of several days to several weeks. Observers agreed that cleaning the city streets and canals was most disgreeable and characteristically unhealthful. Convict laborers were forced to enter the cold, foul-smelling, polluted waters of the canals to remove refuse and other debris, and it was not unusual for the convicts to experience a rapid decline in their health after only a few days exposure to this kind of work.[30] After 1767, persons convicted for major crimes were also sent in large numbers to Vera Cruz, Havana, Puerto Rico, and other distant localities to work in frontier fortifications. Convicts were sentenced to terms of from two to ten years as servants or as unskilled construction workers, with an eight-year sentence to the very unhealthful environment of Havana or Vera Cruz, considered tantamount to a death sentence.[31]

As a matter of law, women were not to be sentenced to rigorous terms of penal servitude in deference to their sex. During the late colonial period, however, women convicted for vagrancy, theft, murder, prostitution, repeated adultery and other offenses of a moral nature, were frequently sold, along with men, to one of the city's artisan workshops. Municipal records for 1740 demonstrate that eleven women were sold to a hatmaker's workshop and several textile enterprises, where they were employed as spinners or as domestics.[32] Women convicted of serious crimes were also incarcerated for terms of from two to ten years in the *Recogimiento de Santa María Magdalena*, a house of corrections for wayward women—a precursor of the nineteenth century penitentiary. The *recogimiento*, founded in 1692 and administered directly by the state after 1767, was established to rehabilitate the inmates in conformity with the guidelines promoted by the Enlightenment reformers of the early eighteenth century. The regulations that governed the administration of the *recogimiento* stipulated that the inmates be given proper moral guidance and be made to work on "moderate" tasks considered suitable for women. Subjected to a strict work regime, the women were employed in the spinning of cotton, sewing, washing, cooking, grinding corn, and in other domestic work considered useful to society. The goods produced by the inmates were destined for internal use or they were sold in the open market to obtain operating funds for the *recogimiento*. The actual purpose of this work, however, was the correction of idleness and bad habits, and the promotion of a work ethic. To this end, the inmates also received two hours of religious instruction and prayer in the evening, as well as suffering harsh disciplinary action for any acts of disobedience or rebelliousness against the authorities.[33]

In the late colonial period, vagrant and wayward women were also placed "*en depósito*" in the household of selected and "honorable" families. These women were usually accused or convicted for minor transgressions of a moral nature, such as adultery, "licentiousness," and disobedience to their husbands. In addition to short jail sentences, the placement of women "*en depósito*" was the principal means of detention and correction for women convicted of minor offenses after the decline of corporal punishment in the latter part of the eighteenth century. As in the case of the *recogimiento*, the objective of placing women "*en depósito*" was rehabilitation. Vagrant and wayward women were placed in "honorable" households for several weeks or several months to learn proper Christian habits and correct female deportment. This practice was, in fact, a thinly disguised subterfuge for involuntary servitude. Each year, hundreds of middle and upper class families were able to secure inexpensive servants through the placement of "*depositadas*" in their households. The women worked as cooks, laundresses, or chambermaids, but there is little evidence that they received the required moral guidance or training. Many women placed "*en depósito*" complained that they were beaten and made to work long hours without food or drink, while others complained of poor living conditions and abuse by the men of the households.[34]

In addition to creating criminal legislation and promoting more effective and rational correctional procedures, the Mexico City urban elite also responded to the challenge of crime by expanding the city's judiciary and law enforcement agencies. From the sixteenth to the early eighteenth century, Mexico City's judicial structure was composed of the *audiencia*, the municipal court, and two Indian courts for the *barrios* of Santiago Tlatelolco and San Juan. First established in 1528, the *audiencia* was divided into a civil and a criminal court. The civil court was composed of eight judges, called *oidores*, who tried cases on appeal and reviewed all sentences given by the magistrates of the lower courts. The *oidores* of the civil court also had important political powers. They formulated legislation in cooperation with the viceroy and the crown, served the viceroy as a council of state, and were often called upon to govern the viceroyalty during an emergency or upon the sudden death of a viceroy. In contrast, the criminal court, or *sala del crimen*, consisted of only four justices called *alcaldes del crimen*. These magistrates, however had no political role or function, and generally enjoyed less prestige than the *oidores* of the civil court.

Throughout the colonial period, the judges of the *audiencia*, both civil and criminal, exercised supreme appellate authority over the lower courts of the viceroyality. The *audiencia*, through the *sala del crimen*, also acted as a court of first instance for Mexico City and its suburbs. This meant that the *alcaldes del crimen* could try cases of theft, burglary, assault, murder, and other crimes, like their counterparts in the lower courts. The day-to-day operations of the *audiencia*

STRUCTURE OF THE CRIMINAL JUSTICE SYSTEM IN MEXICO CITY 1790

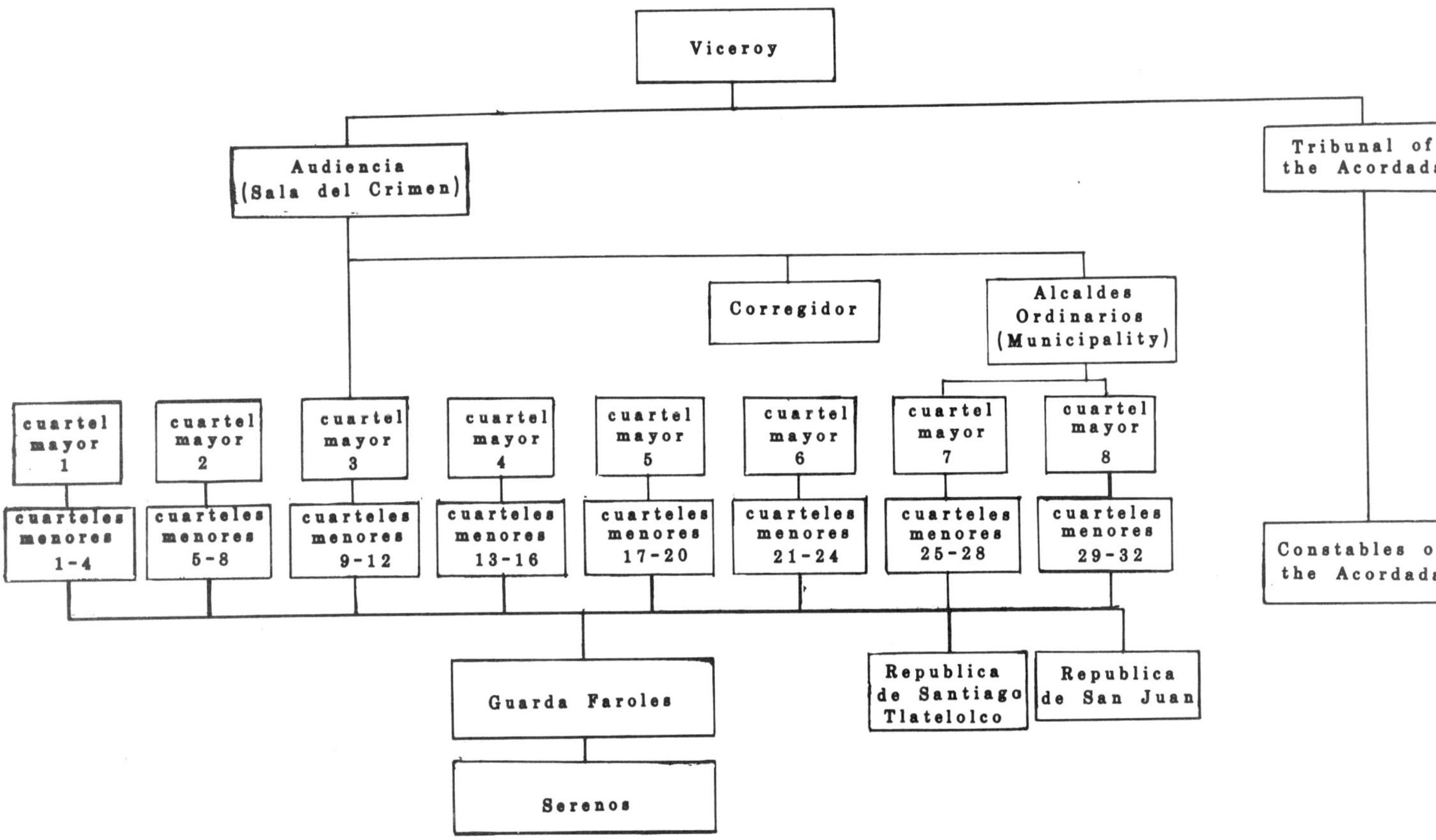

FIGURE 1

were administered by two or three *fiscales*, or chief prosecuting attorneys, who were assigned to the civil or criminal court. In the criminal court, the *fiscal del crimen* directed a complex bureaucracy of scribes, jail keepers, notaries, assistant prosecutors, attorneys for the defense, and special "lawyers for the poor." The *fiscal del crimen* also directed a corps of constables who patrolled the city streets and were responsible for the arrest of lawbreakers and for other law enforcement duties.[35]

Although the *sala del crimen* played an important role in the prosecution of local criminal cases, the municipal court was, in fact, the principal tribunal of first instance for Mexico City until the latter part of the eighteenth century. Established in the early sixteenth century, the municipal court consisted of two judges called *alcaldes ordinarios* or *jueces ordinarios*. The *alcaldes ordinarios* had the authority to prosecute both civil and criminal cases, but they were subservient to the magistrates of the *audiencia*, who reviewed their cases on appeal. The *alcaldes ordinarios* were also responsible for their own bureaucracy of assistants, notaries, jail keepers and scribes, but day-to-day enforcement activities were delegated to an *alguacil mayor*, or chief constable. The *alguacil mayor* directed a corps of constables and municipal watchmen called *guardas de pito*, who were responsible for assisting the inhabitants of the city during fire or personal emergency. There were times, however, when they were called upon to assist the constables in the performance of their duties. In addition to the municipal court, the designated Indian barrios of Santiago Tlatelolco and San Juan had their own judiciary and law enforcement agents. Like their counterparts in the municipal court, the Indian magistates had the authority to try civil and criminal cases within their jurisdictions. There was also a Royal Indian Court or *juzgado general de indios*, a special tribunal established in 1573 to review all cases involving Indians. The *juzgado*, however, had no jurisdictional function in Mexico City, because the city was the seat of the *audiencia*, and the *audiencia* normally reviewed all the cases that were tried by the *juzgado* on appeal.[36]

The Mexico City judicial system remained relatively unchanged during the early colonial period. In the early eighteenth century, however, the crown sponsored an expansion of both the judiciary and the law enforcement agencies in response to what was perceived as an intolerable increase in street crime. The creation of new criminal legislation and the emphasis on convict labor and other "rehabilitative" forms of correction were supplemented with an expansion of the *audiencia* and an increase in the number of constables patrolling the city streets. Nevertheless, the first really significant change to effect the urban judicial and law enforcement structure was implemented in 1756, when the crown authorized the tribunal of the *acordada* to police the city streets, along with the *sala del crimen* and the municipal authorities.[37]

The *acordada* was a special law enforcement agency created in 1719 to deal with the serious problem of rural banditry. In order to destroy the large number of bandit squadrons that infested the major roads of central Mexico, the crown granted the tribunal extra-legal powers to prosecute bandits and lawbreakers and execute sentences without the prior approval of the *audiencia*. In the years that followed, the judges of the *acordada* became famous for their campaigns against bandits and guerrillas. Their success and their ability to restore order in the countryside motivated the crown to grant the *acordada* extra-legal authority to apprehend lawbreakers in Mexico City after 1756. Under the new arrangement, it was understood that the *acordada* would emphasize the prosecution of major property crimes, while the *sala del crimen* and the municipal authorities would emphasize the prosecution of violent crimes and other offenses considered less serious in nature. The extra-legal powers and the independence enjoyed by the *acordada*, in fact, complicated the administration of justice to a considerable degree. In the years that followed, the *audiencia* actively sought to end the *acordada's* independence, which led to frequent quarrels over court records, jurisdictional prerogatives, procedures of arrest and incarceration, and other legal matters.[38]

In recognition of these jurisdictional problems, a somewhat more rational and effective judicial and law enforcement structure was established in the latter part of the eighteenth century. In 1781, the city was divided into eight districts or *cuarteles mayores*, which were then sub-divided into thirty-two smaller sectors called *cuarteles menores* (see figure 1). This structure, which permitted a greater degree of coordination between the *sala del crimen*, the municipal authorities, and their respective law enforcement agencies, was modeled upon the *cuartel* system that had been recently established in Madrid and other Spanish cities. Five *alcaldes del crimen* from the *audiencia*, the two *alcaldes ordinarios*, and the *corregidor* of Mexico City and Tacuba were, henceforth, assigned to one of the city's eight *cuarteles mayores* as judges of first instance. They were also made responsible for the supervision of thirty-two *alcaldes de barrio* and their constables, each of whom was assigned to one of the city's *cuarteles menores*. The *alcaldes de barrio* were, in effect, precinct captains with limited judicial responsibilites. They were authorized to hear pre-trial testimony, prepare legal briefs, and complete other preliminary judicial procedures. Their primary responsibility, however, was law enforcement and the maintenance of public order. As chief law enforcement officers, they were assigned a notary and a corps of constables who patrolled the city streets in search of thieves, muggers, pickpockets and other delinquents. Not limited to the boundaries of the *cuartel menor* to which they were assigned, the *alcaldes de barrio* and their constables were authorized to apprehend lawbreakers and maintain public order throughout the city.

The creation of the *cuartel* system was an important innovation that reflected the "enlightened despotism" of the eighteenth century, as well as a desire to improve the effectiveness of the judicial system in Mexico City. In addition to their role as law enforcement officers, the *alcaldes de barrio* were responsible for duties that were directly related to the preservation of social control and the "proper functioning of society." Each *alcalde de barrio* was required to keep an accurate registry of the number of inhabitants in his district. This registry was to include the number of births, deaths, single women, widows, orphans, and transients, as well as their place of birth, age, ethnic classification and place of residence or destination. In addition, the *alcalde de barrio* was required to keep a careful record of all the commercial establishments and workshops in his district, as part of the general effort to "encourage industry and the arts" among the city's inhabitants. He also had to ensure that the streets and canals in his district were clean, that other essential services were properly maintained, and he was expected to remain in constant communication with neighboring *alcaldes* in order to obtain timely information on events and changes in their districts.[39]

In the years that followed the establishment of the *cuartel* system, other measures were instituted to augment the power of the city law enforcement agencies. Elaborate plans were devised to straighten and reorganize the city streets, especially in the more chaotic outer barrios. Observers and government officials even proposed the construction of a wall around Mexico City in an effort to improve the maintenance of public order. In 1787, Hipolito Villarroel, a chief prosecutor in the *acordada*, enthusiastically proposed the construction of a wall to "secure the King's revenue from smugglers and contrabandists" and to "cleanse the city of the many useless and licentious persons... who have no destiny, nor fixed occupation with which they can support themselves."[40] These ambitious plans, however, were never brought to fruition and the authorities had to satisfy themselves with the implementation of measures that were more modest in character. In 1790, the viceroy, Conde de Revillagigedo, established a street lighting system in Mexico City that employed a corps of watchmen called *guarda faroles*. Each guard was responsible for the care of twelve street lamps and was given permission to carry arms, apprehend lawbreakers, and otherwise maintain public order in his district. Acting as a supplementary force, they assisted the *alcaldes de barrio* and their constables, and worked closely with the *guardas de pito* (by then called *serenos*), by patrolling the patrolling the city streets during the evening hours when thefts, burglaries, assaults, and other crimes were more prevalent.[41]

The expansion of law enforcement agencies and the judiciary in the late eighteenth century was made possible by a general increase in state revenues. Increased revenues were derived from the new taxes, which were imposed on pulque, wine, vinegar, and other products. At the same time, a rise in silver production and the expansion of the export economy also provided the state with an increase in tax receipts. At the beginning of the eighteenth century, New Spain produced annual tax revenues of 3,000,000 pesos. By the end of the century, however, this figure reached an annual average of 20,000,000 pesos. Much of this revenue was used to support the expanded civil and military administration in New Spain during the final decades of the colonial regime. This included increased support for public works projects and expansion of the criminal justice system in Mexico City.[42]

In general, colonial officials appeared to have been satisfied with the reorganization and the improved performance of the criminal justice system. The viceroys of the late eighteenth century, in particular, seemed to be less preoccupied with crime than the viceroys of the late seventeenth and early eighteenth centuries. In fact, in the late 1790s, there seemed to be a greater concern for the activities of foreign subversives and the abuse of suspects in the jails than there was with criminality itself.[43] Nevertheless, other influential persons continued to complain about the prevalence of crime. Begging, vagrancy, public drunkenness, incorrigible children, family disputes, theft, assault, and murder were still seen as serious problems, and despite the expansion and reorganization of the criminal justice system, colonial officials were encouraged to increase their efforts to apprehend and punish lawbreakers.[44] Although there is no clear evidence that demonstrates a proportional increase in the urban crime rate at any time during the eighteenth century, there is reason to believe that, there might have been an increse in the number of crimes in the years between 1770 and 1810 because of a rising population and a deterioration in livng conditions among the urban poor.

The Bourbon reforms of the late eighteenth century generated greater wealth for the upper class and increased revenues for the state. However, the reforms also cultivated greater economic and social inequality in colonial society. The government, for example, initiated a concerted attack on the artisan guilds during the late eighteenth century on grounds that they were a hindrance to economic development. The Bourbon reformers advocated a free labor market as a means of stimulating production in manufacturing and looked upon the guild system as a wasteful holdover of medieval monopoly and privilege. In Spain, where private manufacturing was consciously encouraged by government policies, the attack on the guild system appears to have generated the desired increase in production. In Mexico, however, where independent industry was largely discouraged, the attack on the guild system appears to have resulted in the progressive impoverishment of the artisan class, a process that also affected the urban poor as a whole. Between 1770 and 1810, the artisan and non-artisan workforce was constantly afflicted by monetary inflation, stable or declining wage scales, and increased periods of unemployment and underemployment.[45] The level of crime, as a result, may have increased during the same period, especially the level of crime among lower status artisans. Nevertheless, the criminal justice system should not be judged a failure. As some criminologists have pointed out, the effectiveness of any criminal justice system should be measured, not on its ability to reduce the crime rate, but on its ability to manage, regulate, and otherwise control the level of criminality. In Mexico City, despite a possible increase in crime during the final decades of the colonial regime, it is clear the the criminal justice system was able to maintain the level of criminality at acceptable or tolerable levels. At the same time, it is also certain that individuals dependent on the continued existence of the criminal justice system for their jobs and livelihood, such as judges, prosecutors, lawyers, and law enforcement agents, were not very anxious to reduce the level of criminality to a significant degree.[46]

NOTES

[1]IVMC 1966:53.

[2]For comments on the prevalence of crime in the late colonial urban environment, see Gemelli Carreri (1955, II:176 and *passim*), Cabrera y Quintero (1746:255 and *passim*), IVNE (1867:6-10, 18-19, 303-4, 306-8), IVMC (1966:53, 84-85), Sedano (1880, I:90-93; II:53-54) and Villarroel (1831:34, 37, 45, 62-64, 70, 99, 101-7, 109-11, 114-17, 120-27 and *passim*).

[3]Studies on crime and the administration of justice in late colonial Mexico include: MacLachlan (1974), Taylor (1979), Burkholder and Chandler (1977), Muriel (1974), Fernández-Mensaque (1950), Kagan (1979), Bazán Alarcón (1963) Montgomery (1973), Scardaville (1977), and Haslip-Viera (1979).

[4]This article is largely based on materials consulted in the following Mexico City archives: Archivo General de la Nación, Archivo Historico del Ayuntamiento de la Ciudad de México, Archivo Judicial del Tribunal Superior de Justicia del Distrito Federal, and Archivo General de los Juzgados Unitarios Penales.

[5]For a discussion of general economic and social conditions in late colonial Mexico City, see: Gibson (1964:368-402 and *passim*), Brading (1971:95-128, 159-219, and *passim*), Ladd (1976:53-70 and *passim*), Carrera Stampa (1954), Florescano (1969:85-197 and *passim*), Cooper (1965), Anna (1978:3-34, 140-78, and *passim*), Moreno Toscano (1978), Martin (1972:261-94), Morales (1976:363-402), Scardaville (1980:643-71), Kicza (1982), Patricia See, Social Dimensions of Race: Mexico City, 1753, *Hispanic American Historical Review*, 62 (Nov. 1982), 569-606. Valdés (1978), McWatters (1979), Salvucci (1982), Scardaville (1977) and Haslip-Viera (1979).

[6]For estimates on the cost of living in late colonial Mexico City, see AGN-B 7-33; AHA-CG 495-44-1-4; 48-20-35. For data on daily wages in late colonial Mexico City, see AGN-A 4-168-173; 5-172-178, 187-188, 192-192v; 26-270-273v; AGN-Cr 58-14-205; AGN-Ta 84; AHA-CG 495-2-8-13v; AHA-JP 449-34-1-1v, 1790; AHA-PP 3453-60-1; 3453-74-7.

[7]Carrera Stampa (1954:48-49); Martin (1972:275). For a general discussion of daily wages and their relationship to the cost of living in late colonial Mexico City, Anna (1978: 16, 19, 22-24), see McWatters (1979:153-58, 164-65, 242-47, and *passim*); Salvucci (1982:269-77 and *passim*); Scardaville (1977:66-68, 72, 88-89); Haslip-Viera (1979:56-67).

[8]For the comments of residents and visitors to Mexico City in the late colonial period, see Humboldt (1822, I:184-85; II:71-73), Ajofrin (1958, I:81), IVNE (1867:7, 21, 305-8), Villarroel (1831:74, 90-91, 107-10, 125-27, 131, 134-35).

[9]The quantitative records include judicial hearings, trial inventories, prison registers, arrest records, and *presidio* sentences, which were compiled by the various colonial law enforcement agencies. From the standpoint of quantitative analysis, the most useful documents are the arrest and incarceration records, called *Libros de reos* or *Libros de entradas*. Located in the Archivo Histórico del Ayuntamiento de la Ciudad de México, and the Archivo Judicial del Tribunal Superior del Distrito Federal, and the Archivo General los Juzgados Unitarios Penales, the few remaining volumes cover the years 1708-1711, 1723-1724, 1740-1742, 1794-1796, 1798, 1800, and 1807. Within this group, the books covering the years 1795-1796 and 1798 yield the most detailed or complete bibliographical information on the suspects arrested by the municipal authorities in Mexico City. For a discussion of the advantages of arrest records over other kinds of crime statistics, see Sellin (1931:346).

[10]The proposition that official statistics represent the operational activities of institutions charged with the administration of public order is discussed in Kitsuse and Cicourel (1963:131-39), Newman (1962:144-55), Quinney (1966:45-53) and Wheeler (1967:317-24). For a discussion of the usefulness and the inadequacies of crime statistics as they relate to colonial Mexico, see Taylor (1979:3-9, 73-77, 178-82) and MacLachlan (1974:50-51).

[11]Florescano (1969:128, 130-31, 159-61, 201, 203, and *passim*). MacLachlan has suggested that there existed an informal division of responsibility between the various tribunals and law enforcement agencies that operated in

Mexico City, with some placing their emphasis on the prosecution of major property and violent crimes, and others placing their emphasis on the prosecution of minor infractions, such as vagrancy, public drunkenness, and family disputes. See MacLachlan (1974:22, 51, 53, 78).

[12]See Marvin E. Wolfgang, *Patterns of Criminal Homicide* (Philadelphia, 1958), pp. 65-78 and Federal Bureau of Investigation, U.S. Department of Justice, *Crime in the United States: Uniform Crime Reports, 1979* (Washington, D.C. 1980), p. 198. For a discussion of violent crimes by young adults in the rural areas of Oaxaca and central Mexico during the late colonial period, see Taylor (1979:83-84).

[13]AGN-Cr 60-1-8-9 and *passim;* AJ-LR. *Alcalde ordinario mas antiguo*, 1795-1796, fols. 46-128; Humboldt (1822, IV:292).

[14]IVMC (1966:85), IVNE (1867:10), AFAMBU (1936, II:160-61). Surprisingly, the records show that few women were actually arrested for prostitution Four women were charged with this infraction in 1796, but none were convicted. It was apparently much more difficult to convict a woman for prostitution, especially if she was an "occasional prostitute," than it was to convict her for "fornication," which was considered a lesser offense. A review of the documentary evidence for the years 1795 through 1807 indicates that arrests for prostitution accounted for only 2.5 some form of conviction: a figure that was almost certainly not a reflection of the actual amount of prostitution. Attitudes toward female criminality in early and late colonial Mexico are discussed in Muriel (1974) and Taylor (1979:45, 53, 58, 84-85, 92-95, 108, 154-56, 197n, and *passim*).

[15]Elite attitudes toward crime and its relationship to ethnicity are discussed in MacLachlan (1974:40-41) and Taylor (1979:17, 40-3, 45, 64-65, 103-104, and passim.

[16]The disproportionately large number of caucasians arrested for gambling and indebtedness and the large number of *mestizos* arrested for indebtedness probably reflects the relatively higher socio-economic status of Spaniards, creoles and *mestizos* in colonial society.

[17]For a discussion of this issue leading to similar conclusions, see Scardaville (1977:19-20 and *passim*).

[18]On the problems faced by artisans in late colonial Mexico, see Carrera Stampa (1954:231, 265-75), González Angulo (1979:32-36) and González Angulo and Sandoval Zarauz (1980:173-238). On the relationship between crimes and occupational status, see also MacLachlan (1974:38-39, 44-47, 116) and Scardaville (1977:20-22 and *passim*).

[19]The Spanish law codes and their application to colonial society are discussed in Floris Margadant (1971:123-25), MacLachlan (1974:1-8, 12, 37-39, 42-44, and *passim*), Taylor (1979:74-76, 97-106, and *passim*).

[20]MacLachlan (1974:40-42); Taylor (1979:17, 42-43, 65-66, and *passim*).

[21]Sellin (1970:10).

[22]For a general discussion of these issues, see Gerbi (1960).

[23]Callahan (1971:2-3, 9).

[24]Callahan (1971:7-8); Herr (1958:47-50); Sarrailh (1957:527-37); Cintrón Tiryakian (1978:233-257).

[25]See especially the comments made by the viceroys Duque de Linares and Conde de Revilla-Gigedo (1746-1755) in IVNE (1867:6-10, 302-9).

[26]Bando, Conde de Revilla-Gigedo, Mexico City, May 21, 1748, AGN-B 4-35-15-17; Bando, Marqués de Croix, Mexico City, September, 1766, AGN-B 6-45; Bando, Marqués de Croix, Mexico City, February 26, 1767, AGN-B 57.

[27]IVMC (1966:18, 30); Martin (1972:268, 272, 277). On the tobacco factory and the efforts to establish other state enterprises in late colonial Mexico, see McWatters (1979) and Serrera Contreras (1974:117-22, 146-50).

[28]Sarrailh (1957:537-43). On the failure to establish effective measures to rehabilitate female convicts, see Muriel (1974:115-21 and *passim*). The notion that the use of convict labor increased during the eighteenth century is based, in part, on an analysis of quantitative data for the tribunal of the *acordada*, which is found in *Inventario de Causas de la Acordada*, AGN, vol. 1.

[29]IVMC (1966:63-64); AFAMBU (1936, II:251-52, 257-65). On the use of convict laborers in the *obrajes* of late seventeenth-century Mexico, see Kagan (1979:201-14).

[30]*Ordenanzas para el...Presidio de San Carlos*, Marqués de Croix, Mexico City, April 7, 1769, AGN-B 7-33; AJ, *Libro de Reos de la bara del Señor Corregidor*, 1796, fols. 1-124v; AHA-PSC 3709-2; AHA-CG 495-51; IVMC (1966:76); Humboldt (1822, II:33).

[31]Bando, Marqués de Croix, Mexico City, June 7, 1767, AGN-B 6-68; AGN-RA 14-11-11v, 122; IVMC (1966:63-64). For a description of conditions in the Presidio of San Juan de Ulúa in Vera Cruz, see AGN-CP 29-150-200.

[32]AHA-RACCP 3839-4. On the sentences that women were supposed to receive under the law, see Escriche (1837:456-58, 581).

[33]For a discussion of the *recogimientos* of colonial Mexico and the failure of these institutions to implement effective measures to rehabilitate female inmates, see Muriel (1974:115-21 and *passim*). For the rules and regulations that governed the administration of the *recogimientos* in the late colonial period, see *Reales cédulas de erección y ordenanzas de la casa de recogidas de la ciudad de Guadalajara, 1797*, in Alemán and Iguíniz (1909, I:134-50).

[34]AHA-RACCP 3839-4; AJ-P V, 1791-1792, exp. 8; VII, 1796-1799, exp. 72.

[35]On the criminal courts of colonial Mexico, see Burkholder and Chandler (1977:*passim*); MacLachlan (1974:21-25 and *passim*). Also, see Haring (1947:120-21).

[36]MacLachlan (1974:24-25). Haring (1947:121, 150-52); Greenleaf (1967:248).

[37]MacLachlan (1974:35,70); Bazán Alarcón (1963:85). On the expansion of the Mexican *Audiencia* in the early eighteenth century, see Burkholder and Chandler (1977:46-47).

[38]MacLachlan (:22, 51, 53, 78-79, 94).

[39]Báez Maciás (1969:59-69, 75-106).

[40]Villarroel (1831:110-111). The proposals to straighten streets and improve the Mexico City urban environment in the late colonial period are discussed in Lombardo Ruíz (1979:169-88).

[41]*Reglamiento formado de órden del Exmò. Señor Virrey Conde de Revilla-Gigedo para el gobierno que ha de observarse en el alumbrado de las calles de México*, Mexico City, April 7, 1790, AGN-B 15-158-161v; Bando, Conde de Revilla-Gigedo, Mexico City, April 15 1790, AGN-B 15-60-175; Revilla-Gigedo (1966:177-78).

[42]See Brading (1971:29-30).

[43]See, for example, the comments made by Viceroy Felix Berenguer de Marquina in IVNE (1867:168, 170-71, and *passim*).

[44]On the continued prevalence of crime in the late colonial urban environment, see Villarroel (1831:53, 55-56, 63, 99, 106-7, 109-11, 114-17, 125-27). See also the comments that were made by Lic. Joseph Lebron, a prosecutor in the *Audiencia* of Mexico in AHA-PG 3627-50-3v.

[45]For a discussion of the effects of the Bourbon reforms, and the attack on the guilds in late colonial Mexico, see Carrera Stampa (1954:231, 265-75); Herr (1958:125); González Angulo (1979:32-36); González Angulo and Sandoval Zarauz (1980:173-238); Tanck de Estrada (1979:311-31).

[46]On the management and control of crime, see Silver (1974:2 and *passim*). On the vested interests of lawyers, prosecutor, and law enforcement agents, see the Introduction and the articles by Max Lowenthal, Arthur Millspaugh, Alfred Lindesmith, Donald T. Jackson, and Joseph T. Goulden, which appear in the same volume.

TABLE 1
DIFFERENCES IN THE STRUCTURE OF URBAN CRIME, 1710, 1741, 1796
ARREST RECORDS OF THE MEXICO CITY MUNICIPAL COURT

	1710	*1741*	*1796*
Violent Crimes	29 percent	10 percent	9 percent
Theft and other Property Crimes	16 percent	17 percent	15 percent
Nonviolent Family Disputes (Adultery, Neglect, Abandonment, etc.)	4 percent	9 percent	10 percent
Fornication and other Sex Crimes	10 percent	9 percent	16 percent
Vagrancy, Drunkenness, and Gambling	12 percent	3 percent	10 percent
Selling Prohibited Liquors	8 percent	1 percent	1 percent
Indebtedness	25 percent	10 percent	7 percent
Failure to Pay Tribute	11 percent	0	0
Disorderly Conduct, Obstruction of Justice, etc.	2 percent	5 percent	3 percent
Unspecified Offenses	5 percent	36 percent	29 percent
Total	100 percent	100 percent	100 percent
	N = 334	N = 1898	N = 502

Source: AHA-RACCP, vol. 3839, exp. 1,5. AJ-LR. Alcalde ordinario mas antiguo. 1795-1796 fols. 46–128.

TABLE 2
AGE STRUCTURE OF THE POPULATION OF MEXICO CITY, 1790
AND OF INDIVIDUALS APPREHENDED BY THE MUNICIPAL AUTHORITIES, 1796

Age	*Persons Arrested 1796*	*Population of Mexico City 1790*
0-15	6 percent	35 percent
16-39	83 percent	46 percent
40-	11 percent	19 percent

Source: AGN-IO, vol. 51, no. 48, fol. 2. Humboldt 1822, IV:292. AJ-LR. Alcalde ordinario mas antiguo. 1795-1796, fols. 46-128.

TABLE 3
PERCENTAGE OF MEN AND WOMEN APPREHENDED FOR SPECIFIED CRIMES BY THE MEXICO CITY MUNICIPAL AUTHORITIES, 1796

	Men	*Women*
Violent Crimes	16 percent	11 percent
Theft and other Property Crimes	26 percent	16 percent
Nonviolent Family Disputes (Adultery, Neglect, Abandonment, etc.)	11 percent	20 percent
Fornication and other Sex Crimes	17 percent	34 percent
Vagrancy and Public Drunkenness	14 percent	11 percent
Gambling	3 percent	0
Indebtedness	11 percent	5 percent
Disorderly Conduct and Ostruction of Justice	2 percent	3 percent
	100 percent	100 percent
Total	N = 235	N = 121

Source: AJ-LR. Alcalde ordinario mas antiguo. 1795-1796, fols. 46-128.

TABLE 4
PERSONS APPREHENDED BY THE MUNICIPAL AUTHORITIES, 1796
COMPARED TO THE ETHNIC COMPOSITION OF MEXICO CITY'S POPULATION, 1790

Caucasian	*Percent Defined as Indian*	*Percent Defined as Mestizo*	*Percent Defined as mulato*	*Percent Defined as*	
Population of Mexico City, 1790	48	24	20	7	N=104760
Persons Apprehended by the Municipal Court, 1796	33	37	24	6	N=489
Specified Crimes, 1796					
Violent Crimes	21	56	19	4	N=52
Theft and other Property Crimes	24	44	21	11	N=84
Nonviolent Family Disputes (Adultery, Abandonment, etc.)	41	34	20	5	N=56
Fornication and other Sex Crimes	28	30	31	11	N=74
Vagrancy, Public Drunkenness and Disorderly Conduct	38	31	27	4	N=55
Gambling	83	0	17	0	N=6
Indebtedness	46	22	32	0	N=37

Source: AGN-IO, vol. 51, no. 48, fol. 2. Humboldt 1822, IV:292. AJ-LR. Alcalde ordinarios mas antiguo. 1795-1796, fols. 46-128

TABLE 5

SOCIO-ECONOMIC BACKGROUND OF INDIVIDUALS APPREHENDED FOR VARIOUS INFRACTIONS BY THE MEXICO CITY MUNICIPAL AUTHORITIES, 1796

Socio-Economic Background	Percent Violent Crimes	Percent Property Crimes	Percent Family Disputes	Percent Fornication, Sex Crimes	Percent Debt	Percent Vagrancy, Drunk, Gambling, etc.	Total
Elite	0	0	0	0	7	0	1
Pre-Industrial Middle Class	5	3	0	6	3	2	3
Lower Strata							
Higher Status Artisans	16	12	30	16	24	20	18
Lower Status Artisans	58	39	55	46	50	47	48
Unskilled Workers, Street Vendors and the Unemployed	21	46	15	32	16	31	30
Total	100	100	100	100	100	100	100
	N=38	N=61	N=20	N=37	N=30	N=45	N=231

[1] All the persons arrested by the municipal authorities in 1796 were categorized in conformance to the occupational structure based on socio-economic status, which is found in Haslip-Viera 1979:279-88.

Source: AJ-LR. Alcalde ordinario mas antiguo. 1795-1796, fols. 46-128.

THE LEGAL COMMUNITY OF LATE COLONIAL MEXICO: SOCIAL COMPOSITION AND CAREER PATTERNS

John Kicza

From the mid eighteenth century until early in the national period, the legal community of Mexico was organized around the *Colegio de Abogados* (College of Lawyers) which, in any year, consisted of several hundred attorneys who were almost exclusively Spanish by blood, Mexican by birth, and holders of advanced degrees from the University of Mexico. They differed in their places of birth within the colony—although a distinct plurality came from the capital—and in the wealth of their families. The vast majority were from families of property and standing, although only a few belonged to the highest elite.[1]

The crown authorized the foundation of the *Ilustre y Real Colegio de Abogados* in 1760 in response to a petition by prominent creole lawyers from the jurisdiction of the *audiencia* of Mexico. The organization was empowered to determine what attorneys could practice within the boundaries of the *audiencia*, to exclude all nonmembers from employment in the royal bureaucracy, and to elect its own officers annually.[2] These consisted of a rector, nine *conciliarios*, a number of examiners (divided into those who held the post in perpetuity and those who were elected on an annual basis), the *colegio's* own legal representative, a secretary, a treasurer, a notary, and some minor officials. Rectors were eligible for reelection, and although considerable turnover was normal, some were elected to consecutive terms. One rector served for five years between 1806 and 1810.

The rectorship was by far the most powerful and prestigious post in the lawyers' guild. Its occupant was invariably a well-respected member of the profession and typically served in one or more positions of responsibility in the capital. He might be a member of the government bureaucracy, a *regidor* of the city, the proprietor of a professorial chair (*cátedra*) at the university, the rector of a college or of the university, or a member of the ecclesiastical bureaucracy. Conceivably, the rector could be a member of the cathedral chapter, for in this era a significant minority of lawyers were also clerics.

A preliminary survey of the entrance records of the *Colegio de Abogados* and a more detailed examination of notarial and judicial documentation illustrates that the organization was dominated overwhelmingly by creoles and that a substantial plurality of the membership came from Mexico city itself. Table 1 displays this information in a more graphic manner. When judges and prosecutors of the *audiencia* are excluded, well under 10 percent of the lawyers were peninsulars, and the number from other parts of Spanish America is insignificant. Something over a third of the legal community was born in Mexico City itself. The 45 percent figure represented in the table is probably too high because the present study concentrates on lawyers practicing in the capital, usually something like 75 percent of the membership. The only other city that enjoyed disproportionate representation in the College of Lawyers is Puebla. Relatively few lawyers came from the region south of Mexico City or from the extreme northern provinces of New Spain. The prosperous agricultural and mining centers of the Bajío and the province of Valladolid (now Michoacan) were well represented in the membership.

respectable provincial middle class. Very few of these provincial families could rival the highest elite of Mexico City in either wealth or prominence. Few lawyers of provincial origin were themselves sons of lawyers, although it was not uncommon for a brother, cousin, uncle, or some combination to be employed as clerics, lawyers, or government officials.

Those lawyers born in the capital were far more likely to be the offspring of lawyers, physicians, or government officials than those from the hinterland. But once again, a substantial contingent came from well-off mercantile or agricultural families. Still, only a small minority of families at the pinnacle of colonial society sent even one son into the practice of law. Finally, no lawyers emerged from the substantial population of artisans, *rancheros*, and mill and factory owners, whether the parents were of pure Spanish blood or not and whether they were from the capital or the provinces. Regulations of the *Colegio de Abogados* prohibited membership to persons whose parents or grandparents had worked with their hands or had practiced a low-status occupation. In actuality, the expense of higher education and the prejudice faced by any child of low social rank, even if of pure Spanish extraction, were at least as effective as these rules in keeping the offspring of such occupational groups out of the legal profession.

While the above-mentioned factors kept the Spanish craft and manual workers from entrance into the profession, very different ones held down the number of lawyers from the highest ranks of the colonial elite. Offspring from titled Mexican families, wholesale merchants, miners, and large estate owners simply did not flock to the practice of law. They did maintain a presence and supplied some of the country's most influential lawyers, but when one considers the number of families in the colonial elite (including both Mexico City and the provinces) and the membership of the College of Lawyers, usually somewhere around 275 persons, it is accurate to say that only occasionally did the highest elite families send even a single son into the profession, and very few sent more than one. As a result, at any given time, only a small number of *colegio* members came from this elevated social sector.[4]

The reasons why so few children of the elite opted for a career in law appear to be twofold. First, they did not have to train for a professional career in order to obtain suitable employment. The economic holdings of a colonial Mexican elite family were typically so large and diversified—whether based initially in commerce, mining, or agriculture—that they required loyal and competent managers and supervisors in a variety of enterprises and at different levels. As a consequence, many sons obtained employment within the family business, in the most broadly defined sense, and felt no need to enter a profession that demanded many years of schooling with no guarantee of great earnings at the end.

The second reason for not pursuing the legal profession was that it could not offer the colonial elite higher status than they already enjoyed. A lawyer from an elite family gave more prestige to the profession than it gave to him. It was the children of middle-level merchants and *hacendados*, often from the provinces, who looked to the legal profession as an avenue by which to elevate the social standing of themselves and their families. The statement of blood purity, the advanced education, the tradition, the titles and posts to which lawyers alone had access the contact with royal officials and judges, and the good income that many lawyers received were powerful attractions to persons of comfortable but not exalted station in the society. A lawyer in the family certified the family's respectability, provided it with a legal consultant, and, more importantly, afforded it

Both the low number of peninsulars and the large numbers of Mexico City natives in the lawyers' guild can be readily explained. Few peninsulars with advanced law degrees wished to travel to the colonies unless they were already guaranteed employment in the upper ranks of the royal bureaucracy, and even in the late Bourbon period, a time when the number of creole judges in the *audiencia* declined sharply, native-born attorneys were able to maintain a near monopoly over the many court positions below judge and royal prosecutor. Successful careers in this society characteristically depended heavily on personal contacts promoted by family and social ties. Given the generally high quality of legal education offered in Mexico and the surfeit of attorneys practicing, peninsulars understandably had a difficult time developing the types of relationships that would enable them to compete on equal terms with locally born and educated lawyers.

Mexico City maintained a large plurality in the membership of the *Colegio de Abogados* because of the inordinate size of its Spanish population—especially its better-off component—and because it attracted provincial elite families desirous of enrolling their sons in the city's prestigious colleges and university. The notarial documentation presents several instances in which well-to-do families from the provinces moved to the capital specifically to avail their children of the high-quality educational institutions located there. Mexico City was also the center of the colonial and ecclesiastical bureaucracies, whose members, as we shall see below, were more likely than other social groups to send their sons on for professional training.

Admission to the lawyers' guild was by regulation restricted to those who could certify that at least their previous two generations of ancestors had no traces of other than Spanish blood. Normally, an application for membership had to be accompanied by at least twelve sworn statements from reputable individuals who knew the family of the applicant certifying the devout Catholicism, untainted blood lines, and honorable occupations of his parents and both sets of grandparents. In actuality, there is considerable evidence generated by the organization's investigations that at least some of the applicants seeking to enter the body had strains of Negro or Indian blood in their families. Nonetheless, all of the affected candidates were eventually accepted into the *colegio*, although at least a couple were admitted only after they had commenced legal action charging that the honor of their family name was being slandered. These occurrences notwithstanding, virtually all lawyers were regarded by the society at large as being of Spanish extraction. The most glaring exception to this generalization was *Licenciado* Miguel Gerónimo Cequa y Morales, an Indian from Cholula who practiced law in Puebla as an attorney for prisoners and who often represented Indians before the colonial courts. He appeared in the records when he applied for the post of general interpreter for the Mexico City *Audiencia*. Ultimately, he withdrew his application because of inability to speak Otomí, the second language (in addition to Nahuatl) required for the post.[3]

While the lawyers of late colonial Mexico came from a variety of birthplaces, such diversity was not replicated in the livelihoods practiced by their families. Indeed, in this regard, certain generalizations have a broad validity. Most lawyers came from prominent families in the provinces that had made their fortunes from agriculture, commerce or some combination of the two. While some of these families were unquestionably among the most prestigious in local society, regularly holding posts in the local government or representing the colonial government in some capacity or another, many more belonged to the larger contact with influential persons in business, government, and the judiciary. The colonial elite had much less need for these benefits. They already possessed the social standing and respectability that others strove for, while blood ties, marriage, *compadrazgo*, business agreements, and mutuality of interests linked them to high ranking government and judicial officials.

As might be expected, when children of the elite did enter the legal profession, they ascended to the top ranks of its membership more rapidly and surely than did their non-elite colleagues. They rose specifically because they were from the elite, not because of their profession or their skill in it. This can be illustrated by the careers of several sets of brothers who became lawyers. The brothers Flores Alatorre, from a prominent Aguascalientes family, came as youths to study in the colleges of Mexico City. Besides becoming a lawyer, Doctor José Félix joined the church and made his career in the ecclesiastical hierarchy. He served as the curate to the parish of *La Soledad de la Santa Cruz* in Mexico City, already an auspicious beginning. He next used his legal training as a judge of the court of chaplaincies and pious endowments (*Juzgado de Capellanías y Obras Pías*) of the archbishopric of Mexico and simultaneously functioned as a *catedrático* in canon law at the university. From there he advanced to posts as legal representative and vicar general of the archbishopric and finally was elevated to the cathedral chapter, becoming the *canónigo doctoral* and serving several times as chapter governor.[5] His brother, *Licenciado* Juan José, started his distinguished legal career with the post of lawyer for the poor (*abogado de pobres*) for the *Audiencia* of Mexico and advanced rapidly up the legal ladder. Along the way he was elected rector of the College of Lawyers. In the last years of the colonial period he was appointed substitute *alcalde de corte* of Mexico and then *oidor* (first in Guadalajara, then in Mexico). After independence, he became a minister of the Supreme Court.[6]

Born in Valladolid (Morelia), *Licenciado* Melchor de Foncerrada y Ulibarri and his brother *Licenciado* José Cayetano followed career patterns quite similar to those of the Flores Alatorres. Both attended a college in Mexico City, and while one advanced in the government bureaucracy, the other did the same in the ecclesiastical. Melchor entered royal service early in his career. Serving first as a *subdelegado* in the *visita general* of Peru, he advanced to *oider* in Santo Domingo, then to *alcalde de corte* and subsequently to *oidor* of New Spain. He died an *auditor de guerra* in Mexico City in 1814.[7] *Licenciado* José Cayetano became a cleric and eventually attained the post of canon in the Mexico City cathedral chapter. He also served as vicar general of the *conventos* of the archbishopric. In 1810 he traveled to Spain and was designated a deputy to the *Cortes General*. He chose to remain in Spain and was named dean to the cathedral chapter of Lérida, perhaps fearing loss of rank if he returned to independent Mexico.[8]

From a wealthy landed family of Puebla, *Licenciado* Francisco Ignacio and Doctor Luis Gonzaga González Maldonado both pursued successful careers, the former across the globe as a judicial officer of the crown and the latter locally in Mexico City. Once again both brothers were educated in the colleges and the univerity of Mexico City. Francisco Ignacio served successfully as an *oider* of Spain, royal prosecutor for the *Casa de Contratación* in Spain, and finally back again as an *oidor* to Mexico City, where he died in 1800.[9] Doctor Luis Gonzaga remained in the capital after completing his education and obtained the post of attorney for the *parcialidad* of San Juan Tenochtitlan, one of two Indian districts in Mexico City; he also held a chair in the university. Later, he acquired the office of *regidor perpetuo* of the city, then renounced it in his old age to become a cleric.[10] There was at least one other González Maldonado brother, José Mariano; he remained in Puebla as an *hacendado* and became colonel of the city's militia regiment.[11]

Of the five sons of José Melchor de Ibarrola, a prominent wholesaler of Mexico City, two, Ignacio José and Luis Gonzaga, chose the legal profession. The other three (one a half-brother) became wealthy merchants in their own right. Ignacio José did not make his career in the practice of law; despite his training, he apparently preferred to emphasize commerce like his three brothers.[12] Success in the legal profession was left to *Licenciado* Luis Gonzaga. Probably benefitting from the stature of his father and his brothers in the commerce of the capital, Luis Gonzaga served an extended term as head notary of the Mexico City *Consulado* and still found time to work as a lawyer for prisoners of the Inquisition. Laden with honors, in 1784 he became a *familiar* of the Inquisition. He was elected and reelected rector of the lawyers' guild. His highest accolade was appointment as honorary secretary to the viceroy.[13]

Although himself a peninsular merchant, the first Marqués de Santa Cruz de Inguanzo had creole relatives in Mexico. Two of them were the brothers *Licenciado* Francisco and Doctor Marcos Inguanzo Díaz. Natives of Mexico City, both received their education in the capital and attained prominence as royal officials. *Licenciado* Francisco served as an *auditor de guerra* and then as a *fiscal* at Puerto Príncipe, while Doctor Marcos obtained appointment to the *Audiencia* of Manila.[14]

All the lawyers native to Mexico who obtained appointment to an *audiencia* in Mexico, to a cathedral chapter in the colony or abroad, or to any other high-ranking governmental or ecclesiastical post were born into the landed, commercial, or professional elite of New Spain. There were only two possible exceptions: Francisco Javier de Gamboa and Baltasar Ladrón de Guevara. Despite his fame as a government offical, little is yet known of the early life of Gamboa. Born in Guadalajara, he was educated in Mexico City under the sponsorship of an *oidor* who had taken him under his wing while serving earlier in the *Audiencia* of Guadalajara.[15] Still a young man, Gamboa traveled to Spain as representative of the Mexico City *Consulado* and returned to the colony with an appointment as an *alcalde de corte*. Ladrón de Guevara, although born in Guatemala, came to Mexico City while still a child. Even less is known about his family, but he was educated in the capital. Starting out in the government as a *relator*, without leaving Mexico he advanced to *agente fiscal, asesor del virreinato, alcalde del crimen, fiscal de lo civil, oidor*, dean, and ultimately regent of the *audiencia*. In 1760 he was among the lawyers instrumental in the foundation of the *Colegio de Abogados*.

While neither Gamboa nor Ladrón de Guevara were born into the Mexican economic elite, their lives illustrate two characteristics common to the colony's high ranking professionals. First is the tendency for the sons of professionals to become professionals themselves, although perhaps not in the same field as their fathers. Second is the high degree of nepotism acceptable in both the civil and the ecclesiastical hierarchies.

Gamboa's son, José Manuel, profited from his father's exalted position in the government and pursued a career in the church. He received his doctorate in theology at the University and quickly obtained appointment as a curate in the Valley of Mexico. He then rose to the rank of prebend in the *Colegiata* of Guadalupe before transferring to the cathedral chapter of Mexico apparently at the same rank. He was subsequntly elevated to the post of canon, all within ten years of leaving the university.[16]

Of Ladrón Guevara's two sons, one was seemingly of limited capacity and received a middle-level sinecure in the royal mint of Mexico City. However, the other son, *Licenciado* Joaquín José, became a lawyer and a priest; while still young, he was at least twice elected rector of the lawyers' guild and was appointed a prebend of the Mexico City cathedral chapter.[17]

While the commercial, landed, and mining elites of the colony directed few of their sons into the professions, the professional elite—high-level lawyers, doctors, and government officials in Mexico City—regularly sent their offspring into these fields. Although these families often had significant economic interests outside of the salaries and fees earned from their positions (a characteristic of many professions), their prestige derived largely from their achievements in one or more professional fields.

Far and away the most distinguished family of professionals in the colony was the Beye de Cisneros. Apparently the first prominent professional of the family was Doctor Manuel Miguel Beye de Cisneros, a native of Mexico City (as were all the other members of the family to be discussed) born to a peninsular father and a creole mother. In the early eighteenth century he advanced through the college system of the capital and received his doctorate in canon law. He practiced law, occupied a chair in the legal faculty of the university, and ultimately was named *agente fiscal de lo civil* for the *Audiencia* of New Spain.

Two of his brothers also received professional degrees and rose to prominence. The true patriarch of the family was Doctor Manuel Ignacio. A lawyer and priest, he attained distinction in both professions. As a lawyer, he was a founder of the *Colegio de Abogados* in 1760 and served four times as its rector. As a cleric, he was four times rector of the university and was the *canónigo doctoral* of first the *Colegiata* of Guadalupe and subsequently the Mexico City cathedral chapter. The third brother, *Licenciado* Angel, while also a respected lawyer and cleric, did not match the achievements of his siblings.[19]

A sister, María Francisca, married Manuel de Prado y Zúñiga, a *regidor* of Mexico City, and their children, along with those of Manuel Miguel, provided yet another generation of distinguished professionals.

The four sons of Manuel Miguel all achieved prominence as lawyers, clerics or both. Doctor José Ignacio entered the legal profession and prospered as an offical of the government, working at one time for the *audiencia* and for a shorter period as legal representative of the Mining Court. He held the chair of as legal studies first in the seminary of the capital and then in the university. In 1811 he was named to the *cortes* in Spain.[20] Also a cleric, in 1812 he was the *canónigo doctoral* of the *colegiata*. His superior, the abbot, was his brother Doctor Francisco Manuel. Also a lawyer-cleric, Francisco Manuel twice served as rector of the College of Lawyers and once as that of the university. He too occupied a chair in the university.[21] Yet another brother, Doctor Agustín, entered the church, and in 1812 was the *canónigo penitenciario* of the *colegiata*. The fourth brother, Ignacio, became a lawyer and was named *subdelegado* of Actopan. He inherited the post of *regidor* from his uncle and served as such while still a *subdelegado*.

Although the most distinguished family in the professional elite, the Beye de Cisneros were by no means unique. The Villaurrutia family, related through marriage to the wealthy Fagoaga and Sánchez de Tagle clans, achieved distinction in the royal courts, when first the father and then two sons served in *audiencias* in Mexico and abroad. Doctor Miguel Primo de Rivera, a creole, another of that frequent combination of lawyer and priest, earned his degree in the university and went onto employment there as a *catedrático* in canon law. He then became the personal lawyer of the bishop of Puebla before returning to the capital as a judge of chaplaincies and testaments and ultimately rose to the post of prebend of the cathedral chapter before his death in 1790. His nephew, *Licenciado* Mariano Primo de Rivera, although born in Jalapa, was educated and made his career in Mexico City. He read the law, married a daughter of the Conde de Santiago, and became president of the Academy of Jurisprudence as well as a rector of the lawyers' guild.[22] Doctor Félix Venancio Malo de Villavivencio served as an *oidor* of New Spain for nearly thirty years before entering the church after being widowed. He died holding the post of *chantre* of the Mexico City cathedral chapter. Born in Guadalajara, he was himself the son of a peninsular-born *oidor* and was educated in the University of Mexico.[23] One of his three sons, Bachiller José Miguel, also made his career in the church.

While the above cases demonstrate the ease with which individuals and families moved between careers in the law, the church, and government service, the García Jove family best illustrates how a family could disperse itself through several different professions and accumulate honors in all of them. The Patriarch of the family was *Doctor y Maestro* José García Jove, a native of San Luis Potosí, who advanced in the medical profession to serve an extended period as president of the Mexican *Protomedicato*. He also held the posts of professor of surgery in the university and staff physician in several of the hospitals of the capital.[24]

Each of his three sons achieved distinction in the professions, but none of them in medicine. Doctor Pedro received his degree in canon law. In 1804, at about the age of twenty-five, he was named rector of the university and was reelected the following year. At this same period he was lawyer for the poor in the ecclesiastical courts, although not himself a cleric, and *asesor* of the *protomedicato*. In 1824 he was an *alcalde ordinario* in the capital.[25] He was succeeded as rector of the university by his own brother, *Doctor y Maestro* José Alejandro, a priest and lawyer, who that year was also curate of the parish of Salto del Agua in Mexico City.[26] Their other brother, Doctor Alonso, had his degree in theology and labored solely within the church, serving in 1810 as interim curate of the town of Caimaya.[27]

To prepare for professional careers, youths from across the colony journeyed to Mexico City to attend one of its famed *colegios* or the seminary, and then the university. A number of non-clerics received their education at the capital's seminary. San Ildefonso and Santa María de Todos Santos were the schools most popular with the colonial elite, and if the number of students switching from one college to another is any indication, Todos Santos was perceived as the better of the two. San Juan de Letrán did not contribute as many students to the university, but judging from the names and social background of its graduates, it retained a good reputation with the higher levels of society and certainly was not just a school for mestizos, as it had been early in its history.

Quite understandably, many lawyers born in the provinces received their secondary education at a provincial college. None of these institutions, however, could compete with the acclaimed schools in the capital for the number of graduates who entered the legal profession. Furthermore, while no evidence indicates that any youths from Mexico City enrolled in provincial schools, the number of lawyers born in the provinces who attended the *colegios* of the capital was considerable. Some provincial students enrolled immediately in these schools, while others started their education in other colleges but transferred to the capital before completing their courses of study.

Every attorney in the group who studied and graduated from a Mexico City *colegio* went on to receive his degree from the Royal and Pontifical University of Mexico. None went to a university in Spain or in another colony. Youths normally entered the *colegios* in their early to mid-teens and finished their studies in the university, even if they pursued the doctorate, in their mid to late twenties.

All lawyers were trained at last to the licentiate level, at which point the great majority terminated their formal education. In 1804, 45 members of the lawyers' guild (17.4 percent) held doctorates; in 1812, 46 members (15.1 percent); and in 1824 only 36 members (11.3 percent).[28] In each of these three years, a clear majority of those with doctorates were clerics, usually curates of provincial towns, professors at the university or at one of Mexico City's colleges, or members of the Mexico City cathedral chapter. However, at no point did clerics with doctorates compose a majority of the clerics in the lawyers' guild. Attainment of the doctorate seemingly had no appreciable effect on an attorney's career. Many rectors of the guild were *licenciados*, as were many of the highest government officials. Doctors may have been somewhat overrepresented in the teaching profession. This is understandable, given their academic predilection, but by no means did they dominate the field. Priests who had doctorates in law in some cases advanced to the cathedral chapter, but others served as curates in Indian towns and, despite their advanced education, failed to rise in the ecclesiastical hierarchy.

Table 2, assembled from membership lists for the College of Lawyers in the years 1804, 1812, and 1824, provides some perspective on the composition and salient characteristics of its membership. The organization apparently increased in size in the early nineteenth century, and this growth was not hindered by the coming of independence. However, as only a few years are represented, it is probably unwise to make too much of the data. It is clear, all the same, that over 75 percent of the attorneys regularly resided in the capital itself. The 1812 list supplies fewer places of residence than do the other two, and the 62 percent figure indicated in the table is an absolute minimum. Other evidence indicates a percentage similar to those of the other two years. It should be noted that every figure in the table is a minimum; other sources provide evidence that some of the counts could be increased substantially.

The question of the legal profession's ability to provide its practitioners with suitable employment and an appropriate income has been raised in the past.[29] The table points out the wide variety of official positions normally filled by attorneys. No honorary or non-paying posts are included in the calculation of the number of lawyers employed by the royal and municipal bureaucracies. All of the persons cited held such posts as *relator, asesor, agente fiscal, oficial mayor, abogado de Indios, teniente letrado*, and the like in the muncipal government. All city councilmen of the capital and other cities are grouped separately. Surprisingly few attorneys held multiple salary or fee-paying positions, as would have been expected if the pay for each office was quite low.

In any given year after the formation of the *Colegio de Abogados*, perhaps 15 percent of its membership was composed of clerics. Most lawyer-priests worked within the ecclesiastical bureaucracy, handling cases involving canon law; while others served as parish priests, educators, or high administators in the church hierarchy. Thus, there were two parallel judicial systems: civil and canon. However, for our purposes, the important point is that clerical lawyers and civil lawyers viewed and treated each other as peers. They may have handled different fields of jurisprudence, but they came from similar backgrounds followed nearly parallel career paths, and shared much of the same socal position and aspirations. Officials of the guild could come from either group, and no sort of *alternative* was in evidence.

Actually, the separation of the two spheres was not absolute. Some lawyer-priests served at some point in their careers as government officials or in civil tribunals, and both the Inquisition and the archbishopric regularly employed some lay attorneys.

Table 2 lists both the total number of lawyer-priests and their percentage of the total membership of the guild in the three years examined. The curates are listed as a subgroup of these clerics. Finally, while *catedráticos* are not presented as a subgroup of any of the previous headings, in actual fact most of them were clerics.

When the number of attorneys employed in the municipal, royal, and ecclesiastical bureaucracies is combined with the five to seven lawyers (on the average) who were secular employees of the church or the Inquisition but who are not cited in the table, it becomes clear that a minimum of 40-45 percent of all lawyers were employees of one organization or another, and this percentage increases if only those who are citizens of the capital are included. In fact, when corroborating evidence from other sources is added to that available in these lists, there is a strong indication that somewhat over 50 percent of all attorneys were so employed. Two examples from just the first two pages of the 1804 compilation show that *Licenciado* Basilio Arrillaga, listed without an occupation, was serving as an *asesor* of the Mexico City *Consulado* at the time.

As so many attorneys sought employment in the royal and ecclesiastical hierarchies, they were especially attuned to the ebb and flow of politics in Spain and were prominent among those who traveled to the peninsula in search of royal favor or who delegated their powers of attorney to persons with influence there. It is no coincidence that most *oidores* of Mexico after 1750 who were born or raised in the colony traveled to Spain prior to receiving their initial appointments to the colonial court system, whether in Mexico or in another colony. Gamboa went to Spain as a representative of the *consulado* and returned as an *alcalde de corte*. José Arías Villafañe and Antonio Joaquín de Rivadeneira Barrientos y Padilla also journeyed there on rather obvious shopping trips and came away with their first assignments.

All lawyers understood that the Spanish court was the dispenser of high level positions in the colonial judicial and administrative systems, exactly the posts that they most coveted. When just beginning their careers, they dispatched powers-of-attorney to well-paid agents in Madrid. But success in obtaining a post was just the first step in the process, for most significant promotions had to be approved if not initiated in the Spanish court. Thus, at each step in his career, an attorney employed by the government was dependent at last in part upon his good reputation and powerful friends at court. Even the final step, once an attorney had achieved high rank and accomplishments of which to boast, was to again assemble evidence of service and respectability and dispatch them to an agent in Madrid to obtain an honorific title or membership in an order. Thus, although the legal profession was a preserve of the creoles, those in government service well appreciated their dependence on the Spanish court for a large measure of their success.

Although perhaps half of the legal community of late colonial Mexico was employed in either the governmental or ecclesiastical bureaucracies, neither these lawyers nor those otherwise employed had to rely exclusively on their salaries or on their income from individual legal proceedings. Most attorneys came from families with significant business enterprises, properties, or some combination of the two, and they continued to participate in and benefit from these economic undertakings at the same time that they pursued their professional careers. Some lawyers, especially those from very wealthy backgrounds, became the exclusive legal representatives of their family's business and personal interests. Occasionally they rose to become family patriarchs, representing the family socially and directing its diversified business undertakings. Even those attorneys who did not head up their family's business interests were themselves often quick to invest in different forms of enterprise in order to diversify or supplement their incomes.

Lawyers were often owners of rural estates. Some inherited estates, others purchased them, and yet others rented them from their proprietors. In his 1784 will, Doctor Manuel Ignacio Beye de Cisneros, a founder of the *Colegio de Abogados*, bequeathed three haciendas and three ranchos, most of which were apparently organized into a single agricultural complex, to his nephew, Doctor Francisco Manuel.[30]

Attorneys, typical of estate owners in general, were not content simply to gain a small but steady return from their properties; neither did they perceive them primarily as status symbols; rather they actively sought to develop a range of enterprises on their properties, to improve them, and hence to obtain more income from them. *Licenciado* Fernando Fernández de San Salvador, a native of Toluca, enjoyed a notably successful legal career. He served as *asesor letrado* of the Intendancy of Mexico and as *teniente de corregidor* of the capital. Ultimately, he was named an honorary *alcalde del crimen* of New Spain.[31] Simultaneous with his professional career, Fernández de San Salvador developed a diversified rural enterprise. In 1782 he purchased the Rancho del Piñón Viejo and immediately formed a company in it with Andrés de Escalona, an Indian *cacique*. The property was located on the outskirts of the capital and produced cattle, *tezontle* (the red volcanic rock from which many structures in Mexico City were constructed), and canoes used to transport goods on the canal leading to the capital. In 1791 the company was dissolved, the profits and the livestock were divided equally, and the property was then rented out by Fernández de San Salvador to his former partner.[32]

Not content to live solely on his income as head notary of the Mexico City *Consulado* and to leave business investment to his merchant brothers, *Licenciado* Luis Gonzaga de Ibarrola in 1804 borrowed 7,000 pesos from a wealthy widow at 5 percent for one year to rent and equip two haciendas in the Chalco district.[33] He, like the merchants and members of other occupations who rented estates, calculated that he would be able to obtain enough revenue from operation of the estate to pay off the rental fee as well as the principal and interest on the loan and still earn a profit.

Licenciado Juan José Barberi, a native of Mexico City, achieved prominence as rector of the lawyers' guild and as a judge and captain of the *acordada*, but he was for many years the owner of substantial agricultural estates and eventually invested in a series of independent undertakings. In 1793, to finance two of his estates near the capital, Barberi contracted with a silver merchant to borrow 8,000 pesos in each of the next five years and to repay the bulk of the loan with wheat and maize from each year's harvest delivered to a mill owned by the lender.[34] Ten years later, Barberi was apparently in a much improved economic condition, as he received over 6,500 pesos upon terminating one of the companies a diversified economic enterprise he had developed with a former administrator of one of his estates. The two men had used the estate as the cornerstone of the undertaking, agreeing to an equal split of the profits from a salt deposit that supplied the estate, from a bread bakery (*panadería*) in the capital that was supplied with wheat from the same estate, and from a coach-building business (*carrocería*) also located in Mexico City.[35] With the dissolution of the company, Barberi retained ownership of his estates, while the former administrator became proprietor of the urban enterprises.

Other lawyers regularly involved themselves in agricultural production and marketing, although usually on a more modest scale. The previously mentioned lawyer and *regidor* of Mexico City, Doctor Luis Gonzaga González Maldonado, the brother of an *oidor* of New Spain and of a successful businessman in Puebla, was active in several different economic fields. As the owner of wheat estates, he contracted for the sale of the harvests,[36] and purchased merchandise and borrowed money for their supply and maintenance.[37] As an owner of pulque ranchos, he entered into agreements to insure the sale of their product.[38] As the legal representative of the Indian *parcialidad* of San Juan Tenochtitlan, he himself first rented the *pulquería* owned by the district and then sublet the establishment with stipulations that promoted his own pulque production. Finally, as the legal and business representative of the other people, he contracted agreements for them.[39]

With few exceptions, lawyers did not take over or manage major commercial establishments, but some did speculate in the sale of small lots of goods or in the commodity markets. We have already seen that Ignacio José de Ibarrola, born into a prominent commercial family, never used his legal education to make a career but rather chose to participate in trade along with his brothers. Doctor Ignacio María Sánchez Hidalgo also came from a mercantile background but decided to pursue a professional career, becoming first a practicing attorney and later a cleric, rising to become a curate of one of the parishes of Mexico City. His three brothers and sisters all became or married merchants. Despite this fact, until he became a cleric, Ignacio María directed the family's mercantile and other business operations.[40]

It was common for a lawyer to purchase a shipment of goods from a merchant to sell on or near his estate or to speculate in a highly marketable commodity such as cacao. *Licenciado* Juan Francisco Azcárate y Legama, known for his activities in the Independence movement, made a credit purchase of 2,189 pounds of Caracas cacao, valued at 780 pesos, from a merchant of Mexico City in 1799.[41] Most such purchases from merchants involved hundred of pesos, but an occasional transaction could involve thousands, and in almost all these deals, the attorney would need to buy on credit, usually offering to pay in installments. Finally, while most attorneys refrained from direct investment in retail establishments, occasional exceptions did occur.

One field of the economy in which lawyers were very active was mining. While a few lawyers acquired mines through inheritance, more often they became owners or partners in mining enterprises through direct investment of funds. Silvestre López Portillo, a *consultor* of the General Mining Court, was typical of those who inherited mines. He owned five-sixths of one mine and was joint owner of a half interest in another.[42]

Licenciado José Domingo Laso de la Vega, a native of Guanajuato, was another attorney who found regular employment in the administrative bodies affiliated with the mining industry. A *fiscal* of the General Mining Court in the colonial era, after independence he became the *apoderado general*, administrator, and director of the mining seminar at the Mexico City School of Mines.[43] His knowledge of mining was not solely theoretical, for in 1793 he had acquired half ownership in the mines of Pablo de León y Pejenaute located in Guanajuato in return for the goods and services that he had provided him to put the enterprise into operation.[44]

Licenciado Manuel José Gutiérrez de Navamuel, holder of the important positon of *agente fiscal de lo criminal* for the *Audiencia* of Mexico, was also a full partner in a mine in Taxco.[45] In 1789, the same year that he was elevated to rector of the *Colégio de Abogados*, *Licenciado* José Mariano de Cárdenas was given a half share of two mines near Toluca that he had financed.[46] Within a month, Cárdenas ceded part of his share to another attorney, Doctor Jóse Cebrián de Ahedo, to settle a debt.[47]

Attorneys overlooked no opportunity or field of enterprise in which they thought they could earn profits. No one seemed concerned that certain types of business investments might taint his reputation or that of the profession. *Licenciado* José Fernández de Jáuregui, a lawyer-priest, owned a press. The enterprise evolved out of his interests in literature and music and his ownership of a bookstore. In a 1790 will, Fernández de Jáuregui listed among his assets books worth 8,408 pesos, sheet music worth 7,912 pesos, and musical instruments worth 2,396 pesos.[48]

Nor were attorneys reluctant to invest in manufacturing or artisan activities, no matter how small. We have already seen that *Licenciado* Juan José Barberi owned both a coach-making shop and a coach-renting service as part of his diversified economic interests. *Licenciado* Manuel García de Aguirre involved himself in a company with similar interests. He and Manuel Prieto both owned *coches de providencia* which they rented out to persons needing transportation around the city. Together they purchased a corral with a coach-making shop in the city for 500 pesos and expended an additional 52 pesos in improvements. They divided all expenditures equally.[49] Still other lawyers rented flour mills, and one even rented the *Real Coliseo*, the major theater of Mexico City, for a period of five years.[50]

Those lawyers with disposable capital sometimes lent their money at the standard rate of 5 percent simple annual interest. Professionals in general were quick to lend money to each other for their various economic enterprises and to finance the purchase of posts in the colonial bureacracies. Finally, they were quite willing to act as bondsmen for each other and also for newly-arrived colonial officials, often for large amounts.[51]

Lawyers frequently served as general business and legal representatives for prominent individuals and families, and as such earned very good salaries. In 1796, the same year that he was elected rector of the *Colegio de Abogados*, *Licenciado* José Fernández Mora, a lawyer-priest, was designated the *apoderado general* of the Conde de Miravalle at the annual salary of 1,000 pesos.[52]

Despite the frequency with which lawyers enjoyed success in their careers, as members of the church or governmental administrations, as participants in family business, and as investors, advisors, or independent businessmen, some of them never did fare well economically. Occasionally, a lawyer's will would state that he had little wealth except for his clothing, household furnishings, and library. Ownership of the last item generally distinguished lawyers from members of other professions.

But even these statements of poverty must be taken in context, for some attorneys then itemized their holdings and described their life situations in greater detail and thereby made it apparent that they were poor only when compared to the most fortunate in their profession and not in terms of the overall society. *Licenciado* Luis Galiano is a case in point. In his 1789 will he stated that he had no wealth; however, as he put forth his bequests, he declared that although a lifelong bachelor, he had an illegitimate daughter whom he had married off with a dowry to an official in the governmental accounting department and that he employed both as a clerk and a concierge. Finally, he left his library to a nephew, also an attorney.[53]

A substantial minority of lawyers never married; this is true even when those who were clerics are excluded. Very few of those who wed received substantial dowries, and the number who wed and received no dowry was large. Certainly there were few cases like those of *Licenciado* José Ignacio Ruiz Calado, *promotor fiscal* of the Intendency of Mexico and a widower, who gained a dowry of over 176,000 pesos upon marrying the widow María Francisca Gómez de Haro. *Licenciado* Mariano Primo de Rivera, another widower and from a distinguished family (his uncle had been a prebend of the Mexico City cathedral chapter) married Rita Gómez Cervantes de Velasco, a daughter of the Conde de Santiago, and as a result saw his eldest son inherit a *mayorazgo* upon her death.[54]

More typical was the marriage of *Licenciado* Francisco de Urrutia y Montoya, a *teniente letrado* and *asesor* for the Intendency of Durango and a *regidor* of Mexico City. Despite being from a well-known family and holding these prestigious positions, he received only 900 pesos from three endowments when he wed María Agusina Galindo Rivera de Santa Cruz.[55] Other lawyers in comparable posts received no dowries upon their marriages.

Overall, lawyers, when compared to merchants, had much less access to substantial wealth through marriage, either from dowries or inheritance, and in general did not marry into the creole elite or into the higher ranks of Spanish officialdom in Mexico. Similarly, they were much less likely to marry their immediate relatives. Only one case was encountered in which an attorney married his cousin.[56]

We have already seen that many sons of professionals themselves became professionals, although often not in the specific career of their fathers. Actually, only a small number of lawyers' children ever entered the church, either as seculars, members of orders, or nuns. None of the lawyers examined established a chaplaincy for a son, although several founded them specifically for nephews or for the closest male relative who entered the priesthood.

No son of a lawyer chose commerce as his primary means of making a living. Very few entered the military. (I am referring here to the sons of Mexico City lawyers. The situation may have been far different in the provinces.) Some entered the municipal or colonial buraucracies, occasionally in very technical positions.[57] Others assumed control over family estates and other businesses and lived out their lives as members of the large respectable middle sector of Mexico City society.

No lawyer of colonial Mexico gained a noble title. A few were accepted into the Order of Carlos III, and several were appointed honorary *oidores* or *alcaldes del crimen*. However, these were primarily creole lawyers who had ascended to become *audiencia* judges in New Spain or abroad and thus were atypical of the broader colonial legal community. Only a few were designated familiars of the Inquisition. Just a few received officer rank in the militia. Professionals seemed to have little enthusiasm for the military. Perhaps this lack of honors at the imperial and colonial levels is understandable because the great majority of lawyers came from the respectable but not the wealthiest sectors of Mexican society, and in the late colonial period, most royal honors went to those able to make large financial contributions. Overall it does not seem that lawyers competed with the great landowners for these very high honors.

But, if largely ignored at the international and colonial levels, lawyers were greatly honored at the local level and occupationally. By the 1760s, at least three or four lawyers were to be found each year in the twelve-member *cabildo* of Mexico City. Even more were named honorary members. Others were city councilmen in provincial cities. Some were elected to the rectorship of the university, others to those of the *colegios*. During the Independence movement from 1808 to 1821, lawyers were notable among the persons assigned to the Spanish *Cortes* and to represent the capital in a variety of political meetings. In the early national period, they were again numerous in both state and local governments and as elected representatives to constitutional and national congresses.

In sum, the lawyers of late colonial Mexico came from a diversity of backgrounds but most came from provincial agricultural and mercantile families, with a substantial minority from Mexico City professional and commercial families. Only a very small number came from the truly elite families of the colony. Almost exclusively creole in composition, lawyers were educated in a number of *colegios*, with a clear majority choosing one or another of the prestigious schools in the capital. Virtually all then received their formal legal training at the university in Mexico City before gaining practical training in the office of an established attorney or judge.

Perhaps half of the membership in the Lawyers' Guild held regular positions in either the church or the governmental administration of the colony. Many of the others represented the business interests of their families or looked after the affairs of the wealthy members of this society. Lawyers themselves were very active in the different aspects of the late colonial economy, but very few ascended into the ranks of the highest elite through their professional activities or their economic exploits. As a group respected and comfortably well off, the lawyers of late colonial Mexico enjoyed status, but little effective power. Rather, they were the well paid administrators of the civil and ecclesiastical governments or the spokesmen and defenders of the interests of the leading families, corporate groups, and institutions of the society.

NOTES

[1]This study is based on applications for membership received by the *Colegio de Abogados* and preserved on microfilm by the Genealogical Society of the Church of Jesus Christ of Latter Day Saints, on wills, business agreements, and other notarial documentation in the Archivo de Notarías del Departmento del Distrito Federal, on census material, judicial cases, and administrative files in the Archivo General de la Nación, on lists of membership in the Biblioteca Nacional, on personal and business announcements found in the *Gazeta de México*, and the *Diario de México*, and on published material dating from the era under examination and from more recent times.

[2]To all appearances, judges and prosecutors appointed by the crown to the *audiencia* were admitted to the *colegio* as a matter of course.

[3]AGN-C 1491-1-16, 21, April 30, 1789.

[4]Kicza 1982:3 and *passim.*

[5]AHN Juan Manuel Pozo, Oct. 16, 1791, Jan. 12, 1799; Osores 1908, I:234.

[6]GM, Feb. 26, 1793; DM, Dec. 6, 1805, Aug. 1, 1813; Osores 1908, I:236-37.

[7]Osores 1908, I:239-40; Lucas Alamán , IV:217,

[8]Osores 1908, I:284.

[9]GM, Jan. 30, 1787, April 23, 1800; Osores 1908, I:284.

[10]AHN, José María de Torija, July 23, 1784; Osores 1908, I:284.

[11]AHN, José Antonio Burillo, Sept. 28, 1784.

[12]AHN, Félix Fernando Zamorano y Barrera, Aug. 6, 1808; AGN-Con 161-9-1, July 8, 1805.

[13]AGN-Con 184-1, Oct., 1802; Fernández de Recas 1956:181.

[14]Osores 1908, I:323-324.

[15]Esquivel Obregón 1941:26.

[16]Osores 1908, I:251; Gómez 1854:392.

[17]AHN, Joaquín Barrientos, May 31, 1792; GM, Feb. 8, 1784, Feb. 5, 1793.

[18]Osores 1908, I:106.

[19]AGN-HJ 350-12, Oct. 23, 1784; Beristáin de Souza 1816-1821, VI:350.

[20]GM, Nov. 20, 1787, Aug. 29, 1804; Alamán , III:52; Howe 1949:88.

[21]GM, Feb. 14, 1786, Jan. 30, 1787, Feb. 5, 1793.

[22]AHN, José María de Castro, July 12, 1816; Beristáin de Souza 1816-1821, VII:504; Osores 1908, II:161-62.

[23]AHN, Barrientos, Mar. 12, 1787; Burkholder and Chandler 1977:173.

[24]AGN-P 53, Dec. 1811; AHN, Barrientos, Jan. 5, 1799.

[25]BNM, *Lista de abogados en el Real Colegio de México*, 1812, 1824; *Lista en que han de poner los señores que fueron Rectores y Consiliarios.*

[26]BNM, *Lista en que han de poner.*

[27]AHN, Barrientos, June 23, 1810.

[28]BNM, *Lista de abogados*, 1804, 1812, 1824.

[29]Brading 1971:213.

[30]AGN-HJ 350-12, Oct. 23, 1784.

[31]Beristáin de Souza 1816-1821, III:114.

[32]AHN, Barrientos, July 20, 1791.

[33]AHN, Zamorano y Barrera, July 23, 1804.

[34]AHN, Barrientos, Dec. 13, 1793.

[35]AHN, Zamorano y Barrera, June 17, 1803.

[36]AHN, Burillo, Sept. 1, 1786.

[37]AHN, Torija, July 23, 1784; Mariano Cadena, Oct. 25, 1784.

[38]AHN, Burillo, July 1, 1782, Aug. 27, 1784.

[39]AHN, Burillo, Dec. 14, 1786.

[40]AHN, Pozo, April 10, 1786, July 4, 1787, Aug. 3, 1792, Aug. 27, 1793, April 9, 1795, Oct. 17, 1796; Burillo, Aug. 29, 1794.

[41]AHN, Pozo, June 25, 1799.

[42]AHN, Burillo, March 17, 1785.

[43]Osores 1908, II:23-25.

[44]AHN, Burillo, Aug. 12, 1793.

[45]AHN, Tomás Hidalgo de los Reyes, April 19, 1792.

[46]AHN, Cadena, March 2, 1789; GM, Feb. 17, 1789. Another case of a lawyer-*aviador* is in Manuel Domingo de Chavero, Aug. 17, 1796.

[47]AHN, Cadena, April 1, 1789.

[48]AGN-T 1334-1-1-150, April 28, 1790.

[49]AHN, Francisco Javier Benítez, July 7, 1812.

[50]AHN, Tomás Hidalgo de los Reyes, Oct. 22, 1802; AGN-C 968-3-58, Feb. 12, 1781.

[51]AHN, Cadena, Aug. 19, 1790; Barrientos, Aug. 7, 1806, Oct. 27, 1810; Francisco de la Torre, Oct. 7, 1807.

[52]AHN, Barrientos, June 2, 1796.

[53]AHN, Burillo, Nov. 14, 1789.

[54]AHN, Cadena, July 27,1790; Castro, July 12, 1816; Vicente Hidalgo de los Reyes, Sept. 1, 1810; Beristáin de Souza 1816-1821, II:504.

[55]GM, Aug. 6, 1793; AHN, Pozo, Oct. 24, 1787.

[56]AHN, Zamorano y Barrera, Dec. 4, 1808.

[57]AHN, Pozo, Aug. 31, 1790.

TABLE 1
KNOWN PLACES OF BIRTH OF THE COLEGIO DE ABOGADOS
EXCLUDING AUDIENCIA JUDGES AND PROSECUTORS

Birthplace	*Number*
Mexico City	37
Puebla	9
Guanajuato	5
Querétaro	3
Aguascalientes	3
Valladolid (Morelia)	3
Guadalajara	2
Antequera (Oaxaca City)	2
Durango	1
Toluca	1
Zacatecas	1
Tlaxcala	1
Pénjamo	1
León	1
Culiacan	1
Jalapa	1
Santa Fé de México	1
Fresnillo	1
Guatemala	1
Spain	7
total	82

TABLE 2
SIZE AND SOME CHARACTERISTICS OF THE MEMBERSHIP
OF THE COLEGIO DE ABOGADOS

Category	*1804*	*1812*	*1824*
Total Membership	258	305	318
Resident in Mexico City	207 (80.2 percent)	189 (62 percent)	242 (76.1 percent)
Employed in Royal or Municipal Bureaucracy	71 (27.5 percent)	76 (24.9 percent)	91 (28.6 percent)
Number Holding Multiple Salary or Fee-Paying Posts	8	3	3

Retired Officials	5	6	3
City Councilmen (Honorary Not Included)	8	5	4
Clerics	42 (16.3 percent)	36 (11.8 percent)	42 (13.2 percent)
Curates	12	13	16
Catedráticos	5	4	1

Source: BNM, "*Lista de los abogados que se hallan matriculados en el Ilustre y Real Colegio de México, 1804, 1812, y 1824.*"

MULTI-LEVEL GOVERNMENT IN NINETEENTH-CENTURY OAXACA[1]

Ronald Spores

Introduction

The nineteenth century was one of the most complex periods in the political development of Mexico—a time of notable social and economic change, political struggle, external interference, and internal transformation. Relationships among national, state, district, and local levels of government changed radically in a century marked by grand design, experimentation, anarchy, and fluctuating centralization. Monarchical colonialism was followed by internal and foreign imperialism, republicanism, reformation, and dictatorship. Only Mexico's sixteenth century with its confrontation and amalgamation of European and native American cultures and peoples is comparable. Developments during the sixteenth century seem far more perceptible, however, when compared to the multiple political, social, economic, and ideological currents running through the 1800s.

Despite the critical importance of the nineteenth century in Mexico's political history, state and local-level developments have received little attention from historians and anthropologists. Except for the great *Reforma* of the 1850s and 1860s, the nineteenth century is less studied and understood than either the sixteenth century or the colonial period as a whole. Since the foundations of modern Mexican government were laid in the century of Independence, Iturbide, Santa Ana, Juárez, Maximiliano, and Díaz, inattention to the politics of the Mexican countryside seems ironic. Recognizing this deficiency, the present article attempts to delineate nineteenth century political developments with particular reference to the evolving multi-level system of government and law as it relates to rural Mexico. Attention is directed to the system in the Province or State of Oaxaca and its regions and communities, with secondary emphasis on linkages between the state and national level of government. Although the period of major concern is from Independence to the end of the nineteenth century, we must begin with Spanish colonial antecedents and end with resultant developments in the early 1900s.

Colonial Antecedents

New Spain was administered and maintained by a multi-level system of law and government beginning with the Crown, extending through the viceroy and *audiencia*, to provincial administrators, and finally to the local, or community, level. Effective control of political, judicial, economic, and religious activities in the colony were delegated by the Crown to the viceregal government in Mexico City. Despite the overarching authority of the Spanish king and the Council of the Indies, the highest level of colonial government resided with the viceroy and *audiencia* of New Spain,[2] and passed directly to provincial *corregimientos* or *alcaldías mayores* and to local *cabildos*.

From early colonial times until the 1780s, the native communities of New Spain were organized into *provincias*, consisting of a few to several dozen communities. These agricultural settlements had their own local governments but came under the general supervision and authority of a Spanish *corregidor* or *alcalde mayor*. At the next lower level stood the *cabildos*, or *ayuntamientos*, consisting of locally elected representatives. It is to be noted, however, that although the official political hierarchy was composed of these three interacting levels, the Catholic clergy and a variable cast of para-political functionaries—traditional *caciques*, *principales*, elders, Spanish civilians and businessmen—also played significant political roles. The functions and relationships among these components have been discussed for the colonial period in the articles by William Taylor and Judith Zeitlin. Of immediate concern to the present discussion is the late colonial period, particularly the time from the late 1780s to 1820.

Between 1786 and 1789, Oaxaca, together with the rest of New Spain, was reorganized through establishment of the intendency system.[3] The colony was organized into twelve intendencies (and three military districts), each governed by a chief executive officer, the *Intendente* or *Intendente General*, who served as principal administrative and judicial authority in each division and who answered directly to the viceroy and *audiencia* in Mexico City. In addition to the *intendente*, there was a court of judicial review and a staff of scribes, accountants, fiscal officers, police, and service personnel. Additional functionaries were appointed, normally from the population resident in the capital center, for special tasks and services. The intendency system, in effect, added a level to the traditional colonial political system. Whereas Crown magistrates (the *alcaldes mayores* of pre-intendency times) had dealt directly with the viceroy and *audiencia*, *intendentes* now intervened at the provincial level between the *alcaldes* (now called *subdelegados*) in the regions and communities and the colonial government. In some ways, the colonial regime provided a foundation for a future state organization for the various provinces but without the division of powers that was to characterize post-Independence government.

As of 1793, the Intendency of Oaxaca—conforming roughly to the modern state of Oaxaca—contained 411, 334 people (88 percent of them Indians) residing in 936 pueblos. The intendency was divided into a central district (*Centro*), with its capital at Antequera (Oaxaca City), and twenty *subdelegaciones* or *partidos*.[4] By 1804, Oaxaca ranked fourth among the twelve intendencies of New Spain with a population of 528,860.[5] Some 24,400 resided in the capital and the remainder in the more than 900 communities of the province.

Each *partido* was governed by a chief administrative and judicial officer, the *subdelegado*, a judge of first instance for civil and criminal matters, and a scribe, a fiscal assistant, a jailer, a small police force, and a few part-time officials or service personnel recruited from the area of jurisdiction. Normally, all political, administrative, and judicial matters involving residents of the communities, haciendas, *ranchos*, and religious establishments that were not resolved at the local level would be processed at the *partido* level. This included a great variety of civil, as well as serious criminal, cases. The *subdelegado* was responsible for enforcement of administrative, legal, fiscal, religious and general regulatory demands placed on the communities by colonial authorities.

Routine administrative matters were handled by the *subdelegado*, and criminal and civil cases involving judicial or legislative action were heard by the judge of first instance, by the *subdelegado* acting in the capacity of judge, or by a special judge (*juez receptor*) appointed to investigate and hear certain cases, particularly those that might involve conflicts of interest or irregularities by *subdelegación* officials. In numerous instances, however, complaints would be taken directly to the *intendente* in Oaxaca. The *intendente* might then refer matters to the appropriate *subdelegado* or, if prejudice or conflict of interest were present, a special investigator could be appointed.

Each *partido* was comprised of a capital center (*cabecera*) and several dependent communities. Resources demanded by the colonial government were drawn from the communities by the *subdelegado*, but this official also served numerous necessary functions for the communities and provided security for the region under his control. He supervised the collection of tribute from the communities, acted as a conduit for demands being channeled from the central government to the villages, and in the opposite direction, and oversaw elections, governance, and maintenance of order at the local level. Serious crime, important land transactions, and many civil matters were also processed by the *subdelegado*.

Certain functions normally regarded as political or administrative were not handled by the *subdelegados*. Throughout the colonial period, birth, marriage, and death records were maintained by priests and housed in local parish archives. Military jurisdiction as well was normally beyond the authority of the *subdelegado*. When military activities came into question or when military intervention was required, requests had to be directed to the *intendente*.

Local-level government in Oaxaca, as in the rest of New Spain, was in the hands of officials elected annually to local community councils, or *ayuntamientos*.[6] The larger communities elected a governor, generally three to five councilors, or *regidores*, and one or two judges, or *alcaldes*. Additional functionaries, scribes, *mayordomos* (fiscal overseers), police, tribute collectors, labor controllers, or messengers (*topiles*) were either popularly elected or appointed by *ayuntamiento* members. Smaller communities were governed by one or two elected *alcaldes* who acted in judicial and administrative capacities within their settlements and represented the community on the *ayuntamiento* of a regional capital settlement (*cabecera de partido*). The *ayuntamientos*, in turn, came under the general supervisory authority of the appropriate *subdelegado*. Unless there were irregularities, however, the *ayuntamientos* functioned independently and without outside interference. They were, nevertheless, required to comply with orders and demands from the *subdelegado*, from the *intendente*, and from the colonial level of government.

Ayuntamiento government originated in the sixteenth century. The institution remained intact and virtually unchanged for nearly three centuries.[7] It was recognized by local populations as well as by higher level authorities as a generally effective form of government, and it provided the model for local level political organization in Republican times.

The Revolution of Independence

By 1812, political dissidence was affecting the colonial status quo in Oaxaca, particularly in the Mixteca. On January 11, there was an attack on royalist forces at Yanhuitlan, but on January 15, the insurgents abandoned the area and retreated north to Cuautla where they joined forces with José María Morelos.[8] In November of 1812, Morelos marched south from Tehuacan, Puebla, and took the city of Oaxaca. By May of 1813, however, the Spaniards regained control of the province and were able to survive attempts by the insurgents to take Tlaxiaco and Silacayoapan and other communities. Sporadic resistance followed and Spanish power gradually declined. However, Spanish authority was strongly challenged throughout New Spain, and by 1821 it became clear that the Europeans could no longer control the colony. In June, 1821, Antonio León, functioning at the time in Tezoatlan of the Mixteca, proclaimed Oaxaca's independence from Spain. By July 1, León had entered the city of Oaxaca and assumed military and political control of the province. The Revolution was over in Oaxaca.

The takeover of Oaxaca by Independence forces was quick and relatively easy. Spanish political domination ended, but many colonial institutions remained in force. The form and function of *intendencia-subdelegación-ayuntamiento* government remained. Although official nomenclature was affected, political and legal procedures continued as they had before Independence. Criminal and civil cases, such as intercommunity conflicts over land and resources, continued to be processed as in colonial times.[9]

At the local level, *ayuntamientos* continued to be elected and to function as before. In the Valley of Oaxaca the designation of governor was dropped in most localities, the title and office being replaced by *alcalde primero*. In the larger communities of the Mixteca, however, there was a continuation of the office of governor, and other traditional *cabildo* offices. On November 25, 1821, the community of Tidaa in the Teposcolula area elected a governor, two *alcaldes*, four *regidores*, an *escribano*, two *jueces*, four *topiles*, a *mayordomo de la communidad*, and two *fiscales* and two *topiles* for the church, all to serve during 1822.[10] The town scribe wrote that the "election has been carried out with the assistance of our priest and the people, and the above indicated individuals were considered apt for the discharge of the offices for which they are destined and were elected by a plurality of votes." Similar elections were held throughout the Mixteca in such communities as San Juan Teposcolula on December 2, 1821 and San Andrés de Laguna on November 2, 1821. Except for minor rhetorical innovations, elections, offices, and political functions were as they had been in mid-colonial times throughout the Mixteca, the Valley of Oaxaca, and in other regions of Oaxaca.

The *Imperio Mexicana*

The *Imperio Mexicana* under Agustín Iturbide was established in 1821.[11] Intendencies became provinces (*provincias*). The office of *intendente* carried over from colonial times as did most major administrative functions. Officially the title was *Jefe*, or *Jefe Político, de la Provincia de Oaxaca*, but *Intendente* was also used. For the first time, the communities of Oaxaca held elections for representatives to state and national provisional assemblies. Out of these developed the National Congress and the State Congress and the beginnings of true representational government in Oaxaca. Also evolving to replace *intendency* and *audiencia* review of civil and criminal cases was a superior tribunal of justice seated in Oaxaca.

Under the short-lived administration of Emperor Agustín I, orders were sent to the realm that local, district, and provincial government should continue to function as they had under the colonial regime. There was to be no change in offices, in functions, or in relations among local, intermediate, and provincial levels of government. The most visible change was in the design of official stationery employed in government communications.

The Federal Republic: 1823-1836

Antonio León controlled Oaxaca during the *Imperio Mexicano*, but when Iturbide dissolved the Constituent Congress in October of 1822, the tide turned in Oaxaca. León declared against the Empire and on June 9, 1823, he and Nicolás Bravo led the capture of Oaxaca from the imperial government.[12] Oaxaca was declared to be "*Estado Libre y Soberano*," a provisional *junta* was established, and a base was laid for state and local government. Continuity of public order and government was assured.

Local governments were informed of changes and procedures during the critical 1823-24 period. The *partido* of Teotitlan del Valle, for example, was informed of the overthrow of Iturbide on April 8, 1823, and that the community was to come under the provisional control of the *Jefe Político* of the Province of Oaxaca. They were informed of the establishment of a provisional *junta* and of the election of deputies to the state congress. On July 6, the *Jefe Político* of Oaxaca informed the Teotitlan *partido* that "all authorities and public functionaries are to continue in the performance of their duties....Current laws, orders, and regulations remain effective and in force."

Following the collapse of the *Imperio Mexicano* in March, 1823, the responsible citizenry of Oaxaca quickly mobilized to form an interim government until the planned national federation could be established. A provisional congress was instituted, and between July, 1823 and September, 1823, a series of legislative decrees was promulgated to ensure order and continuity.[13] The Province of Oaxaca was declared to be the "*Estado Libre y Soberano de Oaxaca*," loyal to the central government in Mexico City and to the future constitutional federation of Mexican states. Twenty political "*partidos*" were created from the old *subdelegaciones* of the Intendency of Oaxaca. The capital district was to include Oaxaca and its nearby dependencies. The *partidos* were to be the four *villas* of the Marquesado, Huitzo, Nochixtlan, Teposcolula, Huajuapan, Juxtlahuaca, Jamiltepec, Chontales, Quiechapan, Teotitlan del Valle, Villa Alta, Teotitlan del Camino, Zimatlan, Teococuilco, Miahuatlan and Ixtepeji.

Political Organization:

Oaxaca continued to be governed by laws, institutions, and offices dating from the times of the Spanish colonial and Mexican Imperial regimes. The principle of tripartite division of powers was recognized and held to be inviolable: the state provisional congress was in existence, but it was necessary to create the executive and judicial branches and to define the functions and relationships of the three arms of government.[14]

The position of state governor and related executive offices were established and defined. A five member advisory *junta* was to be appointed by the legislature to advise the governor. A system of six *departamentos* was created with six "*gobernadores de departamento*" to be appointed by the legislature to oversee political activity in departments. These officials were responsible for public order and security, for publication and execution of state laws and orders, for working with the local authorities in the operation of local government, and for maintaining connections between the state and local level. Simultaneously, they were to act as the primary conduit for information flowing from the various regions to the central government of the state. The governors of departments were also to oversee the activities of state employees and judges of the first instance, but they were enjoined from interference in the functions of the judges or the courts.

Also included among the sweeping powers of the *gobernadores de departamento* was the right to investigate irregularities and to arrest delinquents, to assist local governments in health delivery and in controlling epidemics and to report to the state government on matters of health and sanitation, to intervene in the case of election irregularities, to foment the development of agriculture and education, industry and commerce, and to prevent circulation of contraband goods within department jurisdictions. They were to collect certain taxes and to submit monthly accounts and descriptions of their jurisdictions to the state government. Provision was also made for a small militia to operate under the control of the department governors.

Department governors had powers of oversight over local government, being required to report abuses and to periodically visit, advise, and instruct pueblo governors in all areas relating to good government. They also had the right to punish local officials found to be negligent, abusive, or inattentive to duties.

With respect to local government, the interim legislature decreed that the *ayuntamientos* of the pueblos were to continue with forms and functions then in effect, most since colonial times. Except for reiteration of the principles of equality, peace, and fraternity, there was little political innovation at the local level.

The State Judiciary System:

Considerable attention was paid to the state judicial system. A state civil and criminal court was established. The supreme court of justice was composed of a regent (or president), nine ministers of justice, and a *fiscal* (administrator)—all named by the legislature. All were to be certified lawyers. Three *salas* (chambers) were created, with three ministers assigned to each chamber. The first chamber reviewed civil and criminal cases and sentences of the courts of first instance (*juzgados de primera instancia*) and otherwise oversaw the lower courts and judges. It was to act as court of first instance in hearing criminal or civil cases involving the *diputados* of the legislature, the governor of the state, the secretary of *despacho*, and the ministers of the supreme court. Further, it required all judges of first instance to submit monthly reports listing pending and completed civil and criminal cases and an account of sentences delivered during the reporting period.

The second chamber of the court acted as a court of third instance in cases originating in the *juzgados de primera instancia* and as a court of second instance with respect to civil and criminal cases involving *diputados*, the governor, secretary of *despacho*, ministers of the supreme court, governors of the departments, and members of the governor's advisory *junta*. They oversaw ecclesiastical matters and regulated and supervised practicing attorneys and scribes (*escribanos*). It was also the responsibility of the second chamber to require monthly reports from the first chamber of cases pending in courts of first and second instance and to provide the regent with such reports.

The third chamber acted as the court of third instance in cases involving higher state officials. It also resolved ambiguities in the law emanating from the other chambers (or to refer persisting doubts to the legislature for its decision) and examined civil and criminal cases remitted by the second chamber.

Sentences in all chambers were to be unanimous (three conforming votes). Cases involving corporal punishment were heard in courts of second instance by no fewer than four judges. Finally, the regent was required to send monthly reports to the governor covering all civil and criminal cases in the territory in order that this information be published.

Although the provisional legislature firmly insisted on the principle of division of powers, it held substantial control over the executive branch through its powers of appointment of the state governor and the governors of the departments, through its powers of review, and through its appointment of the governor's advisory *junta*. The legislature also appointed the regent and ministers of the state court, and it reserved the right to revise, reduce, or set aside criminal sentences handed down by the courts.

The day-to-day administration of justice took place in the *juzgados de primera instancia*, representing continuity from the colonial institutions of the *alcaldía mayor* and the *subdelegación*. The major difference was that judicial, executive, and limited legislative functions were combined in the offices of colonial *alcaldes mayores* and *subdelegados* whereas, in Republican times, the administration of justice became a segregated function. Otherwise, except for the reaffirmation of the principles of equality, peace, and fraternity that guided post-Independence government and law, judges continued their function in accordance with the laws of the Spanish courts, specifically those of March 24, 1813.

Under the decrees of the interim legislature, the state was divided into 18 judicial "*partidos*," each having a *Juez de primera instancia* appointed by the governor of the state. Appointees were to be licensed lawyers over 25 years of age, but under some circumstances individuals schooled in law, but not "certified," could be admitted. Judges were paid a salary and were forbidden to accept payment for services other than for unusual travel expenses.

Judges of first instance heard all civil and criminal cases not specifically reserved to the higher courts. Included within their purview were cases that were either beyond the competence of local alcaldes (aggravated assault, homicide, rape, robbery, etc.) or were within the *alcaldes'* jurisdiction (domestic disputes, property disputes, quarrels) but which could not be satisfactorily resolved within the pueblo. Judges also intervened in disputes between pueblos in their formal judicial capacity or as mediators.

Judges of first instance also had jurisdiction over prisons and were required to conduct tours of inspection of detention facilities every Saturday and report their findings. When judges had doubts on points of law or procedure they consulted a court-appointed *asesor* before rendering decisions.

Government in Oaxaca under the Constitution of 1825

The foregoing discussion serves as a preamble, a model, and a base for the constitutional government that came into existence in Oaxaca with the promulgation of the Constitution of 1825.[15] Under this constitution, the government was declared to be popular, representative, and federal republican. Catholicism was the official religion. The division of powers was retained with the stipulation that none of the three powers could be combined in one person or corporation.

Legislative Branch:

Legislative power was vested in a bicameral institution. Deputies and senators were elected every two years, one deputy per 40,000 population, and seven senators elected by state electors. Elections were performed by parish (*parroquia*), department, and state electoral *juntas*. Parochial elections were by the adult males, with one elector per 1000 population named to the parochial *junta*.

Departmental *juntas* were composed of all electors from the parishes. This body elected one of its own members as representative from the department to the state *junta*. When the state *junta* met in October, it first elected deputies and their alternates based on a ratio of one deputy per 40,000 population. The *junta* then proceeded to elect the seven senators.

The state congress met yearly on July 2 for three consecutive months. After six years, sessions of congress were to be reduced to two months. The chambers of the congress had the customary functions of legislation—linking the state to the federal government and constitution, appointing state employees, taxing/financing state government, borrowing necessary funds, caring for state property, and promoting agriculture, industry, and commerce. The legislature was also empowered to establish schools and supervise education, protect freedom of the press, grant relief to prisoners, provide a state militia, name a state governor, vice-governor, ministers of the state supreme court and a state collector of rents, and promote the general welfare of the citizens of the state and consistently act in their behalf. They were also empowered by the federal constitution to participate in the election of the president and vice president of the republic, ministers of the federal supreme court, and senators of the general congress of the federation.

Executive Branch:

In electing the governor, the chamber of deputies submitted a list of six names to the senate. Within the two succeeding days, the senate was to elect a governor and a vice-governor from the list. The elections were held every three years on July 15, and the governor and vice-governor were sworn into office on August 12. Primary among the functions of the governor was publication and execution of federal and state laws and decrees, preservation of public order and security, composition of laws and regulations to the chamber of deputies, nomination and/or removal of the secretary of *despacho*, nominations of judges of first instance (*jueces de primera instancia*), nomination and recommendation of governors of departments to the senate, collection and investment of state funds, calling congress into extraordinary session when circumstances warranted, dispatching and directing—but not commanding—the state militia, carrying on correspondence with the federal government in matters concerning the state, and having the option of suspending state employees for irregularities.

A governing council (*consejo de gobierno*) composed of the vice-governor and the four oldest state senators advised and oversaw the functioning of the governor. To handle the business of the governor, the congress appointed a *secretario del despacho*, the chief secretary and deputy of the governor, empowered and required to sign all orders and *providencias* issued by the governor. The secretary of *despacho* also submitted to the chamber of deputies an annual report of expenses incurred in administering the government during the preceding year and a proposed budget for the ensuing year.

Administration of Departments and Pueblos:

Each department had a governor to be named as in the provisional constitution of 1823. The term of office was four years, and re-election to one additional term was permitted, either in the same department or in another. The governors ensured public peace and the security of all persons and property within the department. They executed all laws, decrees, and orders transmitted by the state governor, certified municipal elections, and generally articulated local, department, and state levels of government.

The local *ayuntamientos* made up of *alcaldes de los pueblos* (equivalent to former governors, later *presidentes municipales*), *regidores*, and *síndicos*. The number of officials depended on the size of the population of the community. As indicated in the provisional constitution, duties and obligations of *ayuntamientos* were: police, health, education, public works, collection and investment of taxes, imposts, and other funds, agriculture, and local industries. Towns of under 3000 population were to be known as "*repúblicas*," but many smaller communities could and did petition the legislature for "*ayuntamiento*" status: the functional distinction between *repúblicas* and *ayuntamientos* does not seem to have been significant. Elections were held each year. Officers served for one year, except for *regidores* who served staggered two year terms. Any officer could be suspended by the state governor for cause.

The Judiciary:

Judicial power was invested in the tribunals and judges of the state. Penal and civil codes were formed by the legislature to guide the judges and courts in legal procedures, but the actual functioning of the judiciary was controlled by the supreme court of justice. In place of the cumbersome three chamber court of the provisional government, a two chamber body was decreed. It had a regent, a *fiscal*, and several ministers. One chamber was known as a court of second instance for all civil and criminal causes, except in the case of high state officers where the chamber acted as a court of first instance. The second chamber acted as a court of review and as a court of second instance in cases involving high state officers.

Judges of the first instance functioned very much as they had under the provisional constitution, exercising mixed civil and criminal jurisdiction within the *partidos*. Although formal civil and criminal codes were not enacted until later, basic rights, obligations and functions of courts and citizens were defined by legislative decree in 1825. In the case of matters not specifically considered in the 1825 legislation, colonial laws and procedures were followed.

Alcaldes constitucionales functioned in the pueblos as the lowest level of authority in the judicial system, and their activities, obligations, responsibilities, and placement within the judicial branch of state government were carefully delineated under a decree issued on March 12, 1825. They were specifically empowered to process "minor delicts not causing serious injury to the community or its residents," such as quarreling and fighting where weapons or serious injuries were not involved. They also took formal statements from witnesses, and conducted investigations of cases disposed of locally or referred to higher levels for final disposition.

In civil matters, *alcaldes* attempted to mediate disputes between citizens. Conflicting parties presented themselves before the *alcalde* who made a brief notation of the time, the names of parties involved, and the nature of the dispute. Disputants, either personally or through their arbiters (*hombres buenos*), presented their cases without interruption. In some cases, the conflicting parties would retire, and their representatives and a third *hombre bueno* would discuss a case and take a vote. Being advised of the panel's opinion, the *alcalde* would render his decision, summon the conflicting parties, inform them of the decision, and ask them to sign an agreement. If a party refused to sign, it was noted, but the *alcalde* would nevertheless record the decision. Immediate payment was required and, although the constitution prohibited incarceration for debt, the debtor's goods could be embargoed until payment was made.

Alcaldes could function in presentation of wills, conduct inventories, and supervise activities of guardians and executors in civil matters. They were not allowed to act as notaries or maintain formal registries of public documents or to authorize wills, powers of attorney, dowry agreements, incorporations, and other transactions restricted to notaries (*escribanos públicos*) or *jueces de primera instancia.*

Local Level Government

Under the liberal precepts of the law of 1824-25, local communities operated with a relatively high level of autonomy, being free in most cases to govern themselves with little interference from higher authorities. Necessary relations between the local, state, and national levels were mediated by district level officials, but these functionaries made little effort to intervene directly in local affairs. Not only were they enjoined from such interference, but communities had three centuries of experience with successful self-government, and there was little desire or need at the local, state, or national levels to alter the *status quo*. District officials primarily monitored the flow of demands and responses between the state and local level and handled serious cases, both criminal and civil, that could not be resolved at the local level. District and state officials and institutions functioned interdependently to resolve those matters beyond the competence of local authorities and, of course, to intercede in chronically intractible inter-community disputes.

State and Local Government Under the Conservatives

Despite frequent changes in the upper echelons of the federal government, multi-level politics in Oaxaca and relations between the state and national level remained relatively stable until the mid-1830s. By 1836, the faction desiring a more centralized republican form of government was in political control of Mexico, and there was a reversal of the liberal federalism of the early Independence period.[16] In 1837, the conservative national government issued a series of decrees that increased the control of the central government and produced significant changes in the organization of government at the state, district, and local levels.[17] States were designated *departamentos* and were to be governed by *gobernadores*, seven member *juntas departamentales, prefectos* (replacing *gobernadores de departamentos*), *sub-prefectos* of *partidos*, *ayuntamientos*, *alcaldes*, and *jueces de paz*; a legislature; and a state court.

The governor of each *departamento* (formerly *estado*) was appointed by the president of the Republic with the advice of the *junta departamental.* As before, governors maintained order in the *departamento*, employed armed force when necessary, published laws and decrees enacted by the legislative branch, executive orders, circulars, and other communications from the national and state levels of government, and circulated these to the centers of population within the *departamento.* The governor appointed *prefectos*, and reviewed and approved nominations of sub-prefectos and *jueces de paz.* He worked closely with the *junta departamental* in the performance of duties and kept the national government closely informed about the activities of the governor's office and of the *junta departamental.* Other economic, education, health, peace-keeping, and administrative functions were much as they had been before 1837. Under the conservative revisions, however, governors were assisted by a *secretario del despacho* authorized to handle internal government on behalf of the governor and to act as chief of the governor's office. The *secretario* authorized publication and circulation of laws, decrees, and orders from higher levels of government, the dispositions of the *junta departamental*, municipal ordinances of the *ayuntamientos*, police regulations, and orders from the governor. He initiated and signed the governor's correspondence with lower level authorities.

The seven members (and seven alternates) of the *junta departamental* were elected and replaced every four years. This was a legislative body empowered to enact laws relating to taxation, education, commerce, industry, municipal administration, and constitutional "variations." The body established schools, opened and improved roads, encouraged the development of agriculture, industry and commerce, and formed, in cooperation with the governor, municipal ordinances and police regulations. The *junta* oversaw collection and investment of funds, supervised elections of national officials, and proposed to the national government individuals appropriate for appointment as governor of the *departamento.*

Every district was headed by a *prefecto* named by the governor and confirmed by the central government. The *prefecto* served a term of four years and maintained permanent residence in the *cabecera* of his district during his tenure. Re-election was permitted. The functions of *prefecto* were nearly identical to those of the *sub-delegado* of the 1825-1837 period. They were responsible for the good government and order and tranquility of their districts and were directly answerable to the governor. They disseminated, and/or required compliance with, laws, decrees, orders, and circulars issued by state and national governments, including the congress, the governor, and the *junta departamental.* They could impose fines and sentences for violations or non-compliance by individuals or for improper acts or neglect of functions by government functionaries. *Prefectos* resolved conflicts over *ayuntamiento* elections, encouraged (but did not interfere with) speedy and efficient administration of justice by judges, and supervised education. They informed the governor about ways to improve public works, agriculture, and industry within their districts. It was their responsibility to properly divide and redistribute communal lands, supervise the activities and financial dispositions of *ayuntamientos*, name *sub-prefectos* and (with advice from the *sub-prefectos*) *jueces de paz*, and to ensure compliance of *subprefectos, ayuntamientos*, and *jueces de paz* with their respective obligations. *Prefectos* visited each pueblo within their jurisdictions at least once during their terms. They could preside without vote at sessions of the *ayuntamiento* of the district *cabecera* or, if they chose, of any other settlement of the district. Annual salaries were not to exceed 1500 pesos. Upon assuming office, there was a complete inventory of *expedientes*, laws, decrees, orders, and all other "*papeles*" pertaining to the *prefectura*, with all materials to be accounted for by the outgoing *prefecto* before re-assignment to a successor.

Sub-Prefectos

Sub-prefectos were assigned to each "*cabecera de partido*" or principal settlement of sub-districts, or regions, of the *distrito*. Such functionaries were customarily residents of the largest or most important community in the *partido*. *Sub-prefectos* were named by the *prefectos*, with the approval of the governor of the *departamento*. They served for two years without pay, and could be re-appointed.

Sub-prefectos functioning judicially imposed fines of up to 50 pesos and/or sentences of up to eight days for disturbing the peace, disobedience, disrespect, and other delicts. They heard complaints against public functionaries within the *partido* and imposed fines of up to twenty pesos and/or suspension while complaints against them were being referred to the *prefecto* for final disposition. The *sub-prefecto* made annual visits to the communities under his jurisdiction but was enjoined from unauthorized intervention in local political activities. He made recommendations to the *prefecto* on behalf of individuals considered appropriate for service as *jueces de paz*. Although *sub-prefectos* served without salary, they received 75 pesos annually for office expenses.

During the 1830s and 1840s *sub-prefectos* of *partidos* sent monthly reports of notable occurrences to the *prefectos* of *departamentos*. The *Libro del Juzgado de Tlacolula* for 1838 provided the following information:[17]

> January: No deaths and no injuries in the *partido*, except for one case of aggravated assault in Tlacochahuaya.
>
> February: A San Baltasar Guelavila man died of alcoholism; there were three injuries resulting from assaults stemming from *riña* in Mitla and two such assaults in Tlacochahuaya.
>
> March: No pecuniary punishment; no murders; and no injuries resulting from assault. A Matatlan man accused of rape was released for lack of evidence.
>
> April and May: No violent crime or other unusual events.
>
> June: Citizens of Macuilxochitl invaded lands of Teotitlan, killing a Teotitlan resident and destroying property. The *sub-prefecto* indicated frustration at having tried to pacify the communities and with respect to the irresponsible and drunken comportment of Macuilxochitl's *jueces de paz*, his subordinates in judicial matters, and their failure to make arrests and to punish wrongdoers. Also in June, two Tlacolula men were assaulted and injured; a San Dionisio man beat and injured his wife; a Teotitlan man beat his pregnant wife, and she later died.
>
> July: There were no killings or beatings in the *partido*, but charges were brought against a man from San Juan Teitipac for murder.

August: Assaults and injuries occurred in Tlacochahuaya and Tlacolula; a Tlacolula woman died after being "ravaged"; a death resulted from assault in Santa Cecilia Jalieza; an unidentified body was found in the river bed at San Bartolo Quialana.

September: Continued widespread abuses and fraud were being committed by local *jueces de paz*; mutual wounds were inflicted by two women of Guila; a Guelavia man battered his wife; a Tlacochahuaya man assaulted and wounded two men and a woman.

October: Several individuals from Tlacochahuaya were charged with having assaulted the *juez de paz* and his *topil*; a suicide (by hanging) in Tlacolula; assaults with wounds in Guilá and in Santa Ana del Valle.

November: Assault and battery in Santiago Tisaltepec; wife beating in Guilá.

December: Assault and robbery by an armed gang near San Sebastián Teitipac; murder in San Juan del Río; a Tlacochahuaya man was processed for having injured several people in his community.

Reports very similar to that from Tlacolula were sent to the *prefectos* of the eight Oaxaca districts and, in turn, to the *departamento* governor. Originals and/or copies of these reports may be found in state, district, and municipal archives throughout Oaxaca.[19]

Ayuntamientos

Ayuntamientos were authorized in communities which had possessed them as of 1808 and/or which contained a population of at least 4000. In Oaxaca, however, many communities of less than 4000 had *ayuntamientos*.[20] Jurisdictions of the councils coincided with those of religious parishes. *Ayuntamiento* composition depended on the size and/or importance of the community. The number of functionaries were fixed by the *junta departamental*, with the approval of the *gobernador*. There could, however, be no more than six *alcaldes* (most communities had one or two), twelve *regidores* (most had no more than six), and two *síndicos*. *Alcaldes* were elected for one year; only half of the *regidores* were elected yearly; individual *síndicos* were elected yearly, but if there were two, only one would retire per year. All officials could be re-elected after a two year respite, and none could refuse to serve except with approval of the *goberndor* or the *prefecto*.

Among the specific functions and obligations of the *ayuntamientos* were the following:

a) Maintenance of order; police protection, public health, security, public utilities, and general welfare of the municipality.

b) cleanliness of streets, markets, and public plazas.

c) maintenance of a cemetery.

d) care of hospitals, jails, and public welfare institutions not falling under private control.

e) informing the *prefecto* or *sub-prefecto* of widespread disease or health problems within the municipality.

f) forwarding to the *sub-prefecto* or *prefecto* each semester (half-year) a report of births, marriages, and deaths.

g) overseeing and ensuring the smooth operation of public markets and regulating business, weights and measures, and sale of drugs.

h) ensuring that streets are properly laid out, paved, and illuminated.

i) construction of roads and bridges and advancement of agriculture, industry, commerce, and other enterprises useful to the community, establishment, maintenance, and staffing of primary schools.

k) submission of the preceding year's accounts during the first two months of each year to the *sub-prefecto* or *prefecto* (for re-submission to the governor).

Ayuntamientos appointed a competent salaried *secretario* to record municipal business, the appointment to be subject to approval by the *gobernador*. In the event that municipal funds were insufficient, the position of *secretario* was rotated on a monthly basis among the *regidores*.

Alcaldes

Alcaldes maintained order and preserved tranquility in their communities. They enforced police regulations, laws, decrees, and orders relayed by *sub-prefectos* or, in the absence of *sub-prefectos*, *prefectos*. They circulated such regulations and orders to the *jueces de paz* of the municipality. To discharge their obligations, *alcaldes* were authorized to request armed forces from appropriate military commanders or, in the absence of the military, to recruit forces from the community.

Alcaldes were:

a) to remand delinquents to the custody of the appropriate judge within three days of the commission of a crime or apprehension of the perpetrator.

b) to see that residents of the municipality remained gainfully employed and to reprimand idlers, vagabonds, and other undesirables.

c) authorized to impose fines of 25 pesos or sentences of up to four days of public labor (or double the sentence in the case of flagrant or repeated violations) for drunkenness, disturbing the peace, disobedience, or disrespect.

d) to preside over sessions of the *ayuntamiento* and to cast a deciding vote in the case of impasse.

In case of temporary absence, *alcaldes* were replaced by the most senior *regidor*.

Jueces de Paz

The number of *jueces de paz* in the municipalities was fixed by the *junta departamental*. *Jueces* were appointed by the *prefectos* of the *distritos* with the advice of the *sub-prefectos*. They came under the general supervision of the *sub-prefecto*. Communities of 1000 or more were authorized to have *jueces de paz*, but they were also authorized for remote communities of under 1000, barrios and *rancherías distantes de las poblaciones*. Functions in larger or smaller settlements appear to have been identical. They had duties and obligations that were roughly equivalent to the *ayuntamientos* and *alcaldes* of larger entities.

In communities where *ayuntamientos* were dissolved and replaced by *jueces de paz*, an inventory of all records was made and submitted to the *gobernador* who relayed the reports to the *junta departamental*.

Jueces de paz served without salary and could be re-elected after a two-year hiatus.

As can be ascertained from the previous discussion, there was a strong inclination under the centralist constitution not only to maintain firmer control of local level politics but, at the same time, to mix, rather than separate, executive, judicial, and legislative functions at local, sub-district, and district levels. This tendency was generally less pronounced at the state (*departamento*) level, yet there was apparently an increasing diffusion of power and authority away from the legislative branch to the governor. Generally, the judicial function and authority of the superior tribunal of the state remained stable and effective. Although the balance of political power shifted between liberal and conservative forces between 1834 and 1846, the conservative-centralist group dominated federal and state government. The liberal provisions of the 1824-25 federal and state constitutions were shelved as authority increasingly became vested in the central government. At the same time, state governors (*gobernadores de departamentos*), appointees, and direct representatives of the federal executive gained increased control of state politics.

The struggle for greater political liberalization led to claims of sovereignty for Oaxaca and to disaffiliation from the centralistic republican designs of Santa Anna. In 1844, Antonio de León, Oaxaca's governor, broke with the Republican government and proclaimed the existence of the first "*Soberanía de Oaxaca.*"

Political Change in the 1840s and 1850s

By the mid-1840s there existed sufficient dissatisfaction with the ineffectual centralist government, particularly with respect to conduct of the disastrous war with the United States, to promote a shift away from centralist philosophy and policies.[21] In August of 1846, the state constitution of 1825 was reinstated in Oaxaca.[22] Simultaneously, there was movement toward national reform, and a series of innovations was enacted under the *Acta de Reformas* to the *Constitución General* of the Republic of 1847. During this period of unrest, however, there was remarkable stability in the principles and practice of multi-level law and government. Recognized types of crimes and criminal procedures remained as before. The same was true for civil matters.

Many civil cases, particularly those involving proprietorship and transfer of property, could not be resolved at the local level. Both legal and technical competence was at the district level. When cases were referred from the local to the district level, the local *alcalde* both investigated (often at the direction of the Judge of First Instance) and referred cases. In many instances, however, individuals carried their complaints directly to the district level.

During the summer of 1847, a resident of San Marcos Tlapazola died intestate.[23] The matter of inheritance and division of the dead man's property between a daughter and a son lay beyond the competence of the *alcalde* and was referred to the Judge of First Instance of the Tlacolula district for disposition.

In June of 1847, Francisco Pérez of San Miguel Albarradas brought suit against José Olivares of the same community over dispossession of land. The matter was resolved by the Judge of first instance in Tlacolula.

Also in June of 1847, María Juana Martínez claimed that her deceased husband's family was attempting to "deprive me of everything I have." Her case was heard and resolved in Tlacolula *Juzgado*.

Among the functions of the judge of first instance was the resolution of intercommunity conflicts over boundaries. Some, as in the case of an 1848 suit between San Juan Guelavia and Santa Cruz Papalutla, were resolved—at least temporarily—through conciliation (*convenio*), with the judge acting as conciliator.[24] "In order to preserve peace" the two sides came together in San Juan Guelavia on December 6, 1848. Guelavia was represented by one *alcalde*, two *regidores*, a scribe, and others from the community; Papalutla's contingent included one *alcalde*, three *regidores*, one scribe, and several townspeople. An agreement was made to restore destroyed boundary markers, clean the boundary line, and, in future, respect boundaries between the communities. The agreement was committed to writing, signed by representatives of both sides, and submitted to the Judge for approval.

A long-standing, virtually intractable, boundary dispute among Tlacochahuaya, San Antonio de la Cal, and San Agustín de las Juntas re-emerged in 1849. Citizens of Tlacochahuaya complained that their opponents were destroying boundary markers, cutting trees, and allowing livestock to graze on Tlacochahuaya lands. Pending resolution of the dispute, twelve burros captured by Tlacochahuayaya officials were placed under custody of the Judge of first instance in Tlacolula. This conflict, further complicated by the fact that Tlacochahuayaya was in the Tlacolula district and the opposing communities were in the Centro district, began in the seventeenth century and persisted into the twentieth. Simple conciliation was ineffective. The conflict required full litigation and repeated intervention of district, state, and national judicial authorities.[25]

Local Criminal Justice

Many cases of assault and murder took place within families. A typical case came before the *juez de primera instancia* of Tlacolula on January 28, 1847.[26] María Antonia Morales of Tlacolula, reported that on the previous Saturday night she was in her kitchen preparing *agua de nixtamal*. Her father-in-law, Pedro Méndez, entered and "struck me with a *tapajo* that he carried in his hand." He gave her about five *cueridas*, but she did not know what she had done to deserve such treatment. The immediate justification for the act was that she had not served the meal to her husband when he came in from the field. She attempted to run to the *juzgado* to report the incident and make her declaration, but the father-in-law would not permit it and beat her further. She complained that these abuses occurred repeatedly, that they were worse when the father-in-law was drunk, and that she wanted official intervention by the district judge.

On January 9, 1847, María Martín Sánchez of Santiago Matatlan complained to the Tlacolula *juez* about her husband of two years.[27] "I have had a bad life with him. He is always attacking me with insolent words as well as beating me repeatedly...." She had come to the *juzgado* to complain the previous year, and during the preceding week he had beaten her and her mother. María felt something had to be done or she would be killed.

During, before, and after the 1840s and 1850s, relatively minor family disputes were usually settled within the community through the local *alcalde*, but not with universal success. José Miguel García of Lachigoló went to the Tlacolula *juzgado* on January 28, 1847 to register a complaint.[28] He had had a problem with a nephew over an ox. They could not reach an agreement, so the matter was taken to the *alcalde*. When José could not pay an exorbitant (and probably extorted) 1 peso, 7 *reales* in costs, the *alcalde* ordered him jailed in Tlacolula. Subsequent to swearing out a complaint against the *alcalde* and petitioning for release from jail, the judge intervened on behalf of the petitioner.

It is worthy of note that the types of cases and the range of activities associated with the management of civil complaints (inheritance, land transfers, property loss, and so forth) in the period from 1847 to 1849 are virtually identical to cases, activities, and procedures occurring in colonial times, during the *Imperio Mexicano*, early republican times, through the 1850s, the *Reforma*, French Intervention, and the *Porfiriato*, and, in fact, until the present. To recount such cases and procedures for these periods would be largely repetitious.

Rampant factionalism during the 1840s and 1850s impeded movement toward liberalization-decentralization until the war of Reforma in the middle to late 1850s. Manifestations of reform were promulgation of the liberal state constitution of 1857 and establishment of the second *Soberanía del Estado de Oaxaca*. Except for general reforms relating to church/state relations and land reform, the state constitution of 1857 represented a return to the constitution of 1825. Many liberal principles of government and law were restored. Oaxaca again became a state with a governor, congress, and state court. Districts were recreated and *Jefes Políticos* were appointed to take charge. *Ayuntamientos* continued to function, now led by *presidentes municipales*, with *alcaldes* being assigned to more specifically judicial functions.

Although the amount of power allocated to various levels of government shifted with alternating policies of centralization and liberalization, the traditional four-level system of community, district, state, and national government remained fully intact. Reforms on either side were never directed toward re-organization or displacement of the system itself.

The Reforma

Sweeping political and legal changes were instituted at the national and state levels between 1855 and 1867. Reformed constitutions were enacted at both levels in 1857.[29] The *Reforma* was directed primarily to separation of church and state, re-allocation of civil functions from ecclesiastical to civil jurisdiction, segregation of the military, and land reform. Controversy swirling around the reform movement of the 1850s led to bloody fighting between liberals and centralists and to the *Guerra de Reforma*. Despite the raging conflict, reformation was achieved. The principal reforms and the time of enactment at the national level and promulgation/ratification by the state of Oaxaca were as follows:[30]

> Suppression of civil and criminal jurisdiction by ecclesiastical and military tribunals—the so-called *Ley Juárez*. Enacted at the national

level in 1855, promulgated in Oaxaca in 1856.

Disamortization of unused or monopolized property (*bienes de manos muertas*), primarily those held by the church. National and Oaxaca: 1856.

Nationalization of ecclesiastical property, establishment of independent civil authority, and declaration of religious freedom. National and Oaxaca: 1859. Additional laws guaranteeing freedom of ownership were issued in 1860.

Re-assignment of jurisdiction over marriage and the civil registry of birth, marriage, and death from the church to the civil government; removal of jurisdiction of the clergy over operation of cemeteries; and prohibition of formal involvement of public officials in church affairs and functions. National and Oaxaca: 1859.

Secularization of hospitals and welfare institutions. National and Oaxaca: 1861.

Extinguishment of religious societies (*comunidades religiosas*). National: 1863: Oaxaca: 1867 (following French Intervention).

The years 1861 and 1862 were critical in the development of state and local government in Oaxaca. The spirit and the laws of the Reforma were actualized in government. Numerous changes occurred as government simultaneously modernized, liberalized, and became more effectively centralized than it had during the preceding three decades since Independence. It was also a time when the vultures of European imperialism once again swooped down on Mexico in the form of French intervention. The full force of the intervention did not reach Oaxaca, however, until 1865. So, what of government until that time?

Correspondence of the early 1860s between *jefaturas políticos* and the state Governor's office reveals functions and relationships existing between these levels of government as well as the relationship with the pueblos and the national government.[31] The war with the French was underway in 1861, and the provinces were involved in the war effort to the extent that they were able to contribute men and resources. Men were registered and some were conscripted, primarily for service in Puebla. Taxes were assessed by the state government on a temporary basis and at a low rate, but voluntary donations were also given by certain citizens to aid the war effort. These were collected by the *jefes políticos* and submitted to the governor's office.

The collection of direct contributions to the state had been officially terminated in 1852 by the state congress. *Alcabalas* (taxes on foreign and some domestic goods) were abolished on April 24, 1861, but because of government needs and the war, these were reinstituted on December 14, 1861. District *cabeceras*, such as Nochixtlan, were designated as collection points for funds and personnel during this time.

As was the case throughout the period of their existence, *jefes políticos* and governors were frequently involved in resolving land disputes between communities. Intercommunity land disputes were costly. Often, as in a vigorous and persistent case between Zahuatlan, Tecomatlan, and Jaltepetongo, the former two disputants could not afford to finance their suits independently and asked to have a topographical map made by an authorized engineer and to split the cost.[32] The *jefe político* of Nochixtlan made their request known to the governor, who approved the procedure. During March of the same year, 1862, the *jefe político* of Nochixtlan informed the governor that several pueblos were not in conformity with judicial decisions relating to the fixing of boundaries. As was typical in numerous similar cases, the governor was asked to attempt a final resolution.

In 1861 the registration of births, deaths, and marriages was removed from control of the church and placed in the hands of the civil government. Legislation to transfer responsibility had been enacted in 1859, but not put into effect until 1861. At this time, the position of *juez de estado civil* (judge of the civil registry) was created, with individuals being appointed to serve (at 400 pesos per year) in the *cabeceras* of the *distritos*. They oversaw registration, collected and concentrated records from the municipalities, maintained cumulative census records, or *padrones*, and forwarded copies of all records to the state level. *Jefes políticos*, who had general supervision over activities of *jueces*, informed the governor of activities and/or irregularities in the civil registry or by its administrator.

French Intervention and the Second Empire

On Janury 4, 1865, Juan Pablo Franco was appointed as the first *Prefecto Imperial* of the *Departmento de Oaxaca*, and in February the imperial government of Maximillian established offices in the city of Oaxaca.[33] *Subprefectos* were established in the various districts (e.g., Tlacolula, Teposcolula, Etla, Miahuatlan, Tehuantepec). The legislature was dissolved, but the courts continued to function as before. During the brief period of French control, there was little change in the actual performance of government and judicial activity at the district and local level. *Ayuntamientos* continued to function as before. *Sub-prefectos* exercised the powers of their predecessors, the *prefectos* and *sub-prefectos* of the *distritos* and *partidos*. Judges of the first instance continued to function at the district level, relating to the communities as before, and referring their actions to the superior court of the *departamento imperial* for approval. At the state (*departamento*) level, however, there was greater concentration of power in the hands of the *Prefecto Imperial*. Legislative functions and authority were in a state of suspension. Administrative reorganization of the provinces was undertaken, but there was little or no permanent change effected in the structure or function of law and government.

In compliance with the Law of 3 March 1865 the empire was divided into fifty *departamentos*, including Oaxaca, Tehuantepec, Ejutla, and Teposcolula.[34] However, on 10 April, 1865, the organization was modified. The nation was organized into fifty *departamentos* grouped into eight grand divisions. Each *departamento* was divided into *distritos* and each *distrito* into *municipalidades*. The intent was to retain the basic organization in effect during pre-imperial times but to make it more efficient in operation.

The persistence of traditional problems, as well as the intent of the government to deal with them, is reflected in the law of November 1, 1865. With a view to ending longstanding differences among the pueblos over lands and water, Maximiliano acted "to end the frequent disputes, often lasting for ages, that disturbed peaceful relations among the pueblos or between them and the haciendas."[35] Article One of the law held that

> Any community that demands property or possession of lands or waters against another community or private owner will present to the *Prefectura política superior* of the *Departamento* an exposition of its claim accompanied by documents upon which the claim is based and copies of them on ordinary paper in order that they be compared and certified by the *Secretaría* of the *Prefectura* which will return them.

Private individuals were instructed to do the same. *Consejos Departamentales*, closely supervised by the *Prefectos*, were then empowered to resolve the disputes and to make awards. Although well-intentioned, there is no indication that the imperial reforms were ever instituted in Oaxaca. Edmundo O'Gorman has commented that "... the liberalism of which the *Partido Liberal* boasted so much has in Mexico its best representative in Emperor Maximiliano."[36] This seems to be reflected in the above instance, but as in the case of other reforms instituted by the ill-fated leader and his government, practice could not be brought into line with principle, no matter how well intended. The lasting effect of the Maximilian reforms on the multi-level system of government and justice was practically nil. With the demise of the Empire in 1867, there was a return to the practices and principles of government in effect in pre-imperial times. "In sum," remarks González Novarro, "Mexico emerged from the struggle of the *Reforma* and the *Imperio* with the facade of a republican federal, liberal, and democratic country."[37] The years ahead were to provide strenuous testing for all of these concepts.

Restoration of the Republic

The program of reform instituted in the 1850s and 1860s had not been carried into effect when the French intervened in Mexico. With the restoration of the Republic in 1867, there was a quick return to the laws of reform and to the Constitution of 1857.[38] In Oaxaca, as in most of the nation, the Liberal Party was in power and, although far less than unanimity existed among the various liberal factions, liberal precepts of government prevailed. Although Oaxacans favored Porfirio Díaz, native son, war hero, and future president, Benito Juárez was re-elected president in 1868. In Oaxaca, Félix Díaz, brother of Porfirio, began serving as governor in late 1867 and acted vigorously to control unrest among the state's dissident groups.

The post-Intervention recovery in Oaxaca was difficult. There was factional conflict among political groups; communities continued feuding over lands and boundaries; and the state government was without funds. It was essential, however, that the laws of reform be put into effect and/or enforced, particularly those dealing with separation of church and state and with land reform. The political system extending from community to district to state to nation, however, was virtually unaffected. The chain of authority remained in operation; demands continued to be made; serious cases continued to be handled at the district level with the approbation of the state judiciary; goods and services were mobilized and channeled through the various levels of governments as they had been prior to Intervention. Titles changed, but political norms and functions remained stable.

As provided in the Constitution of 1857, the governor appointed *jefes políticos* of the various *distritos* of the state. The *jefes* continued to function and to be charged with responsibility to maintain law and order in the district and in the communities, to act as the political representative of the governor, and to require compliance with demands from district, state, and national levels of government. Félix Díaz succeeded in appointing *jefes* of his own liberal persuasion during the late 1860s and early 1870s, thereby reinforcing his own position while ensuring good internal government within the state. Communities continued to require judicial services from district and state, and demands were systematically and sympathetically managed at the state level.[39] The state also provided at least token assistance with health (particularly immunization) and education, but the major burden of providing these and other services, as in the past, fell on the communities themselves.

By 1869, Félix Díaz held the loyalty of the state legislature and of the state Tribunal and judges of first instance. Despite his great power within a state that claimed and was granted a high level of political "sovereignty," Félix developed a reputation for able leadership and, initially at least, maintained an open form of government. As often occurs in situations of rising concentration of political power, however, Díaz became increasingly dictatorial, restrictive, and repressive.

The national elections held in June of 1871 were marked by violence in Oaxaca. The state was strongly under control of Félix Díaz and virtually independent of the federal government. After Juárez was elected and later confirmed by Federal Congress, Porfirio Díaz led an unsuccessful uprising in protest. In November of 1871, Porfirio initiated the *Plan de la Noria*, accusing Juárez of abuse of the Presidency and calling for constitutional revision. Félix Díaz, in accordance with the *Plan de la Noria* and claiming election irregularities as justification, declared the separation of the state of Oaxaca from the Federation. He was nearly unanimously supported by the legislature composed of his followers, and he assumed virtual complete military and political control of Oaxaca. As Félix Díaz took over the central district, Félix Romero, a follower of Juárez, assumed control of the remote mountainous Ixtlan district and asserted executive control of the state.[40] A division was created in the state. Romero, loyal to Juárez and the Constitution of 1857, was supported by Juaristas in Tehuantepec, in Juquila, and Jamiltepec, and elsewhere in the state. The federal government responded to the revolution in Oaxaca by sending in a large force under General Ignacio Alatorre, who quickly defeated the Díaz forces and brought the state back under federal control in January of 1872. Félix Díaz fled Oaxaca but was subsequently apprehended, and on January 23, he was executed in Chacalapa near Pochutla.

President Juárez died in July 1872, and was succeeded by Sebastián Lerdo de Tejada. New elections were held in Oaxaca in August, 1872. Liberals supporting the 1857 Constitution gained control of state government which they tenuously maintained for four years.

Lerdo de Tejada sought reelection in 1876, but a group of Oaxacans met in Tuxtepec and, on January 10, 1876, formed the *Plan de Tuxtepec*, which had as its major objective a rebellion against the central government of Lerdo de Tejada. Early attempts led by Porfirio Díaz to overthrow the government were unsuccessful. Meanwhile, there were uprisings in the Sierra de Ixtlan led by Fidencio Hernández and Francisco Meixuerio. This group of rebels soon invaded and captured Oaxaca City and took over the state government. Encouraged by their successes, the rebels prevailed upon Díaz to lead the revolution of the *Plan de Tuxtepec.* On February 18, 1875, a group of rebels led by General Fidencio Hernández fought and defeated the government forces commanded by Ignacio Alatorre in the battle of Cerro Jasmín near Yanhuitlan in the Mixteca. Although Hernández was subsequently defeated in battle at Orizaba, the overall leader, Porfirio Díaz met with success. Díaz defeated the federal armies, captured the national capital, and in the spring of 1876, after Lerdo de Tejada was forced to flee the country, Díaz was named President of the Republic.

The Porfiriato

Serving as provisional president in 1876, Porfirio Díaz was elected to his first full term as President in 1877.[41] During the 34 years from 1876 to 1910, the dynamic Oaxaqueño served 30 years as president. He controlled the government and the economy of Mexico, obtaining the loyalty of the Congress, the courts, the state governors, the vast majority of the Mexican population, and the cooperation of business interests and major foreign governments. He managed to stifle dissent, less by force than by incorporation of dissendents into the government through *pan o palo* politics.[42] Most significantly, Díaz and his supporters brought unity, peace, and stability to Mexico for the first time in its post-colonial history.

In 1883 and 1884, the *Leyes de Colonización* were enacted.[43] This led to formation of companies to identify, survey, and lay out boundaries in the *tierras baldías* of the Republic. In payment for services, the federal government awarded the organizations with grants of lands derived from territory subjected to survey. Other lands were put up for sale at low prices. Rural Communities and the clergy were most affected by the program, as lands were taken from their control and reassigned to private corporations. As a result of the outcry from offended parties, the land grabbing boundary-marking program was discontinued. So far as can be determined, central Oaxaca was little affected by the program. This was due primarily to low demand for the relatively poor, fragmented, and mountainous central Oaxacan lands. Most affected were the lowland areas of Tuxtepec-Valle Nacional and Ixtlan-Tehuantepec. The latifundization of lands in these areas touched off violent interaction between pueblos, and among pueblos, haciendas, companies, and individuals over lands and resources. These patterns became institutionalized and have persisted into the mid-twentieth century. Even more enduring,however, were the long-standing conflicts between the pueblos of central Oaxaca.

The violent intractable conflicts that have characterized intergroup relations in the highlands since Colonial times were as intensified as those in the lowlands, but the private holdings—the haciendas, plantations, and privately held ranches—were smaller and less important as a causal factor in the system of conflict and conflict resolution than in the lowlands. The roots of conflict ran deeper and were nourished by an active, but ineffective, system of administrative-judicial conflict resolution, growing population, demands for productive lands and resources, an atrophied technology, stabilized productivity, and persisting animosities. Further contributing to the conflict syndrome were a lack of viable alternatives for subsistence outside the agriculturally-based settlements and continuing demands on communities by the state and federal levels of government.

Both *jefes políticos* and *jueces de primera instancia* were involved in land disputes and boundary-setting. Typical was a long and bitter dispute in and around Hacienda Xaaga and Mitla that was resolved by the *jefe político* and *juez* of Tlacolula in 1888.[44] The case had at one time or another involved local and district officials, the governor, the state tribunal of justice, and the legislature. Since colonial times, communities petitioned higher level authorities for separation from their "cabeceras." In Republican times, petitions were usually made to, and decided by, the state legislature. Normally such petitions, as in the 1888 cases of Cerro de la Campaña of Tlaxiaco and Nopalera of Santa Lucia Monteverde, were channeled through *distrito jefes políticos* and the state governor.[45] Often, additional information was requested and this was customarily provided by the communities involved and by the *jefes políticos*. Upon approval by the legislature, orders were endorsed by the governors and forwarded to the affected communities and *jefes políticos*.

Jefaturas devoted considerable effort to intervention in local conflicts. Typical of hundreds of such cases was a dispute in the mid-1880s between the communities of San Andrés Lagunas and San Miguel Tixa in the Mixteca Alta.[46] San Andrés sought to drain certain lands for conversion to agriculture. Upon receiving the claim from the San Andrés *ayuntamiento*, the governor directed the *jefe político* of Teposcolula to investigate, delineate affected lands, and assess consequences. The *presidente municipal* of San Miguel, however, complained to the governor of bias and prejudicial behavior on the part of the *jefe político*. Further investigation was ordered before permission was granted to proceed with the drainage project.

With respect to local-level government, it has been claimed that "under the dictatorship of Porfirio Díaz, the *ayuntamientos* lost most of their constitutional faculties, with the result that their activity was restricted to minor transactions."[47] This was clearly not the case in Oaxaca where *ayuntamientos* and local *alcalde* justice functioned actively and effectively throughout the *Porfiriato*. In 1892 there were 22 *ayuntamientos* and 13 *agencias* operating in the 30 pueblos and 5 *villas* of the Teposcolula district.[48] There was a *jefatura política*, a *juzgado de primera instancia*, a *juzgado de estado civil* in the district cabecera. Additionally, there were 40 *juzgados constitucionales* in the cabecera and communities of the district and 6 tax-collection offices in the largest towns. Federal offices included one post office, one tax-stamp office, and a telegraph agency located in the cabecera. In the religious sector there were five parishes falling under control of the *Obispado de Oaxaca*. This organization was repeated throughout the twenty districts of the state of Oaxaca.

Neither local level politics nor the form and function of the multi-level system of law and government was significantly altered during the *Porfiriato*. If the hand of state government was strengthened in local politics, it was more advantageous than detrimental to local interests. Legal cases were handled much the same as they had been in pre-Porfirian times and as they would be after 1910-17, and just as effectively. If anything, the education, health and other welfare services, economic development, marketing procedures, and communication represented substantial improvements over prior practices and certainly were preferable to the periods of anarchy and chaos of earlier republican times and of the 1910-17 Revolution.[49]

Conclusions

The multi-level political and legal system of nineteenth century Oaxaca has been examined against the backdrop of seemingly radical shifts in national political ideology and institutions. What may be most remarkable is that despite the great political upheavals of the century, local level government and relations between local, state, and national levels ended essentially as they began. A practical and basically effective system which evolved during the colonial period survived and persisted through a series of experiments in government. The result was that alternative forms were found to be no more effective in governing and integrating a great collectivity of ideologically, socio-politically, and economically autonomous small communities, than was the system operating during the early decades of the century.

The form and function of government and law changed very little between the 1820s and the beginning of the twentieth century. After 1824, offices changed names, and relations that had been imprecisely defined in colonial times became explicit in republican times. The interposition of the district level between the communities and the state necessitated a re-sculpting of the administrative and judicial offices of the *alcaldes mayores* and *subdelegados*, but basic functions and the mediational stance of the *subdelegados* were virtually unaltered from colonial to republicantimes. These functions were later transferred to department governors and ultimately to district-level judges and *jefes políticos*. Major transformations occurred at the state level where the combined powers vested in the *intendente* were reallocated among the executive, legislative, and judicial branches of government. Although relative allocation of power among the branches fluctuated between liberal and conservative phases of the republican period, functions were persistingly complementary and power was relatively balanced. When imbalance occurred, it favored the executive branch. Recruitment to office at the state level shifted from executive appointment to an elective process, but powers of appointment remained as an essential adjunct to free election. Clearly, intermediate power positions, the regional department governors, *jefes políticos*, and judges of first instance, were controlled by the state governor through his appointive function. Recruitment at the local level remained elective as it had during the colonial period.

Despite attempts to deny or ignore its existence, the *ayuntamiento* remained effectively in operation throughout the nineteenth century. The functions, needs, problems, and responsibilities of local government, if anything, expanded after Independence. The maintenance of peace, settlement of legal cases, construction and maintenance of public works, administration of lands and resources, and custodianship of the civil registry (reassigned in 1867 from ecclesiastical to civil authority) required local action. At the same time, no settlement existed in isolation. None was closed off from social, political, and economic interaction with the outside. Not a few political demands—the processing of minor delicts and the resolution of much intra-community conflict—could be satisfied at the local level. More serious matters within or beyond the community normally involved district, state, and national offices and institutions. In this respect, it could be said that the local communities stood in a position of dependency on the multi-level system of government and justice. At the same time, and more positively, demands that could not be met locally could be processed by the larger system.

The nineteenth century provided a testing ground for local *ayuntamiento* government and the multi-level system of government to which it related. Communities were not inclined to surrender political authority or traditional social, political, economic, and educational functions and allow these matters to be taken over by an impersonal, self-interested, and distant government. Yet there were advantages to be gained and necessary services to be performed by the network of externally-based institutions. The communities accepted and functioned within the system, and the Mexican government accepted the *municipio libre* and local-level government as irreducible facts of national life.

Ayuntamiento government and the basic local-state-national multi-level political system survived with only modest alteration after 1917. By the 1940s, however, it was clear that more than the traditional system would be required for effective government. While the system was functionally "sufficient" during the nineteenth and early twentieth centuries, it is no longer capable of processing the demands of burgeoning national and state government, an encroaching world economy, and greatly increased social and geographic mobility of rural populations. A plethora of new committees, commissions, agencies, and para-political institutions relate communities and regions to the outside world, often bypassing intermediate levels of government. The periphery is linked directly to the center in a way that was neither necessary nor desirable in the nineteenth century.

Although the traditional multi-level system of government and justice persists, it can meet some, but not all, of the political, legal, social, and economic needs of Oaxaca's communities. The system forged in the nineteenth century, in effect, is inadequate to meet the needs of modern Mexican society. On the other hand, local, district, and state offices and courts do continue to serve a variety of critical functions, and unless a better system is consciously devised and accepted, it is unlikely that the traditional system will disappear.

NOTES

[1]I wish to acknowledge monetary support from the National Endowment for the Humanities and from the Center for Latin American and Iberian Studies, Vanderbilt University. Assistance and advice as provided by Judith Gorodetzky and María de la Luz Topete, Director of the Archivo General del Estado de Oaxaca, is also gratefully acknowledged.

[2]For detailed consideration of Spanish colonial government and relations among royal, viceregal, and provincial levels of government see Haring 1947:175-78; Gibson 1966:90-111, 160-81; Lira and Muro 1976; Fisher 1926. Indigenous and local level government is discussed by Zavala and Miranda 1954:75-83.

[3]See Fisher 1929; Haring 1947:144-48; Gibson 1966:170-74.

[4]"Noticia geográfica del Reino de Nueva España y estado de su población, agricultura, artes y comercio (1794)" por Carlos de Urritia (Manuscript in BNM, Cedularios, 1402, ff. 206-296), quoted in Florescano and Gil 1973:117-22.

[5]Based on Alejandro de Humboldt, "Tablas geográficas políticas del reino de Nueva España (1804)," as reported in Florescano and Gil 1973:128-71.

[6]See Taylor 1972; Zeitlin, this volume; Spores n.d., chs. 6-7.

[7]Haring 1947:174-75; Zavala and Miranda 1954:75-83.

[8]Discussion of the Revolution in Oaxaca as presented here and below is derived from Iturribarría 1935:7-32; 1955; "Estado de Oaxaca," 1966-1977:487-88; Dalton Palomo et. al. 1980:15-71; Taracena 1941. For more general discussion, see Villoro 1976:303-56.

[9]AJT, leg "H"; AJTL-Jus; AGEO-Juz, 1821-1823; AMT, legs. 3, 12.

[10]AJT 54-18; AJT 80-16, 17.

[11]For general discussion of the Mexican Imperial period, see Vázquez de Knauth 1974:1-16 and Robertson 1952.

[12]Iturribarría 1935:7-32; Dalton Palomo et. al. 1980:67-71; "Estado de Oaxaca," 1966-1977:486-88; Taracena 1941. Robertson 1952; Vázquez de Knauth 1974:1-16.

[13]Iturribarría 1935:33-79; "Estado de Oaxaca," 1966-1977:488-492; Dalton Palomo et. al. 1980:73-92.

[14]The present section on early republican political organization is based on Iturribarría 1935:81-209; "Estado de Oaxaca," 1966-1977:488-92; Dalton Palomo et. al. 1980:73-92; Oaxaca provisional and state constitutions of 1823 and 1824; and on numerous executive orders and legislative acts. See *Colección de Leyes y Decretos del Estado Libre de Oaxaca, 1851*:5-384; Pérez Jiménez 1959:30-60; and Topete and Spores 1982:9-16, 45-47.

[15]INAH, Oaxaca, Tlacolula, rollos 1-2. Pérez Jiménez 1959:61-103.

[16]Iturribarría 1935:193-321; "Estado de Oaxaca," 1966-1977:491-94; Taracena 1941.

[16]AGEO-DOS, Marzo de 1837; Topete and Spores 1982:13-21; AJT 77, exps. 454, 456, 536, 540. For documentation and general consideration of the conservative movement, conflict between conservatives and liberals, and the pivotal role of López de Santa Anna, see González Novarro 1974b.

[18]INAH, Oaxaca, Tlacolula, rollos 1-2.

[19]Numerus examples may be found in AGEO-G; AJT; AJTL; and AMT, legajos 1-6.

[20]INAH, Oaxaca, Tlacolula, rollo 2.

[21]The period of the 1840s and 1850s is discussed in detail in Iturribarría 1935:227-441. Also see "Estado de Oaxaca," 1966-1977:493-97; Taracena 1941.

[22]*Colección de Leyes y Decretos del Estado Libre de Oaxaca, 1851*; Pérez Jiménez 1959:104-5.

[23]AJTL-Jus, 1847.

[24]AJTL-Jus, 1848.

[25]AJTL-Jus, 1849.

[26]INAH, Oaxaca, Tlacolula, rollo 2.

[27]INAH, Oaxaca, Tlacolula, rollo 2.

[28]INAH, Oaxaca, Tlacolula, rollo 2.

[29]Pérez Jiménez 1959:113-83, 254-55. For detailed discussion of the *Reforma* in Oaxaca, see Berry 1981. More general discussion and references may be found in Torre Villar 1974.

[30]Pérez Jiménez 1959:142; Dalton Palomo et. al. 1980:21-148; "Estado de Oaxaca," 1966-1977; Taracena 1941; González Novarro 1974c.

[31]AGEO, LE, Decretos, 1861.

[32]AGEO, LE, Decretos, 1861.

[33]Various aspects of the French intervention in Oaxaca are discussed in Berry 1981; Dalton Palomo et. al. 1980:161-71; "Estado de Oaxaca," 1966-1977; Taracena 1941; Iturribarría 1955.

[34]O'Gorman 1937:175, 193.

[35]González Novarro 1974c:332.

[36]O'Gorman 1937:173.

[37]González Novarro 1974c:260.

[38]Pérez Jiménez 1959:113-83, 255-56. *Féliz Díaz, Memoria Administrativa presentada por el General Féliz Díaz, 17 de Septiembre, 1869.* For documentation and general discussion of the period of the restoration of the Republic, see González Novarro 1974a:339-64; also Dalton Palomo et. al. 1980:172-83. A highly reputable source on the period is Cosío Villegas 1955.

[39]Abundant supporting documentation for these assertions may be found in AGEO-Juz and G; AJT; AJTL-Jus. Also see Díaz, 1869. Legal substance and procedure were unmodified.

[40]Dalton Palomo et. al. 1980:180-81.

[41]Developments during the Porfiriato in Oaxaca are outlned in Dalton Palomo et. al. 1980:189-219. Among the best of the numerous general studies of the *Porfiriato* is Valadés 1941-1947. For documentation and general discussion of the Porfiriato, see González Novarro 1974a:339-48, 364-432.

[42]"*Pan o palo*": Roughly, "bread or the club."

[43]González Navarro 1974a:371-74.

[44]AGEO-DMA.

[45]AGEO-G, 1888.

[46]AGEO-JP, 1883.

[47]"Ayuntamiento," *Enciclopedia de México* 1966-1977:423. Also see *Ley de Ayntamientos...de 1889.*

[48]AGEO-C, 1892.

[49]Archival support for these conclusions are abundant. For example, see AGEO, Informes y documentos que forman el informe administrativo de 1871; AGEO-G, Relación de los negocios que se despachan en esta sección, 1886. AGEO-G, Copia del inventario general del archivo de esta Jefatura de Huajuapan, 1890. AGEO, Informe de la Jefatura política de Tlacolula, 1905. AMT, legs. 1-37. Bolaños Cacho 1902; Pimentel 1904.

A Political Chronology of Oaxaca, 1787 to 1911

1787 to 1788:	Last *corregidores* and *alcaldes mayores*
1789:	First *intendentes*
July 30, 1821	Last *intendente*
May, 1822 to March, 1823	*Imperio Mexicano* of Iturbide
1823 to 1824:	Oaxaca State provisional constitution of 1823
1824 to 1836:	Federal constitution of 1824 and Oaxaca state constitution of 1825
November, 1834 to August, 1846:	Republican centralist constitution of 1836. First *Soberanía de Oaxaca,* 1844
August, 1846 to February, 1847:	Reinstitution of Oaxaca state constitution of 1825
February, 1847 to February, 1853:	Oaxaca under state constitution of 1825 and *acta de reformas* of the general constitution of 1847
February, 1853 to October, 1857:	Oaxaca under the statute for provisional government of Oaxaca of 1855 and the Revolution of Ayutla
October, 1857 to January, 1865	Oaxaca state constitution of 1856 and War of *Reforma.* Second *Soberanía*
January, 1865 to December, 1866	Oaxaca under the provisional statute of the Empire of Maximillian
December, 1866 to January, 1876:	Reformed constitution of 1857 and the *Plan de la Noria.* Third *Soberanía*
January, 1876 to May, 1911	Oaxaca under the reformed constitution of 1857, the *Plan de Tuxtepec,* and the Dictatorship of Porfirio Díaz

COMPLIANCE AND COALITIONS IN THE MEXICAN GOVERNMENT: 1917-1940[1]

Claudio Lomnitz

Introduction

Political anthropologists studying Mexico have difficulties linking local-level political processes with the regional, national, and international-level politics that these studies are meant to illuminate. As community studies accumulate, it is apparent that the sum of the politics of each of Mexico's localities does not produce a clear picture of Mexico's political system, a situation that has counterparts in the difficulties that macro-sociological and historical studies have in accounting for events at the local and regional levels.

Basically, these problems are related to: 1) researchers' reluctance to study the systematic spatial dimension of politics; 2) insufficient attention to the political system's temporal and spatial structure. Community and macro-level studies cannot provide a generalizable view of politics in a given nation if the historical and regional structures are left to intuition. Analysis of any level in a political system—be it village or national government—requires consideration of that level's relationship to others.

This paper's focus is the temporal structure of Mexico's national-level politics between 1917 and 1940. Using Skinner and Winckler's[2] approach to cyclical change, I will examine power relations between the federal government, four social classes (peasants, workers, the national bourgeoisie, middle class), and two pressure groups (the army and the US government). A preliminary analysis shows that the 1917-40 period can be seen in terms of coalition cycles between the government and these six groups. This approach displays long-term compliance relationships, permitting a better analysis of governmental and intragovernmental relations and actions as they change through time. It is a necessary step for linking local and regional histories to that of the country as a whole.

The Model

Relations between the government and each of the six groups in question are viewed in terms of *compliance*, distinguishing the intentions of the power-holders (goals), the type of power used to attain their ends (power), and the effects this has on those controlled (involvement).[3]

Goals are divided into ideological, economic, and order; power into normative, remunerative, and coercive; and involvement into commitment, indifference, and alienation. The three levels are conceived as homologous in their internal constitutions, with each goal possessing an optimal associated power and involvement. For example, ideological goals are best attained with the commitment of the "lower participants" through normative power.

Skinner and Winckler converted this typology into a dynamic model by asserting that there is an intrinsic cyclical movement in each of the aspects of compliance caused, in part, by this lag. According to them the form of these cycles depends on the nature of the political system in question plus the interaction between the three aspects of compliance.

Regardless of the specific political system, these cycles have an intrinsic movement, that tends towards the following form: normative-coercive-remunerative-normative. This is because once ideological goals are achieved, the only way to demobilize committed "lower participants" is by force (i.e. coercive power); but once the lower participants have been duly repressed, they are alienated from the norms of the upper participants and can only be mobilized via economic incentives, resulting in indifference, so that, finally, the only way to mobilize them further is via commitment. Theoretically, each goal (or kind of power or involvement) can be assigned a point in this field (see figure 1), the intensity of which is expressed in terms of its distance from the "balanced" hexagon—the further from the hexagon in the direction of, say, economic goals, the more strictly economic (and less balanced) the goal.

This model has several problems, not the least of which is its nominalism. What is an "order" goal? How is it distinguished from an "economic" one? How are concrete historical occurrences classified into a combination of, for example, ideological goals, remunerative power, and committed involvement? In addition, even if these concepts are adequately defined, how is their intensity determined? And, finally, if these methodological difficulties are surmounted, why should the cycles occur in the predicted sequence? Cannot a "committed" mob be demobilized with "economic" incentives?

All of these problems are very real. However, this approach also has major advantages. Skinner and Winckler's simplifications allow us to get at a basic and very elusive aspect of power systems—their temporal structure. By forcing the analyst to "plot" the relations between the power-holders and the powerless systematically, by providing for a dialectic between the motives of the dominant group, its means, and the results of its dominance on the group that is over-powered, the method brings us closer to understanding the *reproduction* of power relations. Once this structure is laid bare, detailed historical and ethnographical research can correct the vulgarizations of human relations produced by the initial application of the model. I have modified Skinner and Winckler's model in the following ways:

1. To avoid using vacuous concepts, I redefine the components of the compliance concept for each new compliance relation treated.
2. By comparing the compliance relations between the government and each of the six groups, I construct a coalition cycle that constitutes the most basic temporal rythm in Mexican class politics.
3. I have found that the shape of the compliance cycles proposed by Skinner ad Winckler (e.g. normative-coercive-remunerative-normative) does not always hold. Some of the impediments for compliance relations to change in the direction postulated by Skinner and Winckler are related to the coalitions that upper and lower participants have with other groups.

Methodological Considerations

Compliance relations between the government and the six pressure groups have been modelled on two types of material: yearly statistical data of specific indicators that reflect relations between the government and the lower participants,[4] and an aggregated historical picture of the relations between upper and lower participants.[5] However, since the statistical material is uninterpretable without a qualitative view of the events of the period, I have constructed gross models of compliance based on general qualitative history, and then related some statistical indicators to that model (see table 1).

By way of justification for the breadth of the topic at hand, I must emphasize the exploratory nature of this research as well as some of its limitations. I am not, using this model to analyze the whole of class politics, nor am I treating the classes in their spatial contexts or considering government relations with the vertically organized groups that are so important in Mexican politics.

Class Politics in Mexico: 1917-1940

Upper Participants: Which Government?

At the end of the Revolution, Mexico was a nation of poorly interconnected regions, many with drastically different economies. Most regions were dominated by local strongmen (capitalists, *hacendados*, and/or revolutionary generals) who had a large degree of autonomy from the government. The State had fallen into the army's hands, and the new governing elite was composed of the revolution's main military and ideological figures.[6] Governorships and ministries were given to generals, municipal governments to local *caudillos*, and many posts of the bureaucratic rank-and-file to the literate middle classes.

Until the 1930s, the position of the President vis-à-vis other generals was that of *primus inter pares*,[7] and one of his most difficult tasks was keeping his peer generals under control. Through the revolutionary army, all classes and interest groups could phrase their demands in more or less convincing terms: conflicts within the "revolutionary family" continually occurred, and rebellious factions immediately sought the support of neutral classes and groups or those antagonistic to the President. Factional competition was the prime motive for making and breaking coalitions between the government and the different pressure groups.

There was neither monolithic government opinion nor unified action toward each class, since, invariably, some members of government possessed independent power interests divergent from those of the President and his associates. Nevertheless, I have chosen the President and his faction as representative of the government since his was usually the winning coalition. When it was not (as, for example, during Carranza's last year or during Portes Gil's interregnum), there was soon a change of presidents, and the goals and power of government were correspondingly changed.

Government/worker relations

Between 1917 and 1940, the Mexican working class was divided into non-unionized and unionized workers, the latter further divided into unions of diverse political orientations, and all workers divided by industry and geographical region. For organized labor, I am focusing on CROM and (later) CTM-affilitated unions as they constituted, for practical purposes, the government's own definition of the "working class."[8] Due to their lack of formal organization, unorganized workers were marginal to governmental class politics.

The mechanisms of compliance between the government and this class were and are *sui generis* and follow a different logic than that between organized labor and government.[9]

Since Alvaro Obregón's "red brigades," the organized working class achieved political influence greater than its numerical importance.[10] Workers were concentrated in cities, could harm Mexico's most modern capital investors (especially mining and oil), and were more effectively mobilized than peasants. However, their force alone was insufficient to coerce the government. Since the elaboration of the constitution in 1917, the government effectively established itself as a mediator between labor and capital,[11] and paternalistic relations between government and organized labor characterize this period. The government became the spearhead of working class vindications and the working class became a governmental tool for pressuring other interest groups.

Although compliance relations between the government and the working class are not completely separable from those with other classes, I define governmental goals toward the working (and all other) classes by the nature of immediate, and not general or overall, goals:

> *Ideological goals*: Those goals that, independently of direct working class pressure through class strife, seek to better the conditions or increase the power of the working class.
>
> *Order goals*: Those that seek to quell organized class strife.
>
> *Economic goals*: Those that seek to increase industrial production.

Within presidential periods (basic time units for goals), four general stages can be discerned:

1. An initial period of ideological goals, where the president seeks to bring relative benefits to the working class (and thereby win their loyalty).
2. A shift toward the president's more sincere long-term goals (generally economic; normative in Cárdenas' period).
3. A shift toward order goals because of governmental power crises (this shift often entailed mobilizing workers in favor of government. I define them as "order" rather than "normative" goals because mobilization aims at restoring or maintaining order, not altering the workers' position in society).
4. A disintensification of all goals (end of presidential period) with a preference for the president's long-term goals.

Each of these shifts in goals is relative to those of the preceding and succeeding year: it is not that all periods begin with, say, strong "ideological" goals, pass to economic, then to order, and back to strong economic goals; rather, each president begins his period by shifting toward normative goals, then back toward long-term ideals, then toward order, and so on (see tables 1 and 2).[12]

In the government/worker relationship, power is defined as follows:

> *Normative power*: The manipulation of shared ideologies (notably

nationalism, socialism, and "populism") for the mobilization of workers.

Coercive power: The physical repression of workers.

Remunerative power: Bettering working conditions, increasing union power, or bettering union leaders' conditions.

Involvement is defined as follows:

Commitment: The will to support the government and its policies (measured by mass mobilization in favor of government and by success of governmental programs involving workers' voluntary cooperation).

Alienation: The will for government to fall, the will not to cooperate with governmental plans (measured by lack of pro-government mobilization and support of anti-government groups and policies).

Indifference: The will to do strictly what is most convenient for each individual worker. Workers are only mobilized by direct economic incentives.

Power and involvement (see tables 3 and 4) on a year-by-year basis yield the following general conclusions:

1. Governmental power, like its goals, follows presidential periods as its basic time unit.
2. Each presidential period begins with a shift toward normative power.
3. There is a shift toward remunerative power in the second year.
4. Governmental power crises (that provoked order goals) are met with a shift toward either normative or coercive power.
5. The final year shows a tendency toward remunerative power.[13]
6. Involvement is less sensitive to presidential changes than goals and power and does not neatly follow their four-stage development. Changes in involvement lag behind changes in goals or power, and generally fluctuate between commitment/indifference at the outset of each presidential regnum and indifference/alienation.
7. Nevertheless, governmental goals and power did affect workers' involvement. Initial presidential promises all produced increases in commitment that generally changed to indifference or, when commitment was strong and adversity great, to alienation. The workers also responded to presidential power crises—by either alienation or commitment.
8. Shifts in involvement were less extreme than shifts in goals or power. This unveils the basic nature of the mode of production, in which the workers' position was far from priviledged (see figures 3 and 4).

According to the analysis above, compliance between the government and the working class has the presidential period as its' basic reproductive time-unit, each period being subdivided into four stages. Are these stages visible in the available statistical indicators?(see graph 1).

Graph 1 shows the number of strikers per year between 1920 and 1940. This variable should generally be interpreted as follows: the more strikers in a given year, the more the regime is interpreted as pro-worker.[14] Classifying each year's values as high, medium, or low within its presidential period, and then classifying each presidential period as a whole, produces the following:

PERIOD	*YEAR OF THE PRESIDENT'S TERM*					
	1	2	3	4	5	6
Obregón (pro-worker)	HIGH	HIGH	MID	MID	LOW	
CALLES (anti-worker)	HIGH	MID	LOW	LOW		
Maximato (anti-worker)	MID	MID	LOW	MID	LOW	HIGH
Cárdenas (pro-worker)	HIGH	HIGH	MID	LOW	LOW	LOW

Except for the *Maximato*, the trends within presidential periods are homologous and fit the goal-power-involvement framework well; high mobilization at the beginning of each presidential term, declining toward the end. Strikes were not incited by the government during power crises, thereby limiting this type of mobilization to the beginnings of each period.[15]

Finally, the presidential periods with more strikers in their first year than during the last year of the preceding president were those of Obregón (although we have no statistics before 1920), Portes Gil, and Cárdenas. Increasing the number of strikers is a sign of the initiation (or attempted initiation) of new eras for goals.[16]

Government/peasant relations

In discussing governmental goals for, and power over, the peasants, and the kinds of involvement these produced, some long-term projects to which the government elite was committed must be mentioned. The first and most important is the ***sonorense*** ideal of changing Mexico from peasant to farmer agriculture. Land grants were one route toward creating the mythical capitalist farm. The emphasis in agro-politics was on increasing commercial production, eliminating unproductive land, and creating an internal market for industrial goods. The other main ideological goal was ***agrarismo***—distributing land to the peasants, while encouraging agricultural growth based on cooperatives and small-holdings.

General governmental goals for rural Mexico ranged from elimination of the peasantry to creation of a socialist countryside. Short term goals ranged from directly opposing either of these ideals (ideological goals), to reaching a desired level of production (economic goals), to keeping the peasants quiet (order goals), to mobilizing peasants for the government's self-defense (ideological-order goals).

The government tried to attain these various goals in several ways: 1) distributing ***ejido*** and communal land (remunerative-normative power), 2) granting credit, constructing an agricultural infrastructure, promoting commerce, and opening new markets (remunerative power), 3) repression (coercive power), 4) mobilizing people on the basis of shared ideals such as nationalism, *agrarismo*, and patronage (normative power).

Peasant heterogeneity hinders clear analysis of the kinds of involvement entailed in their response to government power. Peasant involvement in governmental politics was "balanced," but charged with contradictions. In analyzing workers, "balanced involvement" means most *individual* workers feel a mixture of commitment, indifference, and alienation, whereas in analyzing peasants, it means some *groups* are alienated, others committed, and others indifferent, thus prohibiting generalization of the mood toward government. As a corrollary of this condition, extreme commitment or extreme alienation is less common among the peasantry than among the workers.

Contrary to Etzioni's model, the use of remunerative power toward peasants produces commitment. Indifference is caused by governmental non-interference, and alienation by government support of landowners, tax increases, inflation (usually attributed to government), and government repression. Commitment also stems from identification of government with important community values such as nationalism in most *mestizo* communities, identification of government with paternity and paternalism, and identification—for some individuals—of atheist beliefs, education, science, and patriotism with government. Peasant rebellions and lack of cooperation with governmental projects (even those involving economic incentives) are indices of alienation; indifference is reflected in lack of cooperation, and commitment is manifested in voluntary cooperation and spontaneous support for government.

Analysis of Table 5 suggests the following conclusions:

1. Goals. Each presidential period marks a change in the immediate short-term goals that justifies their use as temporal units. Years with economic goals predominate (18 years have "economic goal" components, 14 have "order," and 9 have "ideological"). Ideological goals appear most strongly when global governmental projects change (from Carranza to Obregón and from Ortiz Rubio to Cárdenas). Goal cycles can thus be thought of in terms of projects: the Carranza project, the *sonorense*-project, and the Cárdenas project.

The goal shifts in these projects fit Skinner and Winckler's predictions: each period begins with ideological goals, shifting to order goals as a result of efforts to calm the peasants, and then to economic goals because they are the result of the government's ideological goals, or because of the government's need for revenue, or of the country's need for food.[17]

In contrast to Skinner and Winckler's model, the goal cycle (I-O-E) is inverted in Cárdenas' period due to differences between his and the preceding presidents' goals, and shifts toward order goals are often provoked by crises *external* to government relations with the peasantry.

2. Power. Use of the three types of power is more balanced than either the goals they are intended to fulfill or the involvement they cause. The beginning of each cycle corresponds closely with presidential changes. Each period (*Maximato* counts as 1) begins with an appeal to peasant ideals and with distribution of land. Coercion, then, becomes necessary to quell peasant dissatisfaction with the unaccomplished promises of the new president, and the government uses economic incentives to achieve its economic and political goals.

During national crises, usually army-related (1923, 1927, 1929, 1938), the government used a combination of normative and remunerative power to mobilize the peasantry in its favor. The exception was the government's response to the threat of military rebellion before 1920: instead of allying with the peasants, Carranza continued his coercive rural policy, permitting the peasants to ally with his rivals, which contributed to Obregón's success.

During the four-year presidential regimes (Obregón and Calles), the use of remunerative power was cut short due (presumably) to the brevity of these periods.

3. Involvement. Of the three components of compliance, involvement changes most slowly and least extremely. Only 42 percent of the periods of involvement occur in clusters of two years or less before shifting, while it is 45 percent for goals and 63 percent for power, indicating continuous power shifts in relation to both goals and involvement.

Commitment is usually strongest during changes in government projects (Obregón and Cárdenas) or crises in peasant-oriented regimes (especially in 1923 and 1929). Commitment is usually of short duration and only to push for specific changes (or maintenances). The exception is the Cárdenas regime, whose presidential goals were more sympathetic to the peasants than previous regimes.

The apparent irregularity of changes in involvement during Obregón's period illustrates peasant commitment in non-*agrarista* regimes—short-term, goal-specific, and not analyzable in a strict cyclical fashion. During Cárdenas' period, commitment was of greater duration and in greater conformity with theoretical expectations. For the *sonorenses*, peasant involvement went from indifference to alienation, commitment coming only with the threat of another revolution, at the upsurge of pre-revolutionary agrarian politics, or against the United States (see figure 5).

One concrete indicator (number of hectares distributed per year) shows a straightforward relationship between peasant involvement and agrarian reform (see graph 2). The 1917-1940 period is divided into three stages or projects (the Carranza project, the Obregón project—lasting until 1934—and the Cárdenas project), each internally homogenous but containing common elements of change.

Presidential changes toward the peasantry are related to succession, occurring during each president's initial year in office and at the time his successor is determined (see graph 2).[18]

Mexican/United States governments relations

In the compliance relations between the American and Mexican governments, the former held more power. However, the Mexican government had resources over which the US government had no direct control.

The Mexican government's goal vis-à-vis the United States was to decrease US power over it. However, in years of political and economic crisis the goals were gaining American recognition, avoiding military intervention, securing loans, negotiating better treatment of Mexican migrant workers, exercising greater control over US industries in Mexico, and increasing exports. These diverse goals can be subsumed under the following general categories: 1. lessening US power over the Mexican economy and government (ideological goal), 2. securing US political and economic support (economic and order goals), 3. avoiding armed intervention (order goal).

The following types of power were available to the Mexican government: 1. raising the costs of military intervention (usually achieved via mobilization of Mexican masses and through support from other powers), 2. attracting investment or political support from competing powers, 3. attracting investment by guaranteeing peace and property or by attractive tax and interest rates, 4. harming US interests by not guaranteeing peace or property.

The power to attract US economic interests is classified as remunerative, but it is a power beyond the government's control. The power to mobilize masses is coercive. Finally, the appeal to certain principles considered valid within the US, such as national independence, the capacity of each nation to forge its own destiny, and so forth, are classified as normative (however, this kind of appeal was always weak, since it depended on pressure from the US citizenry).

Mexican government compliance can be classed as follows: 1. alienation (caused by lack of respect for US property, refusal to pay debts, or inability to maintain internal order), 2. commitment (caused by the reverse of these propositions), 3. indifference (caused by the belief that all alternatives are equal).[19] See table 6 and figure 6.

The relation between power and involvement is direct and sensitive, while that between goals and power is not, reflecting the US government's inability to feel indifference toward government policy (due to its position as a hegemonic power) and the Mexican government's relative weakness.

Involvement fluctuates between commitment and alienation, with short intermediary periods of reserve. The US government felt more committed at the end of each Mexican regime's term than at the beginning, indicating success in imposing US terms, although the recurrent alienation shows the revolutionary government's capacity to pressure the United States (optimally, in the initial years of a president's term).

Government/middle class relations

Although many members of the "revolutionary family" had middle class origins, there is no substantial identity of interests between the government and the middle class. The "middle class" falls into at least two distinct groups—owners of means of production (petty bourgeois) and salary earners (white collar workers and liberal professional)—each, in turn, subclassified by occupations into rural and urban, and so forth.

Governmental goals toward the petty bourgeoisie paralleled those of the national bourgeoisie, as the latter comprised much of the former.[20] Consequently, for analytical purposes, this class is subsumed under the national bourgeoisie (a step inadmissible for later Mexican history).

Government goals for white collar workers and liberal professionals differed, as the government subsumed private employees under other categories—petty bourgeois if they were in the liberal professions, working class if they were not. The bureaucracy, however, was a different story, and one for which information is scarce. The specific goals for Mexico's 150,000-employee bureaucracy are unclear, but, in general, the bureaucracy was permitted sufficient latitude to represent different class and group interests, but not sufficient to ignore presidential desires. It was an arena for contending groups seeking hegemony yet forfeiting their power to dissent with the ruling elite.

FIGURE 1

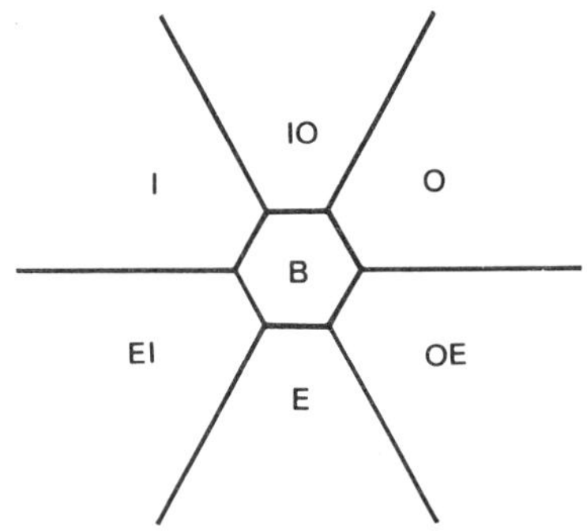

I - IDEOLOGICAL GOALS   O - ORDER GOALS   E - ECONOMIC GOALS

FIGURE 2 GOALS

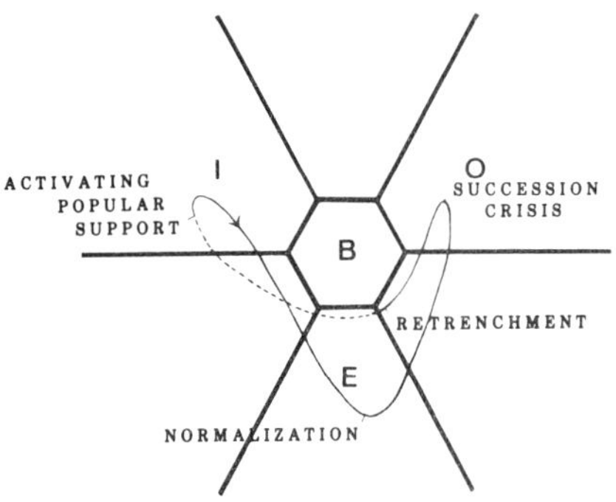

FIGURE 3 POWER

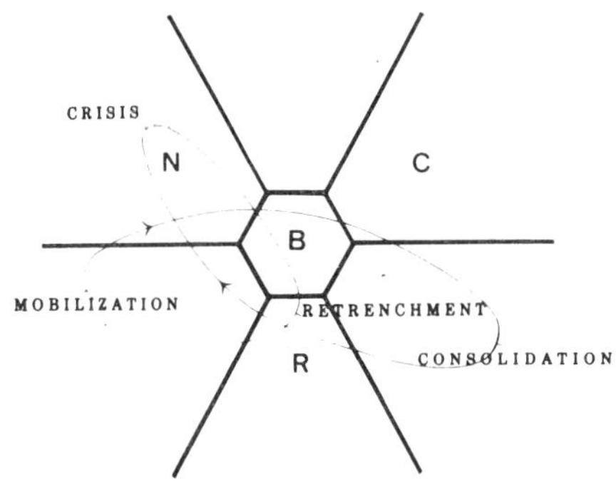

FIGURE 4 INVOLVEMENT

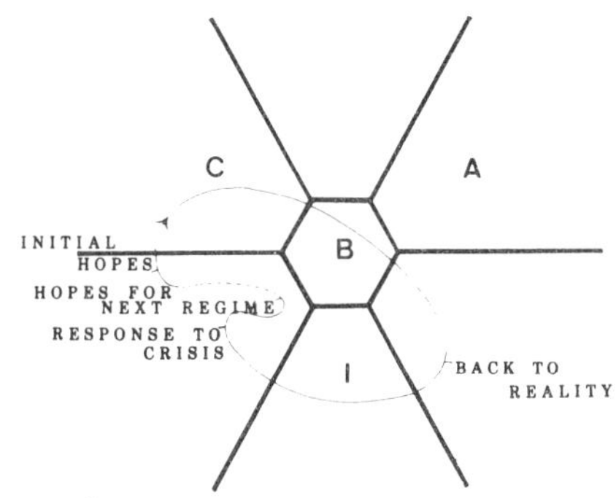

FIGURE 5a GOALS

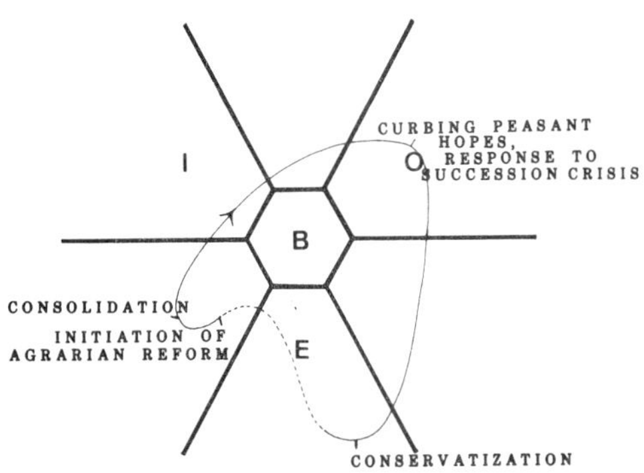

FIGURE 5b POWER

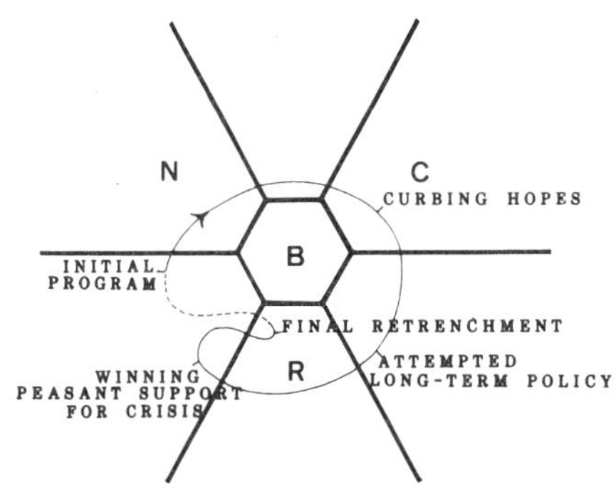

FIGURE 5c INVOLVEMENT

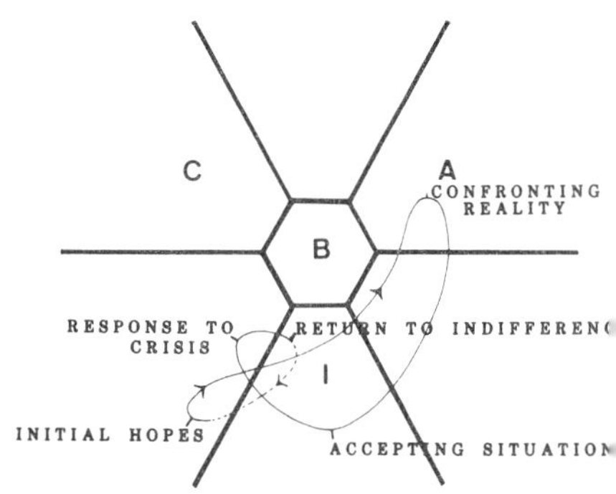

FIGURE 6a GOALS

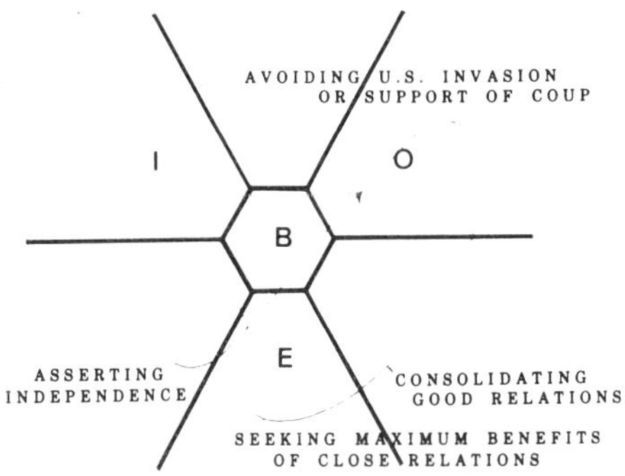

FIGURE 6b POWER

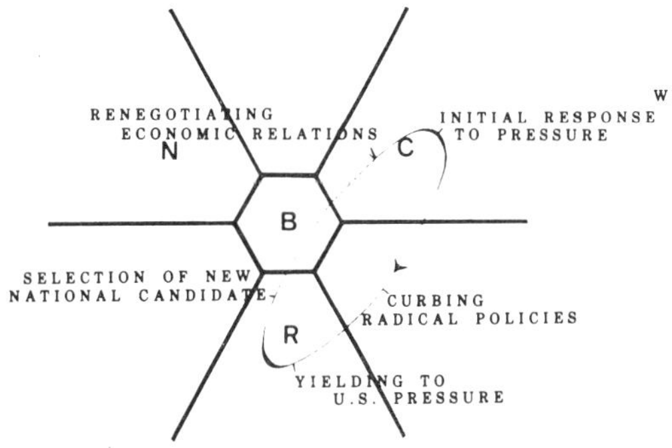

FIGURE 6c INVOLVEMENT

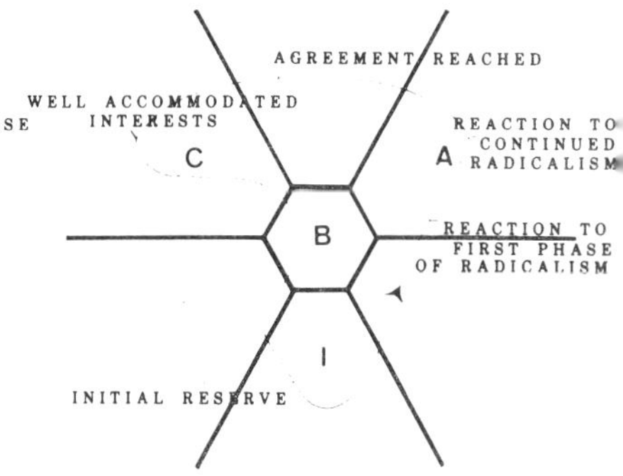

FIGURE 7a GOALS

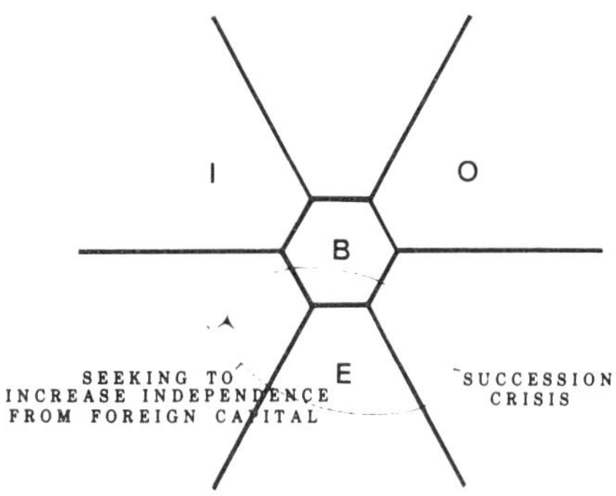

FIGURE 7b POWER

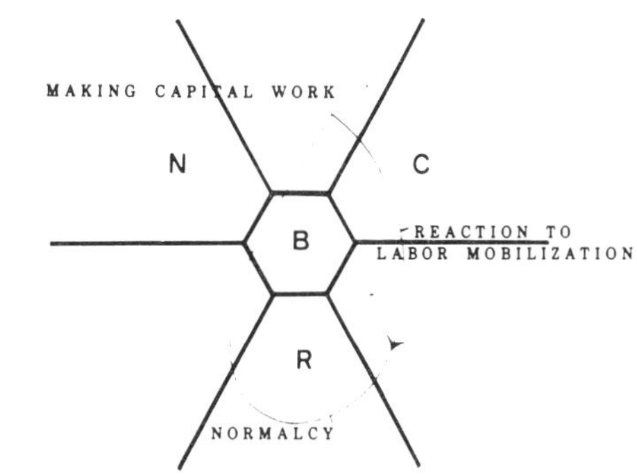

FIGURE 7c INVOLVEMENT

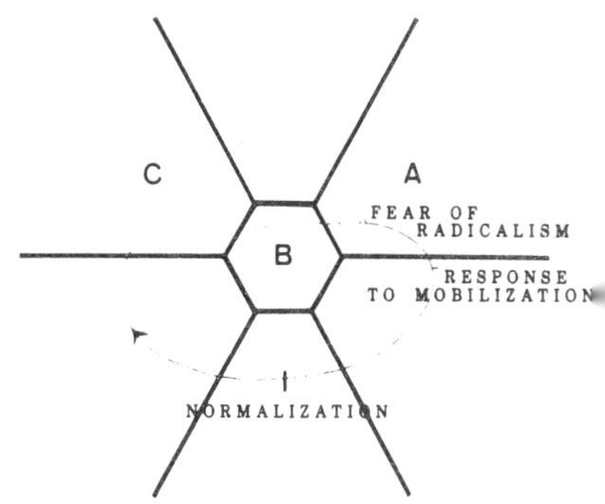

FIGURE 8a GOALS

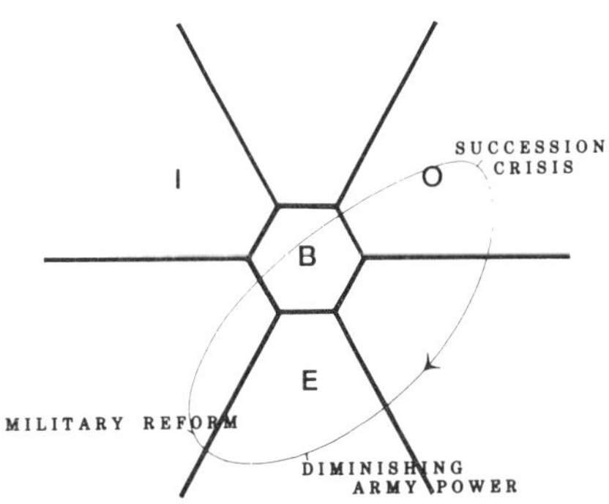

FIGURE 8b POWER

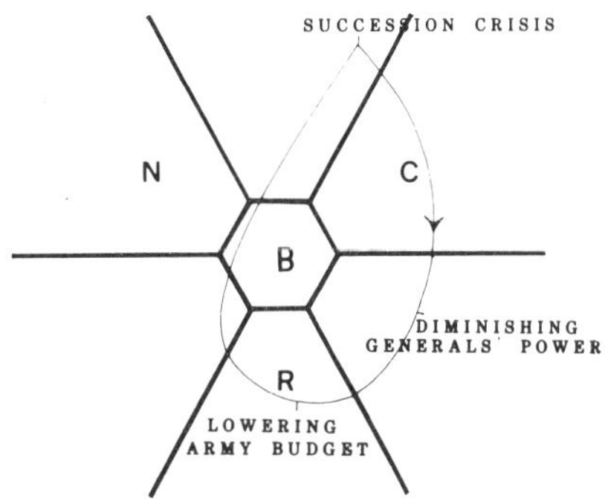

FIGURE 8c INVOLVEMENT

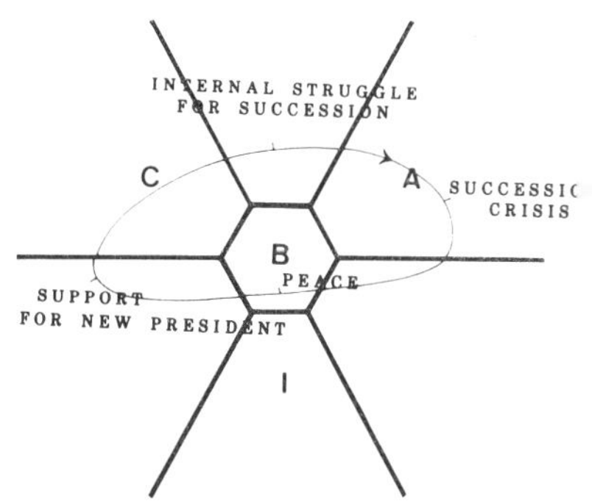

Thus, ideological goals were to increase the bureaucracy's power beyond its internal needs or the nation's administrative demands, and to reorient bureaucratic activity. Economic goals were to increase the efficacy of bureaucratic action, and order goals were to immobilize politically active sectors of the bureaucracy.

Evidently, the ruling elite's power over the bureaucracy was immense: setting salaries, hiring and firing, repressing organized demonstrations and individual organizers, and—through many shared interests—appealing to common ideals (see table 7).[21]

Government/national bourgeoisie relations[22]

The national bourgeoisie's role in the Mexican economic and political systems reveals several long-term governmental tendencies. Some desired a strong, innovative, and modern bourgeoisie to guide the economy and the political system, government economic intervention being considered as a necessary subsidy to the rise of this group. On the other hand, others desired a bourgeoisie subservient to national (and governmental) interests to make Mexico economically independent, and to increase production in the economy's most depressed sectors, but not to become the country's dominant class.

The power wielded by the government over the national bourgeoisie is as follows: to tax, to create protective tariffs, to provide infrastructure (initially roads and railroads, later electricity and gasoline), to convert large tracts of land to *ejido*, to subsidize industry, and to mediate labor disputes. The power that allows the government to close down an industry is coercive; the remainder of those listed are remunerative when used as positive incentives. The government's normative power over the bourgeoisie was largely restricted to general nationalist principles, and the appeal to order and stability.

Bourgeoisie involvement depended on the incentives offered by the government and was rarely indifferent. Like the workers, however, the national bourgeoisie was in a poor position to pressure the government, since it was not a strong class. Instead it appealed to the government's sense of convenience, to shared ideals of what Mexico should be, and to the fact that several important government figures, such as Carranza, were of this class. However, the national bourgeoisie and middle classes were the only classes that could reliably support the government without alienating foreign powers (see table 8 and figure 7).

The following conclusions derive from this table:

1. Except for years of political crises (which provoked order goals), governmental goals were generally economic and ideological.
2. The bourgeoisie's inability to control the government is reflected in its alienation and indifference, exposing ideological differences with the government, historically expressed in terms of populism versus liberalism.
3. The government's infrequent use of normative power indicates the disparity between government and bourgeois interests, as the latter were not usually major policy-making considerations.[23]
4. The general pattern of change for other classes is not clearly reflected in government relations with the bourgeoisie, due to the national bourgeoisie's minor role in class politics. This lack of pressure on the national

bourgeoisie allowed great flexibility (and therefore stability) in its relation with the government.[24] This also allowed an easy flow from government to that class, and the national bourgeoisie served as a kind of asylum for retired or inactive politicians.

Government/military relations

Toward the end of the revolution, the "army" was composed of groups representing diverse classes and interests. Each of these segments could have had independent political weight at the beginning of Carranza's presidency; but, as Tobler and Lozoya[25] have demonstrated, the army quickly lost sight of the peasant interests many of its members were supposed to represent.[26]

The government, however, did not view all of the army's characteristics and aspirations as desirable. Government leaders were often intent on reducing army budgets and individual officers' control over local and regional economies and politics (economic goals), and on controlling the different generals and reducing their ability to rebel against the government (order goals).

The power used to attain these goals were a) normative (the appeal to common revolutionary goals, such as nationalism, democracy, non-reelection, and to peace), b) remunerative (the expansion and reduction of the army's size and budget), and c) coercive (the use of loyal troops and armed peasants and workers against rebelling army factions). See table 9 and figure 8.

There was a gradual reduction of the army's capacity to rebel, and order goals became less urgent. In addition to the secular trend, this era can be subdivided into three periods: Carranza's attempt to subordinate military to bourgeois-civilian rule; Obregón and Calles' periods when Obregón was the undisputed chief of the army, and the PNR and PRM periods (1929-1940) when Calles convinced the generals to forget the Obregón model and become members of a single party that handed concessions to the different power groups in the army. Correspondingly, goals shifted from ideologic, to order, to economic. The main emphasis throughout is on economic and order goals, with ideologic appearing only during major army reforms.[27] Accordingly, the predominant power used toward the army were remunerative (Obregón said: "No one can resist a canonball of 50,000 pesos.") and coercive. Normative power, however, provided the army with a rationale for doing what they were being paid or coerced into doing throughout. But normative power was a decisive factor only after Obregón's assassination, when a commitment to peace made the generals avoid revolution and join Calles' party. Economic power was used unsparingly to control the army. Reducing the size of the army was necessary to balance the federal budget, and expenditures generally diminished. However, budget increases were used to ensure army loyalty in times of crisis. Involvement of the army's *leaders* was divided among groups backing the president and those with their own aspirations for the presidency. Only when it supported Obregón against Carranza was the army unified. Involvement was more unified after unsuccessful military coups, when insurgent generals were purged (1923, 1927, 1929) and the capacity of the main generals to rebel diminished. Commitment and alienation were most common. Invariably, alienation increased in the year succession was determined.[28]

Despite the general trend for federal military expenditure to diminish (see graph 3), of the six years in which military budgets go up (1919, 1921, 1924, 1927, 1929, 1940), five are in response to the army's alienation.[29]

The Coalition Cycle

We have thus far shown that the compliance relation between the government and 6 pressure groups shift in important, often regular, ways. These shifts can be seen as the result of a lack of definitive hegemony of any of these groups over the state. However, this power void did not merely produce chaos and unstructured change; the revolutionary elite filled the void by constantly shifting its class alliances, thereby gaining both stability and power. These class coalitions changed in a regular, cyclical way: shifts in class coalitions were essential to the reproduction of the mexican state.

The government changed the groups with which it formed coalitions because of pressures from opposing groups and in an attempt to strengthen itself and gain independence from all these forces (see table 10). Lack of presidential reelection was a crucial mechanism in gaining independence from the classes: class coalitions changed with presidents because of the mistrust of former allies, but also because of the personal interests involved after a solid coalition with the national and international bourgeoisies had been achieved. Table 10 is a first step in establishing the concrete shape of the coalition cycle: it systematizes the correlations between the relations of the government and each class.

Government relations with workers and with peasants are positively correlated; there is a moderately positive correlation between the government's relation to the US government and to the national bourgeoisie, workers and peasants involvement with the government has a strong negative correlation with the involvement of the national bourgeoisie and the US government. The army and the bureaucracy are ambiguously related to all other groups.

Thus, the president begins his period by establishing an alliance with the workers and peasants, which, with his control of the army, establishes his dominant position within the "revolutionary family." However, winning over the peasants and workers requires concessions (such as landgrants, salary increases, concessions to unions, and nationalizing industries) that invariably alienated the US government and, to varying degrees, sectors of the national bourgeoisie. American economic and military pressure was then exerted, and some presidents reduced their support of peasants vis-à-vis the national bourgeoisie, but not vis-à-vis foreign interests. The opportunity to ally with the United States government and overthrow the president fostered factionalism within the "revolutionary family." American pressure, the danger of a military revolt, and internal economic crises (when the government supported popular interests against those of the national bourgeoisie) led the president to curb his popular policies, often gaining, or re-gaining, American support in time to eliminate internal military threats. Thus, conservatism increased during the post-crisis stage prior to presidential succession (see table 11).

The duration of the coalition cycles increased as governmental stability increased.[30] All military rebellions (with the exception of the Cristero War, which was not a schism in the revolutionary family) occurred during the period of retrenchment before presidential successions (1920, 1923, 1927, 1929, 1938).[31] Since workers and peasants are not intrinsically related (the two classes exist at different levels of the regional systems hierarchies and are not directly related in their modes of production), government relations with these groups need not coincide. Nevertheless, they are actually quite close, since, from the government's point of view, supporting either workers or peasants would alienate the US. Consequently, when such estrangement became necessary, the government attempted to maximize its position and sought support from both peasants and workers.

General Implications of the Model

In conclusion, the above analysis has implications for three general issues: the concept of the nature of the Mexican State; the way national, regional, and community studies of politics are integrated; and the implications of this cyclical model on more linearly-oriented history.

The nature of the Mexican state

Mexico's governing elite in the period after 1917 has been generally characterized as the "revolutionary family," a label suggesting a relation between members of the governing elite and certain ideological and social traits. However, the political-economic bases of that group's idelogical cohesion had not been adequately analyzed previously; no single unified group controlled the government in this period; and the "kin" relations of the revolutionary "family" have been insufficiently researched to assess the relations and ideology within the governing classes.[32]

Although the State frequently submitted to certain class pressures (especially from foreign capital and the US government), the idea of the State as a puppet of those classes finds no support in our analysis. The frequency of submission to the interests of foreign capital is matched by the government's attempts to assert independence, attempts that were occasionally successful thanks to the government's capacity to mobilize and pacify the peasants and the working class. That the State was a puppet of the national bourgeoisie or of the middle classes is also unsupported by our analysis, since the progressive bourgeoisie appears as the weakest partner in class politics. On the other hand, although the bureaucracy had stong ties to the middle classes, this modified the very nature of those middle classes: the bureaucracy had a petty bourgeois origin, but it was not dominated by their traditional interests.

These points are essential for understanding the rise of Mexico's powerful bureaucratic class.[33] The bureaucracy's consciousness of its historical role as a class and of the conditions for its reproduction and growth is attested by the party's insistence on a populist rhetoric that seems independent of all concrete political action, its insistence on the notion of Mexico as an ethnic and racial unity that can represent itself, and its insistence on the most essential condition for its perpetuation—non-reelection.

Implications for regional and community studies

Several hypotheses can be derived from the model: 1) The strength of leaders whose power base is brokerage between government and any given class should rise and fall according to the shape of the compliance cycle toward the class in question; leaders with heterogenous constituencies should be more stable than those with homogenous constituencies. G.A. Collier (1980) has used the scheme developed in an earlier version of this paper to explain why different sorts of leadership emerge in different villages of highland Chiapas. His working hypothesis was that, due to the ebb and flow of government resources toward the peasantry, local political leaders that derive their powers as brokers between the State and the peasants are less stable than those that mediate between government and a more heterogenous group. 2) Pro-government leadership in peasant villages and working class communities should be strongest in the initial and crisis periods, and anti-government feeling (and leadership) most evident during the periods of normalcy and post-crisis periods. 3) If leadership in mixed-class communities lacks ties with the different classes in question, competition between representatives of the different classes should reflect the waxing and waning of government resources toward each class. 4) Because of the smaller oscillations in government attitudes toward the petty bourgeoisie and its relatively privileged position in community interaction, this class is a natural source of stable leadership in peasant and working-class communities—more so than the traditional rural bourgeoisie. 5) Peasant and working-class communities that support the losing side in the crisis stage are doomed to have resources cut throughout following presidential cycle.

Implications for linear history

My analysis of political time provides a relatively rigorous way of periodizing Mexican history that complements the more general notion of this period as one of consolidation. It also specifies the nature of instability during the period and shows how it can occur within a structural framework.[34]

A more general critique of traditional approaches can be derived from the above analysis. Those historians who see history as a trajectory toward a known end, usually "development" or "socialism" in the Mexican case, generally view class politics as gradually leading to that desired end. History is thus a kind of development of Mind; the working class gradually awakens, the peasantry drops tradition and joins modernity, and so on. Teleological history disguises the fact that changes in class conditions are often conjunctural, and not essential.[35]

In conclusion, analysis of the temporal structure of class politics in Mexico is a demonstrably profitable and necessary line of research for the social sciences, and provides a key to numerous methodological and comparative problems.

NOTES

[1]I am grateful to G. William Skinner, to Cinna and Larissa Lomnitz, George A. Collier, and Ross Hassig for their criticisms and support. I also thank Elena Climent for her help with the diagrams.

[2]Skinner and Winckler 1969.

[3]Taken from Etzioni's (1975) characterization of compliance in complex institutions.

[4]The indicators I worked with are: number of strikers, number of workers, workers' salaries, the value of the peso, total foreign investment, percent of foreign investment that is American, percent of total imports from the US, percent of total exports to the US, G.N.P., value of industrial production, percent of federal budget for the army, and average *ejido* grants per year. These figures are all available on a yearly basis, though they are rarely available for the whole 1917-1940 period.

[5]In the original version of this paper, I used quantitative data to determine the scale of changes in the compliance relations, constructing a model of change based on statistical indicators. I have later realized, however, that the three aspects of the compliance relation cannot be derived from a single or a complex of statistical indicators. The meaning of the indicators is always derived from qualitative descriptions of the period. Increases in land grants mean only that government is increasing its use of normative and remunerative power, saying nothing of the goals in this decision or of the participation it provoked; increases in strikes can mean either greater commitment or greater alienation from government.

[6]González Navarro (1760) and Cockcroft (1767) have pointed out the diversity of origins of revolutionary ideologists, most of whom were either repatriated *braceros*, primary school teachers, or urban *licenciados*.

[7]Meyer 1976:115.

[8]An increase in the number of workers affiliated with CROM is interpreted as an increase in commitment or—more frequently—indifference toward the government, while an increase in non-affiliated unions is interpreted as alienation. Because I am attempting to paint an aggregate picture of government relations with the working class, I have averaged out the regional and sectorial variations in this relationship.

[9]C.f. L. Lomnitz 1978a and in this volume.

[10]Workers constituted 11.5 percent of the Economically Active Population in 1921 and 15.5 percent in 1940. However, the productivity of these workers was 4.5 times greater than that of the agricultural population in 1921 and 4.8 times greater in 1940 (NAFINSA 1974).

[11]Carr 1976:125.

[12]The apparent exception—the *Maximato*—can also be broken down into the aforementioned stages: because the president-elect (Obregón) was assassinated (1928), Portes Gil faced a crisis analogous to the succession crises that typify the end of presidential reigns. Thus the goal structure of the *Maximato* is a,c,b,d, and not a.b.c.d, like the other periods. Figure 2 is an heuristic model for the goal cycle of the government vis-à-vis workers.

[13]Except for Carranza's unfinished final year, when the governmental power crisis was not successful resolved.

[14]This relation was pointed out as early as González Casanova's (1965) general treatment of the Mexican political system; however, this fact has not always fazed the mechanistic Marxist view of the State which it clearly contradicts. The Calles regime is an exception to this rule: whereas, according to the statistics, his was an anti-labor period (it is the period with *least* average strikes), his predilection for CROM and his support of union power in government allow us to rate him as more pro-worker than Obregón.

[15]The exceptions to this structure in the *Maximato* can, I believe, be explained with the logic of the same structure. The *Maximato* may have had the ideological homogeneity and constance of a single dominant coalition to be

considered similar to a single presidential term, but it was essentially different from all preceding and succeeding periods. During the *Maximato*, the presidents were not the *primus inter pares* of other times, they were in the last instance subordinated to Calles, who wished to prolong his power indefinitely. Thus, although it lasted exactly six years, this period lacks the bounded qualities of those in which the president was the top of the pyramid. Calles did not expect 1934 to be his last year as *jefe maximo* and therefore it was not like the other final presidential years. On the other hand, the logic of worker mobilization is retained: Portes Gil inaugurated the Calles regnum with pro-worker amendments (that are under-expressed in the strike figures) and the period grew conservative as its stability increased. However, occasional changes of presidents allowed (or forced) Calles to sporadically reactivate his (feebles) relations with the proletariate.

[16]I explored the correlations between number of strikers and increases in salaries, costs of living and foreign investment in the years 1937-47 (the only period for which I could find constant year-to-year data for each of these variables). Although the limited sample and the crudeness of my statistical methods do not allow any definitive conclusion on the matter, my general hypotheses on the nature of strikes during the period and their relation to governmental goals are supported. The only variables that have a significant correlation are number of strikers and increases in foreign investment (a. .06 correlation on Fisher's Exact Test); during this period strikers are *not* significantly correlated to either inflation or salary increases.

[17]Although Carranza's period appears as an exception to the rule, this is because 1917 is not actually the first year of Carranista presidential politics. If we analyzed his period as of 1915 we should obtain the general I-O-E model.

[18]In the case of the Cárdenas period, land distribution was an essential government goal, not merely a tool for peasant control, and therefore the shape of this structure was inverted; land reform being most restricted in periods of national crisis when Cárdenas was forced to make concessions to the national and international bourgeoisies. Thus the structure of change in land reform is maintained, but its contents inverted.

[19]Evidently, indifference is more of a theoretical possibility than a real occurrence, since the US is not *strictu sensu* a "lower participant" in this compliance relation.

[20]C.f. L. Lomnitz 1978b.

[21]Although changes in bureacratic compliance follow a limited number of non-random routes, these cannot be thought of in terms of a single compliance cycle. I have therefore not traced a general model for the period, in accordance with the characterization of the bureaucracy as an arena of expression for the pressure groups.

[22]My analysis of the Mexican bourgeoisie is restricted to the industrial and modern agricultural sectors, and does not comprise government relations with the very important traditional *hacendado* sector.

[23]The exception is Carranza's period, where the President was fully identified with the progressive national bourgeoisie, and where, therefore, the use of normative power was more important.

[24]The two opposing tendencies concerning the ultimate role of the bourgeoisie coincided during this perod on the need to strengthen the bourgeoisie—their ulterior motives for this did not get a chance to materialize in the 1917-1940 period.

[25]Tobler 1971; Lozoya 1977.

[26]The rise of the *hacendado*-general was a common phenomenon during the 1920s, and a predominance of "petty bourgeois" interests in the army's upper echelons was combined with a set of common army interests that went beyond the individual gain of each *caudillo*, namely the goals related to the salaries and privileges of the army and to assuring its prolonged control over government.

[27]Major army reforms were always at the beginning of presidential eras, although not in all eras. Order goals appear strongest in the years when presidential succession is determined, although, of course, it was a dominant theme throughout Carranza's reign over the revolution-stricken country.

[28]Presidential succession usually coincided with a military rebellion. The only rebellion which did not exactly fit this pattern was Cedillo's (1938), who jumped the gun and exploited the oil crisis to attempt a military takeover.

[29] These years are: 1919 (when the army's animosity to Carranza was already apparent), 1924 (following De la Huerta's rebellion), 1927 (the year Obregón's reelection was determined), 1929 (a year of succession crisis caused by Obregón's assassination) and 1940 (a year in which, although there were no important threat of rebellion, the army had discontented sectors that supported the presidential candidacy of Juan Andrew Almazán).

[30]This was particularly the case after 1929 when the creation of the PNR allowed for an institutionalized means for resolving presidential succession.

[31]The only really "irregular" cycle is the Carranza period. Carranza refused to ally himself with the peasants and workers, he was not popular with the Americans, and he tried to maintain his hegemony with the support of the national burgeoisie and the middle classes (and by alloting over 60 percent of the national budget to the army).

[32]Two exceptions to this are Camp (1976) and P. H. Smith (1973), however neither of these constitutes a definitive study of the matter.

[33]Zaid's (1979) analysis of the economic implications of the bureaucratic ideology of "developing Mexico" is a key work. Zaid shows that in Mexico taxes allegedly destined to decrease inequalities actually serve to *increase* them, and that the idiom of "progress" (often shared by even the most radical groups) is the ideology of a bureaucratic mode of production, and the basis for that class's action in and of itself.

[34]There are some periodizations, however, which my study does not support. For example, Wilkie (1967) divided the 1917-1964 period into four stages: the "political revolution" (1917-1930), the "social revolution" (1931-1940), the "economic revolution" (1941-1958), and the "balanced revolution" (1958-1964). From the point of view of the structure of class coalitions, there is little reason to divide the 1917-40 period.

[35]The comparative analysis of coalition cycles might also help resolve some questions in Latin American social sciences. For example, it might help explain why the concept of "marginality" is more recurrent in a country such as Mexico than in Brazil; in Mexico the government keeps (for political purposes) a well bounded and organized working class, it is possible that in countries such as Brazil this binding force is more feeble.

Likewise, a comparative analysis of the effects of stable versus regularly shifting governments would be important. I hypothesize that stable governments would provoke greater class contradictions, whereas unstable governments reduce the preference of government toward a single class. If this hypothesis is correct, governmental stability produces class instability, while governmental instability produces the basis for class stability. The Mexican principle of no-reelection seems an ideal form of resolving this contradiction. Are there other variations?

Finally, comparative analyses of foreign policy, of the nature of the army, and of the force of the middle classes would be much enlightened by comparative studies on the nature of political time.

TABLE 1: A POLITICAL BOOK OF YEARS

1917: President: Carranza. Constitutional convention at Querétaro, radical clauses are included despite Carranza; US alienated by radical clauses and pressure Carranza to modify constitution; Carranza refuses. The State becomes the mediator between capital and labor via its support of the weak working class. The main labor confederacy (*Casa del Obrero Mundial*) is uncertain about its relations with government. Carranza attempts to increase agricultural production for internal consumption, meets with restriction on food exports. Pastor Rouaix threatens merchants with "class struggle" if they don not cooperate with government. Protective tariffs are set for small national industry. Transport subsidy to small agricultural proprietors. New bureaucratic posts are filled by revolutionary intelligentsia and by the petty bourgeoisie. Carranza receives full support from the modern and petty bourgeoisie. US opens doors to Mexican immigration. US claims inflated damages caused by revolution, Carranza refuses to pay. US pressures Carranza to join allies in WWI, Carranza refuses. Banks and several other branches of foreign capital are antagonistic toward Carranza.

1918: US mobilizes troops at the frontier, sends navy to Tampico. Carranza seeks non-American investors. Oil companies pressure Carranza to modify radical clauses of the constitution. Formation of the CROM union; Luis Morones criticizes lack of flexibility of the older anarcho-syndicalist leaders and supports a direct alliance between organized labor and prominent members of the revolutionary elite. Although CROM supports Carranza's foreign policy it is increasingly evident that he is not their ally in internal politics. Morones meets with leaders of the AFL that are being used by the US government to expand control over Latin American labor movements, receives criticism from "old guard." Tax on unproductive rural property. Carranza decides to stop agrarian reform.

1919: Carranza's lack of control over the army becomes evident in his choice of a civilian as his successor. Zapata is assassinated. Strikers against government policy are organized by school teachers of the DF and supported by CROM—strikes are violently repressed and relations with Carranza deteriorate. CROM seeks alliance with Obregón; Morones and Obregón sign a secret pact of mutual support. CROM organizes a textile strike in Veracruz that is interpreted as an aggression against Carranza, who is forced to designate Calles (of Obregón's group) as mediator. Calles resolves conflict in favor of labor and is forced to resign. Carranza violently suppresses socialist party of Yucatan. Bourgeoisie is unhappy with Obregón's group (the *sonorenses*) for their support of the Veracruz strike and of agrarian reform in Sonora (where De la Huerta was governor). Carranza improves transport system. Oil companies decide not to pay the taxes Carranza demands, Carranza decides to close down oil wells. US decides not to invade.

1920: Strikes over presidential succession. Carranza attempts to capture Obregón in Mexico City. Morones's railroad workers allow him to escape. The state of Sonora declares a military rebellion against Carranza. Workers and peasants support Obregón, zapatista movement supports Obregón. Carranza flees and is assassinated. De la Huerta named interim president, is very unpopular with capitalists, foments strikes to a level close to the general strike. Toward end of year, Obregón elected president and begins slowing down strikes. CROM heavily dependent on Obregón. Radical unions leave CROM, but Obregón allows CROM to grow tremendously. Sends Morones to negotiate US recognition of his government. US does not recognize De la Huerta or Obregón's government. Crisis of overproduction in US agriculture provokes unemployment of over 100,000 Mexican workers, 50,000 are repatrated at the expense of the Mexican government. Church begins to organize labor unions. Obregón begins agrarian reform and gives several zapatistas important bureaucratic posts, Morelos is favored for number of land-grants. Obregón was reluctant to split up *haciendas* that produced well. Many army leaders have private deals with *hacendados* and discourage agrarian reform.

1921: First military reform; heads of zones are rotated, number of zones goes from 20 to 35. US continues not recognizing Obregón, wants him to pay damages that Carranza refused to pay and to guarantee mining and oiling interests against constitution's radical clauses. *Acción Social Católica* is formed by the conservative middle classes. Vasconcelos creates new ministry of education. Land distribution continues. Villa assassinated. The current structure of union corruption is created: obligatory membership, obligatory reductions from workers wages, etc.

1922: US again opens doors to immigration. De la Huerta-Lamont agreement makes Mexico pay the inflated charges for damages claimed by the US. Boom in oil industry. US recognition still not accorded to Obregón.

1923: Bacareli agreement, Obregón gives in to US pressure and receives recognition in return. Obregón chooses Calles as successor, and De la Huerta rebells with over 40 percent of the army. Peasants and workers aid Obregón in quelling rebellion. De la Huerta's defeat contributes to decreasing the size of the army. Army plays a conservative role in the agrarian reform, particularly in Veracruz where state government and army interests clashed. Relations with the church are tense because of the anti-clerical character of the *sonorenses*. Archbishop Fillippi is expatriated. The agrarian law of August 2 codifies the agrarian reform, which is also applied to decrease emigration to the US.

1924: Relations with the church are increasingly tense. Minister of agriculture prohibits his employees from wearing catholic symbols or from having them in their homes. Agrarian reform cut down. Relations with US are good, although the selection of Calles as successor was not well viewed. Calles is considered a socialist.

1925: Calles refuses to recognize Bucareli and De la Huerta-Lamont agreements and incorporates CROM into his government. US alienated. Land restitution is renewed. Second military reform, General Amaro reduces the army to less than 2/3 its former size. Calles declares the necessity to raise workers salaries in US industries and to strengthen unions. CROM strikes for 100 percent salary increases in several US factories and wins. Calles attempts and fails to achieve larger government participation in banks. US secretary of state makes impertinent press declaration which raises nationalist support for Calles.

1926: Further antagonism with US. Calles uses massive popular support to continue agrarian reform. *Cristero* rebellion in the central Mexican states. Peasants in *Cristero* region heavily repressed. Agrarista leader Primo Tapia, a De la Huerta supporter, assassinated by Calles' men. Problems between rural school teachers and Christians.

1927: *Cristero* war continues. US change ambassador who's "softer" policy wins Calles over. Calles agrees to pay the American debt and slows down land reform. *Cristeros* are squashed. Obregón decides to be reelected, is opposed by two generals who attempt coups, both are quickly repressed. This is a year that begins a trend of growth for national industry. Morones falls out of favor with Calles.

1928: Obregón elected with an overwhelming majority and assassinated. Crisis within dominant group between Obregonistas and Calles. Obregonista candidate. A. Saena secures the support of much of the army. Calles, in turn, controls the bureaucracy.

1929: Generals decide to approve Calles' project for a party to group all revolutionary leaders (the PNR) and thus avoid civil war. Calles outmaneouvers Obregonistas and has Portes Gil—a relatively neutral candidate—selected as president instead of A. Saenz. Great depression, US frontiers close to immigration, thousands of Mexicans are repatriated. There is an attempted alliance between radical *agraristas* (lead by U. Galvan) and the Communist Party, but the Communist Party misinterprets political meaning of Great Depression and rebells against government. Galvan rests faithful to Calles and Portes Gil and his group survives. Depression has a stronger effect on industry and a few export crops than on the bulk of the peasantry. Portes Gil promotes land reform much more than before, also has progressive labor reforms. Peasants are armed by government for fear of Obregonista *coup de'etat*, this strengthens *agrarista* factions in many states (Veracruz, Michoacán, San Luis Potosi, Hidalgo). Escobar leads an important military rebellion but is repressed. Pascual Ortiz Rubio is Calles' candidate to succeed Portes Gil. Vasconcelos creates his own party of civilians and runs against him. O. Rubio is elected. Small industry oriented to internal market grows.

1930: More extradiction of *braceros*, between 1930-32 over 230,000 are repatriated. O. Rubio takes office and declares the agrarian reform finished, however the local power of several *agrarista* governors is far from diminished; in Veracruz and San Luis Potosi they are still armed. Once succession crisis is resolved, Calles and the president begin disarming *agraristas* and attacking them politically and succeed in splitting the *Liga Nacional Campesina* into two factions.

1931: Governors Cardens, Tejeda, Cárdenas, Vargas Lugo, and Cedillo refuse to halt agrarian reform in their states. New split in *Liga Nacional Campesina* between moderates and radicals, the majority supported the moderate—whose power grew importantly. At the end of the year they triumph over O. Rubio in a supreme court ruling that established the main legal impediment to agrarian reform in the *agrarista* states: *de amparo*. Calles highly irritated with O. Rubin for this. Peasants in Veracruz are disarmed.

1932: Nationalization of electricity in support of the national industry. Ortiz Rubio resigns, Abelardo Rodríguez President. Cárdenas enjoys support of the army and is selected minister of war. *Agrarista* leaders win important positions in federal government, but their local power base is destroyed. Church supports Cárdenas as a future presidential candidate because he is not a Callista.

1933: Government prohibits strikes and gives national industry tax breaks. Calles selects Cárdenas as next presidential candidate because of the need for popular support.

1934: A. Rodríguez gives credit to small producers and rural cooperatives. Boosts agrarian reform, provides for a minimum wage. Bourgeoisie protests. Formation of capitalist associations by branches of industry.

1935: Cárdenas takes office and begins strong mobilization of peasants and workers. Formation of the CNC (peasant union). Organization of school leaders union (SNTE). New ideological generation is in government, uses marxist rhetoric. Cárdenas makes concessions to the church but alienates the most anti-socialist factions. *Ley de nacionalización* gave government jurisdiction over churches and convents. Formation of the CTM (successor to CROM). Popular credit to people with salaries below 3000 pesos a year. Industrialists protest against the insecurity caused by worker mobilization. US alienated by marxist rhetoric and land restitutions.

1936: Cárdenas distributes land from US owned *latifundios*, US shows concern and is worried about Cardens' position on mining and oil. Calles reacts strongly against these moves by Cárdenas and is deported to the US. Cárdenas reforms the party, calls it PRM and divides it into sectors: peasants (CNC), workers (CTM) and military. The "law of expropriations" was passed, US does not protest. Workers and peasants are armed in case US decides to invade. Bourgeoisie creates its own organization: COCAMIN.

1937: Confrontation between workers and oil companies, government mediates, US looks on. Nationalization of railroads. Formation of the extreme right "sinarquist" party. National capitals leave the country for fear of socialism and of the results of the oil problem. Economic crisis. Strikes because of inflation.

1938: Cárdenas signs agreement with oil companies. US decides to end diplomatic and economic harassment due to WWII. Bourgeoisie pressures Cárdenas to choose a conservative successor. Cárdenas does so and selects M. Avila Camacho. Ultra-right still pressures. Sectors of the army and the middle classes want General Almazán as president and he decides to run against A. Camacho. Left wing of Cardenismo will be out of power under next president.

1940: Cárdenas keeps retrenching on his labor and land-reform policies until the end of his period.

TABLE 2: GOALS TOWARD WORKERS

PRESIDENT	YEAR	GOALS
Carranza	1917	high order, mid economic
	1918	high economic
	1919	high order, high economic
Carranza/De la Huerta	1920	high order/h.ideol./mid econ.,m.ideol.
Obregón	1921	m.order,m.economic
	1922	m. economic
	1923	h.order, m.economic
	1924	balanced
Calles	1925	m. ideological
	1926	m. ideological
	1927	h. economic
	1928	m. order, 1.economic
Portes Gil	1929	m. ideological, high order
Portes Gil/Ortiz Rubio	1930	m.ideological/m. economic
Maximato	1931	m. economic
Ortiz .Rubio/Rodríguez	1932	m. economic
	1933	m. economic
	1934	m. economic, l. ideol.
Cárdenas	1935	h. ideol.
	1936	h. ideological, l. order
	1937	h. ideological, m. order
	1938	h. ideological, m. order
	1939	m. order, h. economic
	1940	h. economic

ANALYSIS OF TREND BY PERIOD* WITH INTENSITY OF GOALS EXCLUDED

GOALS:	I	IO	O	OE	E	EI	CHANGE
Carranza		1	4	3	2		IO-E-OE-O
Obregón			1	4	3,5	1,2	EI-E-OE-E
Calles	1,2		4		3		I-E-O
Maximato		1,6			2,3,4,5		IO-E-IO
Cárdenas		1,2,3,4		5	6		IO-OE-E

*The numbers are the year of the president's term (e.g. 1 = first year).

TABLE 3: POWER TOWARD WORKERS

PRESIDENT	Year	POWER
Carranza	1917	m. normative, 1. remunerative
	1918	l. normative, l. remunerative
	1919	h. coercive, l. remunerative
Carranza/De la Huerta/Obregón	1920	h.coer./h.norm.,m.remun./h.norm.,m.remun.
	1921	m. remunerative
	1922	m. remunerative
	1923	m. remunerative, h. normative
Calles	1924	m. remunerative
	1925	h. remunerative, h. normative.
	1926	h. remunerative, h. normative
	1927	m. remunerative, l. coercive
	1928	m. remunerative, l. coercive
Portes Gil	1929	m. remunerative, m. normative.
Portes Gil/Ortiz Rubio	1930	m. remunerative, m. coercive
Maximato	1931	l. remunerative, m. coercive
Ortiz Rubio/Rodríguez	1932	l. remunerative, m. coercive
	1933	m. remunerative, m. coercive
	1934	m. remunerative, l. coercive
Cárdenas	1935	h. normative, h. remunerative
	1936	h. normative, m. remunerative
	1937	h. normative, m. remunerative
	1938	h. normative, m. remunerative
	1939	m. normative, m. remunerative
	1940	m. normative, l. remunerative

ANALYSIS OF TRENDS BY PERIOD WITH INTENSITY OF POWER EXCLUDED

POWER:	N	NC	C	CR	R	RN	CHANGE
Carranza			4	3		1,2	RN-CR-C
Obregón					2,3,5	1,4	RN-R-RN-R
Calles		3		4		1,2	RN-NC-CR
Maximato				2-6		1	RN-CR
Cárdenas						1-6	RN-B

TABLE 4: WORKER'S INVOLVEMENT

PRESIDENT	YEAR	INVOLVEMENT
Carranza	1917	h. commitment, l. alienation
	1918	m. indifference, l. commitment
	1919	m. alienation, l. indifference
Carranza/De la Huerta/Obregón	1920	h. alien./h.comit./h.comit.
	1921	h. indifference, m. commitment
	1922	h. indifference, m. commitment
	1923	h. indifference, m. commitment
	1924	h. indifference, m. commitment
Calles	1925	l. indifference, m. commitment
	1926	m. indifference, m. commitment
	1927	m. indifference, m. commitment
	1928	l. commitment, m. alienation
Portes Gil	1929	h. commitment, m. alienation
Portes Gil/ Ortiz Rubio	1930	l. commitment, m. alienation
Maximato	1931	m. alienation, m. indifference.
Ortiz Rubio/ Rodríguez	1932	m. alienation, m. indifference.
	1933	m. alienation, m. indifference.
	1934	m. alienation, m. indifference.
Cárdenas	1935	m. indifference, m. commitment.
	1936	h. commitment, m. indifference
	1937	h. commitment, m. indifference
	1938	h. commitment, l. alienation.
	1939	m. commitment, l. alienation
	1940	m. commitment, l. alienation

ANALYSIS OF TRENDS BY PERIOD, INTENSITY OF INVOLVEMENT EXCLUDED

INVOLVEMENT:	C	CA	A	AI	I	IC	CHANGE
Carranza		1	4	3		2	CA-IC-AI-A
Obregón	1					2-5	C-IC
Calles		4				1-3	IC-CA
Maximato		1,2		3-6			CA-AI
Cárdenas		4-6				1-3	IC-CA

GRAPH 1. NUMBER OF STRIKERS PER YEAR (RAW DATA)

1920:	88,536		
1921:	100,380	1931:	227
1922:	71,382	1932:	3,574
1923:	61,403	1933:	1,048
1924:	23,988	1934:	14,685
1925:	9,861	1935:	145,212
1926:	2,977	1936:	113,885
1927:	1,005	1937:	61,732
1928:	498	1938:	13,435
1929:	3,473	1939:	14,486
1930:	3,718	1940:	19,784

Source: *Anuarios Estadísticos.*

AVERAGE NUMBER OF STRIKERS PER YEAR BY PRESIDENT

Obregón (including 1920): 69, 138

Calles: 3, 585

Portes Gil (including 1930): 3, 596

Ortiz Rubio: 1, 901

Rodríguez: 7, 867

Maximato (total): 4, 455

Cárdenas: 61, 476

TABLE 5: COMPLIANCE WITH PEASANTS

PRESIDENT	YEAR	GOALS	POWER	INVOLVEMENT
Carranza	1917	h.O.,m.e	h.c,m.r	b (turmoil)
	1918	h.o., m.e	h.c,l.r.	l.a
	1919	h.o,m.e	hc	l.a
Carranza/De la Huerta/Obregón	1920	h.o/h.e,m.i	h.o/m.n,m.r	l.a/m.c
	1921	m.e,l.i	m.n,m.r	m.c,m.i
	1922	m.e,l.i	m.n,m.r	m.c,m.i
	1923	h.o	h.n,m.r	h.c,l.a
	1924	m.o,m.e	balanced	m.c,m.i
Calles	1925	m.e,m.i	m.r,m.n	m.c,m.i
	1926	m.i,m.o	l.n,m.c	m.c,m.a
	1927	m.e,m.o	l.n,m.c	h.i,m.a
	1928	m.e	l.n,m.c	m.i,m.a
Portes Gil	1929	m.i,h.o	h.n,m.r	l.a,l.c
Portes Gil/Ortiz Rubio	1930	m.e,m.o	balanced	l.a,l.i.
Maximato	1931	m.e,m.o	l.n,m.c	m.a,m.i
Ortiz Rubio/A.Rodríguez	1932	m.e,m.o	m.c	l.a,l.i
	1933	m.e	l.r,l.n	l.a,m.i
	1934	m.e	m.r,m.n	l.a,m.i
Cárdenas	1935	h.i	h.r,h.n	l.i,m.c
	1936	h.i	h.r,h.n	l.i,m.c
	1937	h.i,m.e	h.r,h.n	l.i,h.c
	1938	m.i,m.e	h.n,m.r	l.i,h.c
	1939	m.o,m.e	m.n,l.r	m.c,l.a
	1940	m.i,m.e	balanced	m.c,l.a

ANALYSIS OF TRENDS BY PERIOD WITH INTENSITY EXCLUDED

GOALS:	I	I	IO	O	OE	E	EI	CHANGE
Carranza				4	1-3			OE-O
Oregon				4	5		1-3	EI-O-OE
Calles			2		3	4	1	EI-IO-OE-E
Maximato			1		1-4	5,6		IO-OE-E
Cárdenas	1,2	1,2			5,6		3,4	I-EI-OE

POWER:	N	N	NC	C	CR	R	RN	CHANGE
Carranza				3,4	1,2			CR-C
Obregón							1-4	RN-Balanced(5)
Calles			2-4				1	RN-NC
Maximato			3	4		5,6	1	RN-B(2)-NC-C-R
Cárdenas			4,5				1-3	RN-NC-B(6)

INVOLVEMENT:	C	C	CA	A	AI	I	IC	CHANGE
Carranza				2-4				B(1)-A
Obregón	1,4	1,4					2,3,5	C-IC-C-IC
Calles			2,3		4		1	IC-CA-AI
Maximato			1		2-5	6		CA-AI-I
Cárdenas			5,6				1-4	IC-CA

Goals: i = ideological; o = order; e = economic; b = balanced

Power: n = normative; c = coercive; r = remunerative; b = balanced

Involvement: c = commitment; a = alienation; i = indifference; b = balanced

h = high; m = mid; l = low

GRAPH 2. NUMBER OF HECTARES DISTRIBUTED BY YEAR (RAW DATA)
Source: NAFINSA (1974).

1917:	64,207	1929:	1,853,589
1918:	66,563	1930:	584,921
1919:	57,117	1931:	976,402
1920:	192,791	1932:	249,348
1921:	552,129	1933:	542,239
1922:	178,543	1934:	1,517,488
1923:	470,101	1935:	1,923,456
1924:	529,911	1936:	3,985,700
1925:	880,624	1937:	5,811,893
1926:	853,368	1938:	3,486,266
1927:	857,014	1939:	2,223,723
1928:	604,262	1940:	2,705,885

AVERAGE DISTRIBUTED PER YEAR BY PRESIDENT

Carranza: 62,629
Obregón (including 1920): 384,695
Calles: 798,817
Portes Gil: (including 1930) 1,219,255
Ortiz Rubio: 622,875
Rodríguez: 1,030,135
Maximato: 954,088
Cárdenas: 3,356,155

TABLE 6: COMPLIANCE WITH THE US GOVERNMENT

PRESIDENT	YEAR	GOALS	POWER	INVOLVEMENT
Carranza	1917	m.e,h.i	h.c	m.a,l.c
	1918	m.e,h.i	m.c.,l.r	m.a,l.c
	1919	m.e,h.i	m.c,l.r	m.a,l.c
Carranza/De la Huerta/Obregón	1920	m.i,m.o/m.i,m.o.	m.c,l.r/m.c,m.r.	l.a,l.c/l.a
	1921	h.e,l.I	l.c,m.r	l.a
	1922	h.e	l.c,m.r	l.a,l.c
	1923	h.e,h.o	m.r	l.c,l.i
Calles	1924	m.e,m.i	m.r	m.c
	1925	m.i,l.e	n.c,l.r	m.a,l.c
	1926	m.i,l.e	n.c,l.r	m.a
	1927	l.i,m.o	l.c,h.r	l.a,m.c
	1928	m.o,m.e	l.c,h.r	m.c
Portes Gil	1929	m.o	balanced	balanced
Portes Gil/Ortiz Rubio	1930	l.e	h.r.	m.c
Maximato	1931	l.e	h.r	h.c
Ortiz Rubio/Abelardo Rodríguez	1932	l.e	h.r	h.c
	1933	l.e	h.r	h.c
	1934	l.e	h.r	h.c
Cárdenas	1935	h.i,l.e	m.c,l.r	l.c,l.a
	1936	h.i,l.o	m.c,l.r	m.a
	1937	h.i,l.o	m.c,l.r	m.a
	1938	h.i,m.o	h.c,l.r	h.a
	1939	m.e,m.o	l.c,m.r	h.a,l.c
	1940	m.e,m.o	l.c,m.r	m.c

ANALYSIS OF TRENDS BY PERIOD, INTENSITY EXCLUDED

GOALS:	I	IO	O	OE	E	EI	CHANGE
Carranza		4				1-3	EI-IO
Obregón		1		4	3	2,5	IO-EI-E-EO-EI
Calles		3		4		1,2	EI-IO-OE
Maximato			1		2-6		O-E
Cárdenas		2-4		5,6		1	EI-IO-OE

POWER:	N	NC	C	CR	R	RN	CHANGE
Carranza			1	2-4			C-CR
Obregón				1-3	4,5		CR -R

Calles				1-4			CR
Maximato					2-6		B(1)-R
Cárdenas				1-6			CR

INVOLVEMENT:	C	CA	A	AI	I	IC	CHANGE
Carranza		1-4					CA
Obregón	5	3	1,2			4	A-CA-IC-C
Calles	4	1,3	2				CA-A-CA-C
Maximato	2-6						B(1)-C
Cárdenas	6	1,5	2-4				CA-A-CA-C

TABLE 7: COMPLIANCE WITH THE BUREAUCRACY, INTENSITY EXCLUDED

GOALS:	I	IO	O	OE	E	EI	CHANGE
Carranza			4	3	1,2		E-OE-O
Obregón		1		4	3,5	2	IO-EI-E-OE-E
Calles	1	2,4	3				I-IO-O-IO
Maximato			1	2,5,6	3,4		O-OE-E-OE
Cárdenas		2,4	1	5,6		3	O-IO-EI-IO-OE

POWER:	N	NC	C	CR	R	RN	CHANGE
Carranza	1			4		2,3	N-RN-CR
Obregón				4,5		1-3	RN-CR
Calles				3,4		1,2	RN-CR
Maximato		1,2			3,4	5,6	NC-R-RN
Cárdenas		1,4				2,3,5,6	NC-RN-NC-RN

INVOLVEMENT:	C	CA	A	AI	I	IC	CHANGE
Carranza	1,2	3,4					C-CA
Obregón		4			5	1-3	I-CA-I
Calles		3,4				1,2	IC-CA
Maximato		1		5,6	3,4	2	CA-IC-A-AI
Cárdenas		1,2,4,5		6		3	CA-IC-AI

TABLE 8: COMPLIANCE WITH THE NATIONAL BOURGEOISIE, INTENSITY EXCLUDED

GOALS:	I	IO	O	OE	E	EI	CHANGE
Carranza				1		2-4	OE-EI
Obregón				1,2	3-5		OE-E
Calles					3,4	1,2	EI-E
Maximato					2-5	1,6	EI-E-EI
Cárdenas				4,5	6	1-3	EI-OE-E

POWER:	N	NC	C	CR	R	RN	CHANGE
Carranza		1				2-4	NC-RN
Obregón		1			4,5	2,3	NC-RN-R
Calles		1,2		3	4		NC-CR-R
Maximato		1		6	2-5		NC-R-CR
Cárdenas			1,2	3,4	5,6		C-CR-R

INVOLVEMENT:	C	CA	A	AI	I	IC	CHANGE
Carranza	2,3,4	1					CA-C
Obregón				1	2	3-5	AI-I-IC
Calles				1,2		3,4	AI-IC
Maximato	3-5	1,6				2	CA-IC-C-CA
Cárdenas			4,5	1-3	6		AI-A-I

TABLE 9: COMPLIANCE WITH THE MILITARY

PRESIDENT	YEAR	GOALS	POWER	INVOLVEMENT
Carranza	1917	h.o	h.c,h.r,h.n	h.c,h.a,h.i
	1918	h.o,h.e	h.c,h.r,h.n	h.c,m.a,h.i
	1919	m.o,h.e	h.c,h.r	l.c,m.a
Carranza/De la Huerta/Obregón	1920	h.o/m.i	h.r/h.n,h.r	h.a/h.c
	1921	m.o/h.e	h.n,m.r	h.c,l.i
	1922	m.o/m.e	h.n,m.r	h.c,l.i
	1923	h.o/m.e	h.n,h.c	h.c,h.a
	1924	m.e	m.n,m.r	h.c,l.a
Calles	1925	h.e	m.r	m.c,m.i
	1926	m.e	balanced	m.c,m.i
	1927	h.o	m.r,m.c	m.c,m.a
	1928	m.e	m.r,m.n	balanced
Portes Gil	1929	h.o	h.n,h.c	m.c,m.a
Portes Gil/Ortiz Rubio	1930	Mme	m.c,m.r	m.c,m.a
Maximato	1931	m.e	m.c,m.r	l.c,m.i
Ortiz Rubio/Abelardo Rodríguez	1932	m.e	m.r	l.c,h.i
	1933	m.e,l.o	m.r	l.c,h.i
	1934	m.e,l.o	m.r,m.n	l.c,h.i
Cárdenas	1935	m.e,m.i	m.r,m.n	h.c,l.i
	1936	m.e,m.o	m.r,m.n	h.c,l.i
	1937	m.e	m.r,m.n	h.c,l.a
	1938	h,o	h.n,m.c	m.c,l.a
	1939	mo	m.n,m.r	m.c,m.a
	1940	lo,m.e	m.r	m.c,m.a

GOALS:	I	IO	O	OE	E	EI	CHANGE
Carranza			1,4	2,3			O-OE-O
Obregón	1			2-4	5		I-OE-E
Calles			3		1,2,4		E-O-E
Maximato			1	5,6	2-4		O-E-OE
Cárdenas			4,5	2,6	3	1	EI-OE-E-O-OE

POWER:	N	NC	C	CR	R	RN	CHANGE
Carranza				3	4		B(1,2)-CR-R
Obregón		4				1-3,5	RN-NC-RN
Calles				3	1	4	R-B(2)-CR-RN

Maximato		1		2,3	4,5	6	NC-CR-R-RN
Cárdenas		4			6	1-3,5	RN-NC-RN-R

INVOLVEMENT:	C	CA	A	AI	I	IC	CHANGE
Carranza		3	4				B(1,2)-CA-A
Obregón	1	4,5				2,3	C-IC-CA
Calles		3				1,2	IC-CA-B(4)
Maximato		1,2				3-6	CA-IC
Cárdenas		3-6				1,2	IC-CA

GRAPH 3. PERCENTAGE OF FEDERAL BUDGET ALLOCATED TO ARMY BY YEAR

1917:	69.9 percent	1929:	37.3 percent
1918:	55.5 percent	1930:	30.9 percent
1919:	97.4 percent	1931:	29.9 percent
1920:	48.4 percent	1932:	28.8 percent
1921:	53 percent	1933:	24.6 percent
1922:	46.4 percent	1934:	22.7 percent
1923:	36.6 percent	1935:	20.9 percent
1924:	42.6 percent	1936:	17.3 percent
1925:	30.9 percent	1937:	17.4 percent
1926:	29.8 percent	1938:	16.7 percent
1927:	31.9 percent	1939:	15.8 percent
1928:	32.3 percent	1940:	19.7 percent

Source: Wilkie 1967

TABLE 10: CORRELATION BETWEEN TYPES OF POWER USED BY GOVERNMENT TOWARD EACH GROUP.*

	WORKERS	PEASANTS	US	BURO	BOURGEOISIS	ARMY
WORKERS						
PEASANTS	++(1)					
US GOVT.	- (2)	-				
BUREAUCRACY	+ (3)	Ø(5)	Ø(7)			
BOURGEOISIE	- (4)	-	+ (8)	Ø(10)		
ARMY	Ø	Ø(6)	Ø(9)	+ (11)	Ø(12)	

* ++ = a strong positive relation; +=mild positive relation; Ø= no significant correlation; - =mild negative correlation; - - = strong negative correlation. Relations are taken via examination of trends (with intensity included when possible) in tables 2-9.

(1). Rythm of government changes is not exact at the end of the Cárdenas and Obregón periods.

(2). Correlation not significant for Carranza's period.

(3). Øfor *Maximato*, ++ for Calles, + for rest.

(4). Relation under Obregón is not strong; global relation not as negative as Worker/US.

(5). ++ for Carranza; + for Obregón and *Maximato*; - for Calles; Øfor Cárdenas.

(6). ++ for Obregón and Cárdenas.

(7). + for Obregón; - for Carranza and Calles.

(8). ++ for *Maximato*; + for Cárdenas and Calles; Øfor Obregón; - for Carranza.

(9). - - for Obregón and Cárdenas; + for Carranza and Calles; Øfor *Maximato*.

(10). ++ for Carranza; + for Obregón and *Maximato*; - for Calles; Øfor Cárdenas.

(11). ++ for all but Carranza and Calles, for whom there is no correlation.

(12). - for Carranza; + for Calles.

TABLE 11: COALITION CYCLE

Cycle 1: 1917- Coalition with popular base in the creation of a radical constitution; U.S. estranged. (Phase 1)

1918- No support for peasants or workers but no alliance with US. (Phase 2) Government best represents national bourgeois and middle class interests.

1919- Same as above. Lack of army support for Carranza's presidential candidate.

Cycle 2: 1920- Obregón overthrows Carranza with a *popular* coalition. Carranza was without important class (or military) allies. US antagonism (phase 1).

1921-22- Mobilization of peasants and workers. US estrangement grows (phases 2 and 3).

1923- Retrenchment. Bucareli agreements represent end of popular coalition and beginning of coalition with US. De la Huerta rebellion unsuccessful (phase 4).

1924- Conservatism in last presidential year. (phase 5)

Cycle 3: 1925- Revival of agrarian reform and alliance with unions; no recognition of Bucareli agreements. Calles considered "socialist" by US government. (phase 1)

1926- Prolongation of same politics; *cristero* war, further US antagonism (phases 2 and 3).

1927- Retrenchment before succession is determined. Two minor military rebellions quashed. The way for Obregón's candidacy is paved (phase 4).

Structural crisis: 1928- Obregón reelected and assassinated. Succession crisis. Calles avoids civil war by appeasing Obregonista generals.

1929- PNR created. Portes Gil selected as interim president, makes coalition with peasants and workers (attempted phase 1); Escobar attempts to take power without important class coalitions. Internal antagonisms get channeled through party, so conservative parts of the cycle get longer. Portes Gil's lack of autonomy from Calles gives his popular reforms a marginal character.

Cycle 4: 1930- Ortiz Rubio (Calles' puppet) presidency begins conservative reforms but also seeks popular base to avoid another military coup (inverted phase 1).

1931-33- Attempt at end of agrarian and labor reforms. Pro-US government (inverted phases 2 and 3), alienation of popular bases and radical elements of government.

1934- Concessions to pressure from popular base (agrarian and labor reforms), *agrarista* presidential candidate selected (inverted phase 4).

Cycle 5: 1935- Cárdenas mobilizes popular forces; US and national bourgeoisies react (phase 1).

1936- Restructuring of Party; more mass mobilization; Calles deported. (phases 2 and 3).

1937-38- Crisis with US Agrarian reform, socialist education, oil expropriation. (phase 3).

1939- Retrenchment; agrarian reform slows; Cedillo rebellion is squashed; agreement with oil companies is reached. Conservative presidential candidate selected (phase 4).

1940- Conservatism in last presidential year (phase 5).

COMMUNITY POLITICAL SYSTEMS AND THE EXPANSION OF THE MEXICAN STATE 1940-1980

John G. Corbett

The four decades between 1940 and 1980 define a critical watershed in Mexican history. During this period Mexico experienced a profound transformation; a rural, agrarian society still shaken by the strife of the Mexican Revolution gave way to an urban, industrial country pressed by many of the same issues and challenges confronting other large, technologically advanced nations. The population grew from 19,000,000, to 67,000,000, with most crowded into burgeoning cities. The scope and volume of governmental activity increased many-fold. While uneven in distribution and impact, governmental programs fostering agrarian reform, agricultural development, education, electrification, and a host of other services spread across the countryside. Improvements in communications, the expansion of literacy, and greater mobility of people between cities and villages contributed to the emergence of new concerns and new values in rural areas. In little more than a generation, the life of most Mexican peasants has been altered dramatically. Social institutions adquate for the needs of an earlier era experienced new demands and new pressures; at the local level much of this period's history reflects efforts to accommodate or contain the stress such changes imposes on community institutions and on the people dependent on them.

Among these institutions, the community political system stands out as one of the most important. Traditionally, political systems mediated conflict, mobilized, and allocated and controlled relations between the community as a corporate entity and extra-local political actors. In Mexican communities many of the governmental structures and processes were fused with or submerged in other elements of community life—they were "intermittent"[1]—a factor contributing to the fragmented and peripheral attention commonly accorded local politics by authors of community studies. During the period 1940-1980, political institutions, proceses, behavior, and system performance emerged as permanent, vigorous, and significant components of community life; their continued charcterization as intermittent or peripheral gradually became anachronistic and inaccurate. In one sense this emergence reflects a community-generated response to increased internal complexity, to the new needs and new demands mentioned earlier. In another sense it reflects a variety of extra-community actors, notably the national government.

The impact of socio-economic modernization and the passing or alteration of traditional forms of governmental organizations place considerable strain on political institutions. Systems geared to processing a limited volume and range of demands within an established framework find performance pressures rising at a time when broad social change challenges their capacity to manage conflict, mobilize resources, and secure compliance. New expectations and new needs may prove incompatible with long-standing practices and norms. A major factor contributing to internal stress is the progressive penetration of communities by external political actors. Some penetration efforts reflect organizational responsibilities to deliver programs and services, e.g., water or education, while others seek to control political behavior or channel local energies toward national priorities. Either way, the process of "nationalization" involves the displacement of local concerns and the subordination of community autonomy to national institutions and national imperatives. Subordination may bring benefits as well as costs, and differing perceptions as to the net effect may determine whether communities (or distinct groups within them) accept or resist penetration.

Approaches to the Study of Community Political Systems: 1940-1980

Given the increasing visibility and centrality of community political systems, one might anticipate a parallel evolution of scholarship and research priorities. In practice, however, the literature reveals an extended lag in problem conceptualization and research design, a lag that has begun to disappear only within the last decade.[2]

To some degree the lag in scholarship is traceable to the narrowly-based assumptions about Mexican society that shape the operational models utilized by social scientists. American political scientists interested in Mexico commonly conceptualize the political system concentrating as one characterized by a high degree of state centralism, i.e., as a centalized political system concentrating decision power and policy initiatives in the upper reaches of the bureaucracy and the presidency,[3] a view widely shared by scholars in other disciplines and by Mexicans as well.[4] This view offers little theoretical room or motivation to study community political systems. On the assumption tht all key decisions are made by national decision-makers in the *Distrito Federal*, most standard treatments of Mexican politics give little attention to other units of government.[5] In general, American political scientists have ignored community politics or sub-national political systems.[6] After reviewing community power studies in Mexico the Purcells conclude:

> Political scientists....have avoided community studies and have left the field to sociologists and anthropologists who have been only peripherally interested in political processes.[7]

In contrast to the state-centered model favored by political scientists, most American anthropolgists opted for a community-centered model assigning political phenomena low priority, particularly when these are linked to agents and events beyond community boundaries. The intermittent character of political institutions, a concern for ethnographic salvage, an orientation toward culture and personality as causal variables, and a disciplinary tradition of the community as the appropriate unit of analysis—a tradition reinforced both by the wide attention accorded the works of Robert Redfield and Oscar Lewis and by influential articles such as Wolf's[8] discussion of closed corporate communities—channelled research away from politics as a major area of inquiry. While the community-centered model no longer dominates anthropological research in Latin America, including Mexico, to the extent it once did,[9] for two generations it largely defined the direction and scope of inquiry and shaped the data base on which subsequent generations of social scientists would draw.[10]

In the last decade a new approach has emerged, one that takes the community or region as its unit of analysis, but that then interprets events, behaviors, and circumstances within a more dynamic and broadly-defined conceptual framework. Norman Schwartz captures much of this approach in his comment:

> The traditions of a group are dynamic adaptations to ecological and situational conditions. Thus changes in the latter generate behavior changes that lead to modifications in tradition and identity.[11]

Schwartz observes that this approach gives far more explicit attention than others to conflict and to competition among groups for scarce resources and preferred outcomes. Although some foreign scholars have variants of what he terms a "conflict perspective,"[12] the most active, articulate, and imaginative practitioners have been Mexican social scientists, a point to which we shall return later.

One element in the new framework is the emergence of change as a continuing or permanent condition rather than as an anomaly disturbing a patterned and stable state. Change may be economic, organizational, or technological, but the common denominator is the requirement that communities respond to new challenges and adapt to new conditions. Perhaps more important, the frequency of change and the breadth of its consequences for the community foster the development of an institutionalized adaptive capacity. Communities recruit into public office individuals who speak Spanish and understand how to manipulate macro-level political institutions, encourage the formation of political and economic networks, and more generally create or expand information gathering and processing capabilities. Communities learn to tap migrants to Mexico City as part of community-state communications systems, and political leaders develop bargaining skills to interact with bureaucrats and politicians. Adaptation occurs on an *ad hoc* basis through experience and observation, not through grand strategy, and may reflect a composite of individually-acquired skills rather than conscious, collective effort. Both the process of adaptation and the new forms it generates have the potential to stimulate or aggravate conflict within the community, and there is no guarantee that development of an adaptive capacity ameliorates distress caused by change. Whatever the outcome, from a research perspective the important consideration is greater attention to the process and consequences of change.

The second element in the new framework is a steadily growing and very complex web of relationships between the community and the larger world. Not only has the national political system pursued a consistent policy of penetrating community decision-making, but the local economic system is increasingly tied to national and international markets. Craft products from hundreds of villages are sold from Tokyo to Chicago and Geneva, local availability and cost of labor is influenced to a degree by employment opportunities in the United States, and the choice of crops to be planted is affected by consumption demands in Mexico City and export markets. Until the 1970s, when Mexican social scientists began to explore the role of the state and local-national economic integration, most studies over-looked or discounted external linkages, although thirty years ago Howard Cline cautioned against the temptation to do so: "...communities cannot be treated as self-contained cultural units like isolated and remote tribes, but must be considered in their larger real temporal contexts..."[13] Oscar Lewis, whose *Life in a Mexican Village* served as a model ethnography for a generation of American anthropology students, was equally adamant:

> In studying communities in Mexico it is important that the anthropologist become a student not merely of the single community but of the region and nation is well....It seems to me that such a procedure makes for a better sense of perspective in understanding the local scene, and helps to distinguish between that which is local and that which is widespread....It offers an excellent opportunity to study the way in which national events and programs such as the Revolution and the *ejido* program have worked out under local conditions.[14]

The consequences of social change and extra-local linkages, while not the exclusive domain of Mexican scholars, receive extensive treatment in their research.[15] The problem conceptualization and focus of these scholars offer productive insights on the transformation of local political systems. Given the community or regional orientation of individual case studies, the specifics vary, but commonalities among these and related works include:

First, population growth, the emergence of new technologies and markets, the creation of new political institutions, and other aspects of modernization alter historical relationships within communities by challenging values, generating new opportunities, and changing the relative significance of various resources. Confronted by uncertainty and stability, groups struggle to protect or improve their positions.[16] The very ubiquity of social and economic change has at times distracted us from a frequent tendency to treat political sytems as static, and these studies draw our attention to the contradiction and its implications.

Second, extra-local institutions not only penetrate communities to affect *campesinos* in a host of ways, e.g., to deliver services or mobilize support for the regime, but increasingly they define what it means to be *campesino*, and what the prospects of *campesinos*, individually and collectively, will be. Warman captures it best in his introduction to Azaola Garrido and Krotz, when after noting that *campesino* political passivity is in large part illusory, he describes the intimate and complex involvement of the peasant with the state:

> In the Mexican countryside, politics and production are in a direct and immediate relationship, empirically demonstratable. Access to resources essential for production is obtained directly through politics or through conditions imposed by it....Government intervenes directly in the administration of cultivated land through ejidal organization, which has a political origin. Through official credit and state enterprises government intervenes in production, marketing, and processing of campesino harvests. It always intervenes indirectly in production through guaranteed prices, taxes, prohibition of cultivation for technical reasons, through control of irrigation systems or a monopoly of fertilizer production, among many other actions; it also does so through public works built for agricultural purposes. Government intervention is the most powerful force in agricultural activities and economics, and government and policy go together although they are not the same thing.[17]

Warman's analysis suggests that community-state linkages are heavily, although not exclusively, conditioned by economic factors, in particular control of the means of production and appropriation of any surplus created by *campesino* labor. Capital accumulated in this fashion may be expended on community ritual or individual consumption, or reinvested. Its specific utilization is less important at the moment—although given fierce struggles for political control, hardly irrelevant—than the fact that the state shapes and directs the agrarian context within which *campesinos* live out their lives.

Third, there is a continuing process of multiplication of institutional linkages that ties community members directly to higher levels of government, and an increasing subordination of community political authorities to external control and supervision. Peasant unions, credit associations, political parties, cooperatives, and a host of other organizations by-pass local authorities or assign them truncated roles in organization management and decision-making.[18] Local officials face continuing pressures to convert themselves into administrative arms of the state as new laws, policies, and practices replace custom and informal arrangements. The expansion of governmental influence not only forces *campesinos* into more frequent and meaningful contact with a variety of agencies, but acts as a brake on political opposition; few of those dependent on the government for services and problem resolution wish to be identified as opponents of the government.

Caciquismo and Civil-Religious Hierarchies: Community Political Systems in 1940

The late 1930s marked the end of armed opposition to the national government and to its consolidation of control over the countryside. For the vast majority of rural communities, however, the immediate impacts of more effective national administration were limited, episodic, and frequently tied to specific programs and personalities, as in the expansion of agrarian reform under President Lázaro Cárdenas (1934-1940). Routine community management and decision-making remained in the hands of local leaders, although sometimes leadership composition and style changed during the post-Revolution instability. To the extent ethnographic studies from, or of, the period treat political organization, they generally do so with reference to two institutional forms, the civil-religious hierarchy and *caciquismo*. While there is no reason to expect all local systems to fall within this two-fold classification, they have received substantial attention in the literature and mark convenient starting points for an analysis of political change.

Civil-Religious Hierarchy.

Discussions of traditional community social structure and system maintenance often turn to the notion of a civil-religious hierarcy as a descriptive or explanatory concept. Structurally, "civil-religious hierarchy" refers to a ladder-like, pyramid-shaped arrangement of offices ranked on the basis of authority and responsibility, with increasing integration of civil and religious functions as one ascends the ladder.[19] For our purposes, De Walt[20] captures the essential features of a civil-religious hierarchy, or cargo system, as it is sometimes called:

> 1) It involves voluntary service without remuneration (although in most communities there are strong social and/or physical pressures upon individuals to participate in the system); 2) holders of civil or religious offices (*cargos*) perform most or all of the functions necessary for the running of the local government and/or the church; and 3) tenure in these offices is rotated, usually annually, to other members of the community.

Whether the civil-religious hierarchy is of pre-Hispanic[21] or more recent origin,[22] for smooth performance it depends heavily on cultural homogeneity, solidarity, and the significance of tradition. Cámara[23] notes "Centripetal organizations," i.e., civil-religious hierarchies, tend to be "....found in communities where the emotional and utilitarian needs of their members are homogeneous and reciprocal, and where a great majority of the cultural stimuli appear to be determined by tradition and by the community."

From ethnographic profiles of communities fitting Camara's criteria it is possible to construct a list of significant norms and operational characteristics associated with this form of political organization, among them the following:

> 1) Tradition and precedence tend to define both the range of system activities and acceptable approaches to problem-solving. This is par-

ticularly important when political and religious ritual are closely intertwined. The system should do what has been done in the past, and innovation is unwelcome. The centrality of tradition provides guidance and socialization for those with little experience in community governance.

2) Specific demands for action are few, as the emphasis is on passive administration, system maintenance, and conflict resolution. To do less would threaten the system with breakdown, but to attempt to do more would overload the decision-making process, aggravate competition for scarce resources, and raise the possibility of conflict over allocation of costs and benefits. Resources tend to be channeled into collective goods, particularly those associated with public ritual.

3) There will be considerble emphasis on the notion of community harmony and solidarity. Conflict resolution centers on finding broadly acceptable solutions to problems or issues. Recruitment into the civil-religious hierarchy will nominally be broad-based, with substantial participation important to legitimizing decisions and outcomes. Community mythology downplays the existence and significance of class, faction, or other devisive elements.

4) Local affairs are subject to little or no outside intervention, particularly by the state or national governments. Beyond providing some minimal level of security and perhaps such services as a civil register extraloal governments permit a broad latitude of community autonomy. As schools, clinics, electrification, and other services increase vulnerability to external influence, at least some community members resist them.

5) Information gathering and processing capabilities are weak. Skills necessary to deal with the larger world or new problems, e.g., speak Spanish or manipulate bureaucracies, are in short supply. Because of the disadvantages they face in dealing with external actors, communities try to limit their interactions and are frequently victimized by more powerful or knowledgeable outsiders.

Political decision-making in communities with traditional political systems generally places considerable importance on consensus. Decisions are not so much made as emerge through a process of incrementalism, accretion, and community-wide negotiation, never final until they cease to draw opposition. Proposals are tentative and decisions more tacit than explicit.[24] Voting usually serves to ratify a previously-established agreement. The absence of voting on choices makes the division between winners and losers on a given issue less obvious, thereby avoiding cleavages that could threaten community solidarity and harmony. Consensus decision-making works best in communities where the issues are simple and clear, and where the need to make major decisions is infrequent, as consensus-building takes time and is particularly difficult when issues are multi-faceted. For most communities the volume and complexity of issues facing the political system were far more limited in 1940 than in 1980. Consensus also plays an important role in recruiting community officials, as it permits the community to claim unity behind its elected leadership and places heavy social pressures on those selected for office to fulfill their responsibilities.[25] The civil-religious hierarchy, by prescribing routes for advancement and by locating participants at specific stages at any given time, facilitates consensus recruitment by identifying acceptable candidates, legitimizing their availability, and requiring some modest prior demonstration of skill and capacity.

Caciquismo.

If the civil-religious hierarchy is stable, integrated, and deterministic, the second institutional form, *caciquismo*, is personalistic, devisive, and inherently unstable. Definitions of *cacique* differ,[26] but most incorporate violence, territorial control, and acknowledged (though not always unchallenged) dominance of local political decision-making. *Caciques* are self-selected and rarely retire voluntarily.[27]

From the ethnographic record it is clear that at the end of the 1930s *caciques* played a promient role in the political life of many communities. From Yucatan to Michoacan, case studies refer to, and occasionally explore in some detail, the *cacique* as a powerful figure in local politics.[28] Unless one assumes anthropologists have a propensity for selecting communities with *caciques* as research sites, this suggests *caciquismo* played a prominent part in local political systems. In reviewing case studies on *caciquismo*, several aspects of its relationship to community governance merit special attention:

> 1) *Caciquismo* is generally associated with factionalism and violence. To gain and maintain control of a community, or to compete with rivals for power, requires both the ability to mobilize a cadre of supporters and a willingness to intimidate or kill opponents. Much of the concern for community harmony and consensus reflects sensitivity to the insecurity and turbulence that comes with factional conflict.
>
> 2) Over the long term, *caciques* need to supplement the use of violence with distributions of goods and services to their followers, both as rewards for past support and to prevent rivals from luring them away. Distributions commonly include land and privileges, e.g., immunity from social authorities. They may also include the *cacique*'s intervention with outsiders when such assistance is necessary, as in confrontations with the law or a need for a specific service. The role of "broker" or "patron" facilitates *cacique* access to external resources for distribution.
>
> 3) *Caciques* tend to be ambivalent about the growth of extra-local influence in local affairs. To the extent they can control interaction between the community and outside agencies, i.e., play the role of "gatekeeper," they gain additional resources and reinforce their position. On the other hand, the availability of services and resources outside their control reduces their influence and creates a rally point for potential rivals.
>
> 4) As their status rests on personal power, not institutional authority, *caciques* frequently stand outside the formal political structure or occupy formal positions only when it is necessary. The *cacique*'s role in community decision-making may be active, in that nothing is done without his permission, or it may be more passive, with the *cacique* merely exercising a veto to protect his interests. Either way, *caciques* normally seek

to legitimize their rule by claiming they hold power in the interest of community progress or because the community needs a vigorous leader.

Although it might be possible to identify additional institutional forms, e.g., communities manipulated by a oligarchy through peaceful means, *caciquismo* and the civil-religious hierarchy appear to have been the dominant forms in 1940. Even in 1940, however, the changing contexts of local political systems were triggering modifications and adaptations. Cámara, drawing on field studies of the 1930s and 1940s, distinguished between centripetal and centrifugal organizations, claiming the latter were no longer "...oriented toward the conservation of any traditional order or beliefs and practices; it is changing, heterogeneous, weakly integrated, and voluntary."[29] DeWalt,[30] writing a generation later, distinguished four types of organization on the basis of the linkage between political and religious functions, and the level of vigor of the latter. He found traditional civil-religious hierarchies in ten of 26 community studies surveyed, but data for six of the ten were collected before 1950 and their current accuracy is questionable. Of twelve studies undertaken since 1960, nine show substantial deviation from the traditional system, some to the point that even the religious hierarchy shows signs of fading. As DeWalt notes elsewhere,[31] the diminishing power of the civil-religious hierarchy stands in contrast to the continued importance of *caciquismo*, as the latter adapted to new conditions and exploited new opportunities.

Transforming Community Political Systems, 1940-1980

The paucity and indeterminancy of available data complicate tracing the evolution of community political systems between 1940 and 1980. Some early ethnographies provide useful baseline information,[32] but in most cases the coverage of political systems is rather thin.[33]

Prior to the mid-1930s, the primary concern of the national government was its search for a means of institutionalizing the peaceful transfer of power among competing leaders and groups, thereby putting an end to the intrigue, rebellion, and instability that marked Mexican politics.[34] Both to extend the benefits of the Mexican Revolution to its putative legatees and to strengthen his own power base, President Lázaro Cárdenas encouraged the progressive penetration of *campesino* communities by national organizations and the progressive integration of their residents into national life.[35] Almost two generations later these twin goals of development and control continue to shape policy content, and the cumulative effect on community political institutions has been substantial. The extension of national power created stress on, and opportunities for, local political leaders, and it is to these aspects of penetration and local responses to them, that we direct our attention.

In a general sense, control-oriented penetration refers to policies and practices limiting local discretion and autonomy and encouraging compliance with goals and priorities established by state and national leaders. Such penetration may prescribe duties for local officials, define eligibility and selection criteria for recruitment to public office, or circumscribe the authority of traditional courts. Corbett and Whiteford[36] categorize such penetration as institutional transformation, for taken to its logical conclusion it transforms local political institutions into administrative arms of the national government. Control-oriented penetration also includes the establishment of new organizations such as political parties, peasant leagues, or water management committees. Such organizations have their origins in, and are responsibile to, powers outside the community, constituting examples of structural penetration.[37] The existence and effectiveness of specific control-oriented policies and organizations may vary from community to community, but overall they experienced dramatic growth over the forty years. Much the same may be said of development-oriented penetration, which focuses on the provision of services intended to improve the standard of living and productive capacity of the community. Development-oriented penetration ranges from schools and roads to cultural missions, agricultural credit programs, and tourism promotion. In practice, of course, organizations and policies may overlap, as an *ejido* or water management committee may serve both control and development functions.

Control-Oriented Penetration.

One direct means of extending state control over local systems centers on manipulating access to, and responsibilities of, local office, obliging officeholders to be responsive to outside agencies rather than to the community. Clearly there are ill-defined limits beyond which officeholders cannot go without losing local legitimacy, but these will be tested repeatedly through policy and procedural manuvering. Rus and Wasserstrom note that in the late 1930s state officials in Chiapas, responding to pressures from President Cárdenas, took steps "to improve the lot of native people and guarantee their political loyalty."[38] This included appointing bilingual, literate young men from Indian communities as scribes to handle the growing volume of paperwork and communications between villages and government agencies. By 1940 the government decided to recognize only Spanish-speaking *presidentes municipales*, a policy not always successful but which challenged traditional criteria for recruitment to office. Nash and Siverts[39] recount political careers launched by foresighted young men on the basis of their literacy and grasp of the outside world. Governments determine permissable sources of revenue, require myriad reports, and dictate the format in which they must be submitted[40] and involve the *presidente* or other officials in time-consuming, sometimes sensitive negotiations with government bureaucrats. For constitutional, logistical, and operational reasons it would not be feasible for extra-local governments to take direct conrol of community political systems, but institutional transformation offers a feasible alternative to secure cooperation.

Traditionally, community contact with extra-local agencies was channelled through the *presidente* and *principales*, utilizing their formal authority and experience for guidance and support. Direct interaction between bureaucrats and community members erodes the power vested in local authorities as communications gatekeepers, and thereby erodes their ability to command respect and compliance. De la Peña comments:

> A salient feature of *municipio* political life is the multiplicity of agencies concerned with the maintenance of order, administration of civil matters and implementation of public goals. There is the municipal council, the *ejido* committee, the communal land committee, the village *ayudantes* (auxiliary officers), the public works committee, the party (whose delegates sometimes directly interfere in decisions). There is also local interference by the district police, district court, district deputy, etc. There is the district tax collector—who is independent of the municipal council.[41]

This fragmentation of responsibility and authority offers a second form of control-oriented penetration. The bureaucractic expansion of the national state generates continuing pressure on local institutions while undermining the power base that sustains them.[42] Local officials have little to say regarding new organizations, as they represent a projection of state or federal power. Furthermore, new organizations may bring benefits strongly desired by some segments of the community, access to government programs, expansion of physical facilities such as roads and water systems, or entreprenuerial opportunities. Indeed, sometimes officials encourage penetration, counting the loss of control as a reasonable tradeoff for the prestige associated with bringing some benefit to the community or the prospects for personal gain through access to new resources.

A third facet of control-oriented penetration centers on the expansion of outside authority over key resources, e.g., land, water, or forests. The *ejido* program assures that lands distributed through agrarian reform remain under the ultimate control of the national government, which may use its authority over *ejido* membership to reward or discipline members. Although such power may be used directly, it is more common to delegate it to *ejido* officials, who in return for opportunities to use their position for private gain[43] generally support projects and policies of the *Secretaría de Reforma Agraria.*[44]

A final form of control-oriented penetration is the gradual expansion of the political party system, particularly the *Partido Revolucionario Institucional* (PRI), at the community level. PRI, which has dominated Mexican politics since its founding in 1929, attaches considerable importance to its ability to mobilize political support among *campesinos*, for such support validates its claim to be the institutional embodiment of the Mexican Revolution. It also provides a reservoir of votes to offset a gradual decline in party support in urban areas. Historically, PRI ignored purely local elections, concentrating its efforts to mobilize votes for state and national party candidates. Since the 1960s, however, PRI has become more aggressive in controlling local offices.[45] In some cases, PRI counts on voluntary adherence by local authorities seeking to assure PRI assistance in petitions for public works on benefits.[46] In other cases, PRI seeks to identify candidates likely to garner broad public backing and simply proclaims them to be its candidates.[47] In still other cases, PRI simply stuffs the ballot box, counting on local apathy and its close ties with the higher authorities to impose candidates.[48] Given the centralized nature of the party, such arrangements provide PRI with a link to thousands of communities.

Development-Oriented Penetration.

As noted above, development oriented penetration has dual goals, i.e., upgrading local living standards and integrating the community into the nation. It covers a broad ranges of activities and programs accounting for most of the day-to-day contact community members have with state and national governments. In a general way development-oriented penetration may be subdivided into three categories: infrastructure construction, direct services, and formal organization, each of which involves a distinct set of linkages between the community and the outside world. Some penetration takes place through local initiative, while in other cases it represents government programs and priorities established with little or no reference to local needs. The term "development" has a benign, positive ring to it, though in fact the process and consequences may appear otherwise.[49]

Among the various forms of infrastructure construction, e.g., electrification, potable water systems, or roads, associated with development-oriented penetration, the expansion of the road network has received the most attention. Roads facilitate commercial exchange, provide access to opportunities elsewhere, make service delivery easier, and expose the community to new forms of social interaction, e.g., tourism.[50] Road construction in the name of development stimulates the creation of numerous local-national individual and institutional linkages by providing the physical link between the community and the outside world.

Almost all ethnographies make reference to the growing array of governmental services penetrating communities. Some communities receive far more services than others, a function of size, location, or organizational capacity,[51] but even small, isolated communities now have schools and visits by mobile health teams. Unlike infrastructure construction which, once completed, removes outside agencies from the community, serivce delivery requires continuing or periodic presence of government personnel in the community. Ties to extra-community institutions and control over valued distributions strengthens their capacity to act as intermediaries or brokers, and permits them to articulate new standards of achievement and prestige.[52]

The third form of development-oriented penetration—formal organization—refers to the creation of new community-level institutions having the capacity to mobilize local resources and serve as independent channels to extra-local agencies. Formal organization is a form of structural penetration, as it contributes to the multiplication of political structures and to a further fragmentation of power and responsibility within the community. New organizations emerge through the direction, or under the sponsorship of, outside agencies, bypassing the oversight and mediating roles of the *presidente municipal* and other traditional authorities. In practice, some, although not all, new organizations serve both development and control functions. They serve a developmental function when they allocate resources, mobilize labor, and disseminate information, and serve a control function when used to secure compliance. Control implications aside, *ejidos*, water management committees, producers associations, and similar organizations provide government agencies with a specific institutional locus and local management structure for their programs.[53] In some communities such organizations are small, moribund, or of marginal importance, while in others they are sufficiently powerful to overshadow the municipality itself.[54] Lees captures the essential change quite clearly when she writes:

> ...water control is set apart from the ordinary administrative duties of community officials and becomes a function of an arm of the state and federal government; water control officials are set apart from other public officials in the community because they are delegates of the state and federal agencies...the executive arm of the larger society with access to, and support from, the independent and extraordinary power of that government.[55]

Penetration and Brokers

The multiplication of organizational linkages described above has been an important aspect of Mexican political development over the past forty years. Equally important, although far less visible, is the expansion of vast networks of informal ties linking Mexicans with varied needs and resources in a complex exchange system.[56] Carlos and Anderson claim "...these political networks are a principal basis of political activity in Mexico, and...cut across political institutions and often act independently of formal institutions and structures."[57] Such networks both reflect and reinforce the influence of patron-client and personalistic relationships in Mexican politics, and both complement and counter formal organization charts.[58] Their flexibility and complexity[59] allow them to penetrate systems far more thoroughly than formal institutions. Given the ubiquity of political networks, the key role is that of the "broker"—the individual with the skills, knowledge, and contacts to work across groups and subsystems.[60]

Despite the extensive activities of networks and brokers, their informal nature and emphasis on personal contact makes it difficult to trace them in detail, especially across boundaries or political groups.[61] Yet it is precisely this aspect of brokerage that is important in penetration, as can be gauged from the widespread citations of such activity in the literature.[62]

The use of brokers offers communities a mechanism to manipulate penetration, but not without complications of its own. First, service as a broker gives the individual considerable leverage within the community, leverages that might be used to personal benefit. Because they gain access to outside resources, brokers are able to develop a clientele independent of the sanctions or conrol of local authority.[63] Second, brokers seek to hoard rather than disseminate knowledge, as making it widely available depreciates its value to the broker. Third, Rus suggests that as the number of would-be brokers in the community rises, the potential for factionalism rises also.[64] Each aspirant for the position of broker, and perhaps of *cacique*, seeks to gather a clientele, and competition for clients may lead to cleavages and the formation of factions. In addition, competition may lead brokers to assure clients that they offer a better deal than local authorities, thereby undercutting the formal authority system.[65] Finally, as outside agencies become more experienced and sophisticated in dealing with community members, the role of broker or intermediary shifts from community brokers to bureaucratic specialists, e.g., teachers or agricultural agents, who develop local constituencies. Brokerage then facilitates further penetration, as agencies use their resources to promote their programs.

State Penetration of Community Political Systems: An Assessment

A thorough assessment of the impact of state penetration on community political systems awaits additional research, either in the form of explicit comparative studies or more systematic attention to political phenomena in the course of work on other topics. In addition, state penetration is only one of several factors influencing system evolution, e.g., population growth, general social change, or a multiplication of private sector linkages between local and national economies. Nevertheless, the wave of studies during the past decade that concentrate on, or are sensitive to, the political dimensions of community life make possible some tentative judgements about the transformation of community political institutions and community-state relations, and it is to these that we now turn.

The Decline of the Civil-Religious Hierarchy

As noted above, the civil-religious hierarchy as a *political* institution functioned best under conditions of local autonomy, limited demands, and community consensus. Over the past forty years such conditions have become increasingly problematic, confronting communities with a need to accomodate a lengthy list of new strains and pressures. In some communities this led to a process of structural differentiation and specialization, creating separate religious and political hierarchies. In others, the form remains nominally the same, but the issues and patterns of organizational behavior have changed.[66] There is no reason to expect, however, that all elements of the system change at the same rate or under the same circumstances. It appears offices and practices associated with community administration and external relations have experienced heavier pressure, or at least been less able to resist, than those associated with internal conflict management.[67]

Beyond the structural decay of the civil-religious hierarchy, and in some respects even more important, is the decline in community autonomy, particularly the autonomy of the political authorities. The community political system has become increasingly dependent on, and subordinate to, power and resources originating outside the community. Study after study refers to control or development-oriented penetration, and to its tendency to limit and direct local priorities. This is not to argue that there is something inherently undesirable or unsavory about penetration; for many communities it is the only way to secure beneficial inputs of knowledge and capital, and many actively pursue such benefits. Indeed, access to or control over resources available from extra-local agencies may become a sought-after goal, and communities may judge their leaders by how inept or successful they are in attracting social and capital investment. The skills, contacts, and other attributes required to manipulate the larger society become essential parts of the repertoire of political leadership. Whether the goal is increased resource investment or a reduction in intervention, in many communities "...the political activity of local authorities has oriented itself fundamentally in fulfilling the demands and expectations of extra-local society, as it appears to be the necessary and determining factor for the fulfillment of local public goals."[68]

In communities attracting development-oriented penetration, the individual benefits associated with officeholding may outweigh the burdens; in such cases we might see active competition or political office.[69] More common, however, are those communities where increasing penetration and a declining civil-religious hierarchy contribute to the burdens of officeholding. Prestige and authority dwindle, while the financial costs, time commitments, and psychological stress rise. Cleavages within the community may grow more pronounced as the capacity of leaders to orchestrate a consensus diminishes. Conflicting pressures to satisfy the expectations of local and extra-local constituencies simultaneously squeeze local officials unfortunate enough to be caught in the middle, and encourage them to find ways to alleviate the stress. Some officials are very adroit in doing so, while others will find accumulated role strain so burdensome they evade responsibilities and seek to avoid future service.[70] Recognition that community service interferes with personal or familial economic advancement also reduces motivation for participation. Maintenance of the civil-religious hierarchy requires a continuing flow of participants prepared to discharge their obligations, so avoidance of service may well induce a spiral of decay. The more the burdens of service deter participants, the greater the burdens on remaining participants. Eventually the pool of participants may become inadequate to support the structure, or the costs of doing so outstrips their resources. While this dilemma is not unique to the civil-religious hierarchy, it increases the difficulties of sustaining it.

Caciquismo and State Penetration: An Uneasy Balance

Caciques, too, face change. Like the civil-religious hierarchy, ***caciquismo*** must respond to the expansion of national power at the local level. By extending its domain over electoral politics into rural communities, PRI encroaches on a traditional power base of the ***cacique***. In some cases, PRI provides ***caciques*** an arena for non-violent competition for power,[71] furnishing competing groups at the local level the same outlet and oversight it provides at the national level. *Cacique* and party commonly enjoy a symbiotic relationship, with the latter conferring legitimacy and official recognition on the former in return for the *cacique*'s support and mobilization of voters.[72] Conversely, PRI has the capacity to undermine *caciques* by blocking their surrogates and supporters from public office, and by displacing political allies.[73]

For *caciques*, the expansion of state bureaucratic power has been even more important than the expansion of the party system. Most definitions of *caciquismo* incorporate a tacit recognition of the *cacique*'s power by higher officials, but expansion of the activist state brings the bureaucrat and the *cacique* into direct contact on a continuing basis. With government penetration of his community or region, the *cacique* becomes increasingly bound to the state, whether he wishes to be or not. The state becomes a source of resources and opportunities far beyond anything generated locally. By tapping the wealth and authority of the government, *caciques* can strengthen their hold over their followers and their coercive capacity vis-à-vis opponents. The *ejido* system has long been cited as an enormous plum for *caciques*, as it provides land, credit, and other goods to distribute to the *cacique*'s backers, and *ejido* organization offers an excellent means of control over possible dissidents.[74] In addition to the *ejido*, the confusion, inconsistencies, and contradictions associated with almost any government program offers the *cacique* an opportunity to serve as an intermediary and service broker, helping the bewildered and entangled in return for their future support. It would appear, then, that almost any increase in government activity would be beneficial for the *cacique*, as it would expand his resource base and generate more pleas for assistance.

In practice, *caciques* are ambivalent about expanding government programs, recognizing their potentially destabilizing features. They can find themselves acting as little more than conduits for resources generated elsewhere, and therefore vulnerable to events or changes in political fortune that cause resources to dry up. Expansion of programs means expansion of the number of direct contact points between agencies and the *cacique*'s clients, making it increasingly difficult for the *cacique* to monopolize control over the linkages between agency and client. A change in policy or personnel may lead an agency to do away with the intermediary.[75] To survive, a *cacique* must establish political networks and alliances that enable him to profit from his association with the government without falling victim to shifts in policy or wilier rivals.

Community Political Systems and Modern Mexican Politics: A Final Observation

In contemplating the future of community political systems, two well-established patterns seem particularly noteworthy. First, there is little reason to anticipate a shift from the control and development-oriented penetration that has formed the basis for rural development strategies since the 1930s. In addition to a residual commitment to the ideals of the Mexican Revolution, government interest has been rekindled by the agricultural crises of the 1970s, with special emphasis on those economically marginal zones, home to numerous communities of subsistence farmers. Accordingly, programs such as the *Sistema Alimentario Mexicano* are aimed toward further penetration through improved services, infrastructure construction, and organization development. Second, the threads of authoritarianism and personalism so deeply engrained in the fabric of Mexican politics show few indications of weakening. National leaders may publicly condemn these traits, but day-to-day operation reveals how important they are.[76] Access to scarce resources or special privileges may be bestowed from above or negotiated through brokers, usually at the price of political subordination.

What do these patterns signify for the community? Without arguing that the long-term trend at the community level is toward *caciquismo*, it is clear *caciquismo* fits well with the Mexican political system's authoritarian and paternalistic modes of political control. Official rhetoric may condemn *caciquismo*, but tacit policy is to incorporate *caciques* into the political system.[77] Although occasionally disadvantageous to the *cacique*, penetration furnishes new resources and opportunities, enabling him to better reward his supporters; inequality becomes an indicator of the *cacique*'s effectiveness because it reflects his ability to mobilize and distribute benefits. Penetration and personalism allow the *cacique* to replace or supplement overt coercion with less dramatic but equally effective measures—all used with the cooperation, or at least the acquiescence, of the government. In contrast, the civil-religious hierarchy continues to be buffeted by adverse circumstances. It offers the national political system few incentives to maintain it, and its general capacity to resist encroachments continues to decline. Although the civil-religious hierarchy may set on a democratic and equalitarian moral order, as Iwánska and Selby suggest,[78] these values are incompatible with authoritarianism, paternalism, and the elaborate structure of inequalities that marks the Mexican social system.[79] Penetration erodes its institutional framework, transforming it into a marginal entity in the community it purports to serve. Charged by community members to defend them, officeholders find themselves pressured to manage the community in ways acceptable to outside interests. Expected to uphold a community political culture of solidarity and consensus, they confront pressures toward fragmentation and imposition. It is too soon to write an epitaph for the civil-religious hierarchy, but the multiple forces at work in the Mexican political system are moving communities toward other forms of governance.

NOTES

[1]Almond and Powell 1966:215.

[2]Despite the extensive literature on rural Mexico compiled since 1940, specific attention to community political systems and local-level politics has been remarkably limited, a fact reflected in several recent reviews (Chambers and Young 1979; Schwartz 1978, 1981). Nor have contributions from Mexico-based research received more than scant attention in reviews of political anthropology (Vincent 1978; Seaton and Claessen 1979). Even when allowing for the selective character of such reviews, or for discussions of political phenomena buried in works on social change, rural development, group relations, or political economy, the literature remains sparse in volume, variable in coverage, and limited in influence on scholarly research and thought.

[3]Brandenburg 1964; Hansen 1971.

[4]Cf. González Casanova 1965; Reyna and Weinart 1977; P. H. Smith 1979.

[5]There have been some studies of political behavior or issues in urban areas (e.g., Cornelius 1975; Eckstein 1977; Fagen and Tuohy 1972; Graham 1968; Ugalde 1970, 1974b) and of the impact of federal programs and policies on the rural sector (Grindle 1977; Poleman 1964).

[6]For exceptions, see Carlos 1974; Corbett 1976; S. Purcell and J. Purcell 1973; Ronfeldt 1973; Sanderson 1981.

[7]S. Purcell and J. Purcell 1973:71.

[8]Wolf 1957.

[9]Chambers and Young 1979; Schwartz 1978, 1981; C. Lomnitz, this volume; L. Lomnitz, this volume.

[10]There has been nothing in political anthropology comparable to the Harvard Chiapas Project or the UCLA Oaxaca Market Study Project. Some politically-oriented works have been produced by the former (e.g., Cancian 1965, 1967; J. F. Collier 1973, 1976), but most of its publications ignore political aspects of life in Zinacantan or deal with them only indirectly. W. R. Smith criticizes the project for myopia on this point, contending it neglected the "overarching pattern of class and power" that produced and maintained the cultural and social patterns receiving most of Harvard's attention (W.R. Smith 1977:23). Evon Vogt's *Zinacantan* (1969), which draws together much of the ethnograhic detail generated by dozens of individual field projects, devotes more than ten times as much space to religious beliefs and rituals as it does to the political system. This is *not* to argue community political systems are more deserving of scholarly attention than religious or economic systems, but the low level of interest and effort in anthrpological research, as in political science research, resulted in a failure to monitor and analyze significant changes in the relationship between the community and the state.

[11]Schwartz 1981:316.

[12]Corbett and Whiteford 1983; Margolies 1975; Schryer 1980.

[13]H. F. Cline 1952:220.

[14]O. Lewis 1951:xxi.

[15]Among the more notable examples are the numerous studies of Morelos, including a major project directed by Arturo Warman, and works by de la Peña (1981) and by Arias and Bazán (1979). Comparable efforts elsewhere include studies of Arandas, Jalisco (del Castillo 1979; Martínez Saldaña and Gándara Mendoza 1976), San José de Gracia, Michoacan (González 1974), and various communities in Hidalgo, among them several in the Valle del Mezquital (Bartra, *et al* 1975). Schryer's book on Pisaflores, Hidalgo (1980) complements these.

[16]Del Castillo 1979; Schryer 1980. González goes to considerable lengths to outline the varieties of change affecting San José de Gracia (1974:261-63), concluding: "Ten years ago we would not have believed that the people of San José could change in so many ways."

[17]Azaola Garrido and Krotz 1976:8-9, my translation.

[18]Even in situations where extra-local agencies do not exercise direct control they determine criteria for organizational membership, scope of activity, and other important considerations (Arias and Bazán 1979:41-43). While the multiplication of institutional linkages theoretically offer community members enhanced channels of articulation with the larger system, in fact these channels are unidirectional, passing directives and similar communications from above to below (Azaola Garrido and Krotz 1976:245). Furthermore, the relative significance of local vs. extra-local institutions has shifted markedly in favor of the latter. In Tetela del Volcán, community autonomy, although guaranteed by the Mexican Constitution, has dwindled to the religious organizations and a few committees of local significance (Arias and Bazán 1979:41).

[19]It has been cited widely and forms the subject of several extended reviews (Cámara 1952; Cancian 1967; Carrasco 1961, DeWalt 1975) or specific studies (Cancian 1965; Friedlander 1981, Rus and Wasserstrom 1980), all of which offer more detailed treatment than is possible here.

[20]DeWalt 1975:90.

[21]Carrasco 1961.

[22]Rus and Wasserstrom 1980.

[23]Cámara 1952:143.

[24]Foster 1967:172-75; Miller 1961:58-59.

[25]Kearney 1972:20-21.

[26]Bartra *et. al.* 1975; Friedrich 1968:248; Sabloff 1981:3; Ugalde 1974a:124.

[27]The major reviews on political and religious organization by Cámara and Cancian ignore this form completely, while Wolf's 1967 essay makes frequent references to bosses, leaders, and violent conflict between factions but never deals explicitly with *caciques*.

[28]Friedrich's work in Michoacan deals extensively with *caciquismo* in one village (1965, 1966, 1968, 1971). Beals, although never using the term *cacique*, describes the "real political boss" of Cherán in a fashion that, although perhaps unintended, leaves the reader with a strong impression Beals dealt with one there (Beals 1946:107-13). DeWalt (1979:145) remarks "As recently as 1940, the Temascalcingo region was marked by the violence of caciques imposing their will on others and fighting one another for preeminence." Schryer (1980) and Bartra, *et al* (1975) report *caciques* in Hidalgo during the same period, as do Beals (1946), De la Fuente (1949), and Ugalde (1974a) for Oaxaca. Siverts (1965) analyzes the career of a *cacique* in K'ankujk', Chiapas, while Goldkind (1966) reinterprets Redfield's Chan Kom data to argue the community was *cacique*-dominated during Redfield's research there. After three years of field research in the early 1940s, Whetten concluded *caciquismo* was widespread in rural communities (1948).

[29]Cámara 1952:143.

[30]DeWalt 1975.

[31]DeWalt 1979:128.

[32]E.g., Beals 1946; De la Fuente 1949; Parsons 1936; Redfield and Villa Rojas 1934.

[33]Unfortunately there have been few restudies or updates of early work (for exceptions see Avila 1969; Goldkind 1966; O. Lewis 1951; Leslie 1960), with the last two drawing on data now outdated. Foster (1967) and Vogt (1969) summarize data from extended field research. Historical studies such as those of de la Peña (1981), González (1974), Henao (1980), Schryer (1980), and Warman (1980) are helpful, although only Schryer discusses a community political system in a systematic and extended fashion. The others, particularly Warman, are most useful in assessing the impact of the national political system on communities. Beyond these studies any interpretation of system depends heavily on bits and pieces of data assembled from many sources.

[34]Dulles 1961; Hansen 1971.

[35]Cornelius 1973.

[36]Corbett and Whiteford 1983.

[37]Corbett and Whiteford 1983.

[38]Rus and Wasserstrom 1980:473-74.

[39]Nash 1970; Siverts 1965.

[40]Pérez Jiménez 1968 provides a compilation of rules and style for newly-elected community officeholders in Oaxaca.

[41]de la Peña 1981:240.

[42]Arias and Bazán (1979) report the proliferation of organizations in Tetela del Volcán, many of them sponsored or assisted by outside agencies to further agency activities.

[43]DeWalt 1979:133-39.

[44]Oscar Lewis (1951:128) notes formation of the Tepoztlán *ejido* reduced revenues to the municipal treasury previously generated by fees from communal lands. Control over water resources passed from local to federal jurisdiction (Henao 1980; Lees 1973, 1976), as did control of forests. Trees may be cut only by federal permit, ostensibly as a conservation measures, but the permit process works to the benefit of forest products companies, as they enjoy access

to bureaucrats issuing permits and frequently evade regulations requiring them to hire employees locally and pay stumpage fees to municipal or *ejido* treasuries. Lees, in her study of irrigation in the Oaxaca Valley, notes the federal government provides funding and technical support for water projects, but in the process alters local organization:

> It prescribes the form and membership of the local administration of the facilities, which is responsible not to the local community at large (as would formerly have been the case), but to...an agency of the central government. Simply in terms of formal characteristics, this policy undermines local autonomy and directly integrates local organization with the federal apparatus...federal allocation of irrigation water according to its own political and economic priorities illustrates the growing influence of higher-level control (Lees 1976:203-7).

[45]Corbett 1980.

[46]Kearney 1972:20.

[47]Corbett 1976; Foster 1967:175; Martínez Saldaña and Gándara Mendoza 1976:93-94.

[48]Corbett 1980; Iszaevich 1973:133; Kohler 1982:133.

[49]Warman's description (1980) of the penetration of eastern Morelos by development programs, particularly of those calculated to incorporate it into the national market system, underscores the unintended but adverse effects such programs may have on a substantial portion of the local population.

[50]Cancian (1972) documents the impact road construction had on the corn farmers of Zinacantan by making it possible to expand production in the tropical lowlands. Roads substantially altered the economic base of eastern Morelos by making it easier to export local produce to markets in Mexico City and even the United States, while manufactured goods flowed into the region (de la Peña 1981; Friedlander 1975; Warman 1980). This induced a partial shift from corn to tomato (de la Peña 1981) and onion production (Alonso, Corcuera Garza, and Melville 1974), a shift requiring greater integration into credit, marketing, and commercial production institutions outside the community. The influx of manufactured goods displaced, through lower cost or higher prestige, locally-made goods, simultaneously reducing economic diversity within communities while increasing their dependence on distant suppliers. Conversely, Kearney (1972:41) notes the decline of Ixtepeji, Oaxaca, is linked in part to a change in trade patterns after construction of a highway through the Oaxaca Sierra, and the decline of Tlacochahuaya, once an important town in the Oaxaca Valley, appears related to the construction of the Pan American Highway, which siphoned away traffic contributing to its prosperity.

[51]S. Purcell and J. Purcell 1973.

[52]While sometimes controversial or self-interested, teachers are widely cited as agents of penetration (Friedlander 1975; Krejci 1976; Nash 1970; Nelson 1971; Press 1975). Representatives of agencies such as CONASUPO and the Instituto Nacional Indigensita (INI) play comparable roles. As the national government implements a strategy of direct intervention in rural areas for the promotion of development, as it has in recent years, its presence becomes even more apparent and more influential. Martínez Saldaña and Gándara Mendoza note the proliferation of federal agencies in Arandas after 1960 (1976: 108), and pursuit of development programs such as PIDER (Integrated Rural Development Plan), COPLAMAR (Coordinating Program for Marginal Zones), and the SAM (Mexican Food System) assure a further expansion of service penetration.

[53]*Ejidos* provide government agencies promoting agricultural development with a permanent contact point (DeWalt 1979), while water management committees serve the same function for water utilization (Lees 1976). Contacts may be unsuccessful or counter-productive, but over time the number of contacts and the number of local organizations tends to grow (Arias and Bazán 1979:42).

[54]Ronfeldt 1973.

[55]Lees 1976:86.

[56]Carlos and Anderson 1981; Grindle 1977.

[57]Carlos and Anderson 1981:172.

[58]González Casanova 1965:119-23.

[59]E.g., Bartra *et. al.* 1975:110.

[60]Wolf 1956.

[61]Carlos and Anderson 1981:170-71.

[62]Nash (1970), Siverts (1965), and Vogt (1969) mention cases of individuals who parleyed skills such as literacy or speaking Spanish into brokerage roles, acting as intermediaries between Indian communities in Chiapas and Ladino government officials. Bartra, *et al* (1975) and Sabloff (1981) identify *caciques* who built their power through astute moves as middlemen, while Schryer (1980) recounts a number of transient careers as brokers among individuals whose ability to fill such a role depended in turn on the variable political fortunes of their own patrons. Local elites in Arandas use them as buffers between the community and the national government thereby protecting their interests and validating their status (del Castillo 1979:160).

[63]Vogt's description of the rise of the *cacique* of Zinacantan makes it clear he was able to capitalize on the ability to write to gain control of the Zinacantan *ejido* (a resource that did not exist prior to organizational penetration), and control of the *ejido* offered a springboard to control of the community (Vogt 1969:285-87).

[64]Rus 1982:79.

[65]Rus 1982:80.

[66]Nash 1970:230-68.

[67]Several studies (J. F. Collier 1973, 1976; Hunt and Hunt 1969, Parnell 1978) suggest community legal systems have been remarkably resilient.

[68]Arias and Bazán 1979:160, my translation.

[69]Azaola Garrido and Krotz 1976; del Castillo 1979; Schryer 1980.

[70]Corbett 1977; Dennis 1973.

[71]Ugalde 1974a:129-34.

[72]Azaola Garrido and Krotz 1976:149.

[73]Schryer 1980:139-44.

[74]Bartra *et. al.* 1975; Friedrich 1965; Ronfeldt 1973; Sabloff 1981.

[75]Gutiérrez cited the potential for this in his study of Hidalgo: "While it is certain that the participation of political organizations and State agencies in no way excludes caciquismo, it is possible to see that their more active intervention weakens the caciques because it accentuates concentration of power in the higher levels of the Bureaucracy" (1977:912, my translation). Boege, *et al*, describe how the intervention of a government-owned company intent upon restructuring local tobacco production contributed to the demise of a cacique in Valle Nacional, Oaxaca (1979:89-98). Schryer discusses the emergence of a bureaucratic *cacique* whose power base was neither landholdings nor gunmen, but adminstrative clout and patronage as a consequence of high government office (1980:110).

[76]Grindle's study (1977) of CONASUPO, a key agency in promoting penetration, demonstrates personalism to be critical for effective bureaucratic performance, while González Casanova (1965) laments the ways in which authoritarianism shapes social relations.

[77]Bartra *et. al.* 1975

[78]Iwánska 1971; Selby 1973.

[79]González Casanova 1965.

SOCIAL STRUCTURE AND POLITICAL INTEGRATION IN URBAN MEXICO

Larissa Lomnitz

Introduction

There are two possible approaches to understanding social structure. One approach—social class analysis—postulates an ideal model of class positions and then maps social reality onto it. The result is a set of structural relationships that explain, or seem to explain, the positions of various social groups at different times. This approach interprets politics by judging the extent to which the expected behavior of social classes accords with the ideal model.

Another approach, followed here, examines the interactions between people at different levels within the power structure. The actors describe social structure through their own performance, and through the conceptualizations they derive from their experiences within the system. Political wisdom, from this perspective, is not necessarily an understanding of how the power structure originated, or how it relates to a given model of class domination. In fact, such an understanding can be an obstacle to political wisdom as it is commonly conceived in Mexico. Fundamentally, there is an existing authority structure in Mexico. This authority structure can be altered, subverted or overthrown; yet there is an underlying assumption among actors that alternative structures will ressemble the present one in most relevant aspects. This seemingly "pragmatic" or "cynical" attitude toward political structure is actually common sense to members of Mexican society.

I neither intend to explain the origin of this attitude, nor offer it as an alternate theoretical framework to class structure. However, social structure seen as a set of horizontal layers, much like a layered cake, is almost trivially simple compared to the concept necessarily held by any Mexican politician. But I am not concerned with the relative correctness or validity of images or metaphors, but with the process by which actors are matched to positions within the existing power structure. From an analysis of this process emerges a model of social structure that reflects the complex political and ideological relations between individuals and their positions in the power system of Mexico.

The social structure of Mexico has been likened to a set of free-standing pyramids, each of which duplicates itself hierarchically like a crystal from top to bottom.[1] Although such a metaphor may be reconciled with class analysis, doubts have been expressed on this subject.[2] In this paper I suggest that such a pervasive structural image may reflect the pattern of horizontal and vertical social relations at the interpersonal level. In other words, this metaphor is as much a part of Mexican political culture as is the statified class model of European political culture. It elicits responses of loyalty, competition, and patterns of exchange and is a cultural fact of Mexico.

I shall define tentatively the following pyramids or "sectors" of the social structure of urban Mexico: (1) the "Public Sector," or state apparatus, including the administative bureaucracy and the state-owned or state-operated industries and concerns; (2) the "Labor Sector" or organized industrial proletariat; (3) the "Private Sector" including the national bourgeoisie, their allies, clients, and employees, private business and the independent liberal professions under their respective charters; and (4) the "Informal or 'marginal' sector" amounting to about 40 percent of the labor force in the cities,[3] and including all those not comprised in the three preceding "formal" sectors: under-employed, self-employed, or informally employed workers without job stability, social security, fringe benefits, minimum wage guarantees, bargaining power or nationwide organization.[4]

The flow of resources within the system is determined by the interaction of three variables: the direction of the relationship (horizontal or vertical), the kind of resource exchanged (capital, power, labor, information, political loyalty), and the mode of articulation (formal or informal). The first variable generates the basic pyramidal pattern of the structure; the second variable accounts for the existence of specialized sectors handling different kinds of resources; and the third variable explains the basic distinction between the formal and informal segments of urban society.

The Public Sector

Atop the Public Sector is a small power elite composed of the President, members of the Cabinet, and other high government officials whose political resources are measured by their decision-making power and by the number of dependent officials under their control.[5] Typically, each official is a patron to his subordinates, who depend on him for continued access to power and other resources.[6] Loyalty flows upward to the superior in proportion to the resources dispensed downward. Because each official is in turn a subordinate to a higher official, he may be likened to a broker who deals in political support at his level of the structure.[7] Eventually the entire sector (making allowances for personal rivalries and conflicting interests of power groups) is committed to the existing political system and shares an ideology that stresses state control as morally right and beneficial to the nation.[8]

The Mexican political system has been defined as corporative, populist, authoritarian, and patrimonial.[9] Corporative centralism in Mexico, which emerged from the fragmentation of power and from the regional struggles that followed the Revolution, is often credited with the implementation of economic development policies under conditions of political stability. To achieve such aims, a corporative regime characteristically employs

> cooptation of leaders, vertical or sectorial policy compartmentalization, permanent institutionalization of access, "juridization" or legalization of group conflicts through labor and administrative courts, state technocratic planning and resource allocation, a political culture stressing formalism, consensus and continuous bargaining; symbiotic relations with clientelist and patrimonial practices in certain issue areas and regime levels; periodic but systematic use of physical represssion and anticipatory intimidation.[10]

The system depends to a considerable degree on interpersonal bonding between leaders and officials at all levels. At the National University of Mexico,[11] almost from the time of their initial registration some students embark on a "political life career" independent of the field of study they have nominally chosen. Militant student groups (many of them representing political opposition tendencies) provide opportunities for the training of political leaders who eventually graduate into the public administration. Promotion within student groups depends on loyalty, dedication and personal charisma.[12]

The National University is also the main channel of social mobility providing access to bureaucratic jobs at the lower and middle echelons.[13] Clerks, administrators and technocrats are recruited by officials who supplement their jobs in ministries or federal agencies with part-time teaching positions at the University. This is not considered "moonlighting"—on the contrary, such officials are highly valued as linking the University with the Public Sector to which it ultimately belongs.[14]

If militant student groups are organized on the basis of personal loyalties towards leaders, much the same is true of the professional or technological groups. Able students in science, engineering, medicine, architecture, and so on, are spotted by instructors who become their tutors or thesis advisers. Networks based on personal loyalty to a tutor eventually become the backbone of research institutions, state corporations and technical task forces in the ministries and agencies.[15] As the National University represents the breeding ground for the elites in the Public Sector, so the various private universities provide the Private Enterprise Sector with the necessary leadership in administration and technological know-how.

The Structure of Groups: the Case of the National University

Each official within the Public Sector is a power broker engaged in a permanent process of negotiation for resources in exchange for political support. Each broker has a network of horizontal relations (colleagues, friends, relatives) enabling him to maneuver at his specific power level or to mobilize resources from other power systems, in order to strengthen his bargaining hand.[16] These mechanisms are built into the system and contribute to its flexibility and to its ability to deal with internal conflict.

At the National University of Mexico the internal structure of all groups is similar.[17] At the top there is a leader who generates loyalty and whose personality matches the nature of the group. If political, the student-leader must be well-informed and charismatic; if academic, he must be endowed with academic prestige. Immediately below the leader is an inner circle of trusted assistants or leading activists, followed by a second level, and so on. Social proximity to the leader is the main factor in individual ranking and for solidarity within the group. The entire student body—and indeed the university itself—may be thought of as a conglomerate of pyramidal structures (some formal and others informal), that include faculty, unions, research groups, political action groups, and even delinquent student gangs, all competing for resources, jobs, status, and power within the larger University pyramidal structure.

The formal University authorities are recruited among the faculty and tend to emphasize the explicit functions of an academic nature such as teaching, research, and cultural activities. Yet their implicit obligations include tasks that may conflict with academic objectives. For example, the lenient admissions policy is the result of political expediency rather than academic considerations. Political stability, initially a prerequisite for developing academic activities, is now an end in itself—the cardinal principle of the system.[18]

Since the administration sees political stability as its main task and rates its own members accordingly, the leadership of the informal (non-institutional) groups tends to further the social mobility of groups rising from the lower middle class. Since student unrest brings real problems to the attention of the administration, the activity of student leaders is consistent with the long-range preservation of the system and a basis for compromise can always be found. One result of such compromise is consolidation of the power of individual leaders on both sides of the issue.

When students are finally recruited into the bureaucracy they have undergone extensive informal schooling in the mechanics of group membership, and in the political subtleties of confrontation and compromise. More experienced leaders tend to rise to responsible positions and become power brokers within the civil service hierarchy and they award patronage to subordinates, whose loyalty is their main bargaining asset.[19]

Horizontal Relationships in the Formal Sector

In the Mexican urban structure, the circulation of resources is largely governed by patron-client relations. However, horizontal relationships provide necessary flexibility in the system by making available different kinds of resources at each articulation, each pyramidal sector specializing in a different type of resource: power, labor, and capital. Exchanges of power for capital, capital for labor, and labor for political support occur continuously at all levels of the system, emphasizing the importance of a broker in one sector having friends in the other two. Much of the way such linkages are made results from the personal backgrounds of the civil employees.

Some working-class families send their sons and daughters to the university to become civil servants. Liberal professionals have friends and colleagues in government. There is also some downward mobility among entrepreneurial families, so that some of their children and relatives end up in government positions. Labor leaders have sons and relatives in business, and so on. Professional people may move back and forth between jobs in industry and government.[20]

Brokers in one branch of business or government have friends who are brokers in another branch, a situation owing much to chance. A wholesale reshuffling of appointments occurs every six years in government; this mechanism brings former peers into positions where one of them commands extensive patronage. Brokers may change jobs in order to maneuver themselves under a patron to their liking or in a stronger bargaining position. Horizontal social contacts, especially kinship contacts, are the primary factors of mobility as they are elsewhere in Latin America, e.g. in Chile.[21]

The Organized Labor Sector

The three formal sectors compete for relative advantages and ultimate control over the system, although they are all committed to the maintenance of the system as they share interest in the benefits obtained from industrialization.[22] There is much internal dispute over which sector should have the decisive voice on economic and political matters. Relations between government and business have undoubtedly changed over the years, oscillating between outright opposition and "alliance for production";[23] but the Public Sector continues to keep the upper hand and to impose its political objectives. Private Enterprise has become increasingly dependent on the federal government, habitually relying on government assistance for loans, tariffs, and other protectionist measures, and to restrain the labor unions.

The Labor Sector is not just dependent on the Public Sector but is controlled by it through the Party apparatus. In exchange, the Labor Sector has obtained a uniform wage policy, social security and other fringe benefits, plus safeguards against the informal sector. The government consolidates its dominant position by gradually taking over key industries and basic resources (energy, steel, mining),[24] either alone or in partnership with Mexican and multinational corporations. Labor is the client sector, subordinated to both capital and state. Its resources are loyalty and work—the typical resources of clients.[25] However, the Capital Sector is also moving more and more towards a client position vis-à-vis the State.

Historically, the Labor Movement is a sector of the Institutional Revolutionary Party (PRI), organized as *Congreso del Trabajo* (Congress of Labor Federations). The most important labor federation is CTM, the Mexican Federation of Labor, with over 2,500,000 members in 1974.[26]

The CTM is formally a member of the Party.[27] Thus, in Mexico there is an explicit connection between the majority of organized labor and the corporative state; the latter controlling the former through the Party apparatus.

The CTM represents the largest of about 30 organizations affiliated to the *Congreso del Trabajo*,[28] with a likely total of 3 million members in 1975. The CTM is a complex, partially overlapping, organization of statewide federations, regional and local federations, based on geographical units, and industry-wide unions on a national and regional level. In any industrial plant, the local union is headed by a General Delegate, selected from among the delegates of the various plant departments. At a higher level, there is a Regional Section, with an Executive Committee and a number of commissions. The language of the union is the language of class struggle and mobilization for better wages and better working conditions, within a nationalistic context: "the economic emancipation of Mexico."[29]

CTM's power structure is hierarchical and is an integral part of the political apparatus of the nation, hence its dual function as a pressure group lobbying for greater social benefits and a greater share of the resources for labor and as an apparatus for political control of the working force. Each worker is a client of two patrons: the factory owner, manager of a corporation or state enterprise, and the union leader or Party boss.[30]

The Mexican industrial proletariat has become increasingly differentiated in skills, income, and status: foremen tend to become a privileged group,[31] and the union leadership has become a political bureaucracy headed by the old labor bosses, some of whom have been in power for as long as 40 years. The oligarchic model of union organization permeates all levels of the labor structure. Corruption is said to be endemic.

> Labor legislation affords a wide range of opportunities for government intervention in manipulating the unions. On the one hand, the "white" unions are industry-controlled and resist their incorporation into the official structure; they promote the paternalistic attitudes favored by the private sector. On the other hand, the government uses federations such as CTM. Unions which hold out against affiliation into government-sponsored or industry-sponsored organizations are pressured or co-opted

> through the affiliation of their leadership into the official Party. Leaders who resisted such an affiliation have been unseated, jailed or murdered. Their political movements have been suppressed and disbanded, or, during the 1950s taken over by government-sponsored leadership.[32]

There is an awareness, however, that industrial labor is privileged as compared to the informal sector, possessing steady jobs, fringe benefits, and guaranteed incomes. They usually succeed in obtaining a raise as well as improved conditions of housing, health, and training with each contract negotiation. Service workers and workers in the building trade are worse off than the industrial workers, representing a borderline group between organized labor and the informal sector. At the top of the scale, skilled workers "represent a labor aristocracy often used by patrons as middlemen in their dealings with the workers," some of whom become supervisors on behalf of management.[33]

The union leadership's paternalistic attitudes are encouraged by management. Conformity is obtained in "white" unions through management programs in housing, training, and company stores. Similarly, the government as patron exerts control through its own housing programs, social security system, retirement and pension funds and so on. Groups of workers cannot appear on their own behalf but must go through channels, i.e. through the union hierarchy. Political discipline is monolithically enforced from above; local leaders who refuse to participate, or who attempt to assert their independence, are regularly repressed.

However, the system uses repression only after all incentives have failed. For example, in larger private corporations, management will fire undesirable workers or even close down a plant in the knowledge that any subsequent claims will be settled to their satisfaction at a suitable level. Thus, since individual workers generally have no means of redress against the private corporations, they tend to avoid any action that has not been approved by the union leadersip.

The union, in effect, controls all jobs in the plant: loyal members are awarded better jobs, less dangerous assignments, more pleasant tasks, and better shifts. Such practices encourage the passivity and depoliticization of labor. In the long run, a worker needs the support of his section boss to get access even to the fringe benefits he is entitled to.[34]

In state-owned enterprises the management routinely overlooks the misuse of union funds in return for the loyalty of the union leadership. Jobs are sometimes awarded to the highest bidder and union leaders become wealthy. However, the body of labor legislation and, in particular, the Courts of Conciliation and Arbitration can be used to keep the bosses in line;[35] but young charismatic leaders who began their union careers as rebels against the old bosses were eventually co-opted or liquidated.[36]

Horizontal and Vertical Relations in the Labor Sector

Mexican workers socialize mostly within their extended family, and have little personal contact with co-workers.[37]

While the old pattern of vertical *compadrazgo* persists in smaller industries, and patrons are in demand as godfathers, in larger concerns it is largely the union leaders, foremen, and supervisors who seek such favors from members of management.[38]

Thus, there is a marked similarity between the vertical organization of the Labor Sector and that of the Public Sector, except that horizontal contacts in the former are largely restricted to the extended family and to godparenthood. Close relatives who get jobs in the plant represent the closest horizontal contacts of most workers.

Vertical mobility in the Labor Sector occurs through brokerage. Union leaders are brokers in a double capacity: within the union hierarchy (political brokerage) and between workers and management (economic brokerage). As a result of the union, the entire Labor Sector is upwardly-mobile; more than 50 percent of the sons of working-class parents rise into the "middle class," i.e. become white-collar workers, implying a high degree of contact between the Labor Sector and the lower levels of the state bureaucracy, or the clerical levels of private enterprise.[39]

The Private Sector

The Private Sector encompasses the owners of the means of production (industrialists, bankers), private business and commerce, and the white-collar workers and service workers formally employed in private business, i.e. enjoying some measure of job security and social security. It also includes liberal professionals working on their own, associated with professional associations.

The beginnings of industrialization in Mexico extend into the late nineteenth century. From that time onward, industrial development has been state-sponsored or state-supported.[40] After the Revolution, the Mexican state began nationalizing energy resources, thus subsidizing energy prices for industry. It also built electric power stations, roads, water systems, and communications, and provided a protectionist legal structure designed to benefit local industry and the National Finance Corporation (NAFINSA) supplied financial support. As far as the State was concerned, the Private Sector existed for the sole purpose of industrializing the country, particularly towards the production of consumer goods.[41]

We have studied a family group of around 600 persons, the descendants of a single nuclear family, which identifies ideologically with the Private Sector, but includes a relatively small group of really major industrialists.[42] Most relatives are administrators, employees or clients in the family industries and businesses, or have branched out into small businesses of their own. Self-reliance and the virtues of enterprise were stressed in opposition to civil service. Family business was the norm, since kinship provided the element of trust and loyalty an entrepreneur sought in his partners, associates, and administrators. The entrepreneur became the style-setter for a growing kin group that looked to him for leadership and protection. A vast network of patron-client relations developed as family businesses throughout Mexico began to be connected through intermarriage. Each patron was simultaneously a broker who provided income, protection, and economic opportunities in exchange for loyalty and prestige. After 1960, the introduction of modern technology, mass production, and mass marketing made the family business increasingly obsolete; yet the kinship network continues to operate in a less obvious fashion. Dynasties of entrepreneurs sit on each other's boards of directors; they combine their resources through reciprocal deals and matrimonial alliances, and they consciously support the family tradition.[43]

Hence the Private Sector is organized along hierarchical lines, not unlike those of the

Public Sector. At the top are major industrialists who head a small number of well-known business "groups": the Alfa Group in Monterrey, for example. Below these leaders are successive echelons of businessmen who are related to the leaders as clients, contractors, associates, bankers, and so on. Each of these leaders is also a broker in that he funnels resources (patronage, business, protection) to his associates and employees in exchange for loyalty to the patron and his enterprise.

These structures are duplicated within each industry or enterprise. From the owner(s) down, the hierarchy has a number of levels: directors, managers, vice presidents, production managers, and so on. The line of command is explicit in each case. However, the brokerage system cuts across class lines into the Labor Sector, as supervisors and labor leaders transmit the requirements of management down to the labor force.[44]

In small industries an owner may deal with his workers directly or through a trusted foreman. As the industry grows, so do the number of middlemen—vice presidents, managers, engineers, technicians, union officials, and so on. Ideally (from management's perspective), the supervisors become the union leaders as well. If the union is "red" (i.e. politically dependent on a structure other than management), the direct line of command becomes fuzzy and co-option intervenes, although this is a matter of degree rather than of substance, since negotiation is inevitably a feature of the brokerage process.

At a higher level, there is a hierarchy of industries and enterprises; some industries make parts for others, as in the automobile industry;[45] sons or relatives of major industrialists may set up their own industry which sells the entire production to the patron; or they may commercialize a patron's products or act as brokers on his behalf, or process some by-product, such as yogurt in dairy industries.[46] Every major industry or enterprise generates a large number of second-level businesses and provides work for many relatives.[47] A major industrialist may become associated with others in new ventures: one provides the capital and another the know-how, or (as in the housing industry) one provides the real estate and the other the builders and the capital. Businesses are dependent on financial groups, private or state banks, if they are not directly connected with one of the major financial groups in Mexico. And there are the ties with chain stores and other commercial outlets, many of which buy from each other and have their own brokerage chains all the way down to the lowliest store clerk.

Mexico's Private Sector is formally organized into four major business federations: CONCANACO (Federation of National Chambers of Commerce), CONCAMIN (Federation of Chambers of Industries), COPARMEX (Federation of Employers of the Mexican Republic), and CANACINTRA (National Chamber of the "Transformation Industry," or Consumer Goods Industry). Most industrialists and businessmen are members of one or more of these partially overlapping organizations, which accounted for more than 50 percent of the total investment in Mexico.[48] The rest is from investments of multinational corporations and from the State.

Twenty-nine decentralized state-owned corporations own 68.3 percent of the capital of Mexico's 100 largest corporations, and 17 large state-owned concerns controlled over 1.6 billion pesos (i.e. 71.5 percent of the assets of the 50 largest corporations).[49]

Thus, the state is not only in a position to threaten private business with financial takeover, it also controls the sources of energy and much of the raw materials needed by private industry. This is the basic fact of life of the business federations that mediate between private capital and the corporate state. Economic policy is the result of these top-level negotiations, which are very complex since there is a great deal of interpenetration between the two sectors; the state owns shares of many private corporations, and government industries continue to operate with considerable private investments.

The law makes membership in an employers' organization compulsory for all merchants or industrialists having assets in excess of 2,500 pesos. A local group of at least 20 industrialists or 50 merchants form a Chamber; the regional distribution of these chambers (as of the unions) is controlled by the Department of Industry and Commerce. Thus, the state keeps a registry of businessmen, who must join their local Chamber of Commerce (or Industry) in order to do business. The law also specifies the organization of the Chambers, which is analogous to that of the unions, and the active membership of a local Chamber must be at least 80 percent Mexican-born.

CONCAMIN, the national federation of industrial chambers, includes 60 local chambers plus 14 industrial associations (which have a lower standing than a chamber). CANACINTRA, the federation of consumer-goods industries, has a membership of 18,000 industrial concerns, divided into 60 sections according to the type of industry. COPARMEX, an employers' union (with an affiliation of about 10,000 employers, organized in 32 local chapters in 1970), is mainly concerned with representing the Private Sector in matters of labor legislation. CONCANACO, the Mexican federation of chambers of commerce, incudes all tax-paying commercial establishments. These four business federations are, in effect, brokerage offices engaged in lobbying the government on behalf of their members. And politicians are also interested in dealing with a few well-defined representative bodies rather than with individual businessmen. The representation of the chambers is, of course, limited, since most Mexican small businessmen or traders are not eligible for membership.[50]

The hierarchical structure of the Private Sector is reflected in the membership of the Boards of Directors of Mexican corporations. Many industrial concerns were initially family businesses that branched out along generational lines as a family group developed.[51] As a result of partnerships and marriage alliances, the original families coalesced into industrial "groups" whose members sit on each others' boards of directors. Large and small concerns are organized hierarchically by their relative importance and the business they do with each other.[52] Each group is normally headed by a senior industrialist with his closest associates according to rank in power and prestige; then the heads of the smaller concerns. The pattern is repeated within each corporation.

The Informal Sector

The formal and informal sectors in urban Mexico differ not so much in their social structure or relation to the process of production, but in their different modes of articulation with the economic and social resources of the society.[53] Job stability, or security of economic roles in general, is more relevant to the sectorial categorization than the actual tasks assigned to individuals within the economic structure.

Stability of employment therefore deserves infinitely more attention than it normally receives from social scientists who base their analysis simply on the amount of income received or the differential distribution of wealth.[54]

Security means membership in a formal structure. In urban Mexico, all structures are built on the principle of the pyramid: resources are channeled down from the top and loyalty and support are radiated up from the bottom. Such pyramidal structures exist in the ministries, corporations, unions, and shantytown action groups.[55] The difference between them lies in the mode of articulation to resources, formal and permanent in some cases and informal in others.[56]

"Marginality" or "the informal sector" refers to the broad social sector excluded from access to organized labor, bureaucratic jobs, and stable employment within one of the three formal sectors in general. Its members do not enjoy the specific benefits of industrialization—social security, stability of income, labor legislation, union membership, public housing, public health, access to institutional loans or credit, and so on.[57]

The informal sector also includes small family enterpreneurs, who produce goods and provide services comprising a considerable share of the urban economy, although, as a rule, they pay neither wages nor taxes. There are also jobbers, labor recruiters, and political brokers or organizers: a kind of "shantytown bourgeoisie" that, in some ways, represents a social transition between the informal and formal sectors.[58] All these brokers channel resources from the formal to the informal sector, in exchange for labor, services, and political support. But their articulation is informal and therefore the flow of resources is unstable and intermittent. Shantytown dwellers rely on informal networks of relatives and neighbors that provide a minimum of security through reciprocal exchange of goods and services, to survive.[59] Such horizontal neighborhood networks are characteristic of shantytowns; but similar forms of reciprocal exchange are also found among all levels in the three formal sectors, where they enhance social mobility and the circulation of resources among social peers.

Thus, regarding horizontal and vertical relations, the structural features of the informal sector are not essentially different from those of the formal sectors. For example, the shantytown networks are also labor pools that the more enterprising members can organize into action sets for unskilled or semi-skilled trades, as in the construction industry. The joint activities of such an action set may attain a certain degree of stability and specialization; then it becomes a quasi-group consisting of a leader (or patron) and his followers (or clients). The leader may control valuable resources, such as contacts outside the shantytown, that provide employment or political support. He may eventually become a small businessman, labor recruiter or political organizer.[60]

The three formal pyramids feed on the existence of the informal sector.[61] The leadership of the Organized Labor Sector can enforce discipline and cohesion (and maintain its privileges) because of the availability of large masses of unorganized labor eager to work at minimum wages and that can be quickly mobilized by shantytown recruiters. The Private Sector systematically uses unorganized labor in key industries (construction and garment industries, for example) and as strikebreakers in labor conflicts. Finally, the Public Sector manipulates the political support of the "marginals," as, for example, when thousands of shantytown dwellers are ferried by bus to participate in mass demonstrations and other public spectacles organized by the state.[62] None of these uses of "marginality" are institutionalized and none gives rise to formal brokerage roles.

As Worsley[63] has pointed out, the existence of a large informal sector has important implications for the question of class structure and the role of the state in developing countries. From the point of view of the society there is little actual difference between the standard of living of a worker in the formal sector and that of a minor civil servant in the bureaucracy. An industrial worker who is a union member but who is covered by social security becomes in fact, if not in name, a member of the middle class. The new exploited class is the informal sector.[64]

Integration

A conceptual model of the structure of interpersonal and group relationships in urban Mexico is proposed, entailing the following variables: (1) direction of the flow of exchange (horizontal and vertical); (2) kinds of resources exchanged (capital, power, work, loyalty, services, information, and so on);[65] (3) mode of articulation within the structure (formal or informal).

Every ego may be seen as placed at the center of a social network extending in all directions within the social structure. Horizontal bonds are between relatives, friends, and peers or associates at the same hierarchical level. The existence of horizontal bonds conditions, and is conditioned by, the flow of reciprocal exchange to and from ego, and consisting of goods, services, and information.

On the other hand, the structure also has a vertical dimension—hierarchy. Vertical bonds between ego and a superior or inferior imply a relationship that differs fundamentally from the horizontal relationship between peers—a patron-client relationship. These relationships are the main channels that distribute the resources of the system throughout the structure; capital and power flow downward, and work and loyalty are siphoned upward. The asymmetry of the exchange conditions the asymmetry of the relationship. Individuals receive loyalty and service from their subordinates and render loyalty and service to their superior. As a corollary of these services and loyalties, they receive material rewards and power from superiors and yield material rewards and power to their subordinates.[66] The amount of material rewards and power retained by ego defines the status of the individual as a broker in the structure.

The structures formed by horizontal bonds are reciprocity networks, such as kindred networks, friendship circles, cliques, and other ego-centered social networks, and are informal social fields without permanent or well-defined boundaries; they extend or contract according to the flow of exchange between their members.

In contrast, the flow of vertical resources tends to create formal groups, quasi-groups or action groups.[67] In urban Mexico, these groups, quasi-groups, or action groups have a similar configuration, no matter where in the structure they happen to be found. Each is a pyramid with a leader at the top and clients situated at various levels below the leader, ranked according to their proximity to the top. The leader is a broker who derives resources from his articulation to the larger structure, and who distributes a share of these resources to each follower according to his rank. In return, each client contributes services and loyalty to his superior, according to his proximity. The flow of loyalty toward the leader determines the social cohesion or solidarity within the group. This solidarity in turn determines the efficiency (political or otherwise) of the group, which enables the leader to derive additional resources from the structure. To understand these structures and exchange relations, "it is important to realize that traditional kinship and social exchange ties have been incorporated into exclusive structures and political institutions."[68]

Several groups that are equal and independent at a given hierarchical level may be subordinate to the same leader or broker at the next higher level. Leaders at a given level thus have an ambiguous relationship to each other. They are loyal to the same higher leader and they compete for the same resources. The principle of the organization may be defined as concentrating power at the top and fragmenting it downward. As the system increases in size, it generates more resources and thus allows the creation of more subordinate positions under each leader, more groups under each broker, and eventually more hierarchical levels throughout the structure.[69]

In Mexico, the structure is vertically segmented into sectors according to the kinds of resources generated by the various groups. In the Public Sector, the resource generated is political power while in the Private Sector, the resource generated is capital. One sector controls, the other produces. This entails a specialization in the kind of services rendered, the kind of work performed, the expectations attached to roles, the ideology and value systems, and the life styles. Each sector has its preferences in terms of residential neighborhoods, status symbols, entertainment, art forms, public posture and presentation of self.[70]

A third pyramid, officially defined as the Labor Sector, generates the third resource—labor. It supplies labor and political loyalty to the other two sectors and is therefore a client to both. Labor is basic to the production of capital and to the generation of political power. The Private Sector extracts surplus value and the Public Sector extracts political allegiance. The Labor Sector is also organized hierarchically and has its own leadership, which serves the dual purpose of exerting negotiating power vis-à-vis the other two sectors (in stability of jobs rather than wages) and controlling the labor base that might otherwise be an unstable element in the system.

The organizational principle of the system (concentration of power at the top and fragmentation of power at the base) is thus confirmed by the existence of three separate pyramids, or sectors. Each sector is loyal to the nation but competes against the other sectors for an increased share of access to resources. The State is materially embodied in the President, the ultimate patron of all sectors of Mexican urban society. According to most analysts, the Public Sector enjoys a controlling position over the other two sectors and over the system as a whole.

Articulation between the three sectors is provided at a formal level by the State: legal and compulsory organizations of capital and labor, formal instances of mediation and conflict-resolution as in the National Tripartite Commission, and political mediation at the level of the Party (actually, a federation of hierarchies in the Public and Labor Sectors which alternately confront and placate the Private Sector across the negotiating table). But the system of formal articulations alone is overly rigid and might lead to a society of castes permanently battling each other. Flexibility and fluidity in the system are provided by individual networks of reciprocal exchange that informally cut across hierarchical boundaries between the sectors. These networks circulate resources from one pyramid to another: bureaucratic information toward the Private Sector, economic information toward the Pubic Sector, political support, vital services of a bureaucratic and economic nature, and jobs or other opportunities among members of all networks. It is advantageous to have relatives or friends in all three sectors. Industrial workers may have a son or daughter in the civil service or the professions, or they set up a repair shop or service business. Industrialists have sons who become technocrats in the Public Sector. Politicians become investors or office-holders in private corporations,[71] while private businessmen are appointed to executive positions in state corporations and agencies. Some labor leaders have family connections with construction firms and may be influential in winning contracts in the Public Sector. The examples are endless and merely serve to underscore the fact that horizontal networks of relatives and friends provide a web of entangled bonds within and between sectors. If social energy is largely channeled along vertical lines within each sector, lubrication and fluidity in the manipulation of resources is provided largely by these horizontal reciprocal exchanges.

From ego's viewpoint, a reciprocity network is not merely a useful mechanism for obtaining certain resources, it is a resource in itself. The network may be mobilized on behalf of ego's job and may enhance his performance, thus making him more valuable to his superior and increasing his prospects for promotion. The entire system benefits from the existence of such informal contacts, which contain and eliminate sources of conflict at all levels. Political rivalry and infighting are kept within reasonable bounds, and a diffuse tacit solidarity is generated that helps assure the stabiliy of the system.

Of course, horizontal networks may also be used to channel public resources into private pockets. The boundary between reciprocal exchanges of favors and corruption is sometimes difficult to determine. As social distance increases between partners, so reciprocity grades into market exchange, and solidarity into complicity.

In the formal sectors, articulation between levels within a pyramidal structure is determined by rules of hierarchy and sealed by documents such as written contracts.[72] This mode of articulation is decisive. It ensures continuity of employment, social security, fringe benefits, and adequate labor protection quarantees and benefits. Each formal sector is undergirded by informal labor: "*eventuales*" or non-union labor in public and private industry, petty traders and artisans in commerce and the services, shantytown organizers and neighborhood leaders in politics.[73]

Their informal mode of articulation with the three sectors implies that these workers, artisans, and traders have no organization and no representatives who might negotiate on their behalf. Their action groups and quasi-groups are organized according to the pyramidal principle, as in the formal sectors, but they may be disbanded at will. Leadership is beset with problems of insecurity; hence the brokerage role is not institutionalized.

The distinction between a union member and an "*eventual*" is not one of culture, skills, or even income; some marginal brokers may earn more than most industrial workers of the formal sector. Yet there is a significant social distinction. Marginals who succeed in gaining access to a formal job tend to break away from shantytown networks and move into a part of town inhabited by members of the formal sector.[74] Access to security of employment means, in a larger sense, their incorporation into the mainstream of modern life as self-defined by the dominant social system and by the state apparatus.

In Latin America, industrialization implied modernization, rising standards of living, and prosperity in the cities at the expense of the countryside. Rural modernization created a population explosion but failed to provide incentives for peasants to stay in the village. Until around 1960, it was still possible to argue that the influx of migrants to the large cities represented a reserve labor pool that would eventually be absorbed into the urban proletariat. Then came the deceleration of industrial growth in Latin America, and—partly due to automation resulting from the appearance of modern corporations on the scene—the rate of creation of new jobs began to lag behind the influx of rural migrants and population growth.

The industrial proletariat responded by consolidating its privileges and, primarily, its access to jobs within the formal system. Labor unions became defensive associations that worked hand in hand with the state apparatus to protect the jobs of their members and families. Union membership also meant social security, government housing, and a recognized and well-defined structural relationship with the state. Marginals were potential or actual strike-breakers, whose presence served to depress the wages of the proletariat. Their natural interests conflicted rather than harmonized with those of the formal working class.

Conclusions

In conclusion, the social structure of urban Mexico may be described as a system of domination (or authority structure) based on pyramidal corporative entities called "sectors." The share of each individual and group in the resources of the system is determined by their position in the hierarchy and by the mode of articulation. The dominant groups are organized in two competing sectors vying for control of the system: the public sector and the private sector, both organized hierarchically. Above their rivalry, both sectors (plus the hierarchy of the Labor Sector) are interested in the maintenance of the system as such. This is expressed in the proliferation of an intricate mesh of social networks based on kinship and friendship, where information, goods, and services are traded along horizontal channels of reciprocity within and between sectors. These horizontal bonds of kinship and friendship represent one of the major resources of the system.

Another way of expressing this finding is to say that a given individual belongs and yields allegiance to two social categories, one horizontal and one vertical. His horizontal allegiance conforms to the metaphor of the social structure in Western urban societies, according to which the social continuum is divided into classes from top to bottom. But in urban Mexico, this metaphor does not exhaust the complexity of the situation. Class is a useful social category nevertheless, because horizontal solidarity is connected with reciprocal exchange, and because this form of exchange takes place between social equals. This is as true for shantytown dwellers as it is for middle-class college professors or for industrialists. A criterion for class identity in Mexico might be provided by the observation of whether a set of individuals engage in reciprocal exchange of information, goods and services.

The efficiency of the system as an apparatus of class domination does not mean that class conflict is absent. The purpose of this paper is not to deny the existence of conflict but to show how stability is maintained despite the enormous socio-economic inequalities and contradictions within Mexican society, and how interpersonal ties are translated into political opportunities.

Obviously, the system is not monolithic, since each power broker strives to gain influence, and to increase his share of the resources in competition with other brokers. However, this can become an element of stability when the formation of horizontal alliances based on common class interests is impeded. One feature of the Mexican political system that discourages such alliances is the complete turnover that occurs every six years in the brokerage structure of the Public Sector. Every incoming president institutes a new set of national powerholders. Disaffected groups do not join forces but bide their time, since they may gain access to power in the next administration.

Class solidarity and sectional loyalties do exist, but they are conditioned by the flow of exchange, one in the horizontal direction and the other in the vertical direction. Therefore, an individual deprived of vertical resources (as a shantytown dweller) will rely more heavily on class solidarity as a political mechanism than an individual who enjoys the trust and protection of a powerful patron. Clients who are formally articulated to the system through competent brokers seldom join protest movements.

The existence, at all levels, of horizontal as well as vertical bonds of solidarity explains the importance attributed to politics in the system. In Mexico, politics is the art of manipulating vertical against horizontal solidarities.

NOTES

[1]See Zaid 1979. Also Reyna and Weinard 1977; P. H. Smith 1979; J. Purcell and S. Purcell 1977; E. Stevens 1977.

[2]"Most forms of class analysis of Mexico are not entirely satisfying....Many important groups and factions do not have a class basis that is clear enough to make the observer feel comfortable with the concept of class 'factions'." (J. Purcell and S. Purcell 1980:224)

[3]Secretaría de Programación y Presupuesto 1979a.

[4]Portes 1978:39.

[5]P. H. Smith 1979:317-28.

[6]J. Purcell and S. Purcell 1980:204-5; Carlos and Anderson n.d.:7-8.

[7]Adams 1970; Wolf 1969a:17; Grindle 1977:10.

[8]Mexico City has by far the largest share of the Public Sector in the country. In 1976, the Federal Government included 18 ministries, 123 decentralized agencies, 292 federally-owned corporations, 187 official commissions and 160 development trusts, most of them in the capital (Grindle 1977:2-3). State enterprises, such as PEMEX, the national oil monopoly. employ tens of thousands of buraucrats and an even larger number of

[9]Reyna 1977:xi; Stevens 1977; Camacho 1980:23-27; Grindle 1977:5; J. Purcell and S. Purcell 1977:194.

[10]Schmitter 1974:101.

[11]L. Lomnitz 1977.

[12]According to P. H. Smith (1979:317-18), up to 70 percent of the top political leadership of Mexico is composed of National University alumni, and "old boys' networks" occur frequently among the upper echelons.

[13]López Cámara 1971:95.

[14]Camp 1980.

[15]L. Lomnitz 1977; Lomnitz, Mayer and Rees 1979. According to a recent study of one faculty at the National University of Mexico, nearly 70 percent of the alumni are currently employed in the civil service (Insunza 1978:4).

[16]Carlos and Anderson n.d.:7.

[17]L. Lomnitz 1977.

[18]L. Lomnitz 1977; Reyna 1974; Pérez Correa 1974.

[19]Zaid 1979:220-30. The negotiating process remains private in order to save face whatever the outcome of a negotiation.

In my work on the National University I showed how student leaders (or leaders of research or professionl groups, for that matter) entered into circumstantial alliances (or conficts) with other groups. Sometimes the informal linkage of leader-brokers extended to the top of the University administration, although when several groups coalesced on an issue, the administation attempted to deal with each group separately and privately.

The process of civil service position recruitment was studied in the Faculty of Veterinary Sciences (Lomnitz, Mayer and Reed 1979). The students were selected by their instructors on the basis of their leadership qualities as well as academic performance and, eventually, might rise to influential positions within the federal technocracy. The group structures described in the National University were closely duplicated in the ministries or state agencies.

Grindle (1977) pointed out, in her study of a Mexico City federal agency, that

> organizations offer incentives to individuals in exchange for contributions which advance the interests of the organization or its leadership. In order to acquire the incentives offered them, actors must accomplish certain explicit tasks in their roles as organized members...

Such tasks frequently require access to resources outside the organization proper, which may be obtained through friends: "Exchange in the external environment tends to be both vertical and horizontal" (Grindle 1977:28). Thus, political support from other segments of the bureaucracy (normally negotiable through hierarchical channels) is often the result of a reciprocal exchange between friends.

[20]Since the State is Mexico's largest employer, some of the big labor unions (e.g. the Union of Petroleum Workers, the Union of Electrical Workers) draw most of their membership from federal employees, and their leaders are formally or informally civil servants.

[21]L. Lomnitz 1971.

[22]Zaid 1979:230.

[23]J. Purcell and S. Purcell 1977; Villarreal 1977; Vernon 1977; Hansen 1978.

[24]Ceceña 1980.

[25]The Mexican Constitution of 1917 provides a separate legal status for industrial workers (Article 123, Section A) as distinct from civil servants and other unionized workers in the Public Sector (Article 123, Section B). They are covered by different social security systems: *Instituto Mexicano del Seguro Social* (IMSS) for Section A, and *Instituto de Seguridad y Servicios Sociales para Trabajadores del Estado* (ISSSTE) for Section B. The distinction is based

on occupational characteristics: industrial labor vs white collar and service personnel. Industrial workers in State enterprises such as PEMEX, the Federal Power Commission (CFE) or the various decentralized concerns are reckoned as industrial labor and their unions are organized under Section A, which provides for unrestricted striking rights as well as union control over hiring and firing. The Organized Labor Sector is therefore adequately defined by the Constitutional provisions. Non-labor unions such as the FSTSE (the Federation of Civil Servants) or SNTE (the National Federation of Teachers), though extremely powerful, are considered a part of the Public Sector.

[26]Zapata 1976:103-4.

[27]For further details, see Zapata 1976; Reyna and Miquet 1976; Roxborough n.d.a; Camacho 1976; Córdova 1979.

[28]Some of the others are the Union of Petroleum Workers, the Union of Electrical Power Workers, the Union of Railroad Workers, the Union of Miners, and some of the smaller rival federations such as CROM, CROC, and so on.

[29]In 1963, the CTM included 11 "confederations," 131 labor federations, and 1059 unions, nearly half of the unions in the country. Yet the organized labor sector represents only 22.9 percent of the gainfully employed population, according to the 1970 census (Zapata 1976:12).

[30]Vellinga 1979:78, 119-25; Stevens 1977; Camacho 1976; Reyna and Miquet 1976.

[31]Reyna and Miquet 1976:14-15; Vellinga 1979:58.

[32]Vellinga 1979:72.

[33]Vellinga 1979:103; Camacho 1976.

[34]Camacho 1976.

[35]Camacho 1976:24.

[36]The monolithic nature of the labor system has been exaggerated. The union leadership is fragmented and weak as a group, and the nature of their control over the membership varies among unions. In general, however,

> the CTM leadership has been able to transform itself into a stratum of professional career bureaucrats, perpetually re-elected in unrepresentative meetings, and enriching itself by the selling of contracts (to the employers) and the selling of jobs (to the workers). Violence and state intervention in this system is used selectively and probably not very frequently (Roxborough n.d.a:11).

[37]In Monterrey it was found that only 17 percent of the workers had any daily personal contact with co-workers, while more than 50 percent said they saw their co-workers "never, or very occasionally" outside of working hours. Those who did usually had a small group of friends from their immediate working environment; workers from another plant were befriended very rarely. The same pattern was found with respect to extra-curricular activities (besides union membership). Only 20 percent participated in any kind of organized activity, and most of them through industry-sponsored sports clubs while only 7 percent of the "activists" were involved in political organizations (Vellinga 1979:196-97).

[38]As many as 17.4 percent of the godfathers in Vellinga's sample belonged to the middle or upper class (Vellinga 1979:207).

About 30 percent of the union membership have occupied some elected post on the executive committee or on a commission at one time or another, but few of them become professional union leaders. Typically, a leader begins his career by assiduously attending union meetings. He becomes a union activist by participating, voting and, mainly, speaking at meetings. Initially he may be elected a section delegate, dealing with personal labor conficts between a worker and a foreman or supervisor and often mediating between workers and the executive committee.

As a next step in his career, the leader may become a member of a union committee (Justice, Treasury, Vigilance, and so on), serving under the executive committee; from there he may be promoted General Secretary of his local union. Vellinga found that these promotions had little to do with rank-and-file support: most workers expressed distrust of the union leadership and were skeptical of their own influence on the decision-making process (Vellinga 1979:210).

[39]Vellinga 1979; Schensul 1976:150-63.

[40]Wilkie 1967.

[41]By 1950, 88 percent of the consumer goods in Mexico were locally produced (Derossi 1977; J. Purcell and S. Purcell 1977; NAFINSA 1971; Mayer 1968; Vernon 1977; Hansen 1978).

[42]Lomnitz and Pérez-Lizaur 1978.

[43]Lomnitz and Pérez-Lizaur 1978; Salazar 1971.

[44]Valenti Nigrini 1978.

[45]Bennet and Sharpe 1977.

[46]Lomnitz and Pérez-Lizaur 1978.

[47]For example, an architectural firm headed by kin from another branch of the family, a trading company owned by a pair of nephews, a son in charge of trucking, another set of relatives who are suppliers or buyers, others who are contractors or jobbers, and so on.

[48]Alcazar 1977.

[49]These state corporations included PEMEX (the State oil monopoly, largest corporation in Latin America); *Banco de México*, the Mexican federal reserve bank; CFE, the National power commission; NAFINSA, the national finance corporation; *Teléfonos de México*, the telephone company; *Altos Hornos de México*, the national steel concern; and finance organizations such as *Nacional Azucarera*, *Banobras*, *Banco de Crédito Rural*, *Somex*, and so on. Among the 50 next prominent corporations (i.e. ranking 51st. to 100th) there are also important state concerns such as AEROMEXICO (the national airline), *Ferrocarriles del Estado* (the national railroads), CONASUPO (the national retail chain for low-income groups), and important national corporations in copper, fertilizers, fishing, truck manufacturing, newsprint, petrochemicals and many others (Ceceña 1980:7A).

[50]Alcazar 1977; Schafer 1973.

[51]Cinta 1980; Cordero and Santin 1977.

[52]Cordero and Santin (1977:8) were able to identify 131 such groups in the Mexican private industrial sector.

[53]Uzzell 1980:40.

[54]Worsley 1978:3.

[55]L. Lomnitz 1977; 1978.

[56]We have described elsewhere the case of a labor recruiter informally known as "El Diablo," who had as many as 400 construction workers in his employment at a given time (L. Lomnitz 1978). "El Diablo" had an elaborate structure of foremen, "sergeants" and "lieutenants" under his command; yet there were no written documents, such as contracts or receipts, between "El Diablo" and the construction company, and certainly none between he and his workers. At the height of a job, "El Diablo" earned more than the engineer who hired him; but on completion, the engineer continued to draw his salary while "El Diablo" went back to the shantytown. The pyramidal structure of his labor organization was not formal, and it disintegrated as soon as the access to resources was broken.

[57]In metropolitan Mexico City, the informal or marginal sector is estimated at 35.5 percent of the income-earning population (Secretaría de Programación y Presupuesto 1979b:14).

[58]Cornelius 1972; Montaño 1976; Eckstein 1978.

[59]L. Lomnitz 1978, 1977; Alonso 1980.

[60]Another example is the widespread use of "*maquila*" or jobbing in the shantytowns, especially in the needle trade (OIT/INFONAVIT 1976). The shantytown brokers farm out work among the female members of the networks; they

require a basic weekly production from each worker. Wages and working conditions are much lower than those required by law. Marginality also means lack of legal protection and vulnerability to all forms of exploitation. The "*maquila*" broker is not a member of a formal sector, any more than his clients: he has no written contract with the clothing manufacturer and he can be dismissed if he fails to fill his work quota.

[61]Portes 1980.

[62]Durazo 1980.

[63]Worsley 1978.

[64]Portes 1980.

[65]See also Blau (1964) and Befu (1977:225-58).

[66]For further understanding of brokerage and political clientism in other contexts, see: Schmidt et.al. 1977; Greenfield and Stricken n.d.; Boissevain n.d.; and Eisenstadt and Roniger 1975.

[67]Mayer 1968.

[68]Carlos and Anderson 1980:6.

[69]Adams 1975:45-48; 1980.

[70]An example of ideological differences between organized workers and the informal sector can be found in the study of Davis, Coleman, et.al. 1980.

[71]Aguilar 1979.

[72]Portes 1980:18.

[73]In 1976, the informal sector in the three metropolitan areas (Mexico City, Monterrey, and Guadalajara) was distributed as follows: 36.2 percent in labor, 23 percent in commerce and 30.2 percent in small-scale production and handicrafts (Secretaría de Programación y Presupuesto 1979b). These figures fail to reflect the importance of the informal sector in the economy. In the petroleum industry, as in the construction industry, most of the non-clerical labor is done by "*eventuales.*" Similarly, a large share of the retail trade is in the hands of unlicensed small tradesmen, and there is a majority of informal workers in the service occupations (domestic help, gardeners, janitors, watchmen, waiters, washerwomen, cleaning women, messengers, carriers and so on).

[74]L. Lomnitz 1977:133-34.

GLOSSARY

Animate objects have plurals in Nahuatl, but inanimate objects do not draw this distinction. Accordingly, we have given both plurals and singulars of animate words in Nahuatl; however, we have used English pluralization in the text, i.e., *s*, to distinguish singular and plural inanimate objects in keeping with the feel of the phrasing in English.

Acordada. Late colonial legal-judicial body empowered to apprehend, try, and punish highway bandits and other provincial criminals.

Agrarismo. Official and quasi-official policy "favoring" the agrarian sector and the distribution of land to the peasantry.

Agrarista. Supporter of agrarismo (q.v.).

Albacea. Executor of an estate.

Alcalde. Judge and cabildo (q.v.) member.

Alcalde mayor. Spanish official exercising administrative and judicial authority over a given district.

Alcaldía. District or jurisdiction of an alcalde (q.v.).

Alcadía mayor. The office and jurisdiction of an alcalde mayor (q.v.).

Alguacil. Constable.

Alhóndiga. Public granary.

Almud. One-twelfth of a fanega (q.v.).

Altepetl. A town; literally, water and hill.

Apoderado general. General grant of power of attorney.

Asesor. Legal consultant or advisor.

Audiencia. Highest court of appeals and council of state, sharing authority with, and/or presided over by, a viceroy.

Aviador. Capitalist; entrepreneur.

Ayuntamiento. Town council, usually of a cabecera (q.v.).

Barrio. District located within or immediately outside an urban center.

Braza. Two varas (q.v.).

Cabecera. A politically independent town; the administrative capital center.

Cabildo. Town council.

Cacicazgo. Institution of cacique (q.v.) rule; patrimony of a cacique.

Cacique. Indian ruler of a town; later, a self-selected strongman.

Caciquismo. Government of control by caciques (q.v.).

Calpixqueh. Aztec tribute collector (sg. calpixqui).

Calpolli. Originially a kin group, but by the time of the Spanish Conquest, a residential and land-holding unit. Commonly spelled calpulli.

Campesino. Peasant.

Canónigo doctoral. Lettered prebend.

Casa cural. Curate house; the religious building of a town.

Casa real. Royal palace; the principal political building of a town.

Catedrático. Professor.

Caudillo. A political boss.

Cédula. Royal order.

Chantre. Precentor; musical director.

Chinampa. Chinampan; man-made aquatic garden.

Cocoliztli. Pestilence.

Cofradía. Sodality; religious brotherhood.

Colegiata. Collegiate church having a charter of canons and presided over by a dean.

Colegio de abogados. Official body empowered to determine which attorneys could practice in the audiencia (q.v.).

Compadrazgo. Relationship through godparents.

Conciliario. An officer of the Colegio de Abogados (q.v.).

Congregación. Concentration of scattered populations.

Consulado. Merchant guild; the court of.

Coquìtào. Great lord (Zapotec).

Corregidor. Spanish officer in charge of a district.

Corregimiento. Institution or jurisdiction of a corregidor (q.v.).

Creole. Mexican-born person of Spanish descent.

Cuartel mayor. A principal district of a city.

Cuartel menor. A smaller district of a city.

Departamento. A political division of the country; at times equivalent to a state of the republic; at other times a district within a state.

Distrito. A political subdivision of a state or departamento (q.v.).

Doctrina. Parochial jurisdiction or district.

Don. Honorific title.

Encomendero. Holder of an encomienda (q.v.).

Encomienda. A grant of Indians as tribute payers.

Ejido. Community lands.

Escribanía. Notoriate.

Escribano. Notary or scribe.

Estancia. Subordinate community; a farm.

Eventuales. Non-union labor.

Familiar. Police of the Inquisition.

Fanega. A dry measure; approximately 1.5 bushels.

Fiscal. Prosecutor.

Fuero. Special corporate privilege.

Gobernador. Governor; highest town official.

Guarda de pito. Municipal constable or watchman.

Guarda farol. Night watchman.

Hacendado. Owner of a hacienda (q.v.).

Hacienda. Large landed estate.

Hidalgo. Minor Spanish nobleman.

Hospicio. Poorhouse.

Intendencia. Intendancy. Form of provincial government introduced to New Spain in 1786 under Bourbon reforms; replaced gobiernos, corregimientos (q.v.), and alcaldías (q.v.).

Intendente. Chief executive officer of each of the regions, or intendencies (q.v.), of New Spain.

Jefatura. Official headquarters.

Jefe. Official title of the occupant of the office of intendente.

Jefe político. Chief administrative officer of a political district.

Joàna. Principales (q.v.) or nobles (Zapotec).

Juez de paz. Justice of the peace.

Juez ordinario. Judge of the municipal court; also called alcalde ordinario or alcalde constitucional.

Juez receptor. Special judge appointed to investigate and hear certain cases, especially those involving official misconduct.

Junta. Assembly.

Juzgado. Court of justice.

Juzgado general de Indias. The Royal Indian Court.

Licenciado. Lawyer.

Macehualli. Indian commoner (pl. macehualtin).

Maximato. Period of political domination of P. E. Calles, 1929-1933.

Mayehqueh. Indian serfs ranking below the macehualli (q.v.) class (sg. mayehqui *or* mayeh).

Mayorazgo. An entail.

Mayordomo. Pre-Conquest: a calpixque (q.v.) or tribute collector; Post-Conquest: a fiscal overseer.

Mestizo. Person of mixed white and Indian ancestry.

Milpa. Milpan; cultivated field.

Mulato. Person of mixed white and black ancestry.

Municipalidad. Political subdivision of a distrito (q.v.).

Municipio. The smallest administrative unit; a township-sized area governed by a cabildo (q.v.) or an ayuntamiento (q.v.).

Obraje. Workshop, especially of textiles.

Oficial mayor. Chief clerk.

Oidor. Judge of a civil court.

Padrón. A census record.

Parcialidad. Large section of a town.

Parroquia. Parish.

Partido. Political subdivision of an intendancy.

Pilli. Aztec noble (pl. pipiltin).

Pochtecah. Aztec merchants (sg. pochtecatl).

Porfiriato. Era of the presidency and political domination of Porfirio Díaz, approximately 1876-1910.

Prefecto. The executive officer of a departamento (q.v.).

Prefectura. Prefecture.

Presidente. The chief executive officer of an ayuntamiento (q.v.).

Principal. Indian noble or honored community elder.

Proceso. Legal process or suit.

Propietario. Tenured parish priest.

Protomedicato. Official body that regulated the medical profession.

Provincia. Province.

Ranchero. Owner of a rancho (q.v.).

Rancho. Ranch, also a small town.

Real. One-eighth of a peso.

Real Audiencia. See audiencia.

Recogimiento. A house of corrections.

Reforma. Reform; specifically, the reformative movement and political system of the mid-nineteenth century.

Regidor. Councilman in a cabildo (q.v.).

Relator. Legal narrator.

Repartimiento. Usually, a labor draft.

República. Republic; towns of under 3000 population.

Sala de crimen. Criminal court.

Síndico. Legal officer and trustee of the ayuntamiento (q.v.).

Sonorense. Ideal of changing Mexico from peasant to farmer agriculture.

Subdelegado. The chief administrative and judicial officer of a partido (q.v.).

Subprefecto. The chief executive officer of a partido (q.v.).

Sujeto. Subject town.

Teccalli. A noble house into which the principales (q.v.) were organized; also spelled teuccalli.

Telpochcalli. Aztec school for commoners.

Teniente. Lieutenant or assistant.

Tepache. A fermented beverage, usually made from pulque, sugar, and fruit.

Tepixqueh. Calpolli (q.v.) officers (sg. tepixqui).

Tequitlahtoh. Steward responsible for assignment of tribute and labor to vassals of a native lord; also spelled tequitlahtohqui (pl. tequitlahtohqueh).

Terrazguero. Farm laborer; serf.

Tlahtoani. Native ruler (pl. tlahtoanih *or* tlahtoanimeh).

Tlahtohqueh. Plural variant of tlahtoani (q.v.); sg. tlahtoh *or* tlahtohqui). **Tlahxilacalehqueh**. Barrio (q.v.) dwellers (sg. tlahxilacaleh *or* tlahxilacalehqui).

Topil. Hispanism for topileh (q.v.).

Topileh. Officer of a calpolli (q.v.) or of a town (pl. topilehqueh).

Tumulto. Uprising, revolt.

Vara. Staff of office; also a unit of measure, about 33 inches.

Vecino. Citizen or resident.

Villa. A major Spanish settlement.

Visita. Official tour of inspection.

BIBLIOGRAPHY

ABBREVIATIONS USED IN CITING MATERIALS

ARCHIVES

-RAMOS (branches)

AGEO		Archivo General del Estado de Oaxaca
	-C	Catastros
	-DMA	Documentos de la Memoria Administrativa
	-DOS	Decretos y Ordenes Superiores
	-G	Gobierno
	-JP	Jefes Políticos
	-Juz	Juzgados
	-LE	Legajos Encuadernos
AGI		Archivo General de Indias, Sevilla
	-AM	Audiencia de México
	-IG	Indiferente General
AGN		Archivo General de la Nación, México
	-A	Acordada
	-B	Bandos
	-C	Civil
	-Con	Consulado
	-CP	Carceles y Presidios
	-Cr	Criminal
	-GP	Generál de Parte
	-HJ	Hospital de Jesus
	-I	Indios
	-M	Mercedes
	-O	Ordenanzas
	-P	Padrones
	-RA	Real Audiencia
	-RCD	Reales Cédulas Duplicadas
	-T	Tierras
	-Ta	Tabaco
AGJ		Archivo General del Juzgado de México
AHA		Archivo Antiguo de Ayuntamiento, México
	-Cd	Cedulario
	-CG	Carceles en General
	-Co	Compendio

	-D	Desagüe
	-JP	Juntas de Policía
	-O	Ordenanzas
	-PG	Policía en General
	-PP	Panaderías y Pulperías
	-PSC	Presidio de San Carlos
	-RACCP	Real Audiencia–Carceles de Ciudad–Presos
AHN		Archivo de Notarías del Departmento del Distrito Federal, México
AJ		Archivo Judicial del Tribunal Superior de Justicia de Distrito Federal
	-LR	Libro de Reos
	-P	Penal
AJT		Archivo del Juzgado de Teposcolula
AJTL		Archivo del Juzgado de Tlacolula
	-Jus	Justicia
AMT		Archivo del Municipio de Teposcolula
BNM		Biblioteca Nacional, México
BNP		Bibliothèque Nationale de Paris
MNA-AH		Museo Nacional de Antropología, Mexico, Archivo Histórico
UT G-15		University of Texas, Nettie Lee Benson Latin American Collection, Mexican Manuscripts, G-15 "Documentos relativos al clero en la Nueva España"

FREQUENTLY CITED MATERIAL

AFAMBU	*La administración...*
DM	*Diario de México*
ENE	*Epistolario de Nueva España*
GM	*Gazeta de México*
HMAI	*Handbook of Middle American Indians*
IVMC	*Instrucción del Virrey Marqués de Croix...*
IVNE	*Instrucceiones que los vireyes...*
LTC	*Libro de Testamentos de Culhuacan*
PNE	*Papeles de Nueva España*

Acosta Saignes, Miguel

1945 "Los pochteca, ubicación de los mercaderes en la estructura social tenochca." *Acta Antropológica* 1:9-54.

1946 "Los teopixque: organización sacerdotal entre los Mexica." *Revista Mexicana de Estudios Antropológicos* 8:147-205.

Adams, R. N.

1970 "Brokers and Career Mobility Systems in the Structure of of Complex Societies." *Southwestern Journal of Anthropology* 26:315-27.

1975a "Harnessing Technological Development." In Peggie and Lynch 1975.

1975b *Energy and Structure.* Austin: University of Texas Press.

La administración de D. Fray Antonio María de Bucareli y Ursua, cuadragésimo sexto virrey de México.

1936 2 Vols. Mexico: Talleres Gráficos de la Nación.

Aguilar, Alonso

1979 "El estado y la burguesía." *Estrategia* 1:20-61.

Ajorfin, Francisco de

1958 *Diario de viaje que por orden de la sagrada congregación de propaganda fide hizo a la América septentrional en el siglo XVIII.* 2 Vols. Madrid: Maestre.

Alamán, Lucas

1883-1885 *Historia de Méjico.* 5 Vols. Mexico: Imprenta de J. R. Lara.

Alcazar, Marco Antonio

1977 *Los agrupamientos patronales.* Mexico: El Colegio de México, CEI, Jornadas 66.

Alemán, Francisco and Juan B. Iguíniz

1909-1910 *Biblioteca histórica jalisciense.* Guadalajara: Imp. de J. M. Yguíniz.

Almond, Gabriel A., Scott C. Flanagan, and Robert J. Mundt

1973 *Crisis, Choice, and Change.* Boston: Little, Brown and Company.

Almond, Gabriel A., and G. Bingham Powell, Jr.

1966 *Comparative Politics: A Developmental Approach.* Boston: Little, Brown and Company.

Alonso, Jorge

1980 *Lucha urbana y acumulación de capital.* Mexico: CISINAH.

Alonso, Jorge, Alonso Corcuera Garza, and Roberto Melville

1974 *Subsistencia y exploitación.* Mexico: CISINAH.

Anales de Cuauhtitlan

1945 *Códice chimalpopoca. Anales de cuauhtitlan y leyenda de los soles.* Feliciano Velázquez, trans., Mexico: Universidad Nacional Autónoma de México.

Anderson, A. J. O., Frances Berdan, and James Lockhart

1976 *Beyond the Codices: The Nahua View of Colonial Mexico.* Berkeley: University of California Press.

Anderson, Bo, and D. Willer

nd *Social Exchange Networks: The Elementary Theory and its Applications.* Forthcoming

Anna, Timothy E.

1978 *The Fall of Royal Government in Mexico City.* Lincoln: University of Nebraska Press.

Antigüedades de México

1965 4 Vols. Mexico: Secretaría de Hacienda y Crédito Público.

Arias, Patricia, and Lucia Bazán

1979 *Demandas y conflicto: El poder político en un pueblo de Morelos.* Mexico: Editorial Nueva Imagen.

Ariés, Philippe.

1981. *The Hour of Our Death.* New York: Knopf.

Armillas, Pedro

1942-1944 "Oztuma, Gro., fortaleza de los Mexicanos en la frontera de Michoacán." *Revista Mexicana de Estudios Antropológicos* 6:165-75.

1951 "Mesoamerican Fortifications." *Antiquity* 25:77-86.

Artiles, Jenaro.

1969 "The Office of Escribano in Sixteenth-Century Havana," *Hispanic America Historical Review* 49:489-502.

Aubin, Joseph Marius Alexis

1886 "Mapa quinatzin, cuadro histórico de la civilización de Tezcuco. Fragmento de la obra de M. Aubin titulada: "Mémoire sur la peinture didactique et l'écriture figurative des anciens Mexicaines," traducido para los "Anales de Museo" por Francisco Martínez Calleja." *Anales del Museo Nacional de México* época 1, 3:345-68.

Avila, Manuel

1969 *Tradition and Growth: A Study of Four Mexican Villages.* Chicago: University of Chicago Press.

Azaola Garrido, Elena, and Esteban Krotz

1976 *Política y conflicto.* Mexico: SEPINAH.

Báez Macías, Eduardo

1969 "Ordenanzas para el establecimiento de alcaldes de barrio en la Nueva España. Ciudades de México y San Luis Potosí." *Boletín del Archivo General de la Nación* 10:5-50

Bailey, David C.

1978 "Revisionism and the Recent Historiography of the Mexican Revolution." *Hispanic American Historical Review* 58:62-79.

Barlow, Robert H.

1945 "Dos relaciones antiguas del pueblo de Cuilapa, estado de Oaxaca." *Tlalocan* 2:18-28.

1947 "Relación de Zacatula, 1580." *Tlalocan* 2/3:258-68.

1949 *The Extent of the Empire of the Culhua Mexica. Ibero-Americana* 28. Berkeley: University of California Press.

Bartra, Roger, et. al.

1975 *Caciquismo y el poder político en el México rural.* Mexico: Siglo XXI.

Bazán Alarcón, Alicia

1963 "El tribunal de la acordada y la delincuencia en la Nueva España." M.A. thesis, Universidad Nacional Autónoma de México.

Beals, Ralph L.

1946 *Cherán: A Sierra Tarascan Village.* Washington, DC: United States Government Printing Office.

Befu, Harumi

1977 "Social Exchange." *Annual Review of Anthropology* 6. Palo Alto: Annual Reviews, Inc.

Bennet, D. and K. Sharpe

1977 "Controlling the Multinationals: The Ill Logic of Mexicanization." Mimeographed.

Berdan, Frances F.

1975 *Trade, Tribute and Market in the Aztec Empire.* Unpublished Ph.D. dissertation, University of Texas–Austin.

n.d. "Aztec Merchants and Markets: Local-Level Economic Activity in a Non-Industrial Empire." *Mexicon*, in press.

Beristáin de Souza, José Mariano

1816-1821 *Biblioteca hispanoamericana septentrional.* 3 Vols. Mexico: A. Valdés.

Bernal, Ignacio

1966 "Teotihuacan, Capital de imperio?" *Revista Mexicana de Estudios Antropológicos* 20:95-110.

Bernal de Bugeda, Beatriz

1975 "Situación jurídica de la mujer en las Indias Occidentales." In Bialostosky de Chazán et. al. 1975.

Berry, Charles

1981 *Reform in Oaxaca, 1856-76.* Lincoln: University of Nebraska Press.

Berthe, Jean-Pierre

1958 "Las minas de oro del Marqués del Valle en Tehuantepec, 1540-47." *Historia Mexicana* 8:122-31.

Bialostosky de Chazán, Sara

1975 "Condición social y jurídica de la mujer azteca." In Bialostosky de Chazán et. al. 1975.

Bialostosky de Chazán, Sara, et. al.

1975 *Condición jurídica de la mujer en México.* Mexico: Universidad Nacional Autónoma de México.

Blau, Peter

1964 *Exchange and Power in Social Life.* New York: John Wiley and Sons, Inc.

Bock, Philip K.

1969 *Peasants in the Modern World.* Albuquerque: University of New Mexico Press.

Boege, Eckart

1979 *Desarrollo del capitalismo y transformación de la estructura de poder en la región de Tuxtepec, Oaxaca.* Mexico: Escuela Nacional de Antropología e Historia.

Bohannon, Paul

1967 *Law and Warfare.* Garden City, NJ: Natural History Press.

Boissevain, J.

1974 *Friends of Friends.* Oxford: Basil Blackwell.

Bolaños Cacho, Miguel

1902 *Memoria administrativa presentada por el Lic. Miguel Bolaños Cacho, gobernador interino constitucional del estado de Oaxaca a la XXI legislatura del mismo, el 17 de septiembre de 1902.* Oaxaca: Imprenta del Comercio.

Boni, Felix G. and Mitchell A. Selligson

1973 "Applying Quantitative Techniques to Quantitative History: Poverty and Federal Expenditure in Mexico." *Latin American Research Review* 8:105-10.

Borah, Woodrow

1982 "The Spanish and Indian Law: New Spain." In Collier, Rosaldo, and Wirth 1982.

Borah, Woodrow, and Sherburne F. Cook

1960 *The Population of Central Mexico in 1548. Ibero-Americana 43.* Berkeley: University of California Press.

Borgonio Gaspar, Guadalupe

1954-1955 "Organización militar de los Tenochca." *Revista Mexicana de Estudios Antropológicos* 14:381-83.

Bosch Gimpera, Pedro

1966 "Pueblos e imperios." *Revista Mexicana de Estudios Antropológicos* 20:9-39.

Brading, D. A.

1971 *Miners and Merchants in Bourbon Mexico 1763-1810.* Cambridge: Cambridge University Press.

1981 "El clero mexicano y el movimiento insurgente de 1810." *Relaciones: Estudios de Historia y Sociedad* II:5:5-26.

Brandenburg, Frank R.

1964 *The Making of Modern Mexico.* Englewood Cliffs, NJ: Prentice-Hall, Inc.

Brioso y Candiani, Manuel

1943 *La evolución del pueblo oaxaqueño.* Mexico: Imprenta "A Su Orden."

Britton, John A.

1979 "Teacher Unionization and the Corporate State in Mexico, 1913-1945." *Hispanic American Historical Review* 59:674-90.

Brooks, Francis

1976 *Parish and Cofradía in Eighteenth-Century Mexico.* Unpublished Ph.D. dissertation, Princeton University.

Burgoa, Francisco de

1934 *Geográfica descripción.* Tomo II. Mexico: Publicaciones del Archivo General de la Nación.

Burkett, Eleanor

1978 "Indian Women and White Society: The Case of Sixteenth Century Peru." In Lavrin 1978b.

Burkholder, Mark A. and D. S. Chandler

1977 *From Impotence to Authority.* Columbia: University of Missouri Press.

Cabrera y Quintero, Cayetano

1746 *Escudo de armas de México: celestial protección de esta nobilísima ciudad.* Mexico.

Callahan, William J.

1971 "The Problem of Confinement: An Aspect of Poor Relief in Eighteenth Century Spain." *Hispanic American Historical Review* 51:1-24

Calnek, Edward E.

1978 "El sistema de mercado de Tenochtitlan." In Carrasco and Broda 1978.

Camacho, Manuel

1975 "La huelga de Saltillo, un intento de regeneración obrera." *Foro Internacional* XV:74-151.

1976 "Control sobre el movimiento obrero de México." *Las fronteras del estado Mexicano* , Mexico: El Colegio de México.

1980 *La clase obrera en la historia de México.* Mexico: Siglo XXI.

Cámara, Fernando

1952 "Religious and Political Organization." In Tax 1952.

Camp, Roderic Ai

1980 *La clase obrera en la historia de México: el futuro immediato.* México: Siglo XXI.

1977 "La campaña presidencial de 1929 y el liderazgo político en México." *Historia Mexicana* 27:231-59.

1976 *Mexican Political Biographies—1935-1975.* Tucson: University of Arizona Press.

Cancian, Frank

1965 *Economics and Prestige in a Maya Community.* Stanford: Stanford University Press.

1967 "Political and Religious Organizations." In HMAI 6.

1972 *Change and Uncertainty in a Peasant Economy.* Stanford: Stanford University Press.

Caplow, Theodore

1968 *Two Against One.* Englewood Cliffs, NJ: Prentice-Hall, Inc.

Cardoso, Lawrence A.

1977 "La repartriación de braceros en época de Obregón." *Historia Mexicana* 16:565-87.

Carlos, Manuel L.

1974 *Politics and Development in Rural Mexico.* New York: Praeger Publishers.

Carlos, Manuel L. and Anderson, Bob

n.d. "Political Brokerage and Network Politics in Mexico." In Anderson and Willer n.d.

1981 "Political Brokerage and Network Politics in Mexico." In Willer and Anderson 1981.

Carr, Barry

1976 *El movimiento obrero y la política en México, 1910-29.* Mexico: SEPSETENTAS.

Carrasco, Pedro

1961 "The Civil-Religious Hierarchy in Mesoamerican Communities: Pre-Spanish Background and Colonial Development." *American Anthropologist* 63:483-97.

1966 "Sobre algunos términos de parentesco en el náhuatl clásico." *Estudios de Cultura Nahuatl* 6:149-66.

1971 "Social Organization of Ancient Mexico." In HMAI 10.

Carrasco, Pedro, and Johanna Broda

1978 *Economía política e ideología en el México prehispánico.* Mexico: Editorial Nueva Imagen.

Carrasco, Pedro, Johanna Broda, et. al.

1976 *Estratificación social en la Mesoamérica prehispánica.* Mexico: SEPINAH.

Carrera Stampa, Manuel

1954 *Los gremios Mexicanos.* Mexico: Edición y Distribución Ibero Americana de Publicaciones.

Caso, Alfonso

1928a "Relación del pueblo de Instlauaca (sic) que está puesto en corregimiento con la jurisdicción del pueblo de Teomastlahuala." *Revista Mexicana de Estudios Históricos* 2:135-63.

1928b "Tehuantepec." *Revista Mexicana de Estudios Históricos* 2:164-75.

1963 "Land Tenure among the Ancient Mexicans." *American Anthropologist* 65:863-78.

1966 La época de los señoríos independientes: 1232-1427." *Revista Mexicana de Estudios Antropológicos* 20:147-52.

Castillo, Gustavo del

1979 *Crisis y transformación de una sociedad tradicional.* Mexico: CISINAH.

Ceceña, José Luis

1980 "El estado, primer empresario." *Excelsior* enero 23, p. 7A.

Chambers, Erve J., and Philip D. Young

1979 "Mesoamerican Community Studies: The Past Decade." *Annual Review of Anthropology* 6. Palo Alto: Annual Reviews, Inc.

Chevalier, François

1952 *La Formation des grands domaines au Mexique. Terre et société aux XVIe-XVIIe siècles.* Paris: Institut d'Ethnologie.

Cinta, Ricardo

1980 "Burguesía nacional y desarrollo." In *Perfil de México en 1980.* Vol. III. México: Siglo XXI.

Cintrón Tiryakian, Josefina

1978 "Campillo's Pragmatic New System: A Mercantile and Utilitarian Approach to Indian Reform in the Spanish Colonies of the Eighteenth Century." *History of Political Economy* 10:233-57.

Clark, James Cooper

1938 *Codex Mendocino,* 3 vols. (Clark, trans. and ed.) London: Waterlow and Sons.

Clausewitz, Karl von

1943 *On War.* O. J. Matthijs Jolles, trans. New York: Random House.

Claussen, J. M. and P. Skolnik

1978 *The Early State.* The Hague: Mouton Publishers.

Clavijero, Fracisco

1976 *Historia antigua de México.* Mexico: Editorial Porrúa, S. A.

Cline, Howard F.

1952 "Mexican Community Studies." *Hispanic American Historical Review* 32:212-42.

1966 "The Oztoticpac Lands Map of Texcoco, 1540." *Quarterly Journal of the Library of Congress* 23:77-115.

1968 "The Oztoticpac Lands Map of Texcoco, 1540, Further Notes." *Actas y Memorias del XXXVII Congresso Internacional de Americanistas* 3:119-37.

1972 "The Oztoticpac Lands Map of Texcoco, 1540, A la Carte: Selected Papers on Maps and Atlases." In Ristow 1972, Vol. 5.

Cline, S. L.

1981 *Culhuacan 1579-1599: An Investigation through Mexican Indian Testaments.* Unpublished Ph.D. dissertation, University of California, Los Angeles.

1983 "Land Tenure and Land Inheritance in Late 16th-Century Culhuacan." In Harvey and Prem 1983.

Cloward, Richard A., and Lloyd E. Ohlin

1960 *Delinquency and Opportunity: A Theory of Delinquent Gangs.* Glencoe, NY: Free Press.

Cobo, Bernabé

1944 "Cartas del P. Bernabé Cobo, de la Compañía de Jesús, escritas a un compañero suyo residente en el Perú." In Vásquez de Espinosa 1944.

Cockcroft, James

1967 "El maestro de primaria en la revolución mexicana." *Historia Mexicana* 16:565-87.

Código civil del imperio mexicano.

1866 Mexico: Imprenta de Andrade y Escalante.

Colección de documentos inéditos relativos al descubrimiento, conquista y organización de las antiguas posesiones Españolas de América y Oceania.

1864-1884 41 Vols. Madrid.

Colección de leyes y decretos del estado de Oaxaca a partir de 1823 a 1901.

1850-1902 22 Tomos. Oaxaca: Imprenta del Estado.

Colección de leyes y decretos del estado libre de Oaxaca, 1851.

1851 Oaxaca: Manuel Rincón.

Coleman, Kenneth M. and John Wanat

1975 "On Measuring Presidential Ideology Through Budgets: A Reappraisal of the Wilkie Approach." *Latin American Research Review* 10:77-88.

Collier, David

1976 *Squatters and Oligarchs.* Baltimore: The John Hopkins University Press.

Collier, George A.

1980 "Land Reform and Local Level Politics in Highland Chiapas." Paper presented at the American Anthropological Association Annual Convention, Washington, DC.

Collier, George A., Renato I. Rosaldo, and John D. Wirth

1982 *The Inca and Aztec States, 1400-1800: Anthropology and History.* New York: Academic Press.

Collier, Jane F.

1973 *Law and Social Change in Zinacantan.* Stanford: Stanford University Press.

1976 "Political Leadership and Legal Change in Zinacantan." *Law and Society Review* 11:131-61.

Cooper, Donald B.

1965 *Epidemic Disease in Mexico City.* Austin: University of Texas Press.

Corbett, John G.

1976 "Aspects of Recruitment to Civil Office in a Mexican Community." *Anthropological Quarterly* 49:160-73.

1977 "Role Conflict as a Local-Level Constraint on Decision-Making in Mexico." *Proceedings of the Pacific Coast Council on Latin American Studies* 5.

1980 "Linkage as Manipulation: The Partido Revolucionario Institucional in Mexico." In Lawson 1980.

Corbett, John G., and Scott Whiteford

1983 "State Penetration and Development." In Kendall 1983.

Cordero, S. and Santín R.

1977 "Los grupos industriales: una nueva organización económica en México." *Cuadernos del CES* 23, Mexico: El Colegio de México.

Córdova, Arnaldo

1973 *La ideología de la revolución mexicana.* Mexico: ERA.

1979 "El desafío de la izquierda mexicana" *Nexos* 1979 (18) Jun:3-15.

Córdova, Juan de

1942 *Vocabulario castellano-zapoteco.* Mexico: Biblioteca Lingüística Mexicana, Instituto Nacional de Antropología e Historia.

Cornelius, W.

1972 "A Structural Analysis of Urban Caciquismo in Mexico." *Urban Anthropology* 1:234-61.

1973 "Nation Building, Participation, and Distribution: The Politics of Social Reform Under Cárdenas." In Almond, Flanagan, and Mundt 1973.

1975 *Politics and the Migrant Poor in Mexico City.* Stanford: Stanford University Press.

Corona Núñez, José

1966 "Los Teotihuacanos en el occidente de México." *Revista Mexicana de Estudios Antropológicos* 20:111-16.

Cosío Villegas, Daniel

1955 *Historia moderna de México. La república restaurada: vida política.* Mexico: Editorial Hermes.

1972 *El sistema político mexicano.* Mexico: Joaquín Mortiz.

1976 *Historia general de México.* Mexico: El Colegio de México.

Covarrubias, Sebastián de

1943 *Tesoro de la lengua castellana o española.* Barcelona: S. A. Horta, I. E.

Crosby, Alfred W.

1967 "Conquistador y Pestilencia: The First New World Pandemic and the Fall of the Great Indian Empires." *Hispanic American Historical Review* 47:321-37.

Dalton, George

1971 *Studies in Economic Anthropology* Washington, DC: American Anthropological Association, Anthropological Studies No. 7.

Dalton Palomo, Margarita, Reyna Moguel Viveros, and Santiago Portillo

1980 *Historia de Oaxaca.* Vol. 2. Oaxaca: Instituto de Investigaciones Sociológicas de la Universidad Autónoma Benito Juárez de Oaxaca.

Davies, Nigel

1972 "The Military Organization of the Aztec Empire." *Atti del XL Congresso Internazionale Degli Americanisti* 4:213-21. Roma-Genova, 1972.

1977a *The Aztecs.* London: Abacus.

1977b *The Toltecs: Until the Fall of Tula.* Norman: University of Oklahoma Press.

De la Croix, Horst

1972 *Military Considerations in City Planning: Fortifications.* New York: George Braziller.

Dennis, Philip A.

1973 "The Oaxacan Village President as Political Middleman." *Ethnology* 12:419-27.

Derossi, Flavia

1977 *El empresario mexicano.* Mexico: Universidad Nacional Autónoma de México/ Instituto de Investigaciones Sociales.

DeWalt, Billie R.

1975 "Changes in the Cargo Systems of Mesoamerica." *Anthropological Quarterly* 48:87-105.

1979 *Modernization in a Mexican Ejido.* Cambridge: Cambridge University Press.

Díaz, Felix

1869 *Memoria administrativa presentada por el general Felix Díaz, gobernador del estado de Oaxaca, 17 de Septiembre de 1868.* .

Díaz del Castillo, Bernal

1974 *Historia verdadera de la conquista de la Nueva España.* Mexico: Porrúa.

Dibble, Charles E.

1941 *Codex en Cruz.* Mexico.

Diebold, A. Richard, Jr.

1969 "The Huave." In HMAI 7.

Dirección General de Estadísticas

1893- *Anuarios Estadísticos.* Mexico: Dirección General de Estadísticas.

Diskin, Martin

1979 "The Peasant Family Archive: Sources for an Ethnohistory of the Present," *Ethnohistory* 26:209-29.

Documentos para la historia de Méjico

1853-1857 primera seria. 21 Vols. Mexico: J. R. Navarro.

Dulles, John W. F.

1961 *Yesterday in Mexico.* Austin: University of Texas Press.

Durán, Diego

1951 *Historia de las indias de Nueva España y islas de tierra firme.* Mexico: Editorial Nacional.

1967 *Historia de las indias de Nueva España e islas de la tierra firme.* 2 Tomos. Mexico: Editorial Porrúa, S. A.

Durazo, Adriana

1980 "La relación existente entre una institución gubernamental y un asentamiento urbano espontáneo de la ciudad de México." Tesis, Universidad Iberoamericana, Mexico.

Eckstein, Susan

1977 *The Poverty of Revolution: The State and the Urban Poor in Mexico.* Princeton: Princeton University Press.

Eisenstadt, S. N. and L. Roniger

1975 "Patron-Client Relations as a Model of Structuring Social Exchange." Mimeographed.

Enciclopedia de México

1966-1977 Mexico: Enciclopedia de México.

Escriche y Martín, Joaquín

1837 *Diccionario razonado de la legislación civil, penal, comercial y forense.* Mexico: Impreso en la oficina de Galvan.

Esquivel Obregón, Toribio

1941 *Biografía de don Francisco Javier de Gamboa.* Mexico: Tallares Gráficos Laguna.

Estado de Oaxaca

1966-1977 "Estado de Oaxaca." In *Enciclopedia de México.* 1966-1977, Vol. 9.

Estas son las leyes que tenían los Indios de la Nueva España.

1886-1892 In García Icazbalceta 1886-1892, 3:308-15.

Etienne, M. and E. Leacock

1980 *Women and Colonialization: Anthropoligical Perspectives.* New York: Praeger.

Etzioni, Amitai

1969 *A Sociological Reader on Complex Organizations.* New York: Holt, Rinehart and Winston.

1975 *A Comparative Analysis of Complex Organizations: On Power, Involvement and Their Correlates.* New York: Free Press.

Excelsior, 18 de diciembre

1979 P. 4A (Farrell, declaraciones sobre el número de asegurados).

Fagen, Richard R., and William S. Tuohy

1972 *Politics and Privilege in a Mexican City.* Stanford: Stanford University Press.

Falcón, Romana

1978 "El Surgimiento del agrarismo cardinista—una revisión de las tesis populistas." *Historia Mexicana* 27:333-86.

Farriss, Nancy M.

1978 "Nucleation Versus Dispersal: The Dynamics of Population Movement in Colonial Yucatan." *Hispanic American Histrorical Review* 58:187-216.

Fernández, Julio Q.

1969 *Political Administration in Mexico.* Boulder: University of Colorado Press.

Fernández, María T., Maurice Swadesh, and Robert Weitlaner

1960 "El panorama ethnolingüístico de Oaxaca y del Istmo." Séptima Mesa Redonda de la Sociedad Mexicana de Antropología. *Revista Mexicana de Estudios Antropológicos* 16: 137-57.

Fernández de Recas, Guillermo S.

1956 *Aspirantes americanos a cargos del Santo Oficio.* Mexico: Librería de M. Porruá.

Fernández-Mensaque, Fernando Casado

1950 "El tribunal de al acordada de Nueva España." *Anuario de Estudios Americanos* 18:279-323.

Finer, Samuel E.

1975 "State- and Nation-Building in Europe: The Role of the Military." In Tilly 1975a.

Fisher, Lillian

1926 *Viceregal Administration in the Spanish American Colonies.* Berkeley: University of California Press.

1929 *The Intendant System in Spanish America.* Berkeley: University of California Press.

Fitzmaurice-Kelley, Julia

1927 "Women in Sixteenth-Century Spain." *Revue Hispanique* 70:557-632.

Flannery, Kent V. and Joyce Marcus

1976 "Formative Oaxaca and the Zapotec Cosmos." *American Scientist* 64:374-83.

Florescano, Enrique

1969 *Precios del maíz y crisis agrícolas en México.* Mexico: El Colegio de México.

1980 *La clase obrera en la historia de México: de la colonia al imperio.* Mexico: Siglo XXI.

Florescano, Enrique, and Isabel Gil

1973 *Descripciones económicas generales de Nueva España, 1784-1817.* Mexico: INAH.

Foster, George M.

1967 *Tzintzuntzan.* Boston: Little, Brown and Company.

Frías y Frías, Valentín

1906 *La conquista de Querétaro.* Querétaro: Imprenta de la Escuela de Artes de Señor San José.

Friedlander, Judith

1975 *Being Indian in Hueyapan.* New York: St. Martin's Press.

1981 "The Secularization of the Cargo System: An Example from Postrevolutionary Central Mexico." *Latin American Research Review* 16:132-43.

Friedrich, Paul

1965 "A Mexican Cacicazgo." *Ethnology* 4:190-209.

1966 "Postrevolutionary Politics and Communal Ritual." In Swartz, Turner, and Tuden 1966.

1968 "The Legitimacy of a Cacique." In Swartz 1968.

1971 *Agrarian Revolt in a Mexican Village.* Englewood Cliffs, NJ: Prentice-Hall, Inc.

Frost, Elsa Cecilia, Michael C. Meyer, and Josefina Zoraida Vázquez

1979 *El Trabajo y los trabajadores en la historia de México.* Mexico and Tucson: El Colegio de México and University of Arizona Press.

Fuente, Julio de la

1949 *Yalalag: Una villa zapoteca serrana.* Mexico: Museo Nacional de Anthropología.

Gallego, Gonzalo.

1927 "Relación geográfica de Culhuacan." *Revista Mexicana de Estudios Históricos* I/6:171-73.

García, Genaro

1907 *Tumultos y rebeliones acaecidos en México. Documentos inéditos o muy raros para la historia de México.* Mexico: Librería de la Vda. de Ch. Bouret.

García Icazbalceta, Joaquín

1886-1892 *Nueva colección de documentos para la historia de México.* Mexico: Andrade y Morales, sucesores.

García Pimentel, Luis.

1897 *Descripción del arzobispado de México hecha en 1570.* Mexico: José Joaquín Terrazas.

1903-1907 *Documentos históricos de Méjico.* 5 Vols. Mexico: En Casa del Editor.

1904 *Relación de los obispados de Tlaxcala, Michoacán, Oaxaca y otros lugares en el siglo XVI.* Mexico: Documentos Históricos de México.

Gemelli Carreri, Juan Francisco

1955 *Viaje a la Nueva España: México a fines del siglo XVII.* 3 Vols. Mexico: Libro-Mex, Editores.

Gerbi, Antonello

1960 *La disputa del nuevo mundo.* Mexico: Fondo de Cultura Económica.

Gerhard, Peter

1972 *A Guide to the Historical Geography of New Spain.* Cambridge: Cambridge University Press.

Gibson, Charles

1952 *Tlaxcala in the Sixteenth Century*. New Haven, CT: Yale University Press.

1960 "The Aztec Aristocracy in Colonial Mexico." *Comparative Studies in Society and History* 2:169-96.

1964 *The Aztecs Under Spanish Rule*. Stanford: Stanford University Press.

1966 *Spain in America*. New York: Harper and Row Publishers.

1971 "Structure of the Aztec Empire." In HMAI 10.

Glade, William P., and Stanley R. Ross

1973 *Críticas constructivas del sistema político Mexicano*. Austin: University of Texas Press.

Goldkind, Victor

1966 "Class Conflict and Cacique in Chan Kom." *Southwestern Journal of Anthropology* 22:325-45.

Gómara, Francisco López de

1943 *Historia de la conquista de México*. Mexico: Editorial Pedro Robredo.

1966 *Cortés: The Life of the Conqueror by His Secretary* L. B. Simpson, trans. Berkeley: University of California Press.

Gómez, José

1853-1857 "Diario curioso de México." In *Documentos para la historia de Méjico*. 1853-1857.

Gómez de Cervantes, G.

1944 *La vida económica y social de la Nueva España al finalizar del siglo XVI*. Mexico: Antigua Librería Robredo de J. Porrúa e hijos.

Gómez de Orozco, Francisco

1927 "Descripción de Teotzacualco y de Amoltepeque." *Revista Mexicana de Estudios Históricos* 1/6:174-78.

Góngora, Mario

1975 "The Institutions and Founding Ideas of the Spanish State in the Indies." In *Studies in the Colonial History of Spanish America*, pp. 67-126. Cambridge: Cambridge University Press.

González, Luis

1974 *San José de Gracia: Mexican Village in Transition*. Austin: University of Texas Press.

González Angulo, Jorge

1978 "Los gremios de artesanos y la estructura urbano." In Moreno Toscano 1978.

González Angulo, Jorge, and Roberto Sandoval Zarauz

1980 "Los trabajadores industriales de Nueva España, 1750-1810." In Florescano 1980.

González Casanova, Pablo

1965 *La democracia en México*. Mexico: ERA.

González y González, Luis

1979 *Historia documental de la revolución mexicana, 1934-1940*. Mexico: El Colegio de México.

González Navarro, Moisés

1968 *La confederación nacional campesina: un grupo de presión de la reforma agraria mexicana*. Mexico: Cota Amic.

1969 "Tenencia de la tierra y población agrícola, 1877-1960." *Historia Mexicana* 14:62-86.

1970 "Efectos sociales de la crisis de 1929." *Historia Mexicana* 14:536-58.

1974a "La era moderna." In *Historia documental de México*. 1974, Vol. 2.

1974b "La era de Santa Anna." In *Historia documental de México*. 1974, Vol. 2.

1974c "La reforma y el imperio." In *Historia documental de México*. 1974, Vol. 2

Gorenstein, Shirley

1963 *The Differential Development of Military and Political Organization in Prehispanic Peru and Mexico*. Unpublished Ph.D. dissertation, Columbia University.

1966 "The Differential Development of New World Empires." *Revista Mexicana de Estudios Antropológicos* 20:41-67.

Graham, Lawrence S.

1968 *Politics in a Mexican Community*. Gainesville: University of Florida Press.

Greenberg, Martin

1970 *Bureaucracy and Development: A Mexican Case Study*. Boston: Heath.

Greenfield, S. and A. Strickon

n.d. "Towards a Populational, Decision-Making Approach to Entrepreneurships." In Greenfield, Strickon, and Aubrey n.d.

Greenfield, S., A. Strickon, and H. G. Aubrey

n.d. untitled Albuquerque: University of New Mexico Press, forthcoming.

Greenleaf, Richard E.

1967 "The Obraje in the Late Mexican Colony." *The Americas* 23:227-50.

Grimes, C. E. and Charles Simmons

1969 "Bureaucracy and Political Control in Mexico: Towards an Assessment." *Political Administration Review* 29:72-79.

Grindle, Merilee S.

1977 *Bureaucrats, Politicians and Peasants in Mexico*. Berkeley: University of California Press.

Guenther, Anthony L.

1970 *Criminal Behavior and Social Systems; Contributions of American Sociology*. Chicago: Rand McNally.

Guridi y Alcocer, José Miguel

1906 *Apuntes de la vida de d. José Miguel Guridi y Alcocer, formados por el mismo en fines de 1801 y principios del siguiente de 1802*. Mexico: Moderna librería religiosa de G. L. Vallejo.

Gutiérrez, Jorge

1977 "El sistema político y la burguesía rural en México: el caso del valle del Mezquital." *Revista Mexicana de Sociología* 37:901-19.

Hall, Linda B.

1980 "Alvaro Obregón and the Politics of Mexican Land-Reform." *Hispanic American Historical Review* 60:213-38.

Handbook of Middle American Indians

1964- Various editors. Austin: University of Texas Press.

Hansen, Roger D.

1971 *The Politics of Mexican Development*. Baltimore: The Johns Hopkins University Press.

1978 *La política del desarrollo mexicano*. México: Siglo XXI.

Hardoy, Jorge

1973 *Pre-Columbian Cities.* New York: Walker and Co.

Haring, Clarence

1947 *The Spanish Empire in America.* New York: Harcourt, Brace and World.

Harvey, H. R., and Hanns J. Prem

1983 *Explorations in Ethnohistory: Indian Culhuacan.* Albuquerque: University of New Mexico Press.

Haslip-Viera, Gabriel

1979 *Crime and the Administration of Justice in Colonial Mexico City, 1696-1810.* Unpublished Ph.D. dissertation, Columbia University.

Hassig, Ross

n.d. "One Hundred Years of Servitude: *Tlamemes* in Early New Spain." In HMAI, supl. 2, forthcoming.

Hellbom, Anna-Britta

1967 *La participación cultural de las mujeres: indias y metizas en el México precortesiano y postrevolucionario.* Stockholm: Ethnographical Museum.

Henao, Luis Emilio

1980 *Tehuacan: Campesinado e irrigación.* Mexico: Ediciones Edicol, S. A.

Hernández, Rafael

1902 *Indice alfabético de la colección de leyes y decretos del estado de Oaxaca a partir de 1823 a 1901.* Oaxaca: Imprenta del Estado.

Hernández Xolocotzin, Efraim

1949 "Maize Granaries in Mexico." *Botanical Museum Leaflets, Harvard University* 13:7:153-211.

Herr, Richard

1958 *The Eighteenth Century Revolution in Spain.* Princeton: Princeton University Press.

Hicks, Frederic

1978 "Barrio Structure of Aztec Texcoco." Paper presented at the American Society for Ethnohistory Annual Convention, Austin, Texas.

Historia de México.

1974 10 Tomos. Mexico: Salvat Editores de México.

Historia documental de México.

1974 Mexico: Universidad Nacional Autónoma de México.

Historia general de México.

1976 Vol. 2. Mexico: El Colegio de México.

Hobsbawm, E. J.

1959 *Primitive Rebels.* New York: W. W. Norton.

Holt, H. Barry

1976 "The Extent of the Dominance of Tenochtitlan during the Reign of Mocteuczoma Ilhuicamina." *Middle American Research Institute* 22:49-62.

1979 *Mexica-Aztec Warfare: A Developmental and Cultural Analysis.* Unpublished Ph.D. dissertation, University of Texas-Austin.

Horn, James J.

1970 "El embajador Sheffield contra el presidente Calles." *Historia Mexicana* 20:265-84.

Howe, Walter

1949 *The Mining Guild of New Spain and its Tribunal General, 1770-1821.* Cambridge, MA: Harvard University Press.

Humboldt, Alexander von

1822 *Political Essay on the Kingdom of New Spain.* 4 Vols. London: Longman, Hurst, Rees, Orme, and Brown.

Hunt, Eva, and Robert Hunt

1969 "The Role of Courts in Rural Mexico." In Bock 1969.

Iguíniz, Juan B.

1909-1910 *Biblioteca histórica Jaliscuense.* 5 Vols. Guadalajara: Imp. de J. B. Iguíniz.

Instrucción del Virrey Marqués de Croix que deja a su sucesor, Antonio María Bucareli

1960 Mexico: Editorial Jus.

Instrucciones que los vireyes de Nueva España dejaron a sus sucesores.

1873 Mexico: Impr. de Ignacio Escalante.

Instrucciones que los vireyes de Nueva España dejaron a sus sucesores.

1867 Mexico: Impr. de Ignacio Escalante.

Insunza, Isabel

1978 "Mercado de trabajo para los médicos veterinarios" *Revista de Medicina Veterinaria.*

Iszaevich, Abraham

1973 *Modernización en una communidad oaxaqueño del valle.* Mexico: Secretaría de Educación Pública.

Iturribarría, J. F.

1935 *Historia de Oaxaca, 1821-1854.* Oaxaca: Ramírez Belmar.

1955 *Oaxaca en la historia.* Mexico: Editorial Stylo.

Ixtlilxochitl, Fernando de Alva

1952 *Obras históricas.* Mexico: Editorial Nacional.

Iwánska, Alicja

1971 *Purgatory and Utopia: A Mazahua Indian Village of Mexico.* Cambridge, MA: Schenkman Publishing Company.

Jiménez Moreno, Wigberto

1966 "Los imperios prehispánicos de Mesoamérica." *Revista Mexicana de Estudios Antropológicos* 20:179-95.

Juárez, Antonio

1979 *Las corporaciones transnacionales y los tabajadores mexicanos.* Mexico: Siglo XXI.

Kagan, Samuel

1979 "The Labor of Prisoners in the Obrajes of Coyoacan, 1660-1693." In Frost, Meyer, and Zoraida Vázquez 1979.

Karttunen, Frances, and James Lockhart.

1978 "Textos en nahuatl del siglo XVIII: Un documento de Amecameca, 1746." *Estudios de Cultura Nahuatl* 13:153-75.

Katz, Friedrich

1966 *Situación social y económica de los aztecas durante los siglos XV y XVI.* Mexico: Universidad Nacional Autónoma de México.

1972 *The Ancient American Civilization.* New York: Praeger.

Kearney, Michael

1972 *The Winds of Ixtepeji.* New York: Holt, Rinehart and Winston, Inc.

Kellogg, Susan.

1979 *Social Organization in Early Colonial Tenochtitlan-Tlatelolco.* Unpublished Ph.D. dissertation, University of Rochester.

Kelly, Isabel

1952 "Appendix B: The Mexican Conquests." In Kelly and Palerm 1952.

Kelly, Isabel, and Angel Palerm

1952 *The Tajin Totonac. Part 1: History, Subsistence, Shelter, and Technology.* Washington: Smithsonian Institution, Institute of Social Anthropology, Publication 13.

Kendall, Carl

1983 *Social Change in Mesoamerica Since "Heritage of Conquest."* Albuquerque: University of New Mexico Press.

Kern, Robert

1974 *The Caciques.* Albuquerque: University of New Mexico Press.

Kicza, John E.

1982 "The Great Families of Mexico: Elite Maintenance and Business Practices in Late Colonial Mexico City." *Hispanic American Historical Review* 62:429-57.

Kitsuse, John I., and Aaron V. Cicourel

1963 "A Note on the Uses of Official Statistics." *Social Problems* 2:131-39.

Köhler, Ulrich

1982 "Estructura y funcionamiento de la administración comunal de San Pablo Chalchihuitan." *América Indígena* 42:117-45.

Krejci, John

1976 "Leadership and Change in Two Mexican Villages." *Anthropological Quarterly* 49:185-96.

Kurtz, Donald V.

1978 "The Legitimation of the Aztec State." In Claussen and Skolnik 1978.

Ladd, Doris M.

1976 *The Mexican Nobility at Independence, 1780-1826.* Austin: University of Texas Press.

Lajous, Alejandra

1979 *Los orígenes del partido único en México.* Mexico: Universidad Nacional Autónoma de México.

Las Casas, Bartolomé

1958 *Apologética historia.* Biblioteca de Autores Españoles. Madrid: Real Academia Española.

Lavrin, Asunción

1978a "In Search of the Colonial Woman in Mexico: The Seventeenth and Eighteenth Centuries." In Lavrin 1978b.

1978b *Latin American Women: Historical Perspectives* Westport, CT: Greenwood Press.

Lavrin, Asunción, and Edith Couturier

1979 "Dowries and Wills: A View of Women's Socioeconomic Role in Colonial Guadalajara and Puebla, 1640-1790." *Hispanic American Historical Review* 59:280-304.

Lawson, Kay

1980 *Political Parties and Linkage.* New Haven, CT: Yale University Press.

Leacock, Eleanor and June Nash

1977 "Ideologies of Sex: Archetypes and Stereotypes." *Annals of the New York Academy of Sciences* 285:618-45.

Lees, Susan

1973 *Sociopolitical Aspects of Canal Irrigation in the Valley of Oaxaca.* Ann Arbor: University of Michigan—Memoirs of the Museum of Anthropology, Number 6.

1976 "Hydraulic Development and Political Response in the Valley of Oaxaca, Mexico." *Anthropological Quarterly* 49:197-210.

León-Portilla, Miguel.

1976 "El libro de testamentos indígenas de Culhuacan, su significación como testimonio histórico." *Estudios de Cultura Nahuatl* 12:11-31.

Lerner, Victoria

1976 "El reformismo de la década de 1930 en México." *Historia Mexicana* 26:188-215.

Leslie, Charles M.

1960 *Now We Are Civilized.* Detroit: Wayne State University Press.

Lewis, Leslie

1978 *Colonial Texcoco: A Study of a Society in the Valley of Mexico, 1570-1630.* Unpublished Ph.D. dissertation, University of California, Los Angeles.

Lewis, Oscar

1951 *Life in a Mexican Village: Tepoztlan Restudied.* Urbana: University of Illinois Press.

Ley de ayuntamientos expedida por el H. Congreso del Estado en 27 de noviembre de 1889.

1889 Oaxaca: Talleres de Imprenta de Julian Soto.

El libro de las tasaciones de pueblos de la Nueva España, siglo XVI.

1952 Mexico: Archivo General de la Nación.

Lieuwen, Edwin

1968 *Mexican Militarism.* Albuquerque: University of New Mexico Press.

Lira, Andrés, and Luis Muro

1976 "El siglo de la integración." In *Historia general de México* 1976.

Lockhart, James.

1981 "Some Nahua Concepts in Postconquest Guise." Paper presented at the American Historical Association Annual Convention, Los Angeles.

Loera y Ch., Margarita.

1977 *Caimaya y Tepemaxalco.* Mexico: Cuadernos de Trabajo del Departamento de Investigaciones Históricas, INAH.

Lombardo Ruíz, Sonia

1979 "Ideas y proyectos urbanísticos de la ciudad de México." In Moreno Toscano 1978.

Lomnitz, Larissa

1971 "Reciprocity of Favors in the Urban Middle Class of Chile." In Dalton 1971.

1975 *Cómo sobreviven los marginados.* Mexico: Siglo XXI.

1977 "Conflict and Mediation in a Latin American University." *Journal of Interamerican Studies and World Affairs* 19:315-38.

1978 "Mechanisms of Articulation Between Shantytown Settlers and the Urban System." *Urban Anthropology* 7:185-206.

Lomnitz, L., L. Mayer, and M. Rees

1979 "The State University Relation: Mexico's School of Veterinary Medicine." Mimeographed.

Lomnitz, L., and Moran A.

1978 "Estudio de un grupo de egresados mexicanos de una universidad extranjera." *Pensamiento Universitario 12* Mexico: Universidad Nacional Autónoma de México.

Lomnitz, L., and Marisol Pérez-Lizaur

1978 "The History of a Mexican Urban Family." *Journal of Family History* 3:392-409.

Lopez de Cámara, Francisco.

1974 "Hacia una concepción dialéctica de la autonomía universitaria." *Deslinde* 53.

1971 *El desafío de la clase media.* Mexico: Cuaderno de Joaquín Mortis.

López y Magaña, Juan.

1980 "Aspects of the Nahuatl Heritage of Juan Bautista Pomar." Master of Arts Paper in Latin American Studies, University of California, Los Angeles.

Loy, Jane M.

1981 "Forgotten Comuneros: The 1781 Revolt in the Llanos de Casanare." *Hispanic American Historical Review* 61:235-57.

Lozoya, Jorge

1977 "El ejército mexicano," In *Lecturas de política mexicana,* edited by El Colegio de México. Mexico: El Colegio de México.

Luttwak, Edward N.

1976 *The Grand Strategy of the Roman Empire.* Baltimore: The Johns Hopkins University Press.

MacLachlan, Colin

1974 *Criminal Justice in Eighteenth Century Mexico: A Study of the Tribunal of the Acordada.* Berkeley: University of California Press.

MacLeod, Murdo J.

1973 *Spanish Central America: A Socioeconomic History, 1520-1720.* Berkeley: University of California Press.

Margadant S., Guillermo Flores

1971 *Introducción a la historia del derecho mexicano.* Mexico: Universidad Nacional Autónoma de México.

Malloy, James M.

1977 *Authoritarianism and Corporation in Latin America.* Pittsburgh: University of Pittsburgh Press.

Marcus, Joyce

1978 "Archaeology and Religion: A Comparison of the Zapotec and Maya." *World Archaeology* 10:172-91.

Margolies, Barbara L.

1975 *Princes of the Earth.* Washington, DC: American Anthropological Association.

Marroqui, José María

1900-1903 *La ciudad de México.* 3 Vols. Mexico: Tip. y lit. "La Europa" de J. Aguilar Vera y CA.

Martin, Norman F.

1972 "La desnudez en la Nueva España del siglo XVIII." *Anuario de Estudios Americanos* 24:261-94.

Martínez Alcubilla, D. Marcelo

1885 *Códigos antiguos de España: colección completa de todos los códigos de España desde El Fuero Juzgo hasta la Novísima Recopilación.* Madrid: Administración.

Martínez Saldaña, Tomás, and Leticia Gándara Mendoza

1976 *Política y sociedad en México; el caso de Los Altos de Jalisco.* Mexico: SEPINAH.

Matute, A.

1972 *México en el siglo XIX. Fuentes e interpretaciones históricas.* Mexico: Universidad Nacional Autónoma de México/Instituto de Investigaciones Históricos.

Mayer, Adrian

1968 "The Significance of Quasi-Groups in the Study of Complex Societies." *ASA Monograph* 4.

McWatters, D. Lorne

1979 *The Royal Tobacco Monopoly in Bourbon Mexico, 1764-1810.* Unpublished Ph.D. dissertation, University of Florida.

Medin, Tzvi

1972 *Ideología y praxis política de Lázaro Cárdenas.* Mexico: Siglo XXI.

Memoria sobre la administración del estado de Puebla en 1849.

1850 Mexico.

Mtodos y resultados de la política indigenista en México.

1954 Mexico: Instituto Nacional Indigenista.

Meyer, Lorenzo

1976a "El primer tramo del camino." In Cosfo Villegas 1976.

1976b "la Encrucijada." In Cosío Villegas 1976.

1977 "Estado mexicano contemporáneo." In *Lecutras de política mexicana.*, edited by El Colegio de México. Mexico: El Colegio de México.

Michaels, Albert L.

1966 "El nacionalismo conservador mexicano desde la revolución hasta 1940." *Historia Mexicana* 16:213-38.

Migdal, Joel S.

1974 *Peasants, Politics, and Revolution: Pressures Toward Political and Social Change in the Third World.* Princeton: Princeton University Press.

Miller, Frank C.

1961 "Cultural Change as Decision-Making: A Tzotzil Example." *Ethnology* 4:53-65.

Montaño, Jorge

1976 *Los pobres de la ciudad y los asentamientos humanos.* Mexico: Siglo XXI.

Montgomery, Barbara V.

1973 *The Evolution of Rural Justice in New Spain, Culminating in the Acordada and Attempts by the Spanish Crown to Institute the Tribunal in Peru.* Unpublished Ph.D. dissertation, Loyola University of Chicago.

Monzón, Arturo

1949 *El calpulli en la organización social de los tenochca.* Mexico: Publicaciones del Instituto de Historia.

Moore, Barrington, Jr.

1966 *Social Origins of Dictatorship and Democracy: Lord and Peasant in the Making of the Modern World.* Boston: Beacon Press.

Moorehead, Max L.

1949 "Hernán Cortés and the Tehuantepec Passage." *Hispanic American Historical Review* 29:372-76.

Morales, María Dolores

1976 "Estructura urbana y distribución de la propiedad en la ciudad de México en 1813." *Historia Mexicana* 25:363-402.

Moreno Toscano, Alejandra

1978 *Ciudad de México: Ensayo de construcción de una historia.* Mexico: SEPINAH.

Motolinía, Toribio

1903 "Memoriales de Fray Toribio de Motolinía, manuscrito de la colección del Señor Don Joaquín García Icazbalceta." In García Pimentel 1903-1907.

1971 *Memoriales o libro de las cosas de la Nueva España y los naturales de ella.* Mexico: Universidad Nacional Autónoma de México/Instituto de Investigaciones Históricos.

Moxó, B. M. de

1839 *Cartas mejicanas escritas por d. Benito María de Moxó, año de 1805.* Genova: Tipografía de L. Pellas.

Muriel, Josefina

1974 *Los recogimientos de mugeres: repuesta a una problemática social novohispana.* Mexico: Universidad Nacional Autónoma de México/Instituto de Investigaciones Históricos.

Nader, Laura

1967 "An Analysis of Zapotec Law Cases." In Bohannan 1967.

Nader, Laura, and Harry F. Todd, Jr.

1978 *The Disputing Process—Law in Ten Societies.* New York: Columbia University Press.

Nacional Financiera

1974 *La economía mexicana en cifras.* Mexico: NAFINSA.

Nafinsa

1971 *La política industrial en el desarrollo económico para la América Latina.* Mexico: NAFINSA, Comisión Económica para la América Latina.

Nash, June

1970 *In the Eyes of the Ancestors.* New Haven, CT: Yale University Press.

1978 "The Aztecs and the Ideology of Male Dominance." *Signs* 4:349-62.

1980 "Aztec Women: The Transition from Status to Class in Empire and Colony." In Etienne and Leacock 1980.

Nelson, Cynthia

1971 *The Waiting Village: Social Change in Rural Mexico.* Boston: Little, Brown and Company.

Newman, Donald J.

1962 "The Effect of Accomodations in Justice Administration on Criminal Statistics." *Sociology and Social Research* 46:144-55.

Novísima recopilación de los leyes de España.

1805-1829 12 Vols. Madrid: J. Viana Razola.

O'Donnell, Guillermo

1977 "Corporatism and the Question of the State." In Malloy 1977.

Offner, Jerome

1979 *Law and Politics in Aztec Texcoco.* Unpublished Ph.D. dissertation, Anthropology Department, Yale University.

1980 "Aztec Political Numerology and Human Sacrifice: The Ideological Ramifications of the Number Six." *Journal of Latin American Lore* 6:205-15.

1981a "On the Inapplicability of 'Oriental Despotism' and the 'Asiatic Mode of Production' to the Aztecs of Texcoco." *American Antiquity* 46:43-61.

1981b "On Carrasco's Use of Theoretical 'First Principles'." *American Antiquity* 46:69-74.

n.d.a *Law and Politics in Aztec Texcoco.* Cambridge: Cambridge University Press, in press.

n.d.b "Aztec Legal Process: The Case of Texcoco." In *Proceedings of the Conference on Late Post-Classic Central Mexican Iconography.* Washington, DC: Dumbarton Oaks.

O'Gorman, Edmundo

1937 *Breve historia de las divisiones territoriales. Trabajos jurídicos de homenaje a la escuela libre de derecho en su XXV aniversario.* Vol. 2. Mexico: Editorial Polis.

OIT/INFONAVIT

1976 *Industrialización y prefabricación de viviendas y efectos sobre el empleo.* Mexico: Informe.

Ortiz Urquidi, Raul

1974 *Oaxaca, cuna de la codificación iberoamericana.* Mexico: Editorial Porrúa.

Ordenanza general formada de orden de Su Magestad y mandada imprimir y publicar para el gobierno e instrucción de intendentes subdelegados y demás empleados en Indias.

1803 Madrid.

Osborn, Wayne S.

1973 "Indian Land Retention in Colonial Metztitlan." *Hispanic American Historical Review* 53:217-38.

Osores, Félix

1908 *Noticias biobibliográficas de alumnos distinguidos del Colegio de San Pedro, San Pablo, y San Ildefonso de México.* Mexico: Viuda de C. Bouret.

Ots Capdequí, José María

1975 *El Estado Español en las indias.* Mexico: Fondo de Cultura Económica.

Oviedo y Valdés, Gonzalo Fernández de

1959 *Historia general y natural de las indias.* Madrid: Editorial Atlas.

Paddock, John

1966a "El fenómeno imperial: algunas enfoques teóricos." *Revista Mexicana de Estudios Antropológicos* 20:69-81.

1966b "La idea del imperio aplicada a mesoamérica." *Revista Mexicana de Estudios Antropológicos* 20:83-94.

1966c "Monte Albán: Sede de imperio?" *Revista Mexicana de Estudios Antropológicos* 20:117-46.

Palerm, Angel

1956 "Notas sobre las construcciones militares y la guerra en mesoamérica." *Ciencias Sociales* 7:189-202.

Paoli, Francisco

1979 "El cambio de presidente, elecciones mexicanas de 1976." *Revista Mexicana de Sociología* 12:325-52.

Parnell, Philip

1978 "Village or State? Competitive Legal Systems in a Mexican Judicial District." In Nader and Todd 1978.

Parry, J.H.

1953 *The Sale of Public Office in the Spanish Indies Under the Hapsburgs. Ibero-Americana 37,* Berkeley: University of California Press.

Parsons, Elsie Clews

1936 *Mitla: Town of the Souls.* Chicago: University of Chicago Press.

Paso y Troncoso, Francisco del

1905-1948 *Papeles de Nueva España.* 9 Vols. Madrid: Est. Tipográfico "Sucesores de Rivadeneyra."

1939-1942 *Epistolario de Nueva España, 1508-1818.* Mexico: Antigua Librería Robredo de José Porrúa e Hijos.

Peggie, J. J., and R. Lynch

1975 *Rethinking Modernization: Anthropological Perspectives.* Westport, CT: Greenwood Press.

Peña, Guillermo de la

1981 *A Legacy of Promises: Agriculture, Politics, and Ritual in the Morelos Highlands of Mexico.* Austin: University of Texas Press.

Peña Montenegro, Alonso de la

1688 *Itinerario para parochcos de indios, en que se tratan las materias mas particulares, tocantes à ellos, para su buena administración.* Amberes: Casa de Juan Bautista Verdussen, 1726.

Pérez Correa, Fernando

1974 "La universidad: contradicciones y perspectivas." *Deslinde* 53.

Pérez Jiménez, Gustavo

1959 *Las constituciones del estado de Oaxaca.* Mexico: Editorial Costa-Amic.

1968 *La institución del municipio libre en Oaxaca.* Mexico: Editorial Costa-Amic.

Periano, Roger

1961 "Descent, Descent Line, and Descent Group in Cognatic Social Systems." *Proceedings of the American Ethnological Society Annual Spring Meeting.*

Phillips, David A.

1979 "The Growth and Decline of States in Mesoamerica." *Journal of the Steward Anthropological Society* 10:137-59.

Pickett, Velma B.

1960 "The Grammatical Hierarchy of the Isthmus Zapotec." *Language* 36, No. 1, Pt. 2, Supplement.

1965 "Vocabulario zapoteco del istmo." *Serie de Vocabularios Indígenas Mariano Silva y Aceves* 3. Mexico: Instituto Lingüístico de Verano y la Dirección General de Asuntos Indígenas.

Piho, Virve

1972 "La jerarquía militar Azteca." *Atti del XL Congresso Internazionale degli Americanisti* 2:273-88. Roma-Genova, 1972.

1974 "Esquema provisional de la organización militar Mexica." *Actas del XLI Congreso Internacional de Americanistas* 2:169-78. Mexico, 1974.

Pike, F.

1974 "The New Corporatism and Latin America—U.S. Religions." In Pike and Strich 1974.

Pike, Frederick B., and Thomas Strich

1974 *The New Corporatism.* Notre Dame: University of Norte Dame Press.

Pimentel, Emilio

1904 *Mensaje leido por el C. Lic. Emilio Pimentel, gobernador constitucional del estado ante le XXIIa legislatura del mismo, y contestación del presidente del H. congreso, C. Andrés Portillo, el 16 de septiembre de 1904.* Oaxaca: Imprenta del Estado.

Poleman, Thomas T.

1964 *The Papaloapan Project.* Stanford: Stanford University Press.

Pomar, Juan Bautista

1886-1892 "Relación de Tezcoco." In García Icazbalceta 1886-1892, Vol. 3:1-69.

Popkin, Samuel L.

1979 *The Rational Peasant.* Berkeley: University of California Press.

Portes, Alejandro

1978 "The Informal Sector and the World Economy: Notes on the Structure of Subsidised Labour." *IDS Bulletin* 9 (4) June 35-39.

n.d. "The Informal Sector and the Capital Accumulative Process in Latin America." In press.

Portes Gil, Emilio

1964 *Autobiografía de la revolución mexicana.* Mexico: Instituto Mexicano de Cultura.

Pospisil. Leopold J.

1971 *The Anthropology of Law. A Comparative Theory.* New York: Harper and Row.

Press, Irwin

1975 *Tradition and Adaptation.* Westport, CT: Greenwood Press.

Puebla en cifras.

1944 Mexico: Talleres Gráficos de la Nación.

Purcell, John and Purcell, Susan K.

1977 "Mexican Business and Public Policy." In Malloy 1977.

1980 "State and Society in Mexico: Must a Stable Polity Be Institutionalized?" *World Politics* 32:194-227.

Purcell, Susan K., and John F. H. Purcell

1973 "Community Power and Benefits from the Nation: The Case of Mexico." In Rabinovita and Trueblood 1973.

Quinney, Richard

1966 "Structural Characteristics, Population Areas, and Crime Rates in the United States." *Journal of Criminal Law, Criminology and Police Science* 57:45-53.

Rabinovita, Francine F., and Felicity M. Trueblood

1973 *Latin American Urban Research,* Volume E. Beverly Hills, CA: Sage Publications.

Raby, David L.

1968 "Los maestros rurales y los conflictos sociales en México (1931-1940)." *Historia Mexicana* 18:190-227.

Ramírez Cabañas, Joaquín

1943 *La ciudad de Veracruz en el siglo XVI.* Mexico: Imprenta Universitaria.

Redfield, Robert

1950 *A Village That Chose Progress: Chan Kom Revisited.* Chicago: University of Chicago Press.

Redfield, Robert, and Alfonso Villa Rojas

1934 *Chan Kom: A Maya Village.* Chicago: University of Chicago Press.

Recopilación de leyes de los reynos de las Indias (1680).

1774 Madrid: Imprenta de Don Bartolomé Ulloa.

Regiones económico-agrícolas de la República Mexicana

1936 Tacubaya, Mexico.

Reglamento para la administración interior de los departamentos del estado de Oaxaca en lo relativo a los gobernadores y subprefectos.

1850 Oaxaca: Ignacio Rincón.

Revilla-Gigedo, Conde de

1966 *Informe sobre las misiones e instrucción reservada al Marqués.* Mexico: Editorial Jus.

Reyna, J. L.

1974 "Control político, estabilidad y desarrollo en México." *Cuadernos del CES* 3, Mexico: El Colegio de México.

1977 "Redefining the Authoritarian Regime." In Malloy 1977.

Reyna, J. L. and F. M. Miquet.

1976 "Introducción a la historia de las organizaciones obreras en México: 1912-1966." In Reyna et.al. 1976.

Reyna, José Luis, and Richard S. Weinart

1977 *Authoritarianism in Mexico.* Philadelphia: ISHI Publications.

Reyna, J. L., F. Zapata, M. Miquet Fleury, and S. Gómez-Tagle

1976 *Tres estudios sobre el movimiento obrero en México.* Mexico: El Colegio de México.

Reynolds, Clark

1970 *The Mexican Economy: Twentieth Century Structure and Growth.* New Haven, CT: Yale University Press.

Richmond, Douglas

1976 "El nacionalismo de Carranza y los cambios socioeconómicos." *Historia Mexicana* 26:107-31.

Ristow, W. W.

1972 *A la Carte. Selected Papers on Maps and Atlases.* Washington, DC: Library of Congress.

Robertson, William S.

1952 *Iturbide of Mexico.* Durham, NC: Duke University Press.

Ronfeldt, David

1973 *Atencingo: The Politics of Agrarian Struggle in a Mexican Ejido.* Stanford: Stanford University Press.

Roxborough, Ian

n.d.a ""The Mexican Working Class and the Mexican Labour Movement: 1930-1975." London School of Economics. Mimeographed.

n.d.b "The Mexican Labour Movement in Crisis." Mimeographed.

Roxborough, I. and Zapata, F.

1978 "Algunos mitos sobre el sindicalismo en México." *Diálogos* 84:24-26.

Rus, Jan

1982 "Política de desarrollo y algunas aspectos de las relaciones interétnicas." *América Indígena* 42:69-83.

Rus, Jan, and Robert Wasserstrom

1980 "Civil-Religious Hierarchies in Central Chiapas: A Critical Perspective." *American Ethnologist* 7:466-78.

Sabloff, Paula L. W.

1981 *Caciquismo in Post-Revolutionary Mexican Ejido-Grant Communities.* Albuquerque: University of New Mexico, Latin American Institute, Research Paper 7.

Sahagún, Bernardino de

1950-1969 *The Florentine Codex: A General History of the Things of New Spain.* Charles Dibble and Arthur Anderson, trans. In 13 Parts. Santa Fe: The School of American Research and the University of Utah.

Salazar, Roberto

1971 "El empresario industrial." Centro de Estudios Económicos y Demográficos, El Colegio de México, Mimeographed.

Salvucci, Richard J.

1982 *Enterprise and Economic Development in Eighteenth Century Mexico: The Case of the Obrajes.* Unpublished Ph.D. dissertation, Princeton University.

Sanderson, Steve

1981 *Agrarian Populism and the Mexican State.* Berkeley: University of California Press.

Sarrailh, Jean

1957 *La España ilustrada de la segunda mitad del siglo XVIII.* Mexico.

Scardaville, Michael C.

1977 *Crime and the Urban Poor: Mexico City in the Late Colonial Period.* Unpublished Ph.D. dissertation, University of Florida.

1980 "Alcohol Abuse and Tavern Reform in Late Colonial Mexico City." *Hispanic American Historical Review* 60:643-71.

Schafer, Robert

1973 *Mexican Business Organization.* Syracuse, NY: Syracuse University Press.

Schensul, Jean

1976 *Enseñanza para el futuro y el futuro de la enseñanza en México.* Mexico: SEPSETENTAS.

Schmidt, S. et. al.

1977 *Friends, Followers and Factions.* Berkeley: University of California Press.

Schmitter, Phillipe

1974 "Still the Century of Corporatism?" In Pike and Strich 1974.

Schryer, Frans

1976 "Faccionalismo y patronazgo del PRI en un municipio de la huasteca hidalguense." *Cuadernos del Ces* 16, Mexico: El Colegio de México.

1980 *The Rancheros of Pisaflores.* Toronto: University of Toronto Press.

Schwartz, Norman B.

1978 "Community Development and Cultural Change in Latin America." *Annual Review of Anthropology* 7. Palo Alto: Annual Reviews, Inc.

1981 "Anthropological Views of Community and Community Deveolpment." *Human Organization* 40:313-22.

Scott, James C.

1976 *The Moral Economy of the Peasant.* New Haven, CT: Yale University Press.

Seaton, S. Lee, and Henri J. M. Claessen

1979 *Political Anthropology: The State of the Art.* The Hague: Mouton Publishers.

Secretaría de Programación Y Presupuesto

1979a *Características del empleo y el desempleo en las áreas metropolitanas de México, Monterrey y Guadalajara.* Mexico: Coordinación del Sistema Nacional de Información.

1979b *Características de los marginados en las áreas urbanas de México.* Mexico: Coordinación del Sistema Nacional de Información.

Sedano, Francisco

1880 *Noticias de México.* 2 Vols. Mexico: Ed. de la "Voz de México".

Selby, Henry A.

1973 "Comments." In Glade and Ross 1973.

Seler, Eduard

1908 "Das Dorfbuch von Santiago Gueva." *Gesammelte Abhändlungen zur Amerikanischen Sprach und Alterurnskunde* 3: 157-93.

Sellin, Thorstein

1931 "The Basis of the Crime Index." *Journal of Criminal Law, Criminology and Police Science*. 22:335-56.

1970 "Criminology." In Guenther 1970.

Sepulveda, Cesar

1961 "Sobre reclamaciones de Norteamérica a México." *Historia Mexicana* 11:180-207.

Serrera Contreras

1974 *Cultivo y manufactura de lino y cañamo en Nueva España, 1724-1810.* Seville: Escuela de Estudios Hispano-América.

Silva Herzog, Jesús

1959 *El agrarismo mexicano y la reforma agraria.* Mexico: Fondo de Cultura Económica.

Silver, Isidore

1974 *The Crime Control Establishment.* Englewood Cliffs, NJ: Prentice-Hall, Inc.

Silverblatt, Irene

1980 "'The Universe Has Turned Inside Out... There Is No Justice for Us Here : Andean Women Under Spanish Rule." In Etienne and Leacock 1980.

Siméon, Rémi

1889 "Annales de Domingo Francisco de San Antón Muñón Chimalpâhin Quauhtlehuanitzin, sixième et septième Relations (1558-1612)." *Bibilothèque Linguistique Américaine* 12.

Siverts, Henning

1965 "The 'Cacique' of K'ankujk." *Estudios de Cultura Maya* 5:339-60.

Skinner, G. William

1977a *The City in Late Imperial China.* Stanford: Stanford University Press.

1977b "Cities and the Hierarchy of Local Systems." In Skinner 1977a.

Skinner, G. William and Edwin Winckler

1969 "Compliance and Succession in Rural Communist China: A Cyclical Theory." In Etzioni 1969.

Smith, Peter H.

1973 "Continuity and Turnover within the Mexican Political Elite, 1900-1971." In Wilkie, Meyer, and Wilkie 1973.

1979 *Labyrinths of Power.* Princeton: Princeton University Press.

Smith, Robert F.

1972 *The United States and Revolutionary Nationalism in Mexico.* Chicago: University of Chicago Press.

Smith, Waldemar R.

1977 *The Fiesta System and Economic Change.* New York: Columbia University Press.

Soustelle, Jacques

1961 *Daily Life of the Aztecs.* Stanford: Stanford University Press.

Spores, Ronald M.

1965 "The Zapotec and Mixtec at Spanish Contact." In HMAI 3.

1967 *The Mixtec Kings and Their People.* Norman: University of Oklahoma Press.

1976 "La estratificación social de la antigua sociedad Mixteca." In Carrasco, Broda, et. al. 1976.

n.d. *Ñu Dzahui Ñuhu: The Mixteca Alta in Ancient and Colonial Times.* Norman: University of Oklahoma Press. In press.

Stanislawski, Dan

1947 "Tarascan Political Geography." *American Anthropologist* 49:46-55.

Stein, Stanley, and Barbara Stein

1970 *The Colonial Heritage of Latin America.* Oxford: Oxford University Press.

Stenzel, Werner

1976 "The Military and Religious Orders of Ancient Mexico." *Actas del XLI Congresso International de Americanistas* 2:179-87. Mexico, 1976.

Stephan, A.

1979 *The State and Society.* Princeton: Princeton University Press.

Stevens, Evelyn P.

1977 "Mexico's PRI: the Institutionalization of Corporatism?" In Malloy 1977.

Swartz, Marc J.

1968 *Local-Level Politics.* Chicago: Aldine Publishing Company.

Swartz, Marc J., Victor M. Turner, and Arthur Tuden

1966 *Political Anthropology.* Chicago: Aldine Publishing Company.

Tanck de Estrada, Dorothy

1979 "La abolución de los gremios." In Frost, Meyer, and Zoraida Vazquez 1979.

Taracena, Angel

1941 *Efemerides oaxaqueños.* Oaxaca, Mexico.

Tarrow, Sidney

1977 *Between Center and Periphery: Grassroots Politicians in Italy and France.* New Haven, CT: Yale University Press.

Tax, Sol

1952 *Heritage of Conquest.* New York: Macmillan Company.

Taylor, William B.

1972 *Landlord and Peasant in Colonial Oaxaca.* Stanford: Stanford University Press.

1974 "Landed Society in New Spain: A View from the South." *Hispanic American Historical Review* 54:387-413.

1979 *Drinking, Homicide, and Rebellion in Colonial Mexican Villages.* Stanford: Stanford University Press.

Tena Ramírez, Felipe

1957 *Leyes fundamentales de México, 1808-1957.* Mexico: Editorial Porrúa.

Tezozomoc, Hernando Alvarado

1944 *Crónica Mexicana.* Mexico: Editorial Leyenda.

Thomas, Norman P.

1974 "The Linguistic, Geographic, and Demographic Position of the Zoque of Southern Mexico." *Papers of the New World Archaeological Foundation* 36.

Tilly, Charles

1975a *The Formation of National States in Western Europe.* Princeton: Princeton University Press.

1975b "Reflections on the History of European State-Making." In Tilly 1975a.

Tobler, Hans-Werne

1971 "Las paradojas del ejército revolucionario: Su papel social en la reforma agraria mexicana, 1920-35." *Historia Mexicana* 21:38-79.

Topete, María de la Luz and Ronald Spores

1982 *Indice de documentos. Transformaciones económicas y políticas del Oaxaca colonial y independente, 1684-1894. Archivo General del Estado de Oaxaca.* Oaxaca: INAH.

Torquemada, Juan de

1975 *Monarquía indiana.* 3 Vols. Mexico: Porrúa.

Torre Villar, Ernesto de la

1974 *Imperio y reforma. Historia de México.* Tomo 8. Mexico: Salvat Editores de México.

Toussaint, Manuel

1931 *Tasco: su historia, sus monumentos, características, actuales y posibilidades turísticas.* Mexico: Editorial "Cultura."

Tutino, John

1977 "Indian Rebellion at the Isthmus of Tehuantepec: A Socio-Historical Perspective." *Actes du XLII*[e] *Congres International des Americanistes,* 1976, Paris, 3:197-214.

Ugalde, Antonio

1970 *Power and Conflict in a Mexican Community.* Albuquerque: University of New Mexico Press.

1974a "Contemporary Mexico: From Hacienda to PRI, Political Leadership in a Zapotec Village." In Kern 1974.

1974b *The Urbanization Process of a Poor Mexican Neighborhood.* Austin: University of Texas at Austin, Institute of Latin American Studies.

Uzzell, Douglas

1980 "Mixed Strategies and the Informal Sector: Three Faces of Reserve Labor." *Human Organization* 39:40-49.

Valadés, José C.

1941-1947 *El porfirismo. Historia de un régimen.* 3 Vols. Mexico: José Porrúa y Editorial Patria.

1972 *Orígenes de la república mexicana.* Mexico: Editores Mexicanos Unidos.

Valdés, Dennis N.

1978 *The Decline of the Sociedad de Castas in Mexico City.* Unpublished Ph.D. dissertation, University of Michigan.

Valenti Nigrini, Juana Empresa

1978 "Sindicato y conflicto: el caso de Nissan Mexicana." Tesis de grado, FLACSO.

Valenzuela, Arturo

1977 *Political Brokers in Chile: Local Government in a Centralized Polity.* Durham, NC: Duke University Press.

Vargas Rea, Luis

1944-1946 *Papeles de Nueva España colecionados por Francisco del Paso y Troncoso.* Mexico: Vargas Rea.

Vásquez de Espinosa, Antonio

1944 *Descripción de la Nueva España en siglo XVII.* Mexico: Editorial Patria.

Vásquez de Knauth, Josefina

1969 "La educación socialista de los años treinta." *Historia Mexicana* 18:408-23.

1974 *La gestación de una nueva nación. Historia de México.* Tomo 7. Mexico: Salvat Editores de México.

Vellinga, Menno

1979 *Industrialización, burguesía y clase obrera en México.* México: Siglo XXI.

Vernon, Raymond

1963 *The Dilemma of Mexico's Development.* Cambridge, MA: Harvard University Press.

1977 *El dilema de desarrollo económico de México.* Mexico: Editorial Diana.

Vetancurt, Agustín de

1960-1961 *Teatro mexicano.* Madrid: José Porrúa Turanzas.

Veytia, Mariano

1944 *Historia antigua de México.* 2 Vols. Mexico: Editorial Leyenda.

Villarreal, René

1977 "The Policy of Import-Substituting Industrialization, 1929-1975." In Reyna and Weinart 1977.

Villarroel, Hipólito

1831 *México por dentro y fuera bajo el gobierno de los virreyes, o sea enfermedades políticas que padece la capital de esta Nueva España en casi todos los cuerpos de que se compone y remedios que se le deben aplicar para su curación si se quiere que sea útil al rey y al público.* Mexico: Impr. del c. A. Valdés.

Villoro, Luis

1976 "La revolución de independencia." In *Historia general de México.* 1976.

Vincent, Joan

1978 "Political Anthropology: Manipulative Strategies." *Annual Review of Anthropology* 7. Palo Alto: Annual Reviews, Inc.

Vogt, Evon Z.

1969 *Zinacantan.* Cambridge, MA: Belknap Press of Harvard University Press.

Vovelle, Michel.

1978 *Piété Baroque et Déchristianisation en Provence au xviiie siécle.* Paris: Editions du Seuil.

Warman, Arturo

1980 *"We Come to Object": The Peasants of Morelos and the National State.* Baltimore: The Johns Hopkins University Press.

Wheeler, Stanton

1967 "Criminal Statistics: A Reformulation of the Problem." *Journal of Criminal Law, Criminology and Police Science* 58:317-24.

Whetten, Nathan L.

1948 *Rural Mexico.* Chicago: University of Chicago Press.

Whitecotton, Joseph W.

1977 *The Zapotecs: Princes, Priests and Peasants.* Norman: University of Oklahoma Press.

Wilkie, James

1967 *The Mexican Revolution: Federal Expenditure and Social Change Since 1910.* Berkeley: University of California Press.

1975 "On Quantitative History: The Poverty Index for Mexico." *Latin American Research Review* 10:63-75.

Wilkie, James, L. Meyer, and E. Wilkie

1973 *Contemporary Mexico.* Papers of the Fourth International Congress of Mexican History. Berkeley: University of California Press.

Willer, David, and Bo Anderson

1981 *Networks, Exchange and Coercion.* New York: Elsevier.

Wolf, Eric

1956 "Aspects of Group Relations in a Complex Society: Mexico." *American Anthropologist* 58:1065-78.

1957 "Closed Corporate Peasant Communities in Mesoamerica and Central Java." *Southwestern Journal of Anthropology* 13:1-14.

1967 "Levels of Communal Relations." In HMAI 6.

1969a "Kinship, Friendship and Patron-Client Relations." *ASA Monograph* 4.

1969b *Peasant Wars of the Twentieth Century.* New York: Macmillan.

Wolfgang, Marvin E., and France Ferracuti

1967 *The Subculture of Violence: Towards an Integrated Theory in Criminology.* London: Tavistock Publications.

Wonderly, W. L.

1947 "Review of *Mapas Lingüísticos de la República Mexicana,* Departamento de Asuntos Indígenas (1944)." *International Journal of American Linguistics* 13:122-25.

Worsley, Peter

1978 "Social Class in Developing Countries." Paper prepared for the Burg Wartenstein Symp. No. 80.

Zaid, Gabriel

1979 *El progreso improductivo.* México: Siglo XXI.

Zantwijk, Rudolf A. M. van

1970 "Las organizaciones social-económicas y religiosas de los mercaderes gremiales aztecas." *Boletín de Estudios Latino-Americanos* 10:1-20.

Zapata, F.

1976 "Aplicación y organización síndica en México." In Reyna, Zapata, Miquet and Goḿez Tagle 1976.

Zavala, Silvio, and José Miranda

1954 "Instituciones indígenas en la colonia." In *Métodos y resultados* 1954.

Zeitlin, Judith Francis

1978 *Community Distribution and Local Economy on the Southern Isthmus of Tehuantepec: An Archaeological and Ethnohistorical Investigation.* Unpublished Ph.D. dissertation, Yale University.

1982 "Ranchers and Indians in Colonial Tehuantepec: Social, Economic, and Ecological Aspects of the Pastoral Revolution." Paper presented at the American Society for Ethnohistory annual convention, Nashville, TN.

Zorita, Alonso de

1886-1892 "Breve y sumaria relación de los señores, y maneras y diferencias que había de ellos en la Nueva España." In García Icazbalceta 1886-1892, Vol. 3:71-227.

1963 *Breve y sumaria relación de los señores de la Nueva España*. Mexico: Universidad Nacional Autónoma de México.

1971 *Life and Labor in Ancient Mexico*. Benjamin Keen, trans. New Brunswick, NJ: Rutgers University Press.